Passing It On

The Transmission of Music in Irish Culture

Marie McCarthy

CORK UNIVERSITY PRESS

Dedication

For my parents and in memory of my grandparents

109,789
£15-95

First published in 1999 by
Cork University Press
Cork
Ireland

© Marie McCarthy 1999

British Library Cataloguing in Publication Data

A CIP catalogue record for this book is available from the British Library.

ISBN 1 85918 178 3 Hardback
ISBN 1 85918 179 1 Paperback

Typesetting by Red Barn Publishing, Skeagh, Skibbereen

Printed by MPG Books Ltd, Cornwall

Contents

Acknowledgments

This book evolved in two phases. The first was in the late 1980s when I was a doctoral candidate at The University of Michigan writing a dissertation on the history of music education in Irish culture. The second began in 1996 when I returned to the manuscript to rewrite it for publication as a book. I am most grateful to those who assisted me in developing the original manuscript and those who encouraged me to pursue the present book.

I owe a special debt to members of my dissertation committee for their invaluable advice, editorial guidance, and enthusiasm: Judith Becker, Allen Britton, Paul Lehman, Catherine Nadon-Gabrion, James Standifer, and Terrence Tice. The support and insight I gained from scholars in Ireland was of tremendous significance also. The late Aloys Fleischmann showed a keen interest in the study and his words of encouragement later provided me with a strong impetus to rewrite the original manuscript. John Coolahan and Mícheál O Súilleabháin read chapters of the work and provided pertinent criticisms and wise suggestions. Several individuals gave generously of their time to share their perspectives on institutional histories or music education practices that were not documented. Thank you to Gabrielle McCann and Caitlín O hÉigeartaigh for their inspiration and assistance throughout my career in music education.

In the second phase of completing the book, 1996–1998, I was fortunate to be in contact with many leaders in music and cultural studies in Ireland. In particular, I wish to acknowledge the contributions of Harry White who saw merit in the topic and provided advice on publication, Frank Heneghan for inviting me to participate in the Music Education National Debate, (a forum that refocused my attention on music education in Ireland in the 1990s), Martin Barrett for his generosity in sharing materials and information that gave me insight into recent developments in Irish music education, and Michael Cronin for his expert advice on rewriting the manuscript.

Consistent support was forthcoming from my colleagues and friends in the United States. I am particularly indebted to Kari Veblen who provided a wealth of support and encouragement from the beginning. Similarly, I am grateful to Scott Goble who early on in the process helped refine my thinking on many issues basic to the book and who continued to support the project in its later stages. My colleagues at the University of Maryland deserve much credit for their endless patience, reassuring words of understanding, and good humour, as they watched me juggle my academic schedule with the completion of the book. I am also grateful to the University of Maryland Office of International Affairs for a travel grant to support my research abroad.

The collection of research materials involved many individuals and institutions. I appreciate in particular the generous assistance of the library staffs at the Department of Education, Dublin, The National Library, Radio Teilifís Éireann, the Irish Traditional Music Archive, and Comhaltas Ceoltóirí Éireann. Also I wish to express my sincere gratitude to Mícheál O Súilleabháin and the staff at the Irish World Music Centre, University of Limerick, who provided an academic home for me while I was writing this book during a sabbatical in autumn 1997, to the director and staff of the Tyrone Guthrie Centre at Annaghamakerrig where I spent a productive retreat in September, 1997, and to Brendan Graham whose listening ear and encouragement were much appreciated during a critical time in the writing process.

The publication of this book owes much to the support and guidance of Sara Wilbourne at Cork University Press. Her confidence and interest in the topic were especially meaningful throughout the project. A special word of thanks to Anthony McCann for reading the manuscript and for the questions he posed and the suggestions he offered.

I wish to express my most heartfelt gratitude to my family, relatives and friends for their patience, understanding and hospitality. In particular, for the prayers and unfailing encouragement of my parents, míle buíochas. A special thank you to my nieces, nephews and godchildren whose enthusiasm and passion for music served as a constant reminder of the importance of passing on musical traditions with intentionality, dignity and care.

Marie McCarthy
University of Maryland
February 1999

Introduction

*Here in the university the youth of the nation went to receive their educa-
tion under the Filidhe [poets]. Here they were taught the powers of verse
and song by being initiated in the mysteries of metrical cadence, vocal harmony, and graceful action. These branches of knowledge were deemed indis-
pensably necessary to young princes, to candidates for magistracy, and to
the Ollavain.* [1]

A bardic college

*'The Kerry Jig': I learned this jig in early days from hearing pipers and
fiddlers play it; and it has remained in my memory ever since.*

*'Cois Taoibh a Chuinn: Beside the Harbour'; . . . when I learned this
tune from the singing of my grandmother, about 1850, she was then ninety
years of age; and she told me that she learned it by hearing it played on
the violin by* her *grandmother.* [2]

Anonymous traditional musicians

*Then I was sent to a dame-school kept by an old woman who stood us in
rows and had a long stick like a billiard cue to get at the back rows. My
father was still at Sligo when I came back from my first lesson and asked
me what I had been taught. I said I had been taught to sing, and he said,
'Sing then,' and I sang*
Little drops of water,
Little grains of sand,
Make the mighty ocean,
And the pleasant land,
high up in my head.
*So my father wrote to the old woman that I was never to be taught to sing
again; and afterwards other teachers were told the same thing.* [3]

William Butler Yeats

1

[I have] only recently got over the idea that music is fiendishly difficult. We should encourage the idea in primary schools that music is something natural like speaking. There is an excessive element of stressing the tremendous difficulty of music.[4]

Brian Boydell

Since Comhaltas was founded in 1951, education has been the hallmark of its activities. The movement was conscious of the fact that young people must be given the opportunity of appreciating and knowing the native music, song, dance and language of their country . . . we particularly look to the younger generation to take up the challenge which now faces our individuality as a nation. . . . The movement works with young people from a very early age (sometimes as young as four years) right into adulthood.[5]

Comhaltas Ceoltóirí Éireann

It is curious that U2 are seen as this 'Irish' thing. . . . But if you look at the surface level of music – its obvious contents – there's maybe nothing very Irish about it. It comes from a suburban blank generation culture which I grew up in, watching cartoons on TV, Thunderbirds and Hanna Barbera and designer violence. . . . That's the culture I come from, and that's what our music reflects, on the surface at least. It is very 'un-Irish' in the accepted sense.[6]

Paul Hewson (Bono), U2

Each of us is introduced to music in a unique way through experiences in home, school and community. Those experiences can be fruitful and fulfilling leading to a life-long engagement with music, or they can fail to nurture our innate musical impulse. What is common across all time and cultures is the fact that the transmission of music is an integral part of the generational transmission of culture, occurring primarily during childhood and adolescence: 'Children as carriers of culture, and childhood where so much learning occurs, must be seen as crucial to the reproduction of culture.'[7]

As a cultural practice, music can initiate the young person into a number of communities – from the home outward to the local school and church, extended to the national community, and beyond to more culturally distant communities such as those of one's ancestors, one's ethnic diaspora, or those of different ethnic or national communities. In addition to the informal absorption of sounds and the internalisation of musical practices through enculturation, there exists a variety of formal systems and institutions whose *raison d'être* is to pass on to the next generation music that is regarded as valuable and indispensable to the future life of a community.

Ireland is internationally renowned for the vitality of its traditional music and dance. As a national community, the Irish are generally regarded as a people who value their musical traditions and pass them on to succeeding generations. Yet, a survey of formal music education in the mid-1980s concluded that the young Irish person has 'the worst of all European "musical worlds"'.[8] Similar views are found consistently in the history of music education during the last two centuries. These two contradictory images of music in Irish culture bring to the surface many questions regarding the scope and nature of music education in Ireland. Any effort to explore this paradox requires an historical perspective to provide insight into the circumstances that created it. A striking feature of music education across the centuries in Ireland is the richness and diversity of transmissional contexts, as illustrated in the vignettes that opened this introduction. Also noteworthy is the manner in which these varieties reveal perceptions about music and its role in individual lives and in national culture.

Passing It On explores the relationship between musical and cultural development in nineteenth- and twentieth-century Ireland.[9] A primary site for such exploration is the music transmission process – how music is passed on, what is passed on, to whom, and with what purpose. Examining these questions necessarily addresses issues of Irish identity, since not only is music itself (rhythms and tones, for example) transmitted but also a set of values and beliefs that are inextricably linked to political, social, cultural or economic power structures and ideologies in the culture at large. The process of passing on or reinventing musical traditions represents a vital connection between the rhetoric of ideologies and the role of music in communal life.

The phrase 'passing it on' carries many connotations that have developed in Western thought over the decades and that need clarification in the context of this book. 'Passing it on' has been associated primarily with the oral transmission of folk culture. The phrase is used here in the broadest sense to describe a generic music teaching and learning process, the means whereby 'the knowledge, traditions, ideas and cumulative musical creations of a society are passed on from generation to generation.'[10] In the Irish context, it can range from the personal or communal transmission of traditional music in a predominantly oral context, the culturally and politically sensitive music curriculum of national schools, the conservatory-based model of intermediate (later secondary) schools, municipal colleges, academies, and universities, to the promotion and transmission of music in social, political and cultural institutions such as the Temperance movement, the Gaelic League, feiseanna ceoil, or Comhaltas Ceoltóirí Éireann. The transmission process implies a dynamic transaction between the learner and the agency of learning, in other words not a mere passive handing on of material culture but also the development of critical listeners and performers – both vital to keeping musical traditions alive.[11]

A cluster of concepts has developed around the music transmission process, each with origins in specific traditions and educational systems: music education, a discipline that emerged in this century and typically refers to the total context of music in schools, especially those of primary, secondary, and tertiary levels in the Western world; music instruction and music pedagogy, which tend to focus on the immediate conditions, methods and materials of music teaching and learning; and music training, which places emphasis on skill development and is typically associated with the education of professional performers and teachers.

In addition to the variety of terms used to identify various contexts of music transmission, within each subcultural setting is typically found a unique way of naming and categorising the phenomenon of 'music'. For example, in the context of Irish traditional music, one is likely to hear such phrases as 'give us a tune' or '*abair amhrán*' (literally, 'say a song'), or reference is made to a *séisiún* (session), a gathering of musicians who engage in intense musical dialogue. In contrast, a student attending an academy or conservatory is likely to use the term 'music' in reference to her studio lesson, theory instruction, or the repertoire itself. In state-supported schools, the subject of music has been classified as 'vocal music', 'singing', 'music theory', 'practical musicianship', or simply 'music'. One could argue that these differences are merely semantic and superficial.[12] However, when one considers that music is a human practice, the manner in which musicality is described, and music is named and categorised, points to its meaning for practitioners, the nature and quality of interaction among musicians and listeners, and how music has been institutionalised.

Although this book provides but one narrative of music in recent Irish history – from the perspective of music education at all times it is conceived and set in the context of the larger discourse of Irish culture and identity. Thus it seeks to bring music into the general history of Irish culture and ideas, a connection that is only beginning to be addressed in Irish scholarship. F. S. L. Lyons, criticising the state of Irish cultural history in 1978, found that no comprehensive works on any major art form were available.[13] Similarly, Harry White argued more recently that 'music does not form much (if any) part of the vigorous discourse which preoccupies thinkers in their assessment of the condition of being Irish and of Ireland.' As a result, he argues, 'our command of the facts about music in Ireland is sketchy and insecure'.[14] Since White made this observation in 1990 music scholarship in Ireland has increased significantly. As part of that movement, this book is intended to provide facts, to nurture the inclusion of music in the 'vigorous discourse' on Irish identity, and to provide a foundational source for those planning an historical study in music education or those interested in a more comprehensive understanding of the dynamics of music education in late twentieth-century Ireland.[15]

Since participation in music is a maker and a marker of identity, this narrative seeks to explore the interrelationships between institutions and communities that transmit music. In the process, it illustrates how cultural values are reproduced through generational transmission and how social hierarchies and mass media shape the musical canon, empowering certain musical practices and repertoires and excluding others from mainstream discourse and educational practice. In this book, musical and educational institutions are viewed as centres of cultural power and reproduction. A group's values, its priorities, and its relationship with ancestral culture are visible in such institutions. They are resonant of musical traditions of the past; they energise the present by reinventing and reincorporating tradition and in the process shape the future of individual lives, communities, and the cultural life of the nation and its image abroad.

In the most elemental sense, a narrative tells a story, in this case the story of music transmission in Irish culture. At another level, when drawing on contemporary usages of the word, narrative can refer to a form of cultural discourse, that is rooted in power relations and hegemonic structures. Richard Kearney approaches narratives as they relate to communal or national identity, in the generic sense of 'stories, myths or other forms of dramatic collective representation – what I call the "political imaginary"'.[16]

Questions then arise as to the forms these narratives take and how they are transmitted in communal and national contexts. In creating a history of music education in Irish culture, it is important to approach primary sources as part of the narrative- and therefore nation-building process. Who authored the sources and what was their role and motivation? What narrative is being formed? Whose culture is being legitimised? Whose bias is being advanced? Whose voices are missing from the sources, excluded from the narrative?

One of the major challenges in providing a comprehensive analysis of music education in Irish culture prior to the twentieth century is the lack of sources documenting the transmission of traditional music.[17] The lack of sources in itself provides insight into where this set of musical practices and its practitioners were placed in the sociocultural power structures of colonial Ireland. Traditional music was passed on in a predominantly oral culture, characterised by low levels of general and music literacy. In addition, it was not usual for tradition bearers to write about or analyse their teaching practices and methods. Those individuals who did observe and write about traditional culture were frequently foreign travellers and outsiders to the music; they brought a different set of basic assumptions and aesthetic criteria with which to interpret what they heard and observed. From the early years of this century, with more widespread literacy and the increased social status of traditional music within the cultural nationalist movement, more literature on traditional music is available. Now at the end of the century the situation has changed to the extent that a number of traditional musicians are simultaneously scholars and ethnographers of their own music making and performance practices. As the narrative of Gaelic Ireland became politically established and legitimised, traditional music rose in the sociocultural hierarchy and is now regarded as part of the birthright of every Irish child, at least in the official rhetoric of Irish education.

A second challenge in presenting a comprehensive survey of Irish music education is balancing a single, official history or a 'national story' interpreted through government documents and state policies with the seemingly infinite variety of regional and local practices gleaned from autobiographies, school records, local news media, or similar sources that provide a contextualised description of the role of music in the lived experience of Irish communities. The latter is beginning to be addressed by scholars investigating other aspects of Irish culture. The contributions of historians and cultural geographers are particularly noteworthy. For example, Kevin Whelan makes the distinction between a centralised national history, predominantly driven by political imperatives and 'the invented homogeneity of official representation', and the diversity of regional histories where the focus has tended to be more social and economic in character.[18] Heterogeneity of subcultures is a hallmark of Irish society, evident also in the ways music functioned as culture. This is illustrated in Feldman and O'Doherty's study of fiddling styles in south Donegal, where numerous substyles were evident within a limited geographical region.[19]

The passing on of music is located in a broad network of institutions responsible for general and professional music education – for example, the parochial primary school, the private secondary school, cultural centres, academies, church communities, extended family settings, or national music organisations. No one study can aspire to a detailed account of the local variation of these settings of music teaching and learning. I consider this book as a preliminary source for unfolding an historical canvas which will stimulate debate and further inquiry into the relationships between music, schooling, and culture in Ireland. This initial exploration discloses the tensions that have existed between various subcultures as manifest in musical practices, and it offers an interpretation of the relationship between music in official cultural and educational policy and its implementation at the local level.

As a result of Ireland's long colonial history, the concept of multiple narratives is of particular significance in any study of culture in Ireland. The tendency has been to approach music in Irish culture as a dualism and to equate classical music with colonial, Anglo-Irish society and traditional music with Gaelic, Irish-Ireland. It would be reductionistic to use this politico-musical dualism for all periods and all communities. Identification with a musical genre and its practices can also be linked to family values, socioeconomic status and values, geographical location, access to music instruction and, not least, individual creativity and biographical experiences. Motivation to pursue music through continued learning results from the influence of multiple cultures to which the individual belongs; this fact cannot be overlooked in efforts to generalise about music education in Irish culture. Thus musical practices and their transmission are viewed in the context of 'a complex web of interweaving narratives'.[20]

Likewise, while exclusive association of traditional music practices with Catholic cultural life is possible, to consequently view the institutional Catholic Church as necessarily supportive of those practices would be misleading. The Catholic Church and its teaching orders (particularly those that originated in continental Europe) reproduced the ideals of music in 'high culture' and assigned to classical music an important role in the education of Irish youth. In fact, in many instances these same religious orders nurtured the culture and practices of classical music to the detriment and exclusion of traditional music. Other factors such as urban or rural location, gender, and the values of sponsoring communities shaped the extent to which educational institutions advanced classical or traditional music.

Music education at the local level, then, was subject to the influence of values manifest in both local and national communities. At another level, the influence of international cultural trends and music pedagogy developments was profound, especially in the reproduction of the values of 'high culture' and literacy. Originating in continental Europe, these values were endorsed by cultural leaders such as Matthew Arnold[21] in Victorian England and implemented in Ireland through a colonial policy that sought to civilise the barbarous native people and to act as '*a magister artium ingenique largitor*, whose chief office should be, to waft civilization and humanization on the waves that bear her commerce to the earth's remotest bounds'.[22]

The cultural nationalist movement that originated in central Europe in the eighteenth century was a second international influence on Irish musical development, serving effectively as it did in countries that were building a national identity. The idea of instituting and diffusing a national musical canon was an outgrowth of this influence, a canon that was founded on the pristine culture of native, rural people. In the context of a rising Gaelic Ireland in the *fin-de-siècle* years, the ideals of this movement elevated the social status of traditional music, brought it into new cultural spaces where its existence began to be acknowledged in mainstream cultural discourse and appropriated to the dominant culture of Western art music. The rise of traditional music in the sociocultural hierarchy was not exclusively related to cultural nationalism; its development was also impacted by the rising tensions between traditionalism and modernism.

Other movements which directed the course of Irish music education can be witnessed in all Western music cultures of the period:

the introduction of music into public education in the early to mid-nineteenth century; the formation of a school music canon founded on the repertoire and pedagogy of Western classical music; the verbal battle between teaching music by rote or by note in late nineteenth-century education; efforts to introduce folk music into the curriculum in the early twentieth century; the use of recordings and educational broadcasting in music instruction; the rise of music competitions and examinations as forms of music assessment; not to mention efforts in the late twentieth century to deconstruct the Western canon of school music and to view all musical genres as a series of different but equal systems. At a global level, then, this book contributes to our understanding of how communities and mass media, through the informal or formal processes of music transmission, shape the identity and values of the next generation.

No general history of the impact of music education on cultural life can be written until we have more studies of music education in particular countries. This book represents one such study, contributing a 'lesson to the world', the reverse process to what Patricia Shehan Campbell describes in her book *Lessons From the World,* where she seeks to enrich American music education through knowledge of other systems of music teaching and learning.[23] Although influenced by international trends and music pedagogy, this Irish case study of music education represents a unique manifestation of these influences, shaped in large part by colonialism but also by cultural heritage, language, ecology, and religion, to name but the principal determinants of local variation.

In an effort to create thematic links between various historical periods of the last two centuries, I have chosen four interrelated concepts that help achieve unity and continuity. They are: music as *culture* (a foundation and motivation for transmission), music as *canon* (a content and set of values that is transmitted), music as *community* (a context of transmission), and music as *communication* (a system of methods, media, and technologies used in transmission). Musical culture is created within community; efforts by communities to pass on their traditions create canons of practice, of repertoire, and of pedagogy; the transmission of music is facilitated by a broad range of communication media and technologies; such technologies can themselves be canonic, analogous to the belief that 'the medium is the message'.[24]

Chapter one sets forth the theoretical framework for the book by approaching the transmission of music from these four thematic perspectives. Based on these points of reference, the book's four principal themes are explored, with application to the Irish context: the changing concept of the term 'culture' and its impact on music education thought and practice; the role of music education in the construction of identity, in terms of a local, national, European, or global community; the shifting canon of music education, dictated by ideologies rooted in religion, language and nationalism; and the communication of music through methods and media that reflect changing technology and imported philosophies and ideas.

In chapter two, political, cultural and educational contexts are established for exploring the transmission of music since the beginning of the nineteenth century. Ireland's culturally diverse musical heritage is described, from the original myths surrounding music in Ireland to the music subcultures and transmissional contexts of the early nineteenth century. Chapter three provides a profile of the mid-nineteenth century in terms of economic, political and social upheavals and their effect on musical and educational developments. Music education is presented in a variety of school and community settings – in ordinary national schools, model schools, denominational schools such as convents and Christian Brothers' schools, the Royal Irish Academy of Music, the Temperance movement, and the Young Ireland movement. The values of diverse subcultural worlds were reflected in and advanced by the efforts of these groups to form the identity of the young through participation in music.

The role of music in constructing Irish identity is highlighted in late nineteenth- and early twentieth-century Ireland when the movement of cultural nationalism paved the way for political independence in 1921. Chapter four describes how Irish music was defined by nationalist intellectuals and how music education practices served to advance ideologies that were rooted in Irish nationalism. Of particular interest and significance was the rise in status and respectability of native music traditions that entered new cultural spaces and mainstream musical discourse. In the context of passing on musical traditions, the change in status and new educational contexts highlighted the problems in transferring a set of musical practices from primarily rural communities, transmitted for the most part orally, and with a strong social context, to academic, classically oriented settings which valued literacy, uniformity, and contextual independence. From the 1890s forward into the new century, the rise of competitions impacted all music subcultures, in some instances bringing a norm of classical, capitalist society to bear on traditional practices founded on cooperative rather than competitive values. The increased power of the Catholic Church, coupled with its support of nationalist ideals and its ever-increasing interest and investment in school music, makes for an important theme in this era.

In chapter five, I explore the role of music in the construction of national identity in the Irish Free State and later in the Republic of Ireland. Two phases are identified: the first lasted until the late 1940s and was characterised by a parochial, essentialist view of Irish culture which drew on images and ideals from a reconstructed Gaelic Ireland of the past. The late 1940s and 1950s witnessed less explicit action towards reinforcing nationalist ideology and a broader definition of Irishness emerged. Two essential hallmarks of Irish culture – the Irish language and Catholicism – provided direction for establishing national identity and also shaped music education in the Irish Free State. In this era, music education served as a political and religious socialiser. Other factors that influenced the transmission of music included the proliferation of mass media, a striking development of school music festivals, and the development of scholarship and academic discourse on music on the one hand and the neglect of music education in national policy-making on the other.

The cultural dynamic of the period between the early 1960s and the late 1990s reflected an expansion of cultural consciousness due in part to a general movement away from cultural purism and national insularity towards cultural pluralism and global consciousness. Chapter six looks at the impact of this expansion on the nature, role and transmission of music is assessed by examining topics such as changing contexts of Irish music, the leadership of the Arts Council, efforts to develop Irish traditional music pedagogy in settings such as state-supported schools and Comhaltas Ceoltóirí Éireann, and the impact of organisations such as the Music Association of Ireland, the Irish Folk Music Society, the Contemporary Music Centre, and Music Network. While Ireland's musical image abroad assumed a high profile as a result of exposure to Irish classical, traditional and popular artists, results of studies carried out on the formal music education of Irish youth indicated an undemocratic, élitist system of public music education.

The final chapter, seven, synthesises the evidence and evaluates the relationship between musical, educational and cultural development in nineteenth- and twentieth-century Ireland. The four themes examined in chapter one – music as culture, as canon, as community, and as communication – are revisited in light of the evidence provided in chapters two to six. The constant triad of politics, religion and culture in the transmission of music process is highlighted by exploring the principal factors that impacted musical development in the period. The inextricable links between the transmission of music and the formation of Irish identity are thus described, from efforts to establish and confirm a united common identity with Britain to the formation of Irish national identity, and finally to the expansion of Irish cultural identity in the context of a European and global community.

1

Music, Education, and the Changing Canons of Culture

As a cultural practice, music functions in highly complex and powerful ways to advance ideologies and to form and transform the identity of communities. In the context of music education, this is particularly evident. From extended family settings, where music learning is considered a vital part of the socialisation process, to state education systems where music is viewed as a political agent in the formation of national identity, music education is frequently characterised by compelling agendas related to socioeconomic, political, and cultural development. The transmission of music process, then, is not a neutral, innocent activity but one underpinned by a strong motivation to define the parameters of human identity for an individual or group of individuals within a community.

Considering the complicated nature of reinventing or creating traditions through music education, it is important to examine some of the principal constructs that empower the process, and to link music education to the central concept of music as a cultural universal. These constructs of music as culture, as canon, and as community are united by the power of musical participation to communicate 'knowledge'[1] at a variety of levels of human functioning, by means of a broad spectrum of media.

MUSIC AS CULTURE

The degree to which a group passes on its musical traditions to the next generation, indicates the importance placed on music as cultural power. When applied to transmissional contexts, the concept of music as culture embraces at least three fundamental ideas: (i)

13

music education is rooted in and serves to advance the political, religious, and social values of a group of people; (ii) the musical and cultural identity of young people is formed in large part by the informal and formal music education provided by caregivers, by Church and state, by various organisations with an educational agenda, and not least by the mass media; (iii) and the power structures that support music education serve to define subcultural communities and their relationship with dominant culture(s), and beyond. In order to explore these ideas, I focus on the following aspects of the music education process: the perception and role of music in culture, music and cultural processes of transmission, music and identity formation, and the changing perception of culture and being 'cultured' during the period under study.

The forms and meanings that music assumes within and across cultures vary widely. How music is named and valued, what behaviours are manifest in its practices, and how it is related to cultural life at large, all determine what musical capacities are accessible for development in the young.[2] John Blacking wrote:

> The value of music in society and its differential effects on people may be essential factors in the growth or atrophy of musical abilities, and people's interest may be less in the music itself than in its associated social activities. On the other hand, musical ability may never develop without some extramusical motivation.[3]

The perception of musicality and musical talent within a culture is one of those factors determining 'the growth or atrophy of musical abilities'. Based on numerous autobiographical writings in Ireland this century, it is clear that classical music was perceived as a highly specialised, socially élite, difficult subject, suited to female education or for the musically talented minority.[4] Such perceptions of music and musicality were influenced by Victorian values, but it would be erroneous to conclude that all attitudes to music and musicality in Ireland were cast in that mould. In traditional settings, participation in music-making occurred widely at a variety of levels, especially in informal settings.

The generational transmission of cultural knowledge, skills, and values is known as enculturation. Two mutually dependent processes serve to enculturate the young: socialisation and formal education. In the process of socialisation, certain features are dominant: the interpersonal nature of the learning context, the transmission of music by significant adults in the child's environment, and the centrality of affective culture in the learning process, i.e. the values, attitudes and beliefs that permeate the musical practice and the surrounding community. Prolific examples of this type of learning are found in literature describing the transmission of Irish traditional music. For example, Patrick Weston Joyce and his collectors documented many first-hand descriptions of the early education of traditional singers. Since much traditional music was transmitted orally, children's musical memories were challenged from an early age. In these testimonies, singers described how they 'picked up' or learned the named song:

'The Races of Ballyhooly': 'From memory, as learned in my young days.'

'Sweet Colleen Rua': 'I learned this air from hearing it often sung at home when I was a child.'

'Ding, Dong, Bell': 'From memory, as I heard it sung by children, when I was myself a child.'[5]

Socialisation provided the child with a rich network of musical models and constant opportunities to participate in music-making.[6] In contrasting formal contexts such as school music or music lessons in academies, music learning is organised and takes place 'at regular times, in predictable ways, and at set places'. Standardised repertoire, methods, and rewards are allocated for standardised performances and the powerful traits of uniformity and conformity have tended to predominate in these learning contexts.[7] Regardless of the cultural context, learning music involves the transmission of affective culture, defined as 'those cultural manifestations that implicitly and explicitly reflect the values of a given group of people through consciously devised means that arouse emotional responses and that strongly reinforce group identity'.[8]

Since music education in rural settings is a dominant feature of this case study, two examples from other cultural settings illustrate the role of affective culture in music learning and provide some comparative background. In a study of contemporary music education in rural districts of Austria, Ekkehard Jost concluded that music institutions in rural settings 'are of much greater importance for the individual, because there they very often offer the only available possibilities for cultural activities and meetings on a social level'.[9] Learning music within these contexts is imbued with a wealth of affective culture. Learning music and living life in the community share the same platform and are sustained by similar beliefs and values. In Catherine Ellis' research into Central Australian Aboriginal music education she found a system based on a concept of lifelong music education for the entire community: 'the smallest child and the most mature adult can be involved simultaneously in a musical experience which reaches all participants at their own level.'[10] Not only is 'multi-levelled music-making'[11] a hallmark of this type of context but also strong social and cultural cohesion is a likely outcome. Music education in rural, traditional settings is typically characterised by a democratic view of musicality, an awareness of the musical needs of all community members, simultaneous participation of various age groups in music-making, and the dominance of subcultural values in the music-learning context.

The interaction between music education in social and formal, academic contexts can change over time. Irish traditional music, for example, prior to this century, was typically passed on in informal contexts that were personalised and inextricably linked to the general socialisation of the young. In this century, the process of learning traditional music, while it has maintained many qualities associated with informal learning, has become 'schooled' or institutionalised in some instances and has assumed many of the instructional characteristics of formal education. Music in formal schooling, to a lesser degree, has integrated some of the less formal aspects of socialised music learning into its practices, both in content and in methods of transmission.

In many educational contexts such as those described above the teacher or official agency organising the learning is at one with the cultural aspirations of the learner and her family or community. This is not always the case. When groups with differing ideologies come into contact, the process of enculturation changes. A colonial setting such as Ireland in the past presents an example of this form of cultural transmission called assimilation. The political aims of the enculturating agent, Britain, were not consonant with the values of the native Irish. One group's cultural symbols confronted the other's. The goal of both groups was to make their own symbols an integral part of young minds,[12] particularly evident in the context of national education in colonial Ireland. In formal learning contexts, such symbols are exposed and transmitted explicitly. Just as culture itself is 'the very site of the struggle for hegemony',[13] music education can play a significant role in purveying the symbols of a hegemonic culture. However, this does not imply that learners internalise the values of such an education if they conflict with home or community values.[14]

An important feature of the cultural assimilation process is self-definition. A subordinate group seeks not only to construct, maintain and negotiate sociocultural boundaries but also, in the process, 'to articulate differences between self and other'.[15] Musical practices can provide a means by which particular groups are recognised. For example, in Ireland, traditional and classical musical cultures highlighted the dual identification of Catholic with Irish and Protestant with British or Anglo-Irish. Paddy Tunney, in describing the rich musical life of his native county, Fermanagh, recalled an incident where an old woman who was listening to a fiddler asked a neighbour about the musician's identity:

'But tell us now, Johnnie dear, where does he come from?'

'He's a Toura man,' Johnnie told her, 'and a Protestant to boot,' in a tone of finality that brooked no further questions.

'A Protestant fiddler!!' she exclaimed incredulously, 'that beats fighting cocks!!'[16]

While this incident took place in Northern Ireland earlier in this century, the attitudes which surfaced here were deep rooted and applied to Ireland in general.[17] Music-making was inextricably linked to religious and political doctrines and it provided a signifier of people's identity and loyalty. When boundaries were crossed, as in this case, there was confusion and disbelief.

In all contexts of music transmission, the identity of learners is being formed, whether that is identity with a set of religious values or political beliefs, the lifestyle of a particular social class or the values of a subcultural group (e.g. youth culture, popular culture, 'high culture', ethnic culture). Of all the arts, music is perhaps 'the most sensitive indicator of the culture', and is 'most closely tied to the subconscious attitudes and assumptions on which we build our lives within a society'.[18] The transmission of musical knowledge and skills delineates boundaries within which youth acquire a sense of cultural distinctiveness. Alan Merriam speaks of music's function at this level when he says that 'music is in a sense a summatory activity for the *expression of values*, a means whereby the heart of the psychology of a culture is exposed'.[19] The deepening of cultural consciousness through group participation in music depends, of course, on 'a commonality of experience with music'[20] within a community. A consensus about what is essential, desirable, and incidental to musicality, music performance, and musical culture builds identity in community members, thus distinguishing them from other such groups. In a broad sense, the changing perception of culture and the cultured person itself during the last two centuries influenced people's musical identity and impacted considerably on music education practices in the Western world.

The term *Kultur* which began to assume importance in German intellectual circles in the late decades of the eighteenth century, was defined as a 'progressive cultivation of faculties' by Herder, and as an 'amelioration' or 'refinement' by Adelung. Culture thus became the hallmark of the civilised or educated person. This concept of a civilised or cultured person was fundamental to the development of the idea of 'high culture' in the nineteenth century.[21] Cultures formed a hierarchy and the placement of each one was dependent on how near it was to the ideal state of human civilisation.

In a related development, the idea of the arts and culture as autonomous aspects of society came into English thinking during the Industrial Revolution in the early nineteenth century.[22] Art became identified with a particular group of skills and expressive forms and with a particular kind of truth, 'imaginative truth'. The 'arts' were grouped together as having something essentially in common,[23] and the artist began to be recognised as a special person, one who was skilled in particular ways. Accomplishments in the arts identified individuals as having achieved 'high culture'. In this realm, the arts became abstracted from ordinary life skills by the specialised skill and knowledge demanded for their use, appreciation, and judgment. In keeping with the values of the Industrial Revolution, the arts came to be regarded as one of a number of specialised productions, serving to distinguish between the mob and the cultivated few and associated with an ideal social class, 'the highest observable state of men in society'.[24]

Culture in the modern and popular sense of being a total way of life was gradually accepted as a legitimate interpretation in this century. Already in 1871, E. B. Tylor defined it as 'that complex whole which includes knowledge, belief, art, morals, law, custom, and any other capabilities and habits acquired by man as a member of society'.[25] In this view, all people belonged to cultures and were cultured.[26] Behaviours and manners which had been described as barbarous and uncouth in former eras gradually came to be accepted as socially respectable. This is particularly relevant in relation to the social elevation of folk and 'primitive' music and its inclusion in the formal curriculum of schools in the twentieth century. As culture came to be viewed as authentic expressions of all communities, its symbolic nature and its power to create and bestow meaning were highlighted.[27] Clifford Geertz described culture as 'webs of significance' that humanity has spun.[28] James Clifford talked of a polyphonic culture, 'an open-ended, creative dialogue of subcultures, of insiders and outsiders, of diverse factions'.[29] In the context of Ireland, this latter perspective on culture is especially apt since one of the outgrowths of centuries of colonialism was subcultural diversity.

The perception of culture and a cultured person or group has changed over the past two centuries, and the philosophy and practice of music education have changed accordingly – that is, why music is passed on, what is deemed worthy of passing on and in what contexts. Although Ireland does have its own unique set of historical circumstances shaping the development of music education, in many ways it shares the fate of institutionalised music education in the Western world – for example, in the way music was rationalised in formal education. This ranged from the narrow conception of music as a potential transmitter of 'high culture' to an élite group ready to assimilate and appreciate it, to an ever-broadening view of music's educative worth as a binding force in a democratic, pluralistic, and multicultural society. At less extreme points on the continuum are found other perspectives of the value of music education: its civilising and elevating influence on the minds and hearts of all children; its potential to transmit a cultural heritage; its power to instill in the young a patriotic and culturally nationalistic outlook, or its nature as a symbolic and cognitive form expressive of an individual's or a group's identity. These varied interpretations of music's value in general and specialised education illustrate the constant and ubiquitous influence of social, political, and economic factors on the transmission of music. Music in education, education in music, and music education,[30] are conceived in, of, and through culture while also contributing to its transformation.

MUSIC AS CANON

If the concept of music as culture can begin to explain a group's motivation to maintain and develop its practices and traditions

..gh education of the young, then the notion of music as canon
.epens our understanding of what is transmitted and the pedagogical strategies used in the process. In a general sense, canon
means rule, principle, or standard of judgment. In the context of
recent literary and poststructuralist theory, canon is viewed nega-
tively as representing a centralised source of cultural authority that
justifies and reflects the values of the dominant culture[31] and
imposes those values on the young, primarily through educational
agencies.

The institution of a cultural or musical canon can occur incre-
mently and be diffused naturally through generational transmission,
or it can be established consciously and transmitted explicitly as in
the case of cultural nationalism impacting education. Teachers,
artists, and scholars play an important role in instituting a musical
canon, and in helping hegemonic or counter-hegemonic values to
be diffused.[32] The most overt manifestation of canon in music transmission contexts is repertoire – national songs, patriotic music,
hymns, ballads, traditional airs, instrumental pieces, to name but
some categories. Each musical tradition has its own central repertoire; in most instances novices learn a particular set of pieces in
sequential order, sometimes related to technical difficulty, other
times related to the social or spiritual readiness of the learner. Since
song carries verbal messages, participation in communal singing can
create a social cohesion and sense of identity in the group,[33] frequently in the name of political loyalty, cultural nationalism, peace,
or religious belief. Numerous examples can be found to illustrate
how song transmission was used to politicise groups of people.

In nineteenth-century Poland during the Period of Partitions, the
partition powers – Germany, Austria, and Russia – sought to oblit-
erate all national elements in the school curriculum. The native people responded by developing sub-cultural movements to counteract
cultural assimilation, and clubs were organised in the province of
Poznan, 'secret patriotic organizations where the students learned
about Polish music and sang Polish songs.'[34] Less than a century
later, the political ideology of Hitler's Germany was imposed on
Austrian youth after Austria was declared part of Germany in 1938.
Subsequently, in public education, music was an obligatory subject;
the teaching of Nazi songs was the focus of music instruction. Song
texts were regarded as more important than the music and all verses
of songs were to be taught – obligatory collections of songs included
German folk songs, military songs, and Nazi movement songs.[35]

A related form of ideological enculturation was evident in the work of Heitor Villa-Lobos in Brazil in the 1930s and 1940s. In the name of building patriotism, he sought to enculturate the youth of Brazil through education in their native folk music.[36] For Villa-Lobos, collective singing was a powerful activity for causing the individual 'to forfeit at the necessary moment the egotistic idea of excessive individuality, integrating him into the community'.[37] In the present study, there are abundant examples that illustrate how education agencies established a common repertoire of song with the purpose of advancing political or religious ideologies – from 'God Save the Queen' and Moore's *Irish Melodies* in the nineteenth century to Irish language songs and Catholic hymns in post-independent Ireland. As the burden of our history becomes less evident in turn-of-the-millennium education, repertoire used in school music, similar to other Western countries, has moved beyond the limitations set by colonial and nationalist mentalities.[38]

In addition to repertoire-creating canon, music pedagogy or methodology establishes its own canonic structures and procedures, although they are less tangible and accessible than in the area of repertoire. Any pedagogical encounter involves power relations and role play. Western school music, similar to other school subjects, was traditionally teacher-centred, autocratic, with primary emphasis placed on approximating the perfect performance of composed works. A second canonic frame in music pedagogy was literacy. Just as orally transmitted folk and popular music were not deemed appropriate for use in school during approximately the first century of formal Western school music (1830s to the early decades of this century), neither was oral transmission accepted as a legitimate form of learning music. As literacy and the acquisition of theoretical knowledge became autonomous forms of music education, for the most part divorced from the performance of music, canon in the literal sense (knowledge and application of rules and theory) became a core focus of music instruction, especially at the secondary and tertiary levels of Irish education.

A third area in which canon is visible in pedagogy is that of gender. Recent writings in musicology, ethnomusicology, sociology, and music education argue that music as culture is a primary site for the articulation of gender relations, the transmission of gender roles, and the construction of gender knowledge.[39] Lucy Green claims that a parallel process occurs in the music classroom where gendered meanings are re-enacted daily as a microcosm of the wider society.[40] The idea of canon is also evident in the area of assessment. Two forms of assessment have dominated Irish music education: competitions and graded examinations, practical and written. They illustrate clearly what can occur when music is passed on in institutional settings: common repertoire (e.g. set works and performance pieces, national syllabi) is chosen by authorities who are frequently unknown to teachers and students, precise standards are set, various aspects of music are compartmentalised, each having its own set of evaluative criteria, uniformity is expected in performance, and there is minimal consideration given to individual creativity, critical judgment, or musical innovation.

Typically, the schooling of culture (and by inference, music) has occurred by means of a gradual abstraction of formal and informal social-learning contexts into formal institution-learning contexts: 'Even music is rendered into classroom knowledge by emphasising music literacy, musical theory, and divorcing music from its appropriate social occasions and contexts.'[41] Certain sociocultural factors stimulated this change of paradigm. It was initiated by the idea of mass or universal education in the early nineteenth century. The dominant ideology of industrial capitalism was mirrored in institutions which catered to the education of the masses. 'The assembly line, the core of the factory system, . . . became the paradigm for the educational process, in startling contrast to the personal learning context in traditional and primitive societies'.[42]

In addition to music entering public and private schools in the nineteenth century, we also witness the rise of formal colleges and academies with the goal of teaching classical music and inculcating the values of 'high culture'. Examples of such institutions are the Royal Irish Academy of Music (1848), the Trinity College of Music, London (1872) and the Royal College of Music, London (1883). They were established as cultural centres and became symbols and vessels of high culture, providing an opportunity for socially endowed classes to embrace the current ideal of 'high culture' through an appropriate music education.

When one considers education in terms of passing on a cultural canon, it is tempting to associate such transmission with indoctrination. Prior to this century, the words 'indoctrination' and 'education' were used interchangeably and considered synonymous.[43] The teaching or implanting of various doctrines in the young was considered to be basic to education. With an increased awareness of democracy in education, a derogatory meaning became implicit in the word. Individuals who were indoctrinated were seen to be treated merely 'as means to the preservation of a doctrine'.[44] The more usual of these doctrines – religious, political, linguistic, and aesthetic – are rooted in ideologies, versions of reality that give the powerful their legitimacy.[45] Ideological indoctrination signifies the intentional selection of repertoire, methods, or media for pedagogical use, with the explicit purpose of implanting certain doctrines in the young, thereby imposing on them a particular view of reality and with the intent of limiting their access to other views. While many musical traditions existed in Ireland based on the diversity of its cultures, young people were not exposed to the richness of that diversity. The canon of dominant cultures (i.e. colonial, nationalist) reigned supreme. In the contemporary era, the cultural spectrum has opened up and many traditions are evident in cultural development, each mediating between cultural reproduction and the creation of community.

MUSIC AS COMMUNITY

Musical cultures are created within particular communities whose members participate in and share a common musical practice. These communities comprise of performers and listeners who function at various levels of musicianship as defined by the aesthetic criteria of the practice. We generally conceive of community as arising out of the geographical proximity of its members but it is not limited to that factor. An individual may participate in a musical practice at the local level and simultaneously identify with multiple imagined communities across time and space. Benedict Anderson argues that 'all communities larger than primordial villages of face-to-face encounter (and perhaps even then) are imagined'.[46] In a related idea, Ernest Gellner distinguishes between the dominant role of context in intimate, traditional communities (e.g. status of the participants, their tone, expression, body-posture) and the anonymity and invisibility of participants in centralised, institutionalised communities.[47] This distinction is particularly relevant when looking at the manner in which music, once transmitted in traditional communities, enters the culture of centralised institutions.

Music as community, then, can be experienced in a variety of ways – from the lived experience of performing in a local church or school group where a learner knows all the community members, to the less personalised experience of music learning in school contexts where classroom music may be viewed as isolated from other life experiences. This distinction is based on size of community and nature of institution. Music as community can also be experienced in the more imagined, abstract sense of belonging to a regional, national or global community by virtue of common musical interest or expanding cultural consciousness. This is increasingly made possible by electronic mediascapes which facilitate the creation of communities worldwide. In sum, the concept of music as community embraces both the physical and psychological space in which music is experienced, the site where musical and cultural identity is formed and where traditions are legitimised and generational continuity is made possible.

The relationship between music and community is significant as a central, unifying theme in this book. Young children inducted into local musical traditions experience music learning as a vital part of living, bound up with a sense of place, the persona of significant musicians past and present, and unique musical styles that evolve from the intersection of tradition and innovation through the generations.[48] Feldman and O'Doherty address the importance of music education in the transmission of culture in traditional communities:

> If traditional music is considered as a form of inherited knowledge, the musician possessed the emotional and aesthetic history of his culture in his music. . . . The music conferred identity on a vastly decentralised culture; it was history translated into sound. This is why personalised oral transmission of the musical tradition from members of one generation to another was a crucial process in the life of the rural community. This spontaneous transfer of the oral tradition between generations connected the community with its own history.[49]

The dominance of rural settings in Irish cultural development makes this form of transmission even more significant. In 1841 only 14 per cent of the population of Ireland lived in centres of over 2,000 people. Later in the century, the establishment of about four hundred chapel villages and the Catholic Church's rise in political and cultural power laid the foundations for close ties between parochial schools, the church, and the cultural life of communities.[50]

While many communities were immersed in the transmission of their own musical traditions locally, they were increasingly connected to the imagined national community through political and cultural organisations such as the Young Ireland movement, the Gaelic League, and, not least, national education. Whereas musical transmission in the traditional music community evolved naturally from one generation to the next, guaranteeing historic continuity, in the context of the nationalist movement, traditions had to be invented using images and materials from the past.[51] This growing sense of national identity, especially from the *fin-de-siècle* years forward, helped to determine the repertoire used in schools, the social status of traditional music, and it essentially changed the repertoire of music that was deemed worthy of transmitting to the next generation.

The all-pervasive effort to build a sense of national community diminished somewhat in the middle decades of this century and has been replaced by developing awareness of participation in European and global communities. This complication of cultural and, by implication, musical consciousness is not unique to Ireland. It is widely recognised that late twentieth-century identity and sense of community are constructed and situated far and beyond the confines of the immediate environment, although that environment continues to play an important role in their creation. Renowned philosopher Charles Taylor writes: 'People don't have simple identites any more, they aren't just a member of their own nation. They have a complex identity where they relate to their *nation*, and their region, and they also have a sense of being *European*.'[52] Furthermore, Richard Kearney expands the idea beyond the European community and argues that the Irish person should enjoy a triple citizenship of Ireland, Europe and the world. He writes that 'the island [Ireland] is without frontiers, that the seas are waterways connecting us with others, that the journey to the other place harbours the truth of home-coming to our own place'.[53] Although mass media and increasing global consciousness dominate, it is also noticable that there is renewed energy in small, local communities towards nurturing their diversity and cultural life.[54] One difference between the experience of music in local communities in the last century and in this turn-of-the-millennium era is that now local performances are based more on interrelations with other cultures, and less on autonomy.[55]

A discussion of the changing perception and experience of community in Ireland over the last two centuries may not seem related to issues of music transmission. However, the way in which community is conceived impacts musical development in radical ways, from why and how music is organised in communities to what is transmitted and valued and how that is implemented. Communities, whether they be immediate or distant, are the primary sites for the formation of our identities.[56] They represent spaces of significance for individual and collective musical development. Music education serves as a primary agent in generating and maintaining such communities.

MUSIC AS COMMUNICATION

A comprehensive discussion of music as communication is clearly beyond the scope of this book. The focus here is on one aspect of the process: the nature of media used to transmit music and how these media changed over the course of the last two centuries. If we subscribe to the notion that 'the medium is the message', then it behoves us to look closely at the media used to pass on music at any given time and how their presence transformed the content and process of transmission.

The word 'medium' is used broadly as a channel or system of communication used to transmit music. It can take the form of publications, broadcasts, technology, events, agencies, or any structure that facilitates the dissemination of music in educational contexts. The development of media in music education since the early nineteenth century constitutes a fascinating (but nevertheless, underresearched) aspect of the transmission process. Compare, for example, a late nineteenth-century classroom dominated by the oral transmission of song with the assistance, perhaps, of a Tonic Sol-fa chart, to a late twentieth-century studio where students record a group improvisation at a MIDI keyboard, later critically judge the recorded performance, and share their work through the internet with students at another location. Or imagine the difference in the musical journeys of early twentieth-century students travelling outside their parish to perform at a local feis, and contemporary students travelling to an international music festival as part of a global education project, or travelling there vicariously through video- or tele-conferencing. The point that emerges here is that media assist in creating and circumscribing spaces of identity that in a sense determine cultural and musical horizons. Three primary developments in the use of media in music education can be explored by examining the changing relationship between orality and literacy, the advent of mass media of communication, and the various forms of music technology which have transformed music transmission in some countries.

It is important to acknowledge the fact that, during the period described in this book, we witness a transition from a predominantly agrarian society to an industrial and technological society. This transition, as Gellner points out, also represents a change from 'a world in which high (literacy and education-based) cultures are a minority accomplishment and privilege (if they exist at all), to a world in which they become the pervasive culture of society as a whole'.[57] The development of a literacy and education-based society is fundamental to understanding the role of literacy in the transmission of music. Since music is first an aural art form, the interplay between orality and literacy has been uneasy. From the Pestalozzian motto of 'sound before sight', popular in early nineteenth-century music instruction, to the dominance of sight-reading in turn-of-the-century pedagogy, patterns of music transmission now seem to be refocusing on the principle of 'sound before symbol', with less emphasis on music literacy for its own sake.

In describing how oral processes have become technologised, Walter Ong distinguishes between primary and secondary orality in the development of media.[58] Primary orality is a hallmark of music transmitted in traditional communities with literacy serving merely as a memory aid for the students in the absence of the teacher. Secondary orality belongs to the electronic age, manifest when, for example, a student learns to play an instrument from an instructional videotape or learns a song from an audiotape. Primary and secondary orality have different capacities to create community, the former more personalised and context-specific, the latter more objectified and with more global possibilities.

The interplay of orality and literacy in music transmission is not limited to whether or not students learn to read music as they learn to listen to and perform music. It also embraces the entire area of verbal and written knowledge of and about music, a form of knowledge that is easy to transmit and to evaluate. For example, the publication of song collections with text facilitated song learning, most especially in the context of ballads and other lengthy songs that could not be memorised quickly. Other instances of high levels of verbal and written knowledge are found in music history and theory books where students learn about music independent of the sounds of music. The transmission of formal knowledge about music has been a popular form of Irish music education and this orientation was in keeping with the general dominance of the literary medium in the culture at large.

The movement from orality to literacy and a return to orality, albeit of a different quality, has transformed the patterns in which music is transmitted and the form of musical consciousness that is developed. Mass media such as radio and television broadcasting and recordings allow for music to be re-presented in classrooms in unprecedented ways. It is here that issues of identity and cultural policy are most visible in music transmission. Any 'mass' form of communication related to music learning brings people together for purposes such as entertainment, religious worship, political rallying, or cultural celebration. Such occasions create and confirm a sense of public identity. Luke Gibbons addresses two dimensions of media as a cultural phenomenon, both of which have influenced the context and methods of music education in Ireland. He writes: 'The media can act as a means of anglicization (or Los Angelization), spreading foreign influences, but they can also consolidate national culture, bringing technology to bear on tradition.'[59]

On the one hand, media can link heterogenous communities across time and space and in the process expand the cultural spaces of music learning; on the other hand, media can strengthen the bonds among members of homogenous communities and help diffuse a cultural canon in contexts of music transmission. A striking example of the latter is the way in which national broadcasting functioned to revitalise the nation culturally and, by implication, to advance nationalist ideology in post-independent Ireland.[60] The use of media in music education is forever bound up with the advancement of cultural ideologies, the most visible being Anglicisation in colonial Ireland, followed by nationalism and globalism in independent Ireland, at all times set in the context of modernisation and technological advancement.

2

Foundations of Music in Irish Culture and Education

That this country, from an early period, was famous for the cultivation of the kindred arts of poetry and music, stands universally admitted.

James Hardiman, 1831[1]

A survey of Ireland's ancient and diverse musical heritage serves to inform any study of music transmission in recent Irish history. It provides insight into the myths that underlie beliefs about music, the function of music in the various subcultures that evolved over the centuries, and the relationship between music and sociopolitical power. This would hold true for the history of music education in any country, and in Ireland its relevance is of particular significance. In the various phases of nationalism from the late eighteenth to the mid-twentieth century, Ireland's musical heritage was drawn upon consistently as a means of revitalising and legitimising an authentic, Gaelic culture. In the process, myths and images about the origins and development of music were reinvented, and they became part of the cultural canon that was transmitted to succeeding generations.

MUSIC IN PRE-CHRISTIAN AND MEDIEVAL SOCIETY

Knowledge about the origins of music in Ireland is accessible primarily through myths and sagas found in sources documented and interpreted in later eras, or in legends which lived on in folklore. Irish musicologist Ann Buckley points out that even though sources may be classed as 'mythological', they are important, 'for myths are retained, and adapted, only in meaningful ways'.[2] For example, in his social history of ancient Ireland, P. W. Joyce stressed that music was seen by the Gaels as fundamental to human life. He cited a story from the old Gaelic manuscript *Saltair na Rann* that described how Adam and Eve, when expelled from Paradise, were 'without proper food, fire, house, *music*, or raiment'. Joyce continued: 'music is put among the necessaries of life, so that it was a misery to be without it'.[3]

In an earlier history of Irish minstrelsy, James Hardiman drew on historical evidence from the Book of Ballimote to explain the significance of music in ancient Irish society:

> The people deemed each others' voices sweeter than the warblings of a melodious harp, such peace and concord reigned among them, that no music could delight them more than the sound of each others' voices: *Temur* (Tarah) was so called from its celebrity for melody, above the palaces of the world. *Tea*, or *Tè*, signifying melody or sweet music, and *mur*, a wall. *Tè-mur*, the wall of music.[4]

Tara was the administrative capital of ancient Ireland. Its image as a flourishing musical centre lived on and was the subject of one of Thomas Moore's *Irish Melodies* in the nineteenth century, 'The Harp that Once Through Tara's Halls'. Another allusion to music in the Book of Ballimote attested to its significance in Gaelic consciousness. Cahirmore, monarch of Ireland, had a dream or vision in which he saw 'a most beautiful and stately tree, like gold, whose variegated and luxuriant foliage, when moved by the wind, yielded the most melodious music ever heard'.[5] The royal druid, Bree, interpreted the dream as the tree representing Cahirmore and the music as the sweetness of his words in giving laws and ordinances to the people.[6] When comparing the underlying relation between music and power sources in this description to an account of the Battle of Magh Tuireadh, certain parallels emerge. The battle was fought between the Tuatha De Danann, the native Gaels, and the piratical Fomorians. In the description, Uaithne, the Dagda's harper,[7] was captured by the Fomorians. Dagda pursued the enemy and when he saw the harp, it came to him at his bidding. He then plays upon the harp 'the three musical feats which give distinction to the harper. He plays the goltraí until their women weep; he plays the geantraí until their women and youths burst into laughter; and he plays the suantraí until the entire host falls asleep.'[8] In this instance, the division of music into three parts served not only to

explain its role in Gaelic mythology but also to explain its po
induce states of excitement and joy, sorrow, or sleep. In man, legends, music is divided into these three parts.[9] Breandán Breathnach
views this division as 'highly imaginative attempts at explaining the
origin of the music itself or its introduction into Ireland' rather than
'as indicating a technical classification of the music'.[10]

Sources indicate that music played a powerful role in pre-
Christian Irish society. It was perceived as having magical effects
and the power to control and shape behaviour. It had its origins in
the 'other world' with the music of the fairies which was said to be
of exceptional beauty and to have particular powers. The fairies
sometimes conferred the gift of music on human beings.[11] Beliefs
in the interrelationship between music, magic, and supernatural
power lived on in oral tradition and continued to influence the role
of music in medieval society.

In that period, Ireland was seen as *insula sanctorum et doctorum*,
the island of saints and scholars. A high level of music proficiency was
central to that image. From early medieval manuscripts, it is evident
that a principal function of music in society lay in its religious context. In the Christian monasteries, which flourished in the fifth to the
eighth centuries, psalmody figured in all the monastic rules with
poetry and music developing simultaneously.[12] Professional schools
of music were situated in the monasteries and inextricably linked to
religious beliefs and practices. An indigenous art music was nurtured
in these monastic centres and propagated through missionary efforts.
The harp was the official instrument used to accompany chant.[13]
Music was transmitted orally and there is no evidence in any Irish
liturgical manuscript before 1,000 AD that notation was used.

As music was an integral part of the education of religious leaders and visionaries, so also was it seen as central to the education of
scholars and political leaders. In his *Historical Memoirs of the Bards*,
Joseph Walker described instruction in the typical bardic college
under the *filidhe* (poets):

> 'Here they were taught the powers of verse and song by being ini-
> tiated in the mysteries of metrical cadence, vocal harmony, and
> graceful action. These branches of knowledge were deemed indis-
> pensably necessary to young princes, to candidates for magistracy,
> and to the Ollavain.'[14]

A salient feature of education in this and other bardic schools
was the holistic way in which music was transmitted, with 'an

essential overlap between poetry and song, and a close association between magic, chanting, rhythm and song'.[15]

Music performance was widespread in the general population also. When Giraldus Cambrensis visited Ireland in the late twelfth century, he found the Irish to be 'a barbarous people' in most respects but he praised 'the incomparable skill of the people in musical instruments'. 'It is only in the case of musical instruments,' he wrote, 'that I find any commendable diligence in the people. They seem to be incomparably more skilled in these than any other people that I have seen.'[16] His praise is especially significant since the primary purpose of his observations was to vindicate a programme of Anglo-Norman invasion.

Information on the repertoire and methods of music instruction has not been preserved but we do know that a variety of musical instruments were used in this period – stringed instruments such as the *timpán* and *fidil*, military instruments, and pipes. Similar to later historical eras, instruments were associated with various subcultural groups. According to Breathnach, the playing of pipes was legally regarded as an inferior profession,[17] associated with the peasants; harp playing, on the other hand, had strong affiliations with monastic and bardic schools. The association of certain subcultural groups with particular musical instruments is frequently found in cultures as a marker of identity, in this case as a marker of sociopolitical power.

The transmission of music in ancient and medieval Irish culture was influenced by a number of beliefs about music which revolved around its magico-mythical properties, its power to inspire fear and control or manipulate emotions, and its role as a symbol of political power and status.[18] Such beliefs determined who participated in formal education (of which music was an integral component) and how they were prepared to function in religious and political positions in their caste within society. Music held a secure place in general education in early Irish culture, reflecting the way it was perceived as a powerful vehicle for inculcating religious beliefs, transforming behaviour, communing with the 'other' world, and reproducing the values of the social hierarchy.

CULTURAL ENCOUNTERS: THE RISE OF ANGLICISATION IN A GAELIC MUSIC CULTURE

The period of classical court poetry (*c.* 1200 – *c.* 1650) continued the tradition of music as an integral part of the bardic schools. A

system of patronage existed whereby Gaelic ar
chieftains employed an *oirfeadach* or harpei
poems of the *file* or bard which were recited
caire. An 'extensive bardic network of ar
indeed a native Irish art music, almost certainly no.
period. At the same time, this native culture was impacted by u..
Anglo-Norman invasion in 1169, causing an expansion of the function of the music. Increasingly, music served to protect and develop
Gaelic identity. For example, the harp became a symbol of Gaelic
ecclesiastical heritage and political power.[20] As the Irish sought to
mark out political space through musical practices, the chasm
between developments in European and Gaelic art music widened.

According as the Normans gained a stronger foothold in
Ireland, native musical practices began to be transformed. Culturally, many of the colonists integrated with the native Irish and
mutual acculturation occurred. As part of that acculturative
process, they were attracted to native Irish music and welcomed
musicians into their homes. Officially, this entrance of native cultural forms into colonial culture was not viewed positively and laws
were passed to halt such developments. In the Statutes of Kilkenny
enacted in 1366, contact between colonists and native poets and
musicians was forbidden. Although marginally successful, similar
statutes were again decreed during the fifteenth and sixteenth centuries, leading to the more severe campaign by Queen Elizabeth
between 1563 and 1603 at which time Irish poets and musicians
were outlawed. The limited success of the first efforts proved, as his-
torian J. C. Beckett points out, that it was impossible to maintain a
rigid line of division between colonist and native.[21]

While musical practices on the one hand demarcate cultural
space and circumscribe subcultural groups, they can also transcend
those very spaces and ignore sociopolitical differences. Music is
shared and passed on as a function of everyday social interaction as
much as political statement or religious belief. To attempt to silence
musical interaction between people is analogous to forbidding children to play. Music as culture is dynamic and has its own internal locus
of control based on individual and communal sociomusical needs.

In the Pale, the Anglo-Norman settlement around Dublin, and
the area where the colonists had direct control over cultural
development, the music subculture that developed was based on
English models. This was especially evident in church music when
King Henry II in 1172 ordered observance of the English liturgy,

impacting the uniquely Irish form of Latin chant that had olved.[22] Over time, English church music dominated and, as an outgrowth of this phenomenon, affiliated schools of music were founded in Dublin in the fifteenth century. A polyphonic choir was established in St Patrick's cathedral in 1431 and this was expanded in 1432 to include a choir school. In 1495 another music school was founded at Christ Church cathedral. Distinguished English organists were employed at both cathedrals after the Reformation. Development of this subculture of Church music within the Pale was significant in the context of establishing Dublin as second to London as a musical centre in the English empire.

From the arrival of the Normans to the end of the sixteenth century, communities were increasingly preoccupied with the quest for cultural identity. Whereas in medieval Ireland social caste created musical cultural divisions, as time progressed it was ethnicity and religious background that separated subcultures. Music functioned to accentuate those differences and to mark out political and cultural space for various communities. Cultural encounters between the foreign and the native occurred in the province of music making. The English attempted to sever musical links between colonist and colonised since learning native music and language was seen as having the potential to transform power relations and weaken colonial identity. Music education contexts where natives shared their music with colonists came to be viewed suspiciously as occasions of power diffusion and ideological control by native cultural forces. Traditionally, music was perceived as having inherent magical powers and this added to the fear that surrounded its transmission. Already in the early centuries of colonial life, it was clear that music was to be 'centrally involved in power relations and in the construction and reconstruction of identities of both colonised and coloniser'.[23]

INTERACTION BETWEEN MUSIC SUBCULTURES IN THE SEVENTEENTH AND EIGHTEENTH CENTURY

The opening years of the seventeenth century had traumatic effects on the flourishing traditions of Gaelic music, both in its art and folk forms. After the defeat of the Irish forces at Kinsale in 1601, and more significantly the Flight of the Earls in 1607, the old Gaelic order gradually disintegrated, bringing an end for the most part to the Gaelic 'Big House' patronage of music. The harpers and the artistic milieu to which they belonged collapsed under new English laws. In 1603 a proclamation was issued by the lord president of Munster for the extermination by martial law of 'all manner of bards, harpers etc.' Within ten days, Queen Elizabeth ordered Lord Barrymore 'to hang the harpers wherever found'. All through the seventeenth century, harpers were proscribed and banned, hunted and persecuted.[24] All musical instruments 'savouring of "popery"' were ruthlessly destroyed'.[25] Native Irish musicians and those who sponsored their professional schools lost their former patronage, their status and their musical function within society.

Although much was lost in this devastating period, a new definition of native music emerged as a result of a cross-fertilisation in musical styles. The old school of harpers and bards created a bridge between the music subcultures. Some former court harpers joined with folk musicians and, as Gráinne Yeats points out, 'a twofold exchange of traditions' took place.[26] The esoteric nature of bardic poetry and its accompanying harp music were not understood by the peasants, and harpers were forced to alter their style. Many other harpers were employed in the 'Big Houses'[27] of the English-speaking Protestant gentry where they performed their Irish airs and occasionally taught pupils.[28] As they influenced the musical culture of the Big Houses so also did they come under a cultural influence, that of European art music. One such example is found in the life and works of Turlough O'Carolan (1670–1738), a blind harper and composer who succeeded in integrating Gaelic musical idioms with the Italian music of Corelli, Vivaldi, and Geminiani that he heard performed in the Big Houses of his patrons. Carolan's achievement is but one of many examples of musical acculturation that took place in this period.

The various plantations that were established, from the Tudor plantation of the mid-sixteenth century to the Cromwellian plantation in the mid-seventeenth century, brought thousands of English and Scottish settlers to the island. They brought with them their folk music which became part of the culture of their adopted country. These cultural transplantations were evident, for example, in the songs that Oliver Goldsmith heard sung as a child in Longford (*c.* 1740): 'The poet was of English stock, his home atmosphere was English, and the songs he remembered being sung to him by his nurse were "Johnny Armstrong's Last Good-Night" and "Barbara Allan".'[29.]

In the eighteenth century, the music subcultures of Ireland became even more distinctive and more closely identified with the ethnic origins of their communities. The major social groupings were the English-speaking Protestant Ascendancy[30] and the native Irish. The former populated Dublin, provincial towns such as Cork, Limerick, and Waterford, and the Big Houses throughout the countryside. The native peasantry served as tenants to the colonial ruling class and lived primarily in rural areas. Differences in ethnic origins, religious beliefs, socioeconomic status, and political ideology created antagonism and an increasingly deep chasm between these two populations. Difference was also manifest in the musical practices that they developed.

The English and Anglo-Irish aristocracy were affluent and they patronised the arts and recreated the cultural life of London.[31] In this sense, Dublin's musical life was 'a reflection with local colouring of the mainstream of European music'.[32] Music flourished in this society during a period which Brian Boydell described as Dublin's 'golden age'.[33] European composers, teachers, and performers came to Dublin and further influenced the development of musical life in the city.[34] Orchestras were formed, chamber music was cultivated, schools of violin playing were established, musical societies were founded, and music halls were built to accommodate the needs of a burgeoning musically educated population.

In 1729 Lord Mornington (The Rt Hon. Garrett Wesley), composer of secular and church music, established an Academy of Music 'where ladies and gentlemen of the nobility and fashionable life met to practise, and gave a public concert once a year for some charitable object'.[35] He went on to become the first professor of music at the University of Dublin in 1764, and held that position until 1774 (after which the position remained vacant until 1845). Musical life in Dublin and in provincial towns was permeated by English and continental musical values, reflecting an élitist and aristocratic society. In this way it reaffirmed colonial identity for the English Ascendancy.

The musical life of the Irish peasantry developed in a subculture that was radically different to that of colonial Dublin and its network of strongholds throughout the island. Severe penal laws (*c.* 1690–1795) forbade native people to practise their religion or to participate in any form of education. Communal acts of worship were not allowed and, as a consequence, liturgical music did not develop in a way similar to other countries, leaving Ireland with no vernacular hymnology.[36] It was not until the 1780s that the Catholic liturgy could be freely celebrated 'with its full adornments'.[37] This freedom allowed for developments in church music to take place. In his *Tour Through Ireland* in the early nineteenth century, the Revd James Hall remarked:

> The Roman Catholics in some parts of Ireland (which is a new thing) are beginning to pay attention to church-music. At Leighin-Bridge, a few miles south from Carlow, I heard them singing *Te Deum, Gloria Patri*, and other compositions in Latin, in a very correct style. Even ragged boys and girls were thus employed around the altar; they having been taught by a music-master to sing bass, treble, recitativo.[38]

Whereas the arts were patronised in the affluent colonial world, no such development took place in peasant society. Yet, some believe that it was during this period of hardship and repression that 'an enormously creative and vibrant era for the music of the peasantry' emerged,[39] one which produced a rich repertoire which today is known internationally as Irish traditional music. Where, then, did the motivation come from to create and transmit such a prodigious, dynamic musical culture? Sources of motivation were at least twofold: the people's basic need for music-making as part of their daily lives and, at a more abstract level, the desire to assert their cultural distinctiveness and protect their Gaelic heritage against powerful colonial influences.

Native musical life consisted primarily of singing and dancing. Breandán Ó Madagáin tells us that 'there was scarcely a form of human activity, literally from the cradle to the grave, into which song did not enter. . . . [It] had a role in the moulding and perpetuation of the culture, and enhanced the sense of belonging of both singer and audience.'[40] Learning song and dance was an integral part of growing up in these rural communities. Writing in the early nineteenth century, James Hardiman stated that from infancy, people were accustomed to hearing songs that indirectly formed their national identity.

> The words and sentiments are imperceptibly imprinted on their minds, and thus, a taste is formed of which the possessors are generally unconscious. The Irishman, through every vicissitude retains the impress of those early feelings, which so powerfully sway the human heart, and to this source may be traced much of the formation of our national character.[41]

A rich, informal system of music education was available to the young, and their music aptitude was developed through imitation and repetition of music they heard around them, and participation in social music-making.

In the latter half of the eighteenth century, dancing schools or 'rustic dance-academies'[42] were founded and propagated by dancing-masters and their accompanying musicians.[43] These were an itinerant body of teachers skilled in both native and foreign dances, deportment, and social skills of the upper class. The popularity of the dancing school was witnessed by Arthur Young during his travels through the country in 1776–7. He remarked:

> Dancing is so universal among them [the common people], that there are everywhere itinerant dancing-masters, to whom the cottars pay sixpence a quarter for teaching their families. Besides the Irish jig which they can dance with a most *luxuriant* expression, minuets and courtly dances are taught; and I even heard some talk of cotillions coming in.[44]

Documented evidence of the dancing-master and his school is abundant in eighteenth- and nineteenth-century literature. Certain characteristics of this institution deserve mention. The dancing-masters moved in various social milieus teaching young people from a variety of cultural backgrounds. They introduced foreign elements such as the quadrille into Irish dancing. The acquisition of dancing skills was just one dimension of the total learning context of the dancing school. New, 'better' and fashionable ways of life were also taught in these settings. In *The Banks of the Boro*, Patrick Kennedy included a speech made in 1817 by dancing-master Mr Tench. It served to motivate his pupils to attend his dancing lessons and it identified the social advantage of this instruction.

> Now, leedies and gentlemen, I expect the greatest attention to these lessons, which, I must tell you, you are fortunate in getting. I suppose you all admired, more than once, how gracefully the gentlemen of Castleboro' and Mr Blacker walk and bow, and how they do be at their ease, while the likes of you would not know which leg to stand on, or how to keep your hands easy when they are speaking to yous. Well, what's the reason? They were *learned* to mind their positions, and hold themselves in genteel attitudes, and dance when they were young. . . . [So], pay attention to these nine lessons, and you will be inculcated to stand before Mr Carew or Mr Blacker.[45]

Dancing and music, upward social mobility, knowledge and skill to participate in colonial 'high society' were all intermingled in this music learning context.

The dancing schools also provided a stage on which traditional instrumental music could grow and flourish. When available, a piper or fiddler accompanied dances.[46] Music was passed on orally in the context of a master-apprentice system. In his *Tales and Stories of the Irish Peasantry* of 1824, William Carleton provided an example of how a young person might be educated musically:

> A fiddle is procured for him by his parents, if they are able, and if not, a subscription is made up among their friends and neighbours to buy him one. All the family, with tears in their eyes, then kiss and take leave of him; and his mother, taking him by the hand, leads him, as had been previously arranged, to the best fiddler in the neighbourhood, with whom he is left as an apprentice. There is generally no fee required, but he is engaged to hand his master all the money he can make at dances, from the time he is proficient enough to play at them.[47]

T. Crofton Croker, who travelled in the south of Ireland in the early nineteenth century, met a lady who gave him a notated copy of the popular 'Allistrum's March', and is reported as saying: 'Not one of our native musicians understand [*sic*] a note of music, as the pipers in general are blind, and yet the air has been handed or rather (if I may use the expression) *eared* down, I imagine, with very little alteration.'[48] Orality featured less in musical traditions in the urban areas and the Anglo-Irish Big Houses where European art music flourished.

Similar to musical culture in earlier centuries, instruments were identified with various ethnic groups. Hall's description of life in Dublin in the early nineteenth century illustrates this point: 'One Sunday I saw a blind fiddler going through the streets, playing on his fiddle, without the least interruption, as it appeared nothing uncommon. In going through Trinity College, on another Sunday, I heard the students playing on violins, flutes, and other musical instruments.'[49] The first image represented the Gaelic tradition as embodied in the blind fiddler, the second an English-speaking, aristocratic, colonial society as embodied in the student musicians of Trinity College. In a national education system, which of these traditions was likely to be endorsed and whose values were likely to be reproduced? The 'barbarous' music of the common people such as the blind fiddler would have no place in an education system that, in practice, sought to inculcate the values of high culture as enshrined in Anglo-Irish society and in a new 'quasi-anglicised Irish' group who were 'inheritors neither of the Gaelic nor of the English cultural tradition'.[50]

As part of the changing cultural complex, the English language began to replace Irish as the vernacular of the native people from the late eighteenth century onward. This had obvious implications for a native music that had developed in close partnership with the Irish language. Language as a barrier between music subcultures gradually disintegrated, evident in the influence of popular English song on the Irish ballad tradition.[51] Out of this cultural encounter evolved 'a creative reworking of outside ingredients', which had a revitalising effect on traditional music in late eighteenth- and nineteenth-century Ireland.[52]

Deliberate efforts were made to record and recreate a Gaelic art music that had lost vitality after the collapse of Gaelic aristocratic society in the seventeenth century. The primary concern of revivalists such as Edward Bunting was to notate and preserve the ancient music of Ireland.[53] The preservation of this music was part of a larger romantic nationalist movement that aimed 'to recover from the past a state of cultural "purity" uncontaminated by foreign influences'.[54] Bunting's collection of tunes at the Belfast Harp Festival of 1792 and their publication in 1796 attempted to authenticate and 'enshrine this "original identity" in a fixed, literate form'.[55] Concerning the tunes in the collection, Bunting wrote: '[They] bear the impress of better days, when the native nobles of the country cultivated music as a part of education; and amid the wreck of our national history are, perhaps, the most faithful evidences we have still remaining of the mental cultivation and refinement of our ancestors.'[56]

Two points are noteworthy here. First, Bunting's collection represented a pioneering effort to translate the native, orally transmitted airs into a literate form. This and other collections that followed have played an important role in the transmission of traditional music. Second, even in this early phase of nationalism, Ireland's ancient musical heritage was drawn upon to institute a canon. This atavistic approach to musical development continued into the nineteenth and twentieth centuries, placing heavy emphasis on recreating the glories of the past, and creating an imbalance between the roles of tradition and innovation in the process of music education.

Bunting's work also provided the musical context for Moore's *Irish Melodies*, published between 1808 and 1834. Moore's intention was to provide songs in the English language suited to the drawing rooms of the nineteenth century, using the idioms and sentiments of Irish music. The aim of the melodies was not to appeal to 'the passions of the angry multitude', but rather to the rich and educated and those 'who can afford to have their national zeal a little stimulated without exciting much dread of the excesses into which it may hurry them'.[57] At one level, the songs linked the musical worlds of Irish, Anglo-Irish, and 'quasi-Irish'. Throughout the nineteenth century, Moore's collection formed 'the secular hymn-book of Irish nationalism'.[58] Due to the 'cultivated taste' of their lyricist and arranger, this repertoire found an honoured place in the music curriculum of Irish schools in the nineteenth century, a point that will be revisited later in the book.

THE ROOTS OF FORMAL EDUCATION SYSTEMS IN COLONIAL IRELAND

From the fifteenth century forward, various forms of elementary education were developed by the English with the aim of cultural conquest.[59] As colonial presence strengthened after the collapse of the old Gaelic order in the early 1600s, efforts by the English to proselytise through educational agencies increased. The aim of the Charter Schools set up in 1733 was that 'children of the Popish and other poor natives in Ireland might be instructed "gratis" in the English tongue and in the principles of true religion and loyalty'.[60] The majority of Catholics were hostile towards these schools and in the opinion of some, 'the hostility merely strengthened the determination of the society to carry out its messianic aims. The children in the schools were taught militantly to sing "The Battle of the Boyne" and "Thank God, I am no Papist".'[61]

Until the relief acts of the late 1700s, the penal laws forbade Catholics to teach or to receive formal education. To counteract this, Catholics set up their own 'hedge schools', which provided a classical education in Gaelic traditions. Unlike former eras in which these traditions flourished, music was typically not a component of the curriculum since communal vocal or instrumental music would attract attention to these secret, scholarly conventions.[62] In describing school days in the early nineteenth century, Mary Carbery referred to a 'Poor Scholar' who 'helped them with their lessons, played to them on the fiddle, taught them the songs which they dared not sing under the hedge'.[63] In general, hedge

schools served as a vital agent in maintaining native culture.[64]
They continued to exist in the nineteenth century although their
numbers dwindled as the century progressed and as the National
School system became more widespread.

By the end of the eighteenth century, the promotion of religious beliefs had become a major identifying mark of educational
agencies. Protestant societies such as the London Hibernian
Society and Sunday School Society for Ireland 'were avowedly
proselytising in intent'.[65] Efforts to unite members of all religious
denominations within one educational system became the aim of
English education policy in the early nineteenth century. In 1811,
the Society for Promoting the Education of the Poor in Ireland
(Kildare Place Society) focused on being religiously neutral. It
met with certain success in its aim but lost Catholic support in
the 1820s. The Catholic orders that were established at this time
– the Loreto, Mercy, Presentation and Ursuline Sisters, and the
Christian Brothers – opposed multidenominational education and
provided instruction for members of their own communities.

Music was used widely and selectively in private education
prior to the establishment of the National School system in 1831.
In particular, it was used to promote and reinforce religious doctrine and traditions and to inculcate values of 'high society' in
those appropriately disposed to them.[66] The United Brethren
(Moravians) had an academy in Gracehill near Ballymena for
young ladies and gentlemen where they taught music.[67] A visitor
to the academy in 1824 observed that 'the young men are prepared
for college or the military academy or mercentile [*sic*] professions;
the young ladies [are] taught all branches of female education,
music included, dancing excepted'.[68] In several schools of the
same region church music was taught, mostly to female students.[69]
For females, the most popular form of music education was learning to play the piano. Hall's observations during his tour through
Ireland in the early nineteenth century confirmed that the piano
was in widespread use, superceding 'almost every other instrument
among the ladies'.[70] Piano instruction as a component of female
education continued to dominate school culture throughout the
nineteenth and well into the twentieth century.

In private and voluntary education prior to 1831, religious
denomination, social class, and to a certain extent gender, were
powerful factors influencing music education and thus shaping
the course of cultural development. Education was seen as a

sociopolitical context in which the young could be indoctrinated; that coupled with the already well-established view of music as a sociopolitical force placed music education in a highly sensitive position in school culture, a fact that emerged as public, national education became widespread in the nineteenth century.

THE INHERITANCE OF MUSIC IN AN EARLY NINETEENTH-CENTURY CONTEXT

Ireland's history of cultural encounters coupled with its geographical position on the periphery of Europe determined the uniqueness of its musical heritage and the manner in which that heritage was re-invented through generational transmission. Incessant assaults on the country by various groups influenced and directed the growth of musical culture. The incorporation of Norse, Norman, and Anglo-Saxon cultures into the indigenous Gaelic culture from the Middle Ages onward caused a constant reshaping of Gaelic identity. The interplay between music subcultures became increasingly complex as Anglicisation increased from the twelfth century forward. By the late eighteenth century, a shift in relationships took place with many native Irish aspiring to emulate English cultural values as a means of upward social mobility and economic survival.

Music as culture played a major role in defining the identity of subcultural groups. The English and Anglo-Irish population identified primarily with European art music; the poorer native Irish participated in a music culture that developed as a folk music in colonial society. Certain historical developments led to the cross-fertilisation of Anglo and native music subcultures. Itinerant musicians such as harpers and pipers operated in and were influenced by both subcultures. The dancing-masters taught in a variety of cultural contexts and nurtured in Irish youth the social values of 'high culture'.

An intriguing network of private and voluntary education agencies was in operation in Ireland prior to national education. Their educational philosophy was often guided by sectarian or political ideologies, thus causing religious groups to fear the dangers of proselytisation. As public education developed in the nineteenth century, it became a sensitive arena where power relations surfaced and cultures clashed. In his analysis of education systems in Great Britain and Ireland, Graham Balfour addressed the complexity of the Irish context:

> Last comes Ireland, poor and in subjection; passionately attached to her faith; lovable and unreliable and helpless, the child among nations: the Celtic genius, mysterious and unpractical, 'always bound nowhere under full sail,' abandoned to obsolete methods and inadequate instruction, because reform means the calling up of many quarrels.[71]

Forms of music education prior to 1831 were also bound closely to the religious and, by implication, political values of subcultural groups. Inherited conceptions of musicality and musical talent differed between groups. Musical talent in the native Irish subculture evolved from a democratic view of music where it was an indispensable component of everyday community life. The respected musician was known for his technical proficiency, skill in improvisation, and his vast personal repertoire of tunes.

In colonial culture where the values of classical music were dominant, musical talent had different overtones. It was conceived in close relationship with social power and superior cultural capital. A musician's talent was seen more as 'the "property" of a cultural ideology than as a "property" or characteristic of the individual person'.[72] Different perceptions of musical talent in the various Irish subcultures support the theory that the idea of musical talent is a cultural symbol and is inextricably linked to power relations.[73]

If music had been introduced into a democratic educational system in nineteenth-century Ireland, a rich and diverse spectrum of music subcultures would have been represented. However, the embryonic state of formal music education internationally, the political ideology of the English in Ireland, and the agenda of education to reproduce the values of the empowered, did not allow for such a broad representation.

3

Music, Schooling, and Irish Culture: A Mid-Nineteenth-Century Perspective

The middle decades of the nineteenth century were marked by a rapid and traumatic change in Irish life. This resulted in large part from famine and mass emigration, political unrest and a new wave of nationalism, and sociocultural tensions arising out of the confrontation of traditional and modern values.[1] During the same period, the National School system was established in 1831, literacy became more widespread among the lower classes, and English was adopted widely as the spoken language of the native Irish. In effect, the outlook of many communities was transformed and their consciousness expanded by emigration, mass media such as newspapers, and the ability to speak the language of the empowered.[2]

Two conflicting sets of values came into focus, the one rooted in traditional, local communities, the other influenced by mass media and aspirations of upward social mobility among members of the lower classes. At one level, the cultural fabric of life in communities continued to be woven out of local norms and values. Donald Akenson's description of an Islandmagee community off the northeast coast could be applied to many small communities throughout the mainland in this period:

> The hub was the individual family. Religious beliefs and superstitions, social conventions, and instinctive attitudes, were the laws that related the individual and his family to all others. Taken together, these beliefs, attitudes and conventions formed nothing less than a cosmology.[3]

45

In those same communities, the young generation was attending schools of the new National School system where literacy and numeracy skills were given high priority both by parents and teachers. One schools inspector observed:

> So long as their children can read, write, calculate the price of a load of hay, or a bag of flour, they [parents] are perfectly satisfied, and they consider time misspent which is employed in the acquisition of grammar, geography, and other subjects not understood by themselves.[4]

Literacy in particular played a significant role in expanding cultural awareness from the parochial to the national level. Fluency in English changed the nature of interaction between Irish and Anglo-Irish social groups and exposed young people to 'the trappings of Victorian middle class respectability'.[5]

Just as different subcultural groups began to come in contact with each other so also did the musical practices and traditions that were integral to them. The relationship between the Irish language and traditional music was altered as English began to penetrate these practices. In addition, English began to be used in songs associated with Irish cultural and political aspirations, for example, the political ballads developed by Thomas Davis in the 1840s[6] or Thomas Moore's *Irish Melodies* which created a bond between traditional Irish melody and English lyrics. As English became more widely spoken among the native Irish, the interplay of musical traditions increased and became more complex.

PATTERNS OF MUSIC TRANSMISSION

A survey of musical life in this period attests to the diversity and hegemonic structure of music subcultures, each rooted in different social and cultural ideologies. An Anglo-Irish subculture, centred in Dublin and linked to middle-class life in provincial areas, propagated the values of 'high culture' and classical music. The strong classical music tradition that had developed in seventeenth- and eighteenth-century Dublin lost certain patronage after the Act of Union in 1800 when many English aristocrats returned to Britain. Yet the British model of cultivating Western art music continued to dominate Dublin's musical life, evident in the First Grand Musical Festival held in Dublin in August–September, 1831. This festival was patronised by British royalty, and its major attraction was the performance of Signor Paganini.[7] With the exception of a few Irish melodies such as Moore's 'The Minstrel Boy', the works performed were of an English or continental origin. 'God Save the King', a symbol and confirmation of Ireland's allegiance to the crown, was performed in the final concert. This festival was organised by a cultural group that looked outward to London and to the continent for its models, its repertoire, and its pedagogy. Being affiliated with and supportive of the crown, this literate and educated group was in a position to control the discourse on musical aesthetics and subsequently to influence what was worthy of public performance and of inclusion in a music curriculum for schools and academies.

Enthusiasm for music performance spread rapidly in the middle decades of the century, evident in the massed performance of a thousand musicians at the International Exhibition in Dublin in 1853 and in the first Irish performance of Beethoven's *Choral Symphony* in 1856. At the same time, musical leaders began to show concern for the musical education of performers and audiences. Musical societies were founded: The Sons of Handel (1810), later named the Antient Concerts' Society, was the embryo Academy of Music; the Dublin University Choral Society was founded in 1837; and in 1851 John William Glover, professor of music at the Normal Training College, established the Royal Choral Institute. According to Joseph Ryan, the institute represented 'the Catholic response to earlier Protestant initiatives',[8] and was a symbol of the rising social status of Catholics.

Inspired by Thomas Davis' belief that music was the greatest achievement of the Irish people, a group of musicians and music lovers came together in Dublin in 1848 to found an academy with the aim of advancing 'the art and science of music in Ireland by affording systematic musical instruction of the highest class to pupils, both professional and amateur'.[9] Later in 1856, the academy was reconstituted as the Irish Academy of Music.[10] The institution was well supported by musicians, many of whom offered their services without remuneration. Leading ladies and gentlemen of 'high society' gave generous donations towards the development of music in the academy.[11]

The Academy of Music had a clear social agenda and was geared towards a certain class of students who had the appropriate economic background and cultural readiness to benefit from its offerings. The patronage of the academy reflected this socioeconomic bias. 'Queen Victoria became the Patron, the Duke of Edinburgh the President, while the leading magnates in the country as well as the professional and business classes took a keen interest in the project.'[12] In 1870 a grant was voted by parliament to the Royal Academy of Music in London and a similar grant was made to the Irish Academy of Music. The academy was given royal recognition in 1872. It symbolised English influence and presence in Ireland, manifest in its location, patrons, aims, the social background of the students, and the genre of music it sought to transmit to the young. Music at the University of Dublin reflected a similar cultural orientation to that of the academy. In 1845, composer and author John Smith, master of the King's Board of State Musicians in Ireland, was appointed professor of music. His successor in 1862 was Robert Prescott Stewart, organist at St Patrick's Cathedral and professor of music theory at the Royal Irish Academy of Music from 1872.

Music also functioned to promote Irish nationalism in this period.[13] A movement towards the preservation of Irish musical heritage grew steadily during the first half of the century and culminated in the founding of the Society for the Preservation and Publication of Irish Melodies in 1851. George Petrie, a founder member of this society, criticised harshly the bigots who were ignorant of the beauty of native Irish music: 'Could music penetrate their stony hearts', he wrote, 'the melodies of Ireland would make them weep for the ill they were the means of perpetuating on this unhappy island.'[14] Following Bunting, Petrie worked to collect and preserve the music of ancient Gaelic Ireland, evident in his 1855 publication *The Ancient Music of Ireland*, the first of five volumes in this collection. The work of antiquarians such as Bunting, Petrie and Moore focused on heritage art music and ignored the vernacular music of the millions of peasants around them. Alf Mac Lochlainn argues that the peasants had an intense and distinctive vernacular culture 'which owed nothing at all to the chieftains of the Gaelic order'.[15]

Although rooted in a somewhat different cultural background, music within the Temperance movement also functioned to advance nationalism. This movement developed by Fr Theobald Mathew in Cork and supported by the middle class. It was connected not only to nationalist agendas but also to social improvement and the ideals of 'high culture'. Temperance brass bands grew in the 1830s and provided the most popular form of musical entertainment in Ireland until the mid-1850s;[16] they also provided 'a valuable auxiliary' to the Temperance movement, reinforcing the social ideals it sought to propagate.[17] Participation in local bands aimed to educate the people in music, on the one hand endorsing the musical values of high culture while on the other remaining committed to the ideals of Irish nationalism.

Johann Kohl and James Johnson travelled in Ireland in the 1840s and witnessed band performances during Temperance movement meetings. In Kilrush in 1842, Kohl described the scene when Fr Mathew entered: 'the band struck up the English hymn of triumph "See the Conquering hero comes!!"' Later the band played 'Irish and English national melodies, . . .[and] some beautiful old Irish melodies were sung'.[18] In the following year Johnson witnessed a monster political meeting with Daniel O'Connell at Tara Hill. He counted at least thirty-five bands as they arrived on the hill:

> Between 11 and 12 o'clock, the sounds of music burst on our ears, and temperance bands, mostly mounted on caravans or carriages, were seen, winding slowly along all the principal roads, decorated with flags, banners, and devices, and accompanied by huzzaing multitudes.[19]

Kohl and Johnson described two functions of the Temperance bands, the social and the political. The latter function assumed a primary role especially between 1840 and 1848 when the Young Ireland movement was at its zenith. As Kearney put it: 'By playing Irish music, the bands fulfilled the aspirations of the Young Irelanders, who wished to educate the people with regard to their heritage, and thus provide them with a sense of identity.'[20] Music and politics were closely wedded in this musical milieu, and the Temperance movement was instrumental in reviving interest in Irish music.[21]

The need for formal music education surfaced as many people who wished to play in the bands were not musically literate. One writer in *The Dublin Journal* of 1842 described the situation:

> The cultivation of the Irish music appears to have excited considerable interest of late in many quarters. Beginning with the local bands of the temperance societies (which created the movement and rendered necessary a certain degree of study), the desire for musical education extended to the forming of scientific classes, for the study of that delicious accomplishment, in the Mechanics Institutes of Dublin; and, in one most rising country town, the leading Temperance Club had also established meetings for practising the Irish airs.[22]

It is clear that the development of music in the Temperance movement identified with the musical values and traditions of middle-class society. While the movement ceased to function in the 1850s, its development did highlight the need for formal music instruction among the people, a need that was beginning to be attended to in centres such as the Mechanics Institutes and the new Academy of Music in Dublin.

Another genre that emerged was the Irish ballad, associated with the Young Ireland movement. This activity reached a climax in the 1840s in conjunction with the ideas and publications of Thomas Davis and the activities of the movement.[23] Davis and other Gaelic revivalists were striving to eliminate the bigotry caused by class and creed in an effort to create an Irish nation. Some idealists like Davis believed that music had the potential to bind all people together in the name of nationalism. One author writing in 1870 advocated an Irish National School of Music that would transcend politics and religion:

> What a blessing, morally as well as socially, a School of Music would be? Presiding over the Music of the whole country, it would elevate its taste; it would civilise, in many a case, where the ear is deaf to admonition; it would be a bond of union among neighbours; it knows no politics, though mutual foes will drag it, in spite of itself, into party strife. Only the words they put to it bear the sting, the insult, and the bitter meaning. . . . Neither does it know any difference of religion.[24]

Given the embedded nature of music in the political and social realities of the day, it was unlikely that this proposed national school of music would be realised.

A third subculture included the various streams of traditional music and dance that flourished in nineteenth-century Ireland. Hedge schoolmaster Amhlaoibh Ó Súilleabháin compared this music subculture with that of Anglo-Irish Dublin. In rural Co. Kilkenny where Ó Súilleabháin had his school, fiddlers and pipers were held in high esteem. When he visited Dublin Castle in September of 1830 he heard 'a band playing music which was like the music of devils. . . . It in no way resembled the sweet gently moving music of the Irish.'[25] The music he heard reflected a political and social group with which he did not identify and whose music he found offensive, foreign and indeed evil. Identification with particular musical traditions functioned to circumscribe individuals within social and political groups. In the process, otherness was found in musical practices that were rooted elsewhere. Even within the native Irish context, there were cultural tensions arising out of the musical practices of different social groups, for example, traditional Irish musicians of the peasant class and members of Temperance bands who had middle-class backgrounds or aspirations. There was a marked absence of bands in those areas where traditional music was strongest, in Donegal and regions of Galway and Kerry. Certain evidence indicates that traditional musicians were critical of the bands' lack of commitment to national music.[26]

While clear lines of demarcation existed between different ethnic groups in Ireland, in this period those lines began to be blurred by changing sociocultural and political values; some traditional musicians aspired to new social groups and began to assimilate the musical values associated with them; on the other hand, Anglo-Irish groups sought to preserve ancient Gaelic music and appropriate it to their values and musical genres. Such was the complexity of social and musical life in the middle decades of the century. Joseph Ryan's observation regarding participation of Catholics in the Royal Choral Institute may be applied generally to sociomusical values of this era. The development of the institute, he wrote, 'cautions against a simplistic association of Catholics with the indigenous tradition and Protestants with the imported culture'.[27]

Of the various streams of musical life in Ireland, the one which was most likely to be associated with the introduction of music into the National School system was that of the classical music tradition. The primary reason for this was the natural interfacing of the values of this tradition with those of London and other continental centres of music development.

ESTABLISHING A CANON OF SCHOOL MUSIC

As the National School system began to develop in the 1830s, there was considerable discussion about the value of including music in formal education. Such discussion was not unique to Ireland. All nations developing educational systems faced a similar decision: would music be included, why, and in what form? In the process of making these decisions, a canon of school music was formed, the tenets of which continued to underlie school music in Ireland for the greater part of the nineteenth and twentieth century. In effect, a new music culture was created when music entered the institution of popular education, a space within which hegemonic values could be reproduced, scripted, and enshrined in a central institution of Irish culture.

Two major sources guided the development of a philosophy for music in the Irish National School system. They were the *Report from the Select Committees on Foundation Schools and Education in Ireland*, 1835-37,[28] and Sir Thomas Wyse's *Education Reform*[29] of 1836. Based on discussions in these sources, the primary functions assigned to music in education were social, religious and aesthetic. Due to the demands of educating all classes of an increasingly industrialised society, the social influence of music on the lower classes surfaced as a dominant concern. Music would serve to humanise and civilise them, to provide a source of innocent recreation for them, and to elevate their life-style and social manners.[30] Music's value in this instance had a strong utilitarian and social bias. Improving the lives of the lower classes was aimed more at assuring a better and more civilised working population than at educating its musical and aesthetic sensibilities.

Music was also viewed by many witnesses in the report as an important adjunct to religious education in the schools.[31] This function was in keeping with thinking in Britain and the United States at that time, where a rationale for music in popular education grew out of the need to improve congregational singing in the context of Protestant religious practices. The difference lay in the fact that in Ireland over three-quarters of the population was Roman Catholic and a sensitive relationship existed between educational agencies and religious institutions.[32] Basic to the National School system was the principle of keeping literary and moral instruction separate from religious instruction, thus maintaining mixed denominational schools. Evidence from the report indicates the committee's concern to evade allegations of religious proselytisation through hymn singing in school.[33] According as the system's schools became denominational, the religious function of music became more central to its mission in school culture. In fact, it could be argued that music functioned to advance denominational education by creating a vital link between schools and the religious practices of communities.

A third perspective on music's role in education was advocated by Sir Thomas Wyse, a Catholic member of parliament who played a central role in planning the National School system[34] and in advocating a role for music within it.[35] The basic tenet of Wyse's philosophy of music in popular education was presented during a speech in the House of Commons on 19 May 1835, when he said: 'We educate but half the being, give him an intellectual without a moral, or a moral education without an intellectual, or a miserable smattering of both – we make him a reading, writing, and counting machine, whom God designed for a thinking, feeling, acting fellow man.'[36] Having evaluated musical practices in contemporary Ireland,[37] he presented a gloomy picture of his findings. With reference to choral music in religious worship, he asked: 'But why is such music rare? Why are these voices not heard in every church and chapel in the land? We are silent, or worse – discordant.'[38] To correct national musical deficiencies, he advocated that music form an integral part of all public education.[39] Wyse was not willing to accept the popular notion that the introduction of music into education would be fruitless, 'because the people are essentially anti-musical'. He asked:

> But may not they be anti-musical, because it has not been attempted? The people roar and scream, because they have heard nothing but roaring and screaming – no music, – from their childhood. Is harmony not to be taught? – is it to be extended? – is it not a taste to be generated, at least in the period of two generations? Taste is the habit of good things – 'je ne suis pas la rose, mais j'ai vecu avec elle' – it is to be caught . . . No effort is made in any of our schools – and then we complain that there is no music amongst scholars.[40]

Wyse advocated an aesthetic approach that would educate 'the whole spiritual man', become 'an almost secondary morality', and nurture 'all the finer perceptions and higher sensibilities of our nature'.[41] A national education in music would develop a love for the arts, something he saw as lacking in the people generally: 'We should form a nation capable of knowing and loving the arts,' he wrote, 'in a word, we should raise the entire being many degrees in the spiritual scale.'[42]

In a country divided rigidly and antagonistically by sectarian and political bigotry, the realisation of Wyse's scenario for the nation was unlikely in the nineteenth century. The fact that he did not mention the wealth of music and dance traditions alive among the native Irish reflected his own cultural biases. First, he was influenced by the contemporary concept of high culture as that which represented the 'best' examples from each art form. His references to composers such as Mozart, Rossini, Goldini, and the librettist

Metastasio indicated his orientation towards Western art music. This was confirmed by his praise of Thomas Moore's *Irish Melodies* which were popular in the socially élite class at that time. His perception of 'good school music' was influenced by his middle-class background and education. Wyse was not a voice *of* the majority of the Irish people; rather he was a voice *for* the people in that he provided a vision for the role of music in their lives and in the education system.[43] In light of continued neglect of the arts in national policy into the middle of the twentieth century, Wyse's evaluation is historically significant.

A rationale for music in education was based on the social, religious, and aesthetic values of music. These values were similar to those in Britain but local circumstances coupled with the political relationship between the two countries brought to the surface some insightful differences. First, whereas the religious function of music could be discussed with considerable flexibility and freedom in Britain, in Ireland it was referred to with utmost sensitivity and caution. Moreover, the traditions of music in Catholic and Protestant denominations differed, being more exclusive in the former with select choirs, and more inclusive in the latter with mass congregational singing.

A second difference can be inferred from Britain's self-determined cultural policy to civilise and anglicise the barbarous natives of Ireland, without due consideration to the musical needs of Irish communities. This social and cultural objective was basic to the development of music in the curriculum of the Irish National School system in the nineteenth century. Some observers noted that the Irish did not seem to respond to British efforts to civilise them through improved music instruction.

> There is not a nation under heaven that appreciates the Beautiful in music through lower grades of society than the Irish. Their ear is exquisite, and their taste, as far as it goes, singularly chaste; but we regret to think that they are impatient of cultivation; and besides, by a peculiarity more to be regretted than wondered at, turn away moodily from any improvements that may be brought to them through the sister island.[44]

Differences between the British and Irish contexts were also evident in relation to the use of national music. In Britain, music was seen to function as a means of 'diffusing through the people national sentiments', to remind the peasant of 'the traditions of his country's triumphs'. The songs of the people, which frequently embodied national legends, were regarded as important means for engendering the national spirit and for forming an industrious, brave, loyal, and religious working class.[45] While this statement was appropriate for Britain, its application to the Irish National School system would have been in direct opposition to the British policy of cultural assimilation that dominated the system. The diffusion of national sentiments and the transmission of Irish national legends through singing did not take place in the schools. Rather, the aim was to instill feelings of nationality with and loyalty to Great Britain and thereby to bypass and suppress all indigenous Irish music that might arouse loyalty to Ireland.

In general, many Irish communities would not identify with or support the manner in which music's value in education was rationalised. This applied also to the method that was selected to teach music in the schools. With regard to pedagogical models, British educators imitated the continent and subsequently adapted them to the Irish context. This was the case when the British Committee of Council on Education set out in the 1830s to find an appropriate music method for use in elementary education. Having observed and reviewed many continental methods,[46] in 1840 the council sanctioned the use of the French Wilhem method which had been formally adopted in 1820 for use in schools in Paris. John Hullah, British music teacher and composer, was commissioned to prepare an English version of J. L. B. Wilhem's *Manuel Musical*. The resulting textbook, Hullah's *Manual*, was granted government approval for use in British schools.[47] Without further investigation or modification, this method was adopted by the Commissioners of National Education in Ireland. A French method of music teaching designed for use in a monitorial system was imported via an English adoption into Ireland.[48] In 1840, two Irish music teachers were trained in the Wilhem-Hullah method (hereafter the Hullah method) at the Battersea Training College in Britain and they returned to introduce it into the system's model schools.[49]

The Hullah method contained nothing uniquely Irish, and was culturally discontinuous with the experience of the majority of young people it sought to educate. Patrick Keenan, head inspector of the National School system, criticised the tunes in Hullah's *Manual* because they 'do not pretend to any national character, . . . are foreign to all sympathy, . . . belong to no country, . . . [and] are sung in no home'.[50] The weakening of identity with native Irish culture was one of the principal aims of the National School system and Hullah's tunes were in accord with that aim. Both at the philosophical and pedagogical levels, native Irish input was minimal in the establishment of music in the curriculum of the National School system.

MUSIC IN THE CULTURE OF NATIONAL SCHOOLS

Various classes of schools operated within the National School system and the nature and quality of music education available in them varied accordingly.[51] Model schools, ordinary national schools, and denominational schools formed the majority of the system's schools.[52]

Model schools[53]

Lord Stanley's foundation document in 1831 included a plan for a model school for teacher training. This was founded in Marlborough Street, Dublin in 1838. A further plan for a network of district model schools was devised by the Board of National Commissioners of Education. Due to lack of funds, the first district model school was not opened until 1848; this was followed by twenty-five others serving various regions of the country between 1848 and 1867.[54] Since the National Board exercised tight control over these schools, its aims and policies of cultural assimilation were implemented in them. Education was close to that of England,[55] and included 'extra branches' of instruction such as drawing and vocal music.[56] The pupils were typically from middle-class families and their social background was in accord with the values promoted by music education in model schools.[57] Parents and community members recognised in music yet one more of the delights of 'Victorian middle class respectability' that could be developed in the new schools.[58]

The implementation of a music curriculum required qualified teachers. In 1847, James Hill was appointed professor of music at the Church Education Society Training College, and in the following year J. W. Glover was appointed to a similar position at the Marlborough Street Training College.[59] In 1849 the first official music teacher, James Washington, was employed by the board as a peripatetic teacher who worked in model schools.[60] Washington spent six months in each school teaching the pupils and teachers and was the first to bring the Hullah system of music teaching to the district model schools.

The two main aims of vocal music instruction in model schools were to impart a theoretical knowledge of 'the science of music' and to have pupils perform 'appropriate music'.[61] These aims were consistent with the social and cultural expectations of school communities. Emphasis on music literacy and songs from the classical tradition appealed to a middle class already steeped in literate traditions and 'high culture'. The importance of music in school culture was visible to community members particularly on public examination days when administrators and significant local figures evaluated the schools. In that context, music served to improve public relations, to confirm for those present the healthy state of the model schools, to attract students to the school, and not least to lend an air of solemnity to the day.

Songs chosen for public performance originated in three sources, Hullah's *Manual*, the European art music tradition, and Moore's *Irish Melodies*.[62] The most appropriate and indispensable air, and the one which lent solemnity to each occasion, was the British national anthem, 'God Save the Queen', usually sung by all present.[63] At one level, the singing of the national anthem was a culminating musical event on the occasion of public examinations; at another level, it was part of a ritual which confirmed for everyone present the cultural goal of the Irish National School system, a goal intended to strengthen colonial identity.

One song from Hullah's *Manual* that was clearly absent from public performance programmes was 'The English Child', whose verse was included in the pupils' reader, *The Fourth Book of Lessons*. Lines from this song reinforced the hidden curriculum of the National School system: 'And make me in these Christian days,/A happy English child.' It is curious that the song was not included in public performances although many other songs from Hullah's *Manual* were performed regularly. Perhaps its text was thought inappropriate and too explicit for public performance on annual examination days.

Through public performance, music was proven to be a worthy component of education in the model schools, effective in establishing relations between the pupils, the local community, the inspectors, the Board of National Education, and ultimately the British crown. On a typical public examination day when the children performed, audiences of 'respectable and influential'[64] figures were present – clergy, gentry, 'professional men', mercantile classes, members of the corporation, and the parents of the children.[65] In essence, music served as a magnet to attract pupils from all denominations to the new educational system and to impress on the public the goodwill of the Commissioners of National Education.[66] Efforts to attract Catholic children to model schools were halted when in 1863 the Catholic hierarchy declared a ban on their members attending these schools.

Music performance also featured on special occasions that marked the visits of significant political figures. At the Annual Public Examinations at the Belfast model schools in 1862, the lord lieutenant of Ireland and other dignitaries were in attendance. To flatter him, the pupils sang a duet for which he had composed the words.[67] When Queen Victoria of England visited Ireland in 1849, she went to the Marlborough Street model schools where a chorus of 500 to 600 voices sang 'God Save the Queen' 'with taste and feeling'.[68]

Music in the culture of each model school shared common elements founded on the Hullah method and the board's goal of cultural assimilation. At the same time, school music varied from region to region.[69] For example, it flourished in centres such as Clonmel, Belfast, and Marlborough Street, Dublin, due primarily to the presence of enthusiastic music teachers. Music in Dunmanway model schools did not develop in the same way. Why did the board not consider it worthwhile to have a music teacher employed there? Was local support not forthcoming? Did the population of the town and its hinterland not identify with the value of music in education? When music was introduced in Dunmanway in 1853, the inspector observed that it was viewed in the community as 'something ridiculous', and not understood as a school subject. Thus it never thrived there as it did elsewhere.[70] The school's geographical position, rural location, and the values of the school community were likely to have influenced this lack of development.

A second and more pronounced regional difference was found in the model schools of the north-eastern region of the country. Donald Akenson addressed the individuality of this Protestant-dominated region in the nineteenth century.

> By 1800 the northeast had become a coherent regional culture embodying distinct material forms, as well as linguistic and other non-material attributes. This culture was a hybrid, incorporating native Irish and imported English and Scottish components, but dominated by the Scottish elements.[71]

Distinctive features of music in the model schools of the north-east – Ballymena, Coleraine, Belfast, and Newry – emerged during the mid-century and they reflected markedly the coherence of this regional culture. The belief that Northerners were a non-musical people was found in many contemporary sources.[72] In defence of this image, the lord bishop of Down and Connor spoke out in 1860 at the Annual Public Examinations in Belfast model schools. Having heard the students perform, he said: 'With regard to music, we have all been highly delighted. It dispels, in my mind, the charge which has been often made – that we are not a musical people. It has been said often that we Northerns have no love of music and sweet sounds.'[73] One author from the south associated this 'lack of musicality' with Northern Presbyterians. 'They are not musical,' he wrote, 'their ear is formed in Ulster to the melody of fife and drum, supported by the sound of fire-arms – by way of bass.'[74] In this perception of musicality, politics and religion were linked inextricably. The development of music in the model schools of the north helped to dispel the myth of the nonmusicality of northerners.

The tradition of fife-and-drum bands in this region, a tradition closely associated with the Protestant Orange Order,[75] entered the schools and provided cultural continuity with musical life in the community.[76] Repertoire used in Northern model schools displayed a certain independence also. An image of the Northern region as part of the cultural unit of Great Britain was evident from the repertoire chosen for performance. Selections were made from the national music of Ireland, England, and Scotland.[77] The integration of hymns into school music and public performance seems to have occurred in schools of this region. For example, in Ballymena's model schools, vocal music was divided into *hymns* and *songs*.[78] The religious homogeneity of the pupils facilitated the integration of religious and musical instruction. Although bound by the board's rules and regulations, the development of music in North-eastern model schools demonstrated local initiative and assertiveness. Efforts to integrate community resources and values into the schools seem to have been more prevalent in the North-east than in other regions.

Another form of cultural continuity between school and community took place in the model schools of the south and east. The musical traditions and values identified with the network of Big Houses[79] were reflected in model schools. As cultural centres, both served the Anglo-Irish Protestant and rising Catholic middle-class population of rural Ireland. In these contexts, music was valued as a social grace, associated with drawing-room pleasures and the English language, and regarded as reproducing the values of 'high culture'.

Ordinary National schools

School music, as it developed in the model schools in the late 1840s and '50s, formed the basis for music in all national schools. Influential inspectors such as Newell supported the introduction of music into all schools, believing that school songs would supersede those of 'the humbler classes' which were for the most part 'vicious trash, hawked about by itinerant ballad-singers; in times of political excitement often seditious, and frequently obscene and demoralising'.[80] In his idealistic view, music education would elevate the tastes of the people and they would refrain from participation in music or musical events that had political overtones.[81]

The social and political culture of ordinary national schools differed radically from that of model schools. This is nowhere more evident than in the inspectors' reports. They used a different style of language to describe pupils' performances in each school setting. For model schools, the language typically used included singing 'with great ease and correctness', 'in a finished and artistic style', 'with taste and feeling', or 'with a precision, accuracy of taste, and beauty of effect'.[82] In general remarks about ordinary national schools inspected by Newell in 1854, he stated that singing 'was from first to last painfully discordant'.[83] Other less severe remarks of evaluation included 'fair proficiency', 'tolerable', 'tolerably fair', 'very little progress', or 'poor'. The eloquence of the language used to describe music in model schools reflected the strategic role of music in gaining community support through public performance. In ordinary national schools, the reports do not lead one to believe that a public concert was part of the examination day's procedures. It was examined like any other subject and evaluated in categorical terms on a continuum from 'poor' to 'fair' to 'excellent'.

In ordinary national schools, the majority of the pupils came from rural, economically deprived backgrounds. Parents' attitudes towards 'extra branches' of education such as music were not favourable.[84] When vocal music was taught, it was against the wishes of the parents who universally opposed it.[85] The values which surrounded school music, the songs taught, and the manner of performance were alien to the traditional, musical life of rural communities. Among the people, traditional music learning was experienced and valued in an oral context and as a dynamic form of social interaction. Native Irish music pedagogues were teaching countrywide but due to the orality of the tradition in which they taught and the absence of group teaching situations or formal schools, no class method books or music primers emerged until later in the nineteenth century. A master-apprentice system was used for the generational transmission of music. In short, the musical culture of ordinary national schools that provided music instruction and that of surrounding communities were disjunct. An example taken from P. W. Joyce's memories of his schooldays in Galbally, Co. Limerick, illustrates this point:

> I was the delight and joy of that school; for I generally carried in my pocket a little fife from which I could roll off jigs, reels, hornpipes, hop-jigs, song tunes, !&c., without limit. . . . Some dozen or more of the scholars were always in attendance in the mornings half an hour or so before the arrival of the master. . . . and then out came the fife, and they cleared the floor for a dance . . . And not one in the lot was more joyous than I was; for they were mostly good dancers and did full justice to my spirited strains.[86]

The rich musical heritage which pupils such as Joyce absorbed informally during their youth remained outside classroom doors. The joy which surrounded the musical performance described here did not carry over into school music, based on documented evidence of formal music instruction.

In contrast, school music was founded on a rationale that reproduced the values of high culture, ignoring the music familiar to students and meaningful in an Irish context. An attempt to bridge these two musical traditions may be inferred from the extensive use of Thomas Moore's *Irish Melodies* in national schools. In a further effort to minimise the social distance and aesthetic differences between art and folk music, Archbishop John McHale translated the lyrics of the *Irish Melodies* into Irish and they were published in 1842.[87]

The dilemma arising out of the discontinuity between music in schools and their communities was frequently addressed by head inspector Patrick Keenan from the 1850s to the early '70s. He was acutely aware that transmission of native Irish culture was lacking in the National School system, and found this reality 'not at all gratifying to our patriotism'. He drew on the richness of the native musical heritage, 'a national music of a beautiful and elaborate class', and criticised harshly 'that namby-pamby' style of music 'that of late years has been regularly recognised as "school music"'.[88]

> I don't think that I have heard five different Irish melodies sung in all the schools that I have ever visited; . . . The introduction of Hullah's system into the country brought into use a series of melodies, constructed with no idea as to melodic excellence, but to illustrate the intervals, sharps, flats, scales, marks of expression, !&c., to be met with in music.[89]

In the same source of 1855, Keenan issued a warning which had reverberations into the twentieth century. 'We are unfortunately not only *not* disseminating Irish music but we are absolutely laying the foundation of its complete extinction from the tastes and habits of the people.'[90] Keenan recommended songs that would allow the 'national strain' to touch pupils' hearts, bind them to their native land and develop within them a great affection for it. Due to his encouragement, J. W. Glover's *School Songs,* containing some Irish melodies, was published in 1867.[91]

Keenan continued his criticism of school songs in the *Powis Commissioners' Report* of 1870, arguing that the Hullah manual contained songs that were not suited 'to the ears of Irish children', tunes that were prepared entirely for English schools, with not a single Irish air in the book. In his opinion, very little attention was paid to 'the cultivation of Irish music, the class of music which the people could best understand and appreciate'.[92] His definition of 'Irish music' was grounded in Anglo-Irish culture. At that particular stage in the development of Irish traditional music, it could not be readily interfaced with group performance based on European harmonies and part singing. Superimposed on this contrast between the two genres was the rapidly growing association of Irish traditional music with social backwardness among the native Irish themselves. At the same time, they could not identify with the values of music literacy and art music.

Meanwhile, outside the National School system, Thomas Davis was highly critical of the lack of native culture in schools. 'Until the *National* Schools fall under national control,' he warned, 'the people must take *diligent care to procure books on the history, men, language, music, and manners of Ireland for their children.*'[93] Of these aspects of culture, he considered music to be the most powerful in shaping identity. 'Musical characteristics', he wrote, 'are perhaps, the most spiritual and safe from confusion of any that can be imagined, and the surest to last in a country, if it be independent, or if it be rude.'[94] Davis was addressing some fundamental issues about the dilemma of Irish identity at that time. The country was in a state of political, social, and economic turbulence. Rapid developments and changes in music subcultures reflected this. In Davis' vision, Irish music would confirm national identity and serve to unite the Irish people. It grieved him that it was not being taught in the national schools.

> Our antiquaries may rescue treasures from the depths of time, . . .
> our musicians may revive those strains wherein love, mirth, or glory
> are sung with angels' voices; but they are never given to the students
> of our national schools, though little German airs, and English daubs
> and the lore of every other land are put within his reach whenever it
> is possible to do so.[95]

The 'German airs, and English daubs' he referred to were part of the Hullah system, a system which met with limited success in schools.[96] The cultural content of the Hullah songs and the esoteric nature of musical knowledge imparted were generally irrelevant to the communities of ordinary national schools.[97] One teacher writing in 1860 lamented the fact that in music education:

> the theory has been so mystified, and placed beyond the reach of
> the people, that those of the masses who have been endowed by
> nature with capacities, are left to stumble and grope their way
> through its labyrinth for a lifetime, without ever arriving at anything
> really practical.[98]

As dissatisfaction with the Hullah method intensified from the late 1850s forward, other methods such as Tonic Sol-fa and rote singing were advocated.[99] Enthusiasm for the Tonic Sol-fa system spread rapidly since it provided a more accessible way of teaching singing. At the same time, as national schools became denominational in practice, there was an increasing desire on the part of patrons (the majority who were clergymen) to make music part of general education and contribute to the improvement of church music.[100] This development was evident in advertisements for teachers in *The Irish Teachers Journal* beginning with the journal's publication in 1868. Skills in music performance were considered favourable, if not a prerequisite, in applying for many teaching posts:

The master *must* be able to sing, and instruct the Choir in Vocal Music. (Church Education Society school)[101]

Wanted immediately a Female Teacher who can sing well and play the Harmonium. Along with her school salary, she will have 10 pounds a year for playing and singing in the Chapel every Sunday.[102]

Male and female teachers wanted, for a Mixed national school – must be Church of Ireland. If music is taught, teacher will get 15 pounds.[103]

Wanted immediately, a first-classed R[oman] C[atholic] male teacher. He must have a certificate to teach Vocal Music.[104]

Co. Cork – Bantry Parochial national school – must be member of Church of Ireland, must understand music, have a good voice, and assist in Church choir.[105]

It is evident that not only was the character of the National School system denominational at this time but also that music had a meaningful place in denominational education. Clergymen sought to link school and Church and a musically skilled teacher could coordinate musical activities in both institutions. The strengthening of links between the parochial school and the Church was one outgrowth of this function of music in education.

Since no state funding was forthcoming for denominational education, many Catholic orders such as the Christian Brothers and some convent schools remained outside the system. The Church of Ireland set up its own school system, the Church Education Society, in 1839. Presbyterians changed some regulations to suit the schools that served their members. Gradually, the idealistic principle of mixed education was subsumed under the tenets of various religious denominations.

Denominational schools

In late eighteenth- and early nineteenth-century Ireland, orders of religious sisters were established with the intention of educating Catholic Irish children.[106] Their contribution to Irish education increased in significance as the nineteenth century progressed. In the *Powis Commission Report* (1870), convent schools received high commendation for their music instruction.[107] Inspectors referred to the 'scientific' manner in which music was taught, how hymns accompanied religious lessons, the singing in harmony of Irish melodies, and the importance the sisters attached to 'the humanising effects of music'.[108]

In accordance with the current Victorian mentality, the sisters regarded music as an indispensable part of female education. Many community members had a middle-class background and, based on countrywide evidence describing the fine quality of music education in convent schools, it appears that communities typically had trained musicians among their members.[109] Certain religious orders were influenced by continental social and cultural ideals and identified closely with the Jesuit educational aim of 'forming the judgment or developing what the French call *'le gout'* (good taste)'.[110] Music education functioned to achieve the overarching educational goal of blending the aesthetic, the moral, and the religious in the total development of the child. This goal permeated school culture, evident in Jane McCarthy's study of the contributions of the Sisters of Mercy to West Cork schooling:

> Concerts, poetic and dramatic sketches, original playlets and even full musicals, were performed by the children of these schools, in honour of particular occasions, such as the visit of the Bishop, or Reverend Mother's Feast Day, at Christmas or on Convent Anniversary days.[111]

If music assumed such a vital role in these convent schools of a geographically remote region of the country, it is likely that it assumed a similar role in convent schools countrywide. Music was valued within the realm of aesthetic education, providing pupils with musical experiences which were otherwise unavailable to them. The foreign and sophisticated was perceived as being superior to the native. Exposure to 'appropriate' music i.e. harmonised music, Western art music, would develop musical taste which in turn would refine and enrich the child's aesthetic sensibilities. From this perspective, music education in convent schools functioned in a manner similar to that of model schools. Emphasis was placed on the theory of music and the cultivation of part singing.

Instrumental music received attention in addition to vocal music. In the report of the Powis commission, there is evidence that senior pupils preparing to become school teachers were taught instrumental music.[112] The piano was the instrument favoured by members of the upper classes of Victorian society, and piano instruction was a recommended component of female educa-tion.[113] Religious sisters sought to elevate the taste of their female students, and education in instrumental music was deemed a pow-erful medium towards that end.

The aesthetic, the religious, and the moral dimensions of edu-cation came together in music instruction. Participation in music immersed pupils in the good, the beautiful, and the divine. In sum, music assumed a significant role in convent schools. In its capacity to integrate religious and cultural ideals into the fabric of everyday school life, it was perceived not as an 'extra branch', but rather as an indispensable educational ally which offered 'self-fulfilment in the highest forms of human expression'.[114]

Music was also included in the general school curriculum of the Christian Brothers' schools.[115] It functioned around two ideals rooted in religion and politics – the Catholic social ideal and the national ideal. Since Christian Brothers' schools of this period functioned almost independently of the National Board of Educa-tion, the Brothers had the freedom to put their own educational philosophy into practice. In effect, their students were not taught to sing of themselves as 'happy English children'.[116] On the con-trary, the Catholic social ideal and the national ideal permeated school life.

One of the most innovative educators of the period was Br Dominic Burke of the North Monastery in Cork. His pioneering work in music education confirms his role as an educational leader and it illustrates how these two ideals were manifest in school cul-ture. Br Burke ensured that singing was taught in all classrooms; Catholic hymns and plain chant were taught in preparation for the feast days of the liturgical year.[117] To indicate the value placed on sacred music, a German professional musician and organist, James Uglo, was hired to teach music. He also composed and published music books for the pupils' use.[118]

In Christian schools, not only was music regarded as a power-ful source for transmitting Catholic doctrine to pupils but also in fulfilling the Catholic social ideal of moral goodness. One Br Dug-gan reported:

> The children are taught to sing moral and religious songs; and I myself, in walking out in the neighbourhood, have frequently heard them in their houses singing the songs they had learned in school, and I know as regards what we call 'neglected children', who have

not been taught to read or write until a late period of their lives, that it has been a powerful instrument as regards its moral effects.[119]

A commitment to social improvement through music education was evident also in Dublin where Br Hoope organised the first brass band associated with the Christian Brothers in the Glasnevin Orphanage in 1863; this group was formally named the Artane Boys' Band in 1870 and the group functions to this day.[120]

Closely allied to the religious and moral effects of music education in the Brothers' schools was a recognition of music's role in highlighting the national ideal. Moore's *Irish Melodies* represented a genre suitable for developing national sentiments. Again, Br Burke of Cork was active in promoting this new and 'respectable' presentation of Irish airs. Since his favourite songs were these melodies and since many of the airs were slow and majestic of movement, 'they came to be styled by the schoolboys "Brother Burke's Lamentations"'.[121] It seems that other popular Irish music expressing sentiments of nationalism such as political ballads were not acceptable for school use in that period.

As many of the students in these schools had low levels of literacy, it is not surprising to find Br Burke and his colleague, Br O'Mullane, promoting use of the Tonic Sol-fa method. They transposed many of Moore's melodies to Tonic Sol-fa notation, as well as the airs of several hymns and songs, and had them printed for use in the Christian Brothers' schools.[122] The initial adoption of this method in Cork is significant in light of Cork's subsequent leadership role in music education.

Similar to music in other schools, the public relations function of music was important in the Brothers' schools. On the annual public examinations in the North Monastery School, Cork, in the 1860s, 'the delightful rendering of difficult music by the large, well-trained choir of boys' was highly appreciated by the large audience.[123] Just as Queen Victoria was greeted appropriately with song on her visit to the Marlborough Street model school in 1849, Cardinal Wiseman, first Archbishop of Westminster, was received enthusiastically in the Christian Brothers' schools during his tour in Ireland in 1858. On his entrance to the Richmond Street Schools in Dublin, 'all rose from their seats and knelt down to receive his benediction, after which the school choir sang a very beautiful hymn in praise of the Pope, which was said to have been the composition of His Eminence'.[124] In Christian Brothers' schools, the emphasis in music education was placed on moral development in accordance with Catholic ideals, and cultural formation in accordance with the prevailing ideal of nationalism.

The integration of music and religious education was strong in all denominational settings and not limited to schools of Catholic orders.[125] Efforts made by Protestant missions to convert Catholics included the use of hymns. Baptist W. Noel described the work of a Protestant mission on the northern shore of Achill Island.[126] Established in 1833, the Missionary society opened a school there in 1834 in order to make converts from 'popery'. The members communicated with the people in their native language. Some friends in London and York presented the society with a printing press and type. Their publications included an Irish hymn-book containing translations from 'the cottage hymn-book', and original compositions, all completed by the schoolmaster.[127] The Achill case provides just one example of attempts by Protestants to proselytise through music instruction. It is outside the scope of this book, however, to draw conclusions regarding the extent of this phenomenon.

Religious music was also in widespread use in non-denominational schools. When Thackeray visited the Dundalk Infant School during his Irish tour he heard the pupils sing a hymn, and observed that most of the children were Roman Catholic. 'At this tender age', he wrote, 'the priests do not care to separate them from their little Protestant brethren.' Later he heard the same children singing their hymns 'in the narrow alleys and humble houses in which they dwell'.[128] Thackeray's description can be interpreted reasonably in two ways. Either he, 'as a friend from England', was attempting to paint a positive picture of non-denominational education in Ireland, or the chanting of hymns was perceived as a common denominator for all religious groups and offensive to none.

Chanting verses and thus committing them to memory, marching, and singing were frequently presented as occurring simultaneously during instruction or school routines. In his visit to an infant school in Wexford in 1842, Kohl observed similar school activities when the children marched into the classroom, chanting a verse to an old British national melody. 'The instruction,' Kohl remarked, 'is conveyed in a poetical form, the little pupils learning short verses, which they repeat or sing in chorus, accompanying it sometimes even with pantomimic gesticulation.'[129] Rote-learning of moral and religious verses as part of school ritual was likely to leave deep traces and ensure long-term effects. In Kohl's opinion, herein lay the ultimate value of this indoctrinatory method of imparting knowledge.

As music became established in the national schools in the 1850s and 1860s, and as schools became increasingly denominational, the role of music was clarified and confirmed through repeated successful public performances. One author in 1870 advocated the establishment of a national school of music, ruling out the possibility of opposition from any sector of the public. In his opinion, Protestants were a class 'to whose education Music belongs as an accomplishment' and as a necessary component of their church services. Catholics, in turn, were glad to cultivate what the Church delighted in. (He did not deal with Presbyterians since he believed them to be nonmusical.)[130] In the context of Ireland, the juxtaposition of religious denomination and participation in music is not at all surprising. It is a reaffirmation of the deep-rooted connections among music, politics, and religion, connections that were strengthened as music developed in national education.

THE INSTITUTIONALISATION OF MUSIC TRANSMISSION IN IRISH CULTURE

Music education in mid-nineteenth-century Ireland functioned to highlight the values of a diverse range of subcultural groups. As national education developed, music served to identify various religious groups, to immerse new members in religious doctrine, and to socialise them within subcultural groups. Through participation in music, strong bonds were created between the various churches and the parochial schools, a line of development which ran contrary to the board's goal of nondenominational education throughout its system's schools. While music assumed an important role in religious education, this was seldom acknowledged in the reports of the National Board of Education. Such documents concentrated on promoting music as an agent which cultivated a refined taste and raised the moral standards of the people.

The values assigned to music in education reflected those endorsed by Anglo-Irish society – the importance of music theory and sight-reading, the equation of Western art music and good music, and the promotion of Ireland's nineteenth-century answer to classical traditions – Moore's *Irish Melodies* and other repertoire modelled on it. Transmission of these values was made possible by the adoption of the official Hullah method. In practice, this method was implemented chiefly in those schools serving middle- and upper-class students. In Moore's melodies, sentiments of Irish nationalism were expressed safe from explicit political biases and were thus suited to use in schools. The elegance of the lyrics and their harmonised melodies added to their value as school music. The songs were cast in such a mould that they were not seen to rouse sociopolitical sentiments. The raw political, social, and economic needs of the people were glossed over in endearing lyrics that addressed unaffectedly the beauty of the country, the tone in keeping with nineteenth-century romanticism. This song collection found an honoured place in the music curriculum of schools.

Political ballads, on the other hand, did not find a place in the curriculum. Considering the policy of cultural assimilation which permeated the National School system, this exclusion is not at all surprising. Typical of the dominance of classical and literary traditions in Irish education, lyrics determined in large part the worth of any song for school use. This was evident in the *Report of Her Majesty's Commissioners on Endowed Schools, Ireland* (1857–58):

> Pupils who have received instruction in music of a higher kind, listen with distaste to the coarse and too often obscene performances of ballad-singers. Songs embodying noble and virtuous sentiments may be ranked among the most powerful agencies by which the moral nature is elevated and character is formed; and the influence of such music on the human heart is greatly enhanced when it is performed by many persons singing tunefully in concert. The union and harmony of the voices awaken in the singers sympathies by which the effect of the words upon their feelings and imagination is rendered more intense.[131]

In addition to the exclusion of ballads from school culture, traditional Irish music and dance were not included in national education. At an international level, folk music was not considered favourably (if at all) in the context of formal education. It was deeply embedded in community life and was not deemed necessary or appropriate in a social institution such as the school. Second, those who held control of the discourse on aesthetics and music education philosophy were English speaking, committed to Western art music traditions, and psychologically distant from the social and cultural circumstances around which traditional music revolved. Third, Irish traditional music was predominantly transmitted orally while music in education was conceived in terms of literate forms and media. As yet, this music had not entered the realm of scholarly discourse as a living music although much attention was devoted to it as an antiquarian artifact.[132] As a flourishing and rich musical genre, it remained hidden from the formally educated classes of society. Its partnership with the Irish language, albeit a changing one, further inhibited its chances of finding a place in the system. Moreover, Irish language and music were fast losing their status in the minds of socially and economically aspiring Irish and were gradually relegated to the order of social backwardness.

In education, music functioned within powerful social parameters, in which ethnic, religious, and political identities were framed. The timeless values of music, those guiding children towards national pride (defined in a British context), moral goodness, and religious fervour, were dominant. Sacred music, moral verses and hymns, and songs with national sentiments, were perceived as appropriate repertoire for achieving that educational outcome. In denominational schools, religious and social agendas underpinned school music. Catholic sisters sought to elevate the cultural taste of their pupils and Christian Brothers emphasised the social effects of music education and its potential to shape good citizens.

The success of music in any transmissional context was dependent on the cultural continuity which existed between the school, the church, and the local community. Such continuity was made possible by an interfacing of social values, political agendas, and religious beliefs among these institutions. Music education flourished in those contexts where the values of subcultural groups were invested and visibly functioning in the musical culture of schools and other agencies of music education.

4

Music, Education and Cultural Nationalism in Fin-de-Siècle *Ireland*

IN SEARCH OF 'IRISH' MUSIC

The nationalist movement of late nineteenth- and early twentieth-century Ireland influenced the course of musical and educational development. These aspects of cultural life, in turn, served to advance nationalist ideologies. Similar to other countries, the achievement of nationhood was preceeded by a cultural nationalist movement that expressed the new nation as an 'imagined community',[1] relying heavily on images from the past. Superimposed on the struggle for nationhood was the struggle between two social processes: the modernisation of Irish society and the erosion of traditional values and lifestyles.[2]

One of the foremost institutions to advance nationalist ideals in the late nineteenth century was the Gaelic League, founded in 1893 to reconstruct a Gaelic past, build a national identity, and keep the Irish language spoken in Ireland.[3] The remnants of true Ireland, according to the Gaelic League, were to be found in the rural, pristine culture still practised in peasant communities, particularly in the west of Ireland.[4] Traditional music of the people was an important component of peasant community life, seen as 'always spontaneous and original'.[5] Besides being one of the remnants of indigenous culture, singing in the Irish language was viewed as an important medium for reviving the language. Many cultural nationalists expressed deep concern about the decline in traditional music practices and the loss of a vital stream of Irish culture. Addressing

72

the Gaelic League, George Moonan referred to Irish girls' igno-
rance of Irish music and the lack of knowledge about traditional
music among Ireland's musical leaders.

> For our Irish girls to accept without question the silliest jingles that
> have caught the ear of the English populace, and to remain ignorant
> of our varied stores of thousands of delightful melodies – even could
> they appreciate Schumann and Mendelssohn and Gounod, and
> knew not the names of Rory Dall or Carolan, Bunting, or Petrie –
> must also be deplored as a sign not only of our loss of national edu-
> cation, but as a lowering of our standard of culture. For our Irish
> musicians to dogmatise on the comparative merits of the claims of
> Solesmes and Ratisbon, and to be unable to guide us to the mystery
> lying beneath the 'traditional' singers untutored efforts, is but one
> instance of our educated ignorance on national matters.
>
> Not, I repeat, that the Gaelic League is opposed to the apprecia-
> tion of the great masters of art, but it insists upon our national treas-
> ures getting the due attention that would be paid to them were they
> possessed by any other nation of the world.[6]

Similarly Douglas Hyde, president of the Gaelic League, considered that traditional music had 'become Anglicised to an alarm-
ing extent'. 'If Ireland loses her music', he continued, 'she loses
what is, after her Gaelic language and literature, her most valuable
and most characteristic possession. And she is rapidly losing it'.[7]
The spread of the English language among Irish-speaking communities, the acquisition of literacy and a primary education by the
majority of the population, and the growing tensions between traditionalism and modernism, were contributing to the erosion of
Gaelic culture.

A major task faced those who sought to develop Irish music.
Many cultural nationalists drew on an image of the Irish as a musical race having a rich musical heritage. This group was also well
aware that such an image belonged to a time 'very long ago' and
did not necessarily reflect the spirit or quality of contemporary
musical life.[8] Annie Patterson, avid reformer of Irish music,
believed that 'we cannot always live on records of the past'.[9] She
sought to reinvent Ireland's musical past and in October, 1894, presented the members of the Gaelic League with a plan for the revival
of the ancient Gaelic festivals or feiseanna.[10] Subsequently, the Feis
Ceoil or Musical Festival Association was founded in 1895 and the
first feis was held in Dublin in May, 1897. The aims of the Feis
Ceoil were to promote the study and cultivation of Irish music[11]

and music in general in Ireland, to hold an annual Feis Ceoil, consisting of prize competitions and concerts, and to collect and preserve by publication the old airs of Ireland.[12] In the initial years, the Feis Ceoil was exclusively Dublin-based, but at the turn of the century local feiseanna were established, thus giving the institution a national presence.[13]

The Feis Ceoil was modelled on the Eisteddfod, a reputable Welsh competitive festival. It is worthy of note that a competitive spirit seemed to be popular in turn-of-the-century Ireland and interest in competing in music contests had become widespread. Competitions functioned as a powerful medium for centralising and standardising efforts to build national values, and they were central to the transmission of music, especially within the organisational culture of schools and academies. Participation in competitions had the power to instill feelings of conformity, unity, and nationalism, facilitating the institution and diffusion of a cultural canon.

Feis Ceoil activities reached out into the culture of schools and a competition for 'school choirs and singing classes' was included. Schools from urban and rural areas competed in different sections, with choirs from urban schools required to read staff notation while rural school choirs had a choice between staff and Tonic Solfa notation.[14] Peter Goodman, professor of music with the National Board of Commissioners, acknowledged in the 1906-7 report the value of these competitive festivals in consolidating his efforts to raise the standard of music education in the national schools.[15] The primary influences of the feiseanna on the development of music were the increase of Irish language songs in schools, the recognition and appraisal of musical talent in school communities, and the inclusion in school music of culturally relevant activities which created bonds between school, home, communal, and national aspirations.[16]

The Feis Ceoil aimed at representing all genres of Irish music, classical and traditional.[17] In effect, this contest may be regarded as the initiation of traditional Irish music into the arena of mass schooling and competitive performance. Since the competitions were judged by classical musicians, the values of one musical tradition, which evolved from a radically different set of aesthetic criteria, were grafted onto another. Traditional music assumed new performance contexts and expectations, and it was staged and evaluated by musicians from outside 'the tradition'. Syllabi of test pieces were made available and uniformity in performance was demanded. This resulted in an encounter of different musical, pedagogical, and socioeconomic subcultures. For example, renowned fiddle player Michael Coleman made his first known public performance at the Sligo Feis Ceoil in June, 1909, an event that brought him into contact with a social class and musical culture that was quite different to that of nearby Killavil, his native countryside.[18]

Some observers of the Feis Ceoil were sympathetic to the different aesthetic dispositions of classical and traditional music and offered opinions as to why traditional musicians were often not successful on the concert platform. Pádraig Pearse, for example, regarded the performance context as inappropriate for them, arguing that peasant musicians 'are of the countrysides and for the countrysides'.[19] Carl Hardebeck, president of Cumann Ceoil, the musical society within the Gaelic League, expressed a similar opinion when he wrote in 1911:

> The adult traditional singer in the habit of singing in the kitchen by the fireside, be he ever so good, has no business to be dragged on to the concert platform. There he is nervous, and as uncomfortable as a fish out of water, misunderstood by the public, and usually thoroughly unhappy. Except a rabid Gaelic Leaguer, nobody will listen to him singing without accompaniment.[20]

The new context of the concert platform and the competitive element of the festivals were alien to the traditional musician. Thus the performance of traditional music did not develop as it might have within the arena of the Feis Ceoil. Breathnach claims that living traditional music did not receive serious attention in this forum and by the 1920s competitors were not traditional players in the sense that the early ones had been.[21] A similar observation was made by an author who described the character of instrumental music performed at the Feis Ceoil as 'almost wholly alien', rooted in the culture of the music academy and catering for 'the foreign, so-called "classical" element' in music.[22]

While the Feis Ceoil set out to present all aspects of Irish music, its underlying set of assumptions and musical values did not accommodate traditional music. The voice of the insiders – traditional musicians themselves – was not present in the association's leadership, so these musicians were often misunderstood and their practice misinterpreted. On the positive side, the Feis Ceoil brought traditional music into the domain of public performance, academic discourse and public debate. In the opinion of some scholars, this musical practice needed to progress and become modern. Traditional musicians needed to be educated 'in musical science',[23] and brought into the market place and paid for their performance. The forms and repertoire of Irish music needed to be developed using models from European art music.

In former eras, Irish traditional music was perceived as 'barbarous' music and was held in low esteem by 'cultured' classes. Now in the context of cultural nationalism, the attitude towards this music and its cultivation changed with many believing that it was time 'to elevate the study to the dignity of a science'.[24] If this 'science' had been developed by adhering to the aesthetics of the musical practice, then the entrance of traditional music into the schools would have taken a different course than it actually did. For example, Richard Henebry, writing in 1908, focused on the importance of the performance context in passing on traditional music, especially 'the complementary life associations that vivify music and give it a grip'. Likewise the standard of judging the music was 'the aesthetic, the totality of feeling induced by it'. Passing on the music depended on a total immersion in the practice, especially in the early years.[25] Henebry's statement addressed the essence of the tradition, its aesthetic, and its importance in the transmission process. Teaching traditional music in formal education contexts should, in his opinion, be grounded aesthetically in the primary performance context.

Differences between the aesthetics and pedagogy of traditional and classical music surfaced again in discussions about an Irish national school of music.[26] A variety of scenarios was offered reflecting the attitudes and values of both traditionally and classically trained musicians, as well as cultural nationalists. As early as 1892, Douglas Hyde proposed the establishment of music schools that were rooted in Irish traditions.

> I am afraid in this practical age to go so far as to advocate the establishment in Cork or Galway of a small institution in which young and promising pipers might be trained to play all the Irish airs and sent forth to delight our population; for I shall be told that this is not a matter for even an Irish government to stir in, though it is certain that many a Government has lavished money on schemes less pleasant and less useful.[27]

In a publication of Irish songs in 1894, A. P. Graves asked: 'What are our Irish schools of music doing with this inestimable legacy? How many of their professors and teachers are even alive to its existence? If so, how is their knowledge of it influencing the studies of their pupils?' These rhetorical questions were followed by an assertion that 'it is indeed high time for us to restart a school of national Irish music'.[28]

The idea for a national school of music became more popular at the turn of the century as the movement of cultural nationalism intensified. Classical musician Brendan Rogers imagined it as

A class or style, or order of musical art . . . which has sprung from a people's nature, has grown with their growth, has been broadly, deeply and strongly tinctured with their hereditary characteristics, which becomes the fitting . . . which has sprung from a medium by which they give expression to the changeful moods which the varying fortunes of their history have made characteristic of their daily lives.[29]

This school reflected the accumulated musical consciousness of the people and it was rooted in their everyday experiences. However, it was an image that could be applied to any national school of music and one that needed clarification.

To many critics, the academies already established in Ireland were not fulfilling their role as national schools of music. In addition to the Royal Irish Academy of Music (RIAM), two municipal schools of music were founded in this period, the Cork School of Music in 1878 and the Dublin Municipal School of Music in 1890.[30] The latter began under the aegis of the RIAM with a grant from the Dublin Corporation and was taken over by the City of Dublin Technical Education Committee in 1904. Prior to that change, in 1902, W. H. Grattan-Flood had criticised both the academy and the Dublin School of Music for their un-Irish character.[31] After the School of Music changed affiliation in 1904, the curriculum expanded to include aspects of traditional music. Instruction in uilleann pipes and Irish war pipes were among the new subjects. The culture of both municipal schools of music was different to the academy. They were founded to provide 'a thoroughly systematic education' to all classes, and in the case of Dublin, to provide instruction for municipal band members at reduced fees.[32]

Many nationalists believed that separate schools of music needed to be established for traditional musicians, thus maintaining the authentic character of the practices. In 1902, The Revd

Heinrich Bewerunge suggested that such schools be established in Irish-speaking districts.[33] Others saw training in classical music as a prerequisite to training in traditional music. Annie Patterson suggested that traditional musicians be trained in music notation and in 'sight-singing of Irish melodies from ordinary notation'.[34] She also suggested that 'thoroughly cultured' musicians would teach theory and voice production classes at each branch of the Gaelic League. In her opinion, only after a thorough drilling in theoretical and technical work, and exposure to 'all that is best in the literature of music', should the young musician be trained in 'the proper emotional rendering of Irish music and song'.[35] The sequence of instruction advocated here implied a movement from art to folk music. In essence, what Patterson was suggesting came from a distinctly classical world of music pedagogy. Considering that education in classical and traditional music had developed in different sociocultural worlds prior to this, their full integration in a music school or institution was not likely as an immediate outcome. Both genres did expand but successful intersections and interactions were minimal.

MUSIC IN NATIONAL EDUCATION

As a school subject, music creates its own subculture within schools to reflect the prevailing values of school, local and national communities. The music curriulum, then, varies in different school types, each having a different political agenda and set of goals and loyalties. In the *fin-de-siècle* period, the rural or lay school became increasingly connected to the parish community and often the national school teacher was the musical leader of the parish, especially in the context of church music. It was these same schools that responded most enthusiastically to the nationalist movement and taught patriotic and Irish language songs for the cause. Christian Brothers' schools were also reputed as supportive of nationalist values as those values were related to Catholicism. Joep Leerssen points out that the Christian Brothers' schools were 'a breeding ground for that type of Irish separation which flourished in the later decades of the [nineteenth] century'.[36] Many convent schools seemed more attuned to elevating the musical tastes of the students and preparing them for participation in the classical traditions of Catholic Church music. Private, denominational secondary schools were designed to provide a classical education, and music served to develop the values of 'high culture' and ecclesiastical taste. In general, these secondary schools were not as responsive to the demands of nationalist agendas.

NATIONAL SCHOOLS

Music in an age of accountability

Music in national schools came under the influence of economic, sociopolitical and educational trends during this period. Between 1872 and 1899, a payment-by-results system dominated the National School System. As part of this era of educational accountability, a competency-based, examination-oriented system was established. Highly structured syllabi were laid down for each subject, student progress was evaluated regularly by board inspectors, and teachers were paid according to pupils' results. Each school subject became an economic commodity and was ranked in monetary value against other subjects. Since teachers' salaries were dependent on the results of their pupils, they were forced to enter into the system and to succumb to its regulations even if they were opposed to them.

The technical and mechanical aspects of music were emphasised, those aspects which could be standardised, quantified, and measured. As a school subject, music inherited all the characteristic features of the system – monetary rewards, calculated outcomes, competition, accountability, and categorisation. The element of competition was evident at a number of levels – a competition for teachers to win pupils' music fees, a competition between the Hullah and Curwen methods of teaching, a competition between schools in singing contests. The payment-by-results system brought music teaching and learning to a low ebb, resulting in what was perhaps the most destructive period for music in the entire history of that subject in Irish education.

While the curricular status of music improved somewhat in 1883 when it was changed from being an 'extra' subject to being an ordinary and optional subject,[37] there were many obstacles impeding its development. The vocal programme was highly theoretical;[38] dividends for teaching music were low and the risk factor was high in monetary terms;[39] fees paid for pupils in lower classes were dependent on the musical proficiency of pupils in the upper classes, and the annual gratuity for teaching music made available in 1859 was now granted only to teachers employed in model schools, or teachers in ordinary national schools who taught music outside school hours.[40]

An inspector's report from Limerick in 1893 illustrated how music taught before school hours actually improved school attendance and punctuality. 'The pupils are enthusiastic about Tonic Sol-fa; they beam with delight when asked to sing by it. This ardour has been utilised to insure punctuality in several schools'.[41] Whether this practice was regional or national, it does provide evidence of the success of the Tonic Sol-fa system, a method of sight-singing that received strong official support.[42] By the end of the nineteenth century, it had displaced the Hullah system and became an institution of Irish primary education until the introduction of *An Curaclam Nua* (*The New Curriculum*) in 1971. In the initial stages of adopting this method, there was some resistance to change, especially by those who believed it did not use standard musical notation.[43]

The rote-note controversy (singing by ear versus from staff notation) was widely debated during this period, as it was in other Western countries. The fact that singing by ear was not recognised as legitimate for examination purposes was criticised by many, considering that in Britain, from 1882 forward, it gained half the fees out of the possible grant for singing by note.[44] Many inspectors believed that singing by note was inappropriate for primary-age children and supported the Tonic Sol-fa method because it was more accessible to children.[45] Others, however, made disparaging remarks about music instruction, were not supportive of music in the curriculum, and were quite merciless in evaluating students' progress during music examinations.[46] This caused anxiety for teachers and pupils alike, captured in this description:

> The art of the Inspector lay in finding out if there was any individual not singing, and how he went up and down the line stooping to catch the varied tones from the frightened units who stood trembling lest they should be put out of the class as disqualified and thus come under another eye – the eye of the disappointed master.[47]

Similar to earlier decades of the century, the songs taught were mainly imported and devoid of native material. Advertisements for songbooks in the *Irish Teachers Journal* indicated an influx of English publications, most of which were adapted to the Tonic Sol-fa method of music teaching.[48] To meet teachers' needs, emphasis was placed on preparing pupils for the board's music examinations, as evident in the music textbooks published by Glover and Co. in Dublin, 'Glover's Results Fees in Vocal Music with Corresponding Music: What to do and how to go about it'.[49]

The abstract nature of the music curriculum and the negative conditions surrounding its implementation placed music in a precarious position. The aesthetic dimension of music education was bled in the political economy of the payment-by-results system (1872–99). Teachers became discouraged and irate due to new conditions.[50] Could an 'unprofitable' subject like music flourish in the schools? The amount paid in grants for music requisites in the early years of the system showed a decline of interest in music.[51] The number of pupils presented for music examinations decreased; at the same time the percentage pass rate increased, thus making the subject exclusive and élitist.[52] By 1896, only 14.0 per cent of national schools presented students for music examination, compared to 99.8 per cent of schools in Britain and 96.6 per cent of schools in Scotland in the same year.[53] It is clear that music did not thrive in national schools during the payment-by-results era.

Music in an age of competition

As already evident in the forum of the Feis Ceoil, music competitions were popular in turn-of-the-century Ireland. They provided a platform not only for music performance but also for the appropriation of certain musical practices and the advancement of nationalist ideologies. Competitions became a feature of school music culture beginning in the 1890s. They developed in Cork and Dublin and in both centres their growth was associated with the Catholic Church which played a dominant role in educational and political life in *fin-de-siècle* Ireland. At one level, Catholicity was increasingly associated with Irish independence, being a mark of identity that was 'distinctively un-English'.[54] At another level, the Catholic Church's interest in musical matters was linked to international efforts to improve congregational singing and church music in general. A diocesan synod held in Thurles in 1879 produced a decree which addressed liturgical music. This development, combined with the activities of the Irish Society of St Cecilia and the steadfast leadership of Catholic clergy such as Archbishop William Walsh, The Revd Heinrich Bewerunge, and The Revd E. Gaynor, and church organists such as Brendan Rogers and Joseph Seymour, highlighted the importance of Catholic Church music in education.

The favourable state of music education in Cork city and surrounding areas was in large part due to the efforts of The Revd E. Gaynor of the Congregational Missions in Cork who visited many of the larger schools, organised singing classes, and promoted the Tonic Sol-fa system.[55] In addition, an Association for the Advancement of Music in Primary Schools was founded, with a £50 grant from the City of Cork Corporation. Within this environment the first singing competition was held in the School of Art in late 1892.[56] Indicating the competition's close connection with the Catholic Church, it was described in *Lyra Ecclesiastica* as 'an event of some significance for Irish Cecilians'.[57]

In Dublin, singing competitions began in 1893 under the influence of the Catholic Church, with support from head inspector with the Board of National Education, Sir Patrick Keenan,[58] and music inspector Peter Goodman. Monitored by the governors of the Royal Irish Academy of Music,[59] the first competition took place on 29 June 1893, at the Antient Concert Rooms. Similar to the Cork competition, one of the aims was to prove the Tonic Sol-fa method superior to the Hullah method,[60] the former receiving open support from the Catholic clergy.[61]

In promoting public singing competitions, Goodman and other organisers believed that they were liberating music from the narrow focus of the board's program. They saw the need to provide teachers with some motivation to go beyond mere examination of syllabi. However, the mentality of the era was so grounded in competition, examinations, and 'payment-by-results' that any efforts to broaden the scope of music in the schools were influenced by that mentality. Motivation to participate in competitions came in two forms – first, the prospect of honour and glory and second, substantial monetary prizes. The media of the day provided positive encouragement for these events stating that there ought to be more competitions and more schools competing.[62]

Competitions were continued annually under the auspices of Dublin Corporation.[63] The Dublin Catholic clergy played a significant role in their development and thus influenced music in the Dublin schools, most especially in convent schools. Aware of the value of music in national schools as a means of improving the quality of church choirs, Archbishop William Walsh of Dublin, among others, encouraged schools to participate and acknowledged the winners of the competition by inviting them to participate in a major Church festival in honour of St Cecilia.[64] In turn, the board's inspector of music, Peter Goodman, approved of the interest displayed 'by our highest ecclesiastical authorities' in the music education of children in national schools, and their support of the Tonic Sol-fa system of instruction. He publicly acknowledged the positive effect such encouragement had on the standard of school music, especially in convent schools.[65]

Beyond the convent schools and those in urban areas such as Dublin and Cork, the clergy's influence was evident in provincial and rural areas also. In the late 1870s and 1880s, an era of reform in Catholic Church music, priests had been encouraged to look to their own parish primary schools to improve congregational singing. It seems that many priests responded to this advice. For example, in 1887, Inspector Downing of Galway observed: 'Several choirs consisting of the teachers and pupils of the National schools may now be heard, even in Connemara, on Sundays, performing sacred music in a becoming manner, and, in at least three instances, the organ or harmonium played by pupils of the National schools'.[66] Music inspector Peter Goodman, being a church organist and staunch member of the Irish Society of St Cecilia, not only supported the use of Catholic Church music in education but also compiled *The Catholic School Hymn-Book* which contained fifty English hymns, twenty-four Latin hymns for Benediction, and a unison mass by Singenberger.[67] The role of music in transmitting Catholic ideals expanded during this period to reflect the increased influence of the Catholic Church in school and community life. Similar to the mid-century period, this was most true of music education provided by Catholic religious orders.[68]

One striking pattern that emerges from sources describing music in national schools of this era was the impact of the competitive mentality on the way school music was evaluated and how it excluded major sectors of the school-going population from music instruction. First, the urban-rural worlds of music education became farther removed from one another by the growth of public singing contests in the urban areas of Dublin and Cork. While positive reports of music in the schools in previous decades were generally directed at model schools and convent schools throughout the country, in this period a distinction between urban and rural schools was evident, one which favoured urban schools, with convent schools maintaining the same positive image. Inspectors' reports frequently identified the musicality of Dublin and Cork children.[69]

Second to the rural-urban distinction was a clear gender discrimination in the Dublin singing competitions. Boys' and girls' competitions took place on separate days at different venues because, 'as things musical are at present in the Dublin schools, the boys would have no chance in competition with the girls'.[70] This prevalent Victorian attitude of music belonging peculiarly to female education was reinforced through the medium of these competitions. For example, in 1894, the competition for girls' schools took place in public on the 27 June, but only the winning choir of the boys' competition held on the previous day performed, and that choir's performance took place during the interval in the concert.[71]

The urban-rural distinction and the gender bias were paralleled at a more global level in terms of a north-south regional difference, a theme which was already apparent in music education in earlier decades. While Inspector Skeffington commented in 1899 that 'the people here in the south are musical, and the pupils readily learn singing',[72] there were numerous remarks in the reports on the non-musical nature of Northerners.[73] Such comparisons based on gender, school type, ethnic background, or geographical location, resulted in music being perceived as an exclusive subject available to certain populations. Inequality of educational opportunity ensued and some of these factors continued to be prevalent into the late twentieth century.

The negative effects of music competitions were acknowledged officially in the 1890s. Singing contests were changed in 1897 from inter-group competition to individual group examination. All groups who obtained 75 per cent of the total marks received £10, a certificate for the school, and individual book prizes for pupils. While the tensions of competition were, in theory, obliterated and exposure to humiliation and failure minimised, the nature of music performance and its rewards were similar to previous years. In national schools, the ills of competition in children's music education – fear, compulsion, humiliation, jealousy – were discussed as part of the greater recognition of the ills of the payment-by-results system. In 1899, Goodman stated:

> Payment by results of individual examinations has not succeeded in making our teachers cultivate art for art's sake. Would it not be well, therefore, to seek to make Music loved and cherished in the school for its own sake, and so to deal with it that each teacher will come to

regard it, not merely as a source of money making for himself, but rather as a means of bringing pleasure and happiness into the lives of the little ones entrusted to his care?[74]

Music in an age of changing educational philosophy

With the abolition of the payment-by-results system in 1899, the early twentieth century brought reform within education and much thought was given to making the system democratic and more in touch with the realities of the surrounding culture.[75] Music in national schools came under the influence of this new thinking: it began to be valued as a medium for establishing self and group discipline, for confronting moral issues, and for linking home, school, and society. Attention was focused on the needs and characteristics of the child and the provision of age-appropriate instruction. In addition, national schooling became increasingly associated with the process of nation-building and the promotion of patriotism, civic responsibility and common national ideals.[76] When taken as a whole, the new education movement addressed the total development of the child – physical, social, intellectual, aesthetic, and emotional – and set it in the larger sociocultural context. Music was to become a living and significant component of the child's education, a subject which radiated beams of pleasure and delight not only in school culture but also in homes and communities.

In 1900, vocal music became an obligatory subject of the new *Revised Programme of Instruction in National Schools*[77] and the beginning years of the century were marked by waves of reform in national-school music. The élitist attitude towards music which dominated previous decades gave way to a more democratic one. An effort to disseminate music to the remotest regions of the island was at the forefront. Music in education was to be 'national' both in its presence in the schools and in its content. The commissioners' mandate to introduce music 'into all schools as soon as possible' was reflected in the increasing percentage of schools who offered music instruction, from 17 per cent in 1899 to 78 per cent in 1907.[78]

To assist teachers with the goal of universal music education, an intensive teacher inservice programme was provided by the commissioners.[79] Care was taken to reach teachers in remote, 'culturally deprived' rural districts, based on the assumption that 'outside the towns, Music in Ireland is practically an unknown art'.[80] The will to expand music education in national schools was strong and the philosophy for music education changed accordingly. Yet the methods used to teach music and the values that surrounded it seemed to change little in certain respects. Emphasis continued to be placed on sight-singing and the democratic notion of music for every child was not embraced, for the most part, until much later in the century. Tonic Sol-fa was the recommended method of sight-singing over staff notation,[81] and Curwen's music education charts and modulators were supplied to schools. The mechanical, formal aspects of ear-training and sight-reading were given much instructional time and attention.[82]

A second feature of singing in the schools, and more especially in rural schools, was the practice of ignoring those pupils labelled as 'non-singers'.[83] Inspector Dalton issued a warning with regard to the growth of this phenomenon in the Portarlington district:

> 'The singing classes are reserved for rigidly selected pupils and sometimes limited to a small minority of the pupils; all the pupils who are supposed to be in any way deficient in "voice" being rejected. If this practice is not checked it will eventually kill singing as a popular accomplishment, and go far towards destroying musical voice power in the next generation.'[84]

A dichotomous view of singing ability was in operation here: you can sing or you can't. The idea of nurturing a singing voice seemed to be foreign to teachers. Owing to the highly personal nature of the voice as a musical instrument, rural children would typically be at a disadvantage compared with their urban counterparts since they tended to be more introverted and shy. The cult of excellence in performance and the either-or dichotomous view of musicality were values brought forward from nineteenth-century practice and reinforced through the medium of singing competitions beginning in the 1890s.

In addition to vocal music, this period saw the development of instrumental music in the National School system. While it had been granted status as an extra subject in 1859, a new regulation of 1885 elevated it to a subject that could be taught to fifth and sixth classes within school hours. The curriculum described a two-year programme for piano similar to the syllabus of the Royal Irish Academy of Music and other colleges of music of the day.[85] Instrumental music was primarily available in the schools of affluent communities and in convent schools where 'daughters of respectable well-off parents' had many opportunities for practising at home.[86] The number of schools presenting pupils for examinations in instrumental music increased from 47 schools in 1884, 168 in 1891, to 180 in 1899.[87] Similar to vocal music in this era, however, instrumental music teaching was exclusive and available only to a minority of students.

As the new century was ushered in, the impact of the cultural nationalist movement became more evident in education. Accordingly, the music curriculum began to reflect nationalist values and aspirations.

Music in an age of nationalism

Literature on Irish education in the early years of the century reflected the countrywide preoccupation with nationalism.[88] The National School system was viewed critically as 'a colourless, unnational thing, from which every element has been eliminated that might serve as a link between the future and the past, or help to make his country dear to the child'.[89] Music was seen by nationalists as a primary source for stimulating nationalist ideals, and the inheritance of native music traditions was considered central to the formation of Irish cultural identity. One author questioned the absence of native music in the system's schools:

> Why are the children not taught, first and foremost, to sing all the better-known national melodies before they touch melody of any other kind? This learning of the 'Songs of Our Land' should be a *sine qua non*, and go hand in hand with the study of the Gaelic tongue.[90]

In official circles, the *raison d'être* for music in national schools remained remarkably consistent with that of the nineteenth century, focusing on its value as 'a refining and intellectual pursuit, . . . beneficial in most cases to the health and spirits of the pupils, . . . [and] calculated to have a cheering influence on school life generally'.[91] A circular issued by the London Board of Education to teacher-training colleges throughout the islands and issued in Ireland in 1902 suggested that students in teacher training should be impressed with the importance of passing on the national songs of England and Wales, Scotland and Ireland to the next generation, thus setting 'a wholesome standard in musical taste'.[92] The 'wholesome standard' envisioned here through use of national music was not the standard embraced by Irish cultural nationalists.

The political agenda of the London statement was Ireland's continued union with Britain; the nationalist agenda was diametrically opposed to this, as its goal was independence from Britain.[93]

From the perspective of Gaelic League leaders and supporters, national school teachers were vitally important in the task of transmitting the native cultural heritage. The teaching of Irish music in the schools received support from the teaching profession, but certain challenges needed to be overcome. First, no general consensus existed as to what constituted Irish music; in addition, opinions on the future of Irish traditional music varied. Traditionalists battled with modernists, conservatives with progressivists, leading to a lack of consensus as to what the child should learn as an inheritor of Irish music traditions. Second, the Irish language was only being revived, with the introduction of Irish in a bilingual programme in 1904. Third, a repertoire of Irish music appropriate for primary school pupils was needed. From the early years of the century, those who published song materials began to balance their collections between Irish language songs and Anglo-Irish music. Examples of such collections were Peter Goodman's *The Irish Minstrel* (1907),[94] and Fr Walsh's *Fuinn Na Smól* (1913) and *Songs of the Gael* (1915).[95]

The Irish Minstrel served as a symbol of official recognition of native Irish music in the curriculum of national schools. Its exclusive focus on Irish songs and airs may be interpreted as a response to the demands of cultural nationalists. Viewed from another perspective, it may be seen as part of the wider British discourse on the use and value of folk-song in education which was maintained during the early years of the century.[96] A second song collector, Fr Walsh, visited the Gaeltacht (Irish-speaking) regions, 'those favoured glens and mountains where anglicisation has not yet triumphed'.[97] There he transcribed songs which were still part of the living tradition and published them with Tonic Sol-fa notation in a series of seven booklets, *Fuinn na Smól*. Recognising that a great number of teachers and students did not understand the Irish language sufficiently well to be able to sing songs in Irish, he compiled another collection of 200 Anglo-Irish songs and ballads and wedded them to traditional Irish airs in *Songs of the Gael*. His efforts may be compared to Moore's *Irish Melodies* published one century earlier. The primary difference arose in the source of the airs. Moore composed lyrics for Stevenson's arrangement of airs from the notated collection of Bunting, while Walsh's collections depended more on field research with living musical traditions. Goodman's and Walsh's efforts to provide Irish music for the national schools represent but a fraction of the rising tide of native Irish song materials in both languages in the early decades of the century.[98]

Collections of hymns in the Irish langauge were also published, *Dia Linn Lá Gus Oidhche* (1917) and *Raint Amhrán* (1917).[99] The provision of hymns in the Irish language in these decades was aimed at wedding Catholicism and nationalism and, in the process, developing homogenous Irish characteristics in the next generation. Irish language songs and Catholic hymns, the staple diet of singing in independent Ireland, were already established as the canon of Irish school music by 1920. Two examples taken from the autobiographical writings of Patrick Shea (1908–86) and Paddy Crosbie (1913–82) provide support for this conclusion. Shea described his Irish childhood in Deerpark in the midlands and recalled singing class at Deerpark National School around 1916: 'We fairly belted out "The Minstrel Boy", "Let Erin Remember", "A Nation Once Again", and, out of respect for the Principal's native county, "The Bells of Shandon".'[100] While Shea's recollections described repertoire with a strong patriotic spirit, Crosbie's description of his early convent-school music education focused on hymns. He wrote:

> We were taught plenty of hymns e.g. 'I'll sing a hymn to Mary', the Lourdes hymn, and a hymn which we all thought was 'Oh Mother I could sweep the earth', but which in reality was 'Oh, Mother I could weep for mirth'. We learned also 'Sweet heart of Jesus', 'To Jesus Heart All Burning', 'Hail Glorious, Saint Patrick', and so on. We knew all of these songs and sang them lustily on the many occasions offered, particularly at the May Processions.[101]

Crosbie comments that he was aware of the difference between the songs he learned in the convent school and the British songs such as 'God Save Our Glorious King' that he heard sung in the nearby Protestant school in Blackhall Place on his way home from school.

In this era of cultural nationalism, it is not surprising to find a school devoted to the ideals of an Irish-Ireland. This was Scoil Éanna founded by Pádraig Pearse in September of 1908. Pearse was involved with the activities and publications of the Gaelic League and in particular with its Education Committee. This involvement, coupled with his keen interest and research into educational reform, prompted him to design an educational experiment in the form of an Irish school. Music and dance were an integral part of the school's culture and ethos from the beginning. The repertoire and musical instruments taught reflected a deep commitment to the Irish language and to Irish music and dance traditions.[102] Links were created with cultural and political events outside the school.[103]

With the onset of World War I, the climate of war at home and abroad had positive and negative effects on music in schools. On the negative side, it brought a crass, utilitarian mentality back into the education system. The 1916 Irish National Teachers' Orgainzation (INTO) congress criticised the overloaded curriculum of the revised programme issued in 1900 and demanded a return to the basic subjects.[104] Music was once again relegated to the periphery as an additional subject, its availability dependent upon the staffing of the school and local needs and resources.[105] No argument could rationalise the centrality of the arts in primary education. It is ironic that the body representing the national teachers of Ireland should make this 1916 congressional statement to coincide with the assassination of some of Ireland's idealists and cultural visionaries, and in particular their leader, Pádraig Pearse.

On the positive side, the climate of war highlighted the power of school music to unite people for a common cause and to instill patriotic sentiments for the homeland. During World War I, for example, many school concerts were organised 'on behalf of local distress caused through the war'.[106] Public performance had functioned in important ways since the early days of music in national education. In the mid and late nineteenth century, it provided entertainment on public examination days and prize-giving days. In the 1890s it assumed the form of competition. In the early twentieth century, there is ample evidence to show the rise in popularity of the school concert so that by 1907 Goodman wrote that it had become 'a fixed institution' in many places.[107] The school concert provided opportunities for the performance of instrumental music. Although class instruction in instrumental music was not organised officially in national schools, it did occur haphazardly, its development dependent on individual teachers, school traditions, or local musical traditions. The first two decades of the twentieth century witnessed major developments in group instrumental teaching both in Europe and in the United States. The method of the British Maidstone violin classes was adopted successfully into violin class teaching in America,[108] and advertised widely in Irish teachers' journals.[109] Political and economic conditions in Ireland did not support the development of instrumental music in formal education, and this absence marks a major difference between music education in Ireland and other Western countries to this day.

Instrumental school music flourished when it was linked to community music groups which were a feature of many towns around the country. Bands developed in nineteenth-century garrison towns where the local militia usually supported their growth. The social milieu of the Temperance movement also nurtured the growth of brass bands, and bands in general, whether fife and drum or brass and reed, served an important function in nineteenth-century political movements such as the Land League. In fact it was a report on 'The State of National Bands in Ireland' in 1887 that stimulated the establishment of the Dublin Municipal School of Music in 1890.

Traditions of instrumental ensembles in urban and rural communities were well established when the idea of class instruction in instrumental music for children emerged at the beginning of the twentieth century. The first example of school-community partnerships in instrumental music comes from Foxford, Co. Mayo, where the Sisters of Charity founded a convent in 1891; in the following year the Sisters opened the Providence Woollen Mills and a primary school. Certain members of the religious order were accomplished musicians and they established choir and orchestra for the young students.[110] In 1923 a music school was built. Local children came there to learn piano and violin at a nominal fee. A children's orchestra continued to function into the 1930s,[111] and out of this centre of musical activity emerged a men's brass band. Music education thrived in this closely-knit rural community. Children participated in music performance groups from an early age and, due to the pervasiveness of music in the community, they regarded it as a life-long engagement. The flourishing economy, coupled with strong leadership from the members of the Sisters of Charity, provided a firm base for the future development of music in the town.

Another example of music thriving in a small community in the early decades of the century is Buttevant, Co. Cork. A writer in the *Irish School Weekly* described the development of the musical groups.

> The Buttevant School Band, like the orchestra, is the natural offshoot of the musical training given in the school. The orchestra was

improvised, and subsequently developed, in connection with the school concerts, dances etc., and in the same way the band was organised in order to bring physical drill to perfection.

A local committee, under the patronage of the Very Rev. Manager, provides the necessary funds for the instruments, and the instruction necessary to keep up a supply of players. Its functions are very popular, and they are carried on non-political and non-sectarian lines. Candidates for admission to the band must have a very high school record, and the competition is very keen. It has been eight years in existence, and its effect on the morale of the school is very marked.[112]

The determining factor in the growth of instrumental music in Buttevant was the presence of interested and musically oriented teachers in the boys' school and the strong tradition of music which the Sisters of Mercy had developed since 1879 when their convent was founded in the town. When the Buttevant School Band disbanded, Mother Nalasco founded the Buttevant Brass and Reed Boys' Band in 1937, a band which functions to this day.[113] While leadership in music education was forthcoming from the teachers and Sisters, the local community and clergy provided support for their projects. Various ensembles, in turn, fulfilled social functions within that community.

Both examples from Foxford and Buttevant illustrate the role of local communities in shaping instrumental music in schools – the interest of teachers or community members, economic conditions of the locality, the perceived social value of investing in such a project, and the presence of music teachers in the community. Instrumental music education was perceived as ultimately serving important communal needs. These examples indicate that geographical location played a less significant role in determining whether children had opportunities to learn instruments: other factors such as local leadership, musicians, communal values and traditions, and economic conditions were more significant.

INTERMEDIATE EDUCATION

Classical roots of music in secondary education

The Intermediate Education Act of 1878 represented the first step towards state control of secondary education. The Act itself was a response to repeated demands from the middle class for a post-primary system of education. There was a long-standing tradition of classical education in Ireland prior to the Act, designed for middle-class Catholics and Protestants.[114] In that tradition, the curriculum had a strong 'humanist grammar-school' bias, one in which music played a complementary role to a comprehensive classical education.[115] At St Stanislaus college, a Jesuit college in Tullabeg and 'one of the most foremost colleges in Ireland at the time', specialist music teachers were employed in the 1870s to teach piano, violin, school band, and dancing lessons.[116] The role of music at Carlow College was aligned to the tradition of Catholic colleges. In describing a college concert, one observer was critical of the fact that in an Irish college such as this, too little attention was given to native Irish music with overemphasis on Italian repertoire.[117] The values of Anglo-Irish society – art as synonymous with 'high culture' and as a desired accomplishment of the educated classes – permeated the music curriculum of colleges which provided 'superior' or secondary education.

Irish traditional music was worthless, it would seem, in the view of those who sought to transmit the values of 'high culture' to students. A writer in the *Carlow College Magazine* conveyed this attitude.

> It is true that the National Board of Education, has, within certain narrow limits, . . . taken measures to promote a knowledge of the rudiments of Music among our peasantry. By the encouragement it has given to vocal music, especially to part singing according to the Hullah system of teaching, it has contributed much to elevate the musical taste of the rising generation of our humbler classes to a something that will not rest quite satisfied with the strains of the Ballad singers, fiddlers, pipers, and such other wandering minstrels, as they were obliged to put up with for many a year.[118]

Such a view of the music of the peasants was not limited to any one political group or religious denomination. Irish traditional music and Catholicism, the denomination of the vast majority of its practitioners, now began to be dissociated. In other words, while traditional musicians were typically Catholic, not all Catholics endorsed the values and culture surrounding traditional music. This growing separation was but another indication of the degree to which the Catholic clergy had appropriated Anglo-Irish cultural values. The monopoly of European art music with its connotations of 'high culture' was also evident in the schools of other religious denominations.[119]

The establishment of music in intermediate education

During the initial years of music in a state-supported, centralised system of secondary education, patterns were laid down that influenced the shape of music instruction in this sector of Irish education in the twentieth century. The acquisition of musical knowledge and skill was viewed as an accomplishment of an educated person and in particular that of females. The music curriculum was modelled on conservatory training, i.e., the education of professional musicians; a strong theoretical orientation underpinned music instruction; the curriculum was organised in terms of assessment procedures and syllabi; the evaluation of student achievement was based on a final product (e.g. performance and written examination), and expressed in terms of marks, categories, honours-pass-fail rates, and monetary outcomes; a gender bias gradually led to the exclusion of boys from music examinations; and a strong competitive element was evident at a variety of levels. Each pattern mirrored the dualistic nature of the payment-by-results system which also operated in the Intermediate Education system: you are musical or you are not; you pass or you fail; you win or you lose; you compete and succeed or you are selected out of music.

Subjects in the curriculum were arranged in seven divisions, the last being 'Music, or Drawing, or such subjects of secular education, as the Board may prescribe from time to time'.[120] Reflecting the payment-by-results system, each subject was designated marks according to its perceived value and the results' fees granted reflected the scale of marks set out for each subject.[121] Students were examined at three grade levels and the curriculum and examinations were guided by the standards of the Royal Irish Academy of Music, an institution that had expanded rapidly in the 1870s, having been granted royal recognition in 1872.[122]

The character of music education in the academy was mirrored in the Intermediate Education system. Those who prepared the papers held music doctorates and functioned in a highly academic music milieu, removed from the reality of teaching in secondary schools and the capabilities and interests of secondary-school students. The music curriculum had a strong academic and theoretical bias, one which concentrated on knowledge about music and ways of reproducing that knowledge in examination contexts.[123] The theoretical bias of the programme was reinforced in 1882 when the examination subject 'Music' was altered to 'Theory of Music'.

The standard of theoretical knowledge demanded to pass was raised. In addition, a distinction was made between the number of marks granted to boys (300) and to girls (500) in the examination.[124] This marked the beginning of discrimination against boys' music education within intermediate education. Gender bias in music education was not peculiar to this system. It was a product of Victorian society and reached a climax in Irish music education in the last two decades of the nineteenth century.[125] The music examiners of the Intermediate Education Board were displeased with boys' performance in examinations.[126] Complaints continued through 1888, at which time a regulation was passed stating that 'music shall cease to be a subject of examination for Boys'.[127] This regulation was in place until 1903.

Participation in music examinations decreased also for girls in the 1890s. The élitism of music in intermediate education in this period was clear. The shortcomings of the programme were identified by a music teacher writing in 1902 who posed three legitimate questions: 'First, could not boys as well as girls be included? Secondly, is "theory of music" the only branch of musical art within the scope of the Board? Thirdly, could not the Board err on the side of leniency in drawing up the programme?'[128] Nor was the students' own musical culture or the nationalist movement in the surrounding culture acknowledged. T. O. Russell blamed the lack of Irish content in the curriculum on the fact that 'music-doctors, whether Irish or not, are very seldom Nationalists . . . [They are], as a rule, mortal enemies of Irish music'. He referred to one eminent Dublin music-doctor 'over thirty years ago, an Irishman too, if he heard any of his children playing an Irish air, he'd box their ears'.[129]

Between 1878 and 1900 music was acknowledged in the Intermediate Education system but it assumed a weak and educationally unsound position with no practical component.

Curricular reform in the new century

The weaknesses of the intermediate system of education were acknowledged in the *Report of the Commission on Intermediate Education* (Palles Commission) in 1899. Suggestions made about music included the reintroduction of examinations for boys, the addition of instrumental music, and the introduction of a practical component to the examination.[130] Music reached a low before it was

reformed. In January 1902 it was eliminated from the board's programme. Immediately, a number of groups reacted to this decision,
(the governors of the RIAM, the Leinster Branch of the Incorporated Society of Musicians, and the Catholic Headmasters' Association), each urging the commissioners to reconsider the decision,
since the removal of music from the programme of the board, they
believed, would be fraught with grave results for the study of music
in Ireland.[131] The commissioners responded positively and considered the introduction of practical music. To support the introduction of practical music, a local school examinations system in music
had been in operation in Britain since 1890 and it 'spread its influence to the remotest parts of the British Empire'.[132] Beginning in
1894, local centre examinations were held in Dublin, Belfast, Bray,
and Rathfarnham.

In that context, practical music was established in the secondary curriculum. The governors of the RIAM offered to conduct and
report results of practical examinations to the board, confirming the
status of the academy and identifying reasons why the board should
choose it over other music schools as its official examining body.[133]
The stages leading up to the board's final choice of an examining
body for practical music are vague. The RIAM, claiming to be 'the
only National School of Music', was not invited to fill that position.
An English organisation operating in Ireland, the Incorporated
Society of Musicians, was chosen instead.[134]

The year 1904 was significant both in introducing instrumental
music programmes and in re-establishing theory of music examinations for both boys and girls. However, there was general dissatisfaction with the implementation of the programmes and the
examinations. Complaints from teachers and school administrators
were numerous. They concerned the manner in which monetary
bonuses were granted, the high fees for entering choirs or orchestras for examinations, the difficulty of the theory examinations, the
need for elevating the status of music to honours level,[135] the
employment of an English examining body to conduct the practical examinations, and the lack of opportunity for provincial schools
to enter for the choir and orchestra competitions held annually in
Dublin, starting in 1904.

Sight-reading was also problematic. From 1910 forward sight-
reading in staff notation was encouraged by granting 25 per cent
more credit to choirs reading from staff notation than those reading from Tonic Sol-fa notation, something that provoked a negative

response from the Tonic Sol-fa College of London. The sight-reading tests in themselves were criticised for their difficulty,[136] compounded by the decision in 1912 that the number of parts in which the sight-test was performed by a choir or orchestra would be one of the criteria for determining the amount of the bonus granted.[137]

In the theory of music examinations, the low standard of students was the subject of criticism among third-level music educators. Percy Buck, professor of music at Dublin University (1910–20), appealed to the board to make music 'more of a preparation for students intending to proceed to a university degree in music'.[138] Both he and Charles Kitson, organist and choir master at Christ Church cathedral and later professor of music at University College Dublin (1916–1920), argued that more weight should be given to music theory. music began to be established in other universities during this period,[139] and university and college music professors continued to influence the secondary music curriculum in terms of content and student evaluation procedures.

An Anglo-Irish music culture

The ethos, content, and examining body of intermediate music education of this period had strong British affiliations. It operated within a highly political and strategic framework. Participation was encouraged by offering extrinsic and non-musical rewards such as monetary bonuses, certificates, prizes, and competitive placements. A British examining body conducted the practical examinations from 1902 forward, a situation that seemed absurd to many critics. Theo Gmur asked:

> Why, in the first instance, should exclusively Englishmen be selected to examine Irish schools, who, as a rule, are not only not in touch with the working of our educational establishments, but who are, in many cases, still prejudiced against Ireland and its institutions?[140]

A bias in favour of British presence was not unique to music in intermediate education. One critic stated in 1908: 'There is nothing distinctly Irish in the whole system. No stimulation of patriotism. The whole outlook is English, and English in its most shallow and unreal form.'[141] Policies, rules, and curriculum content did not reflect the changing political values of early twentieth-century Ireland.

In the selection of choral pieces for examinations a list of twelve prescribed pieces for two-, three-, and four-part choirs was compiled by the board and issued in 1908.[142] With the exception of one of Moore's melodies, there was a marked predominance of songs of British origin. After the Irish rebellion in 1916, a national element began to surface in the choral set pieces: 'Shule, agra' (1917); 'The Minstrel Boy' (Thomas Moore) (1918); 'Turn Ye to Me' (Old Gaelic) (1919); and 'The Minstrel Boy' (1920).[143] Only in the event of the War of Independence was there any evidence of Irish repertoire found in the music curriculum of intermediate education. Up to that point, it followed closely the model provided by conservatory music education.

Similar to national school education, public examinations were also a feature of music education at this level. One of the first steps taken to encourage the growth of choral and instrumental music was to initiate an examination for school choirs and orchestras in Dublin in 1905.[144] All groups were awarded prizes and the competition was dominated by Dublin schools. Compared to the number of groups examined annually by the board, only a small minority entered for these competitions.[145] The year 1916 marked the last reference to these events in the commissioners' reports. The competition's geographical location, the expense involved in participation, and the disturbed social and political climate of the time were all factors which influenced the demise of this event.

The Catholic Church observed closely the progress of school music in intermediate education, as it did in national schools. *Lyra Ecclesiastica* published a series of articles on music in intermediate schools and its effects on public and ecclesiastical taste. In this survey Brendan Rogers found that, compared to other nations, Ireland had fallen behind in musical standards. He criticised the quality of music education and said that it was here that antidotes were to be found, one being 'the study of high class, i.e., classical music'. In contrast, the repertoire used in schools, in his opinion, was 'unintellectual, commonplace, and trivial', exerting no refining influence but the opposite on the students. He urged the Catholic headmasters to take music education seriously, it being part of their responsibility to society and to the Church.[146] Rogers' exposition is yet another confirmation of the burgeoning alliance between reform in school music and in music within the Catholic Church. Classical music was seen as the nurturer of acceptable public and ecclesiastical taste.

Some cultural nationalists accused convents of shoneenism, an education which aimed to make 'lively-minded Irish girls "respectable" and "more English than the English". 'They teach any music except Irish music, any language except the Irish language, any literature except Irish literature.'[147] One cannot generalise from this observation to all convent education. For example, British visitors to Listowel Convent School in 1887 found that the music teacher and girls sang 'God Save Ireland' with great ease and enthusiasm, but when asked to sing a verse of 'God Save the Queen', 'nobody knew it, and it was plain that nobody cared to sing it. They will sing it at some future time, gently said the Mother Superior'.[148] What is true of convent schools is that the religious sisters believed in the value of teaching art music, whether for nationalist, sociocultural, or ecclesiastical reasons.

In general, music in intermediate education was built solidly on the aesthetics of Western art music. Such instruction transmitted the values of 'high culture', and presented music as an élitist subject.[149] Those features continued to dominate secondary music education well into the twentieth century.

THE TRANSMISSION OF TRADITIONAL MUSIC

Transmission, community, and socialisation

Efforts to develop the native Irish vocal tradition met with many obstacles. The loss of the Irish language as the vernacular of the majority of the people was one factor that affected its transmission. Richard Henebry observed the effects of this change on young singers.

> So, too, I have noticed in a district where a National School has substituted English for Irish in the last ten years, the young girls from their non-use of Irish speech have entirely lost the Irish singing voice. For this habit of English has a physical effect on the speaking organs, and destroys the full, soft, and mellow Irish voice so necessary for singing, and the acquisition of new ideas has ousted the Keltic outlook, and with it the subjective state from which Irish music sprang.[150]

Carl Hardebeck highlighted the importance of socialising young children so that they valued traditional singing and felt confident about singing traditional songs in school. He wrote:

> Let us suppose a Gaelic speaking child comes to the school who has
> learned songs traditionally from his mother or someone else, he is
> now taught the 'strong-weak, medium-weak' accent of the Sol-fa; he
> naturally comes to the conclusion that the school teacher is right
> because of his authority as school teacher, and that those who taught
> the traditional singing must be wrong.[151]

In the spirit of cultural nationalism, many viewed the transmission of traditional music as being the most natural and true way
to learn music. Bewerunge commented frequently on traditionalism in singing, describing it as the way that music is 'handed down
from mother to child, from one peasant singer to his younger companion, without any interference of theoretical knowledge, or of
acquaintance with other kinds of music'. He claimed that while the
child could be trained in both Irish and 'modern' scales, 'we must
not overlook that only really good musicians would learn singing
from mere oral transmission, while in schools even a lot of
mediocre talent is trained up to the rendering of a song'.[152] He
provided an example of this phenomenon from a country feis held
in Ardmore, Co. Waterford, in 1900. A young girl sang her Irish
melody exactly as she had learned it from her mother and a media
report stated that 'her superiority over the artificially-trained children was glaring'.[153] In this instance, the increasingly popular belief
in the superiority of native Irish culture is evident. An unaccompanied, solo tradition in a language barely resurfacing in educational and social realms was difficult to integrate into formal
education. Even if practical measures were not easily found, a
philosophical base for traditional vocal music in formal education
was articulated.

In this *fin-de-siècle* period, the conditions which impeded the
entrance of vocal music into formal education did not arise in the
transmission of traditional instrumental music. Conversely, many
current trends and developments facilitated the development of
music education in this domain. On the social side were the rapidly
growing movements of cultural nationalism, the proliferation of
town bands, the climate of war, and the growing interest in group
music making. The climate of practical education and the development of class teaching methods encouraged the growth of ensembles. Traditional instrumental music education of this era can be
explored in two contexts – first, the master-apprentice context, well
established since the nineteenth century, and second, the forum of

the feiseanna, which motivated pupils to take lessons and prepare for competitions.

In contrast to vocal music, instrumental music was not transmitted to the same degree within the home (the exception being those families who had built a tradition for generations). Master teachers were identified in the immediate community or in a neighbouring community and pupils were sent to them for lessons. In other cases, these masters were itinerant and travelled around to the pupils' houses. When the master and pupil met for a lesson, the master would often inscribe a tune in the pupil's book to help him recall it after the lesson in the master's absence. As Breandán Breathnach points out, music literacy among traditional players was more frequent than one might expect, many men acquiring the skill when they served as a bandboy in some regiment in the British army.[154] Textbooks *per se* served a minimal function, since 'in performance, the printed text has no function. A traditional performer playing in public from music would be regarded as an object of curiosity'.[155]

A variety of indigenous and non-orthodox systems of notation were in use in the transmission of traditional music. Letters, numbers, signs, and the staff (used in a non-orthodox way) were the primary media used to notate tunes. A notational system was selected based on the instrument being taught. The orality of the transmission remained in the forefront. Examples of non-orthodox notational systems for fiddle were those of Pádraig O'Keeffe[156] and Bartly McMagh.[157] The letters of the alphabet were also used to teach fiddle tunes, a system which was also popular with pipers. Describing the renowned, blind fiddle master, Tom Billy Murphy (1879–1944), Ward reported that 'unable to write music, he called out the notes by name and got the pupil to write them down'.[158] Another example of a musician using this system was Billy Heffernan, the 'musical genius' in Kickham's portrayal of Knocknagow, Co. Tipperary. When Heffernan was asked to write down his own composition, 'The Frolic', he replied: 'I don't know how to write music, though I could tell her the names of the notes wan [one] by wan.'[159] Numerical notation systems were also in use and one particular system combined numbers and other non numerical symbols, the dash (−) and the caret (^). Breathnach reported this system as being popular for teaching melodeon and accordion.[160]

Indigenous notation systems displayed individuality, uniqueness, and parochialism, all characteristics which were in keeping

with the nature of the tradition. They also reflected the ineffective-
ness of the exclusive use of any one system of notation in transmitting this repertoire. Unlike the value placed on music theory and
sight-reading in formal music education, instructors in Irish traditional music viewed notation merely as a means to an end which
was independent of that means. This relationship between notation
and the transmission of the music was expressed by one author as
he described musical life in the little hamlet of Kickham's Knocknagow. There, 'life sang and sobbed its course to music. The dry
bones of the art – its symbols – may have been unknown to the
greater number of the dwellers, but its spirit flourished with all the
strength of a living growth'.[161]

The manner in which music was valued in these communities
provided a strong motivational base for young children to participate in music. Music was an integral part of everyday life. As children grew, their musical identity was formed. Personal investment in
music gave many intrinsic delights and rewards. For example, Julia
Clifford, one of Pádraig O'Keeffe's prodigies, recalled:

> I remember, I was mad for music, and I was only very small, and
> Taidy . . . and Denis [brothers] and my father in the evening when
> any bit o' work – doing turf or hay or something – was finished,
> they'd get in the kitchen and start playing music – and the three o'
> them'd be sitting there playing away y'know and they'd play for about
> a couple of hours and they'd leave the fiddles lovely in tune also y'
> know. And they'd get up and go away out . . . 'rambling' . . . And the
> very minute they'd go I'd go for the fiddle, and m' mother 'd say 'Put
> that away or you'll break it' . . . I was so small you know!! . . . But
> 'twas Taidy that learned me the first tune – I'd be craving him to
> learn me one.[162]

In these moments, the innate musicality of the child was tantalised
and the motivation to participate was heightened. As Julia grew
older, she showed great promise on the fiddle but no formal lessons
outside of the home were provided. It was only when she entered
herself for a local music competition and won it that her parents
decided to bring in O'Keeffe to give her lessons.[163]

A less favourable musical atmosphere, but one with no less passion for music, was found in John O'Donoghue's recollections of his
musical childhood. The first instrument he received was a melodeon
which he and his sister learned to play from a neighbour, Shaun
Heila. The enthusiasm and personal investment in this activity were

obvious from the following description of the journey to his teacher's house. 'Many a frosty night Bridget and I ran barefoot across the wild lonely slieve [hill] that led to his house at the foot of a grey rock near the banks of the river to pick up tunes from him.' Although the slieve was said to be haunted, a fear-instilling fact for a child, 'nothing would have daunted me with the joy I felt to be learning a power of tunes'. Motivation for learning was intense and when he heard about a miniature fiddle for sale in a local shop, he ran there 'in a fever of wild excitement, hurrying for fear someone else might get it before me'.[164]

On another occasion, he attended a local open-air concert and heard the Killarney Pipers' Band play. The 'wild spirited music swelling out into the air' was mingled with a secondary observation that the players 'wore a uniform of green jackets and yellow kilts, the last word in Irish national colours'.[165] This musical event motivated him to experiment with reeds and make his own set of pipes. In O'Donoghue's case, the will to learn music was overwhelming. No formal contexts of music education seemed to have been available to match it. Both examples point to the passion for music which was engendered in these children as a result of natural curiosity and musical talent on the one hand, and a nurturing environment on the other.

FORMAL SCHOOLS OF TRADITIONAL MUSIC

As the new century progressed, social and cultural awareness began to be extended beyond the local community. This was in part due to the spread of literacy, and increased general education of the masses, but also emigration, and the growing acceptance of the English language as the vernacular by the majority of Irish people. With the rise of cultural nationalism and the establishment of forums such as feiseanna, traditional music began to enter new public spaces and be observed and evaluated by musicians outside the tradition. Resulting from all of these changes, the need to formalise instruction in traditional music became clear.

Some elements of traditional music did not lend themselves to school settings or to the methods of music education popular at the time. The solo nature of performance, and the unaccompanied, strictly melodic, and highly ornamented style of the vocal tradition stood in contrast to the contemporary preference for concerted and harmonised works.[166] Traditional music notation was inadequate when transcribing the nuances of the live performance. In addition, the Irish language which was wedded to traditional vocal music was only now being introduced into the schools. Finally, teachers were typically unable to stand inside both traditional and classical musical worlds, respect and develop the uniqueness of each tradition in formal music education, and not merely impose the values and methods of the classical world onto traditional music. So the passing on of music in schools and in traditional music contexts continued to develop primarily in separate worlds, although the cultural nationalist movement did promote the introduction of Irish language songs and ballads in national education.

As traditional music entered new cultural contexts in the late nineteenth and early twentieth centuries, organisations of performers were established and the need for primers emerged. The idea of a training school for pipers was advocated by Douglas Hyde as early as 1892, and it is not surprising to find that pipers' clubs were founded as offshoots of the Gaelic League. The Cork Pipers' Club is said to have been founded in March, 1898 but there is no evidence of its activities before early 1899.[167] The Dublin Pipers' Club was established in February, 1900, and by 1904 a similar club was in operation in Limerick. These clubs, although established to revive and popularise the pipes, expanded their activities to include other instruments of the tradition (such as the fiddle), the vocal tradition, and dance. Starting in 1902, the Dublin Pipers' Club held a *píobaireacht* (piping festival) which was competitive in nature like all other music festivals of that era, with a special competition for those learning pipes included in the 1904 festival.[168]

The pipers' clubs (*de facto* representative of the entire spectrum of traditional music) were the first formal schools to organise and provide instruction in traditional music in urban centres.[169] Placed on a larger historiographical canvas, only now in the early twentieth century was the hegemony of British values being challenged in the Pale. Cultural spaces were shifting and so also was the music which had lived in exile outside the Pale for many centuries. An institution such as the Dublin or Cork Pipers' Club was symbolic of this change.

The idealism and activities of the movement of cultural nationalists uplifted Irish traditional music and spread its practice to make it a nationwide phenomenon. The need and demand for education in traditional music emerged in this new phase. While the itinerant master teacher continued to function, more formal educational contexts developed.

MUSIC EDUCATION IN THE *FIN-DE-SIÈCLE* YEARS

Music in formal education in the *fin-de-siècle* period was influenced by four factors – the payment-by-results system, the cultural nationalist movement, the dominance of Victorian cultural and musical values, and the spread of the Tonic Sol-fa method of sight-reading. Music functioned in a strong subculture of competition and examination that was in part imported from the British system and its royal colleges of music. This capitalistic enterprise developed hierarchies at economic, social and musical levels; it served as an organising principle and motivational force for music instruction. In a more general context, educational, religious, and cultural institutions built their power structures around competitive hierarchies. Music education bore the mark of this development, since 'every code of music is rooted in the ideologies and technologies of its age, and at the same time produces them'.[170] The influence of competition reached a climax in the 1890s with the establishment of the Feis Ceoil and the involvement of the Catholic Church in promoting singing competitions to improve church music and elevate ecclesiastical taste.

The cultural vitality and political dynamism of the years 1900–21 were mirrored in the various forms of music transmission of this period, in the National School system, intermediate education, the colleges of music, the movement of cultural nationalism, and in the living traditions of native music. Each form was anchored to one or more cultural ideologies – political, social, religious, or educational – and can be placed along a continuum ranging from the personal tuition of the oral and living native Irish tradition to the culturally sensitive music curriculum of national schools to the highly theoretical and impersonal character of music education in intermediate education. In the native living tradition, music continued to be transmitted primarily through oral media. The role of home and community values and the centrality of music in everyday life were significant in motivating youth to learn music. As general literacy grew in these communities (now in both rural and urban settings), so also did the use of written notation systems become popular in the transmission of music.

The transmission of music in national schools drew from and responded to a rich variety of ideological movements abroad. For a subject that had just become obligatory in the school curriculum, its pacing and development during the early years of the century were considerable. With the spread of the Irish language in national schools, Irish songs were taught, and this practice reinforced the ideology of cultural nationalism while binding the repertoire to the Tonic Sol-fa sight-reading method then in widespread use. A vast repertoire of Irish folk songs and ballads was translated into this notation. Motivation to teach and learn Irish music was intensified by the rise of local feiseanna which provided a competitive forum for displaying individual or group musical talent.

When music in intermediate education is compared to that of primary education, a different dynamic is evident. Here music was anchored to the conservatory model of music education. Motivation to teach or learn music continued to be founded on extrinsic rewards such as money, prizes, marks, all mediated through examinations and competitions. As a curricular subject, music was philosophically weak and pedagogically unbalanced. The theory of music in its most reified form was the only aspect of the subject considered by the board prior to 1902. London-dominated models of music instruction and evaluation permeated the curriculum and when practical music examinations were introduced in 1904, the British influence was furthered by the employment of the Incorporated Society of Musicians as the examining body.

Efforts to form a collective national identity through music education were channelled through numerous cultural organisations and educational systems which were more or less receptive to the agenda of the cultural nationalists. All forms of music education in the *fin-de-siècle* period arose out of specific cultural ideologies. Some percolated down to individual schools from a physically and culturally distant bureaucratic centre, as in the case of intermediate education. Others evolved naturally out of 'art as experience' in the everyday lives of small communities. The rest interplayed between dictatorship and democracy, music as a narrow, specialised domain of institutionalised activity and music as part of shared community life and values.

In the process of advancing nationalist ideals, native Irish music entered the cultural canon of school music to form a counter-hegemony to the high culture which dominated formal music education. In keeping with the philosophy of Irish-Ireland at the time, a narrow definition of Irish music emerged, one that focused on promoting the Irish language, on the one hand, and Catholicism on the other. The respected culture, and the one to be transmitted to the next generation, originated less in social class and more in political ideology, although the two are sometimes inextricably linked. Some native musical leaders such as Annie Patterson struggled between adherence to sociomusical and political values, attempting to elevate the status of traditional music to 'the dignity of a science' worthy of serious academic consideration. Others such as Richard Henebry recognised the importance of accepting the music as it was practised, in its total aesthetic context. The interaction of sociomusical and political values was paralleled by an interaction between religious and political values, manifest in efforts by the Catholic Church to improve liturgical music as part of a greater effort to strengthen the Church's power in Irish culture, and to advance its own brand of nationalism. Music in formal education served as an important forum for achieving these aims.

The concept of community changed in this period, with an expansion in awareness from the local, lived community to the imagined national community. Music played a significant role in realising this transition in the minds and lives of the next generation through transmission of Irish music, particularly Irish language songs and Catholic Church music. Herein lay the seeds of Irish cultural identity in independent Ireland.

5

Constructing Ireland: The Role of Music Education in the Nation State

In the history of any country, the transition from colonialism to independent nationhood is a traumatic one. What was dreamed of and imagined in the prelude to independence was now to be realised in the new Irish Free State after 1921. As in all new nation states, there was a rush to establish identity,[1] an identity that would define a national community and set it apart from other nations. One of the hallmarks of colonial Ireland was the plurality of its political parties, religious denominations, and cultural symbols. In the nation state, the circumstances which created such plurality were greatly eliminated, although the plurality in some ways remained.[2] Nations are 'exclusive clubs', as Ernest Gellner points out, working towards the achievement of 'one culture, one state'.[3]

In the process of nation-building, Ireland experienced an identity crisis during which deep-rooted fears were brought to the surface concerning difference and separateness: where did the core of difference, the justification for separateness lie?[4] Resolution of these deep-rooted fears was central to the struggle for self-definition. The Irish language, Catholicism and other aspects of rural life, markers of Irish culture and of cultural separateness that had mobilised nationalists towards the achievement of independence, continued to dominate educational and cultural policy after 1921. In essence, the values of one Irish tradition formed the national ideology of the new state and were dominant during at least the first four decades of independence.

Policies in new states are deliberately intended to achieve cultural unity. As a result, national cultural policies in the emergent nation state were decisive and absolute. Clear cultural boundaries separated Irishness from otherness and cultural isolation resulted. Two different approaches to nation-building have been described by anthropologist Clifford Geertz and they are useful in understanding cultural development in the Irish nation state.[5] The first, an essentialist approach that was prominent between 1922 and the early 1940s, established clear markers of national identity defined by native cultural heritage. In contrast, the epochalist approach to nation-building which developed in the mid to late 1940s focused more on the spirit of the time, the present needs of the people, and the modernisation of the nation.

DEVELOPING MUSICAL CULTURE IN THE NEW NATION

Musical development, both in formal education and in the culture at large, was influenced by a number of factors during the early decades of independence: a state cultural policy that focused almost exclusively on the revival of the Irish language to the neglect of arts education in general, the prevailing Catholic ethos, the expansion of mass media, and the organisation of music at the national level. The first two reproduced the values of nationalist ideology while the latter two, although at times committed to a nationalist agenda, tended to broaden the vision for music in Ireland.

The language revival movement exerted the single most dominant influence on Irish cultural transmission in independent Ireland. Music's role in education was shaped by state language policy. Fr Corcoran of University College, Dublin, a zealot for language revival and an active educational policy-maker, was consultant in the planning of the National Programme of Primary Instruction that came into operation in April, 1922. Corcoran advocated two forms of vocal music in general education: Irish traditional singing and plain song,[6] the former reinforcing the language and the latter Catholic beliefs and practices. Both of these song repertoires gained official support. In fact, songs in the Irish language were in widespread use in primary schools by 1932 after which the language received a further official impetus during the De Valera administration.[7] Its dominance in the national music curriculum continued throughout this period, particularly in national and vocational schools and to a lesser degree in secondary schools.

Catholicism, a second marker of Irish identity, also affected the direction of music in Irish culture and education in the Free State. In 1926 a summer school of plain song was founded by Fr John Burke, dean of University College, Dublin. Resulting from widespread and consistent efforts of the Catholic Church since the late nineteenth century, the plain chant movement had been quite successful in Ireland, a fact that was recognised widely.[8] Liturgical festivals in many provincial centres such as Tuam, Ennis, Limerick, and Kilkenny were evidence of its countrywide appeal. Even in remote country areas, there is evidence of its influence.[9] These festivals provide a clear example of how ecclesiastical musical taste influenced musical standards in Ireland, an idea that is explored by Fintan O'Toole who argues that the Catholic Church in the early decades of the new state was 'by far the largest patron of the arts', and an important source for shaping musical taste.[10]

The technology of music transmission expanded significantly during these decades. The national radio broadcasting station, RN2 (later Radio Éireann), was founded in 1926 and, along with other mass media, played a major role as an instrument of 'intentional policy' in the new state and opened up possibilities for the manipulation of culture.[11] The first two directors of the radio station, Séamus Clandillon and Séamus Brennan, were Gaelic revivalists and performers of Irish traditional music and dance.[12] It was in this cultural environment that a policy for music in the national radio service was developed. In the realm of educational broadcasting, the radio was viewed as a medium with the potential to reinforce national identity, to promote Irish music, and to raise the standards of musical culture in Ireland. Cultural leaders seeking to build a national identity were aware of the power of radio to shape musical taste and objected when jazz music became popular in broadcasting.

In the early 1930s, Conradh na Gaeilge launched an anti-jazz campaign, believing that jazz had a denationalising influence on Irish culture. The organisation sent a deputation to the Minister for Posts and Telegraphs in 1933, asking for more Irish music on radio and less jazz. In 1935, the Conradh passed resolutions asking for a boycott of jazz music.[13] This issue continued to be debated through the 1930s, and in the early 1940s the minister banned jazz from the airwaves.[14] In this instance, radio acted as a medium of cultural control and a site for establishing a canon of Irish music and for excluding 'other', non-Irish music, regardless of its popularity among the people.

This era also witnessed the development of national networks of communication set up to disseminate musical culture. There was an awareness that for music to progress nationally, it needed to be organised at the national level. The years between 1935 and 1948 witnessed the establishment of numerous music associations, beginning with the Cork Music Teachers' Association in 1935 and culminating in the Music Association of Ireland (MAI) in 1948.[15] Among the MAI's national goals were to further musical education, to improve conditions for composers and musicians generally, to submit recommendations on music policy to the authorities concerned, to organise popular lectures, concerts and recitals, and to awaken musical consciousness in the nation. One of the first tasks undertaken to implement these aims was the submission of a memorandum on music education to the Irish government.[16] In 1953 the MAI was invited to sponsor the launching of the Music Teachers Association, and in 1956 it was admitted to the International Music Council of UNESCO as the Irish National Council.

A number of national agencies and groups assumed responsibility for the development of musical culture. Of primary importance were Radio Éireann, the Garda Síochána Band, the Army Band, and orchestral societies. They performed and broadcast live music concerts and thus advanced the cause of music appreciation, and performed and promoted the works of Irish composers. With heightened awareness of the appreciation of 'good' music, and its increased access and availability through radio and recordings, music appreciation became central to the mission of music education between 1922 and 1960. Such a phenomenon was not unique to Ireland; it had featured prominently in the United States and in certain European countries since the early years of the twentieth century.

TOWARDS A NATIONAL MUSIC AND A NATIONAL SCHOOL OF MUSIC

Fragmented and differing definitions of 'Irish' music brought major obstacles when defining a national musical image that was all-encompassing. In discussions on the future of music in Ireland, essentialist and epochalist approaches to nationality can be found at work. The former concentrated on Ireland's musical heritage, sometimes in a narrow manner; the latter focused on developing the musical creativity of the people and responding to their musical

needs and preferences. This tension was evident in Aloys Fleischmann's criticism of those with an atavistic[17] outlook who sub-
scribed to the essentialist view of Irish national identity, focussing
on the musical achievements of their ancestors. In two 1936 articles, he elaborated on the futility of atavism as a means towards
progress in Irish music.

> Continuity or fidelity of tradition is not best achieved by atavism, by
> a slavish use of the materials of the past. While welcoming the
> spread of Irish traditional music among the people and in the
> schools, while having profound respect for the work of preserving
> and embellishing this centuries-old music (provided it be the work
> of thorough-going scholars and musicians), we must remember that
> the task before us lies in . . . making of music a medium for the
> expression of the life of present-day Ireland, by the use of present-
> day methods elsewhere.[18]

Other Irish musicians, while one cannot accuse them of atavism,
remained loyal to the Gaelic musical ideal. Prominent among this
group was Seán Neeson who believed that only 'When Gaelic Tunes
are Whistled in the Streets' and are sung in the schools, would Ireland produce a school of native composers. In his opinion, folk
music was the vitalising factor in any nation's music.[19] Although
Irish traditional music never gained the status of the Irish language
in the revival movement, it did receive a boost in March 1937 when
minister for education Thomas Derrig declared the official recognition of Irish traditional music 'as second only to the Irish language'.[20] In the late 1940s it received increased official support and
attention and in 1951, the governmental post of director of Irish
Folk Music was created and filled by Donal O'Sullivan.

Musical leaders were aware that in order for a national music to
develop, a national school of music was necessary. What musical
culture or cultures would such a school represent? Music in post-
colonial Ireland lacked cohesiveness and unity. Various musical subcultures had developed autonomously; now there needed to be
interaction among them at socioeconomic and artistic levels in
order for a unified national image to emerge. Many musicians and
cultural leaders had offered scenarios for a national school of music
in the early years of the century and this idea surfaced again in the
1920s and '30s. John Larchet argued that 'there should be but one
endowed musical establishment, a central Academy of Music'.[21]
Composer Frederick May proposed an all-embracing National

Academy of Music that would serve as 'a musical dynamo for the whole country', with all schools and smaller institutions in the provinces affiliated with it. Students from the provinces would be trained in the academy and return to their native towns to stimulate musical activity there. In this and other ways, the academy would encourage amateur music-making and provide an education not only in classical music but also in traditional Irish music and folk music of other lands.[22] Neither Larchet's nor May's ideas for a government-supported national academy materialised in the 1930s and only now in the late 1990s is the idea receiving serious consideration.[23]

Similar to earlier eras, public and private institutions with responsibility for music education were criticised harshly for their discrimination against traditional music, and for their failure to develop an appreciation for music among the people in general. Eamonn O'Gallchobhair described some of the 'many charges laid against our academies'. First, they were seen to be anti-Irish or West-British based on their indifference to traditional music, and second they tended to be divorced from the musical life of the people, 'living within themselves and failing to extend musical culture to those outside the magic circle'.[24] The provision for traditional music in academies and institutions of higher learning expanded to some degree in the nation state. For example, academic positions in Irish music were founded or retained at University College, Dublin, and University College, Cork.[25]

The formal system of general education was criticised for its lack of provision for music in the curriculum. As early as 1924, Larchet addressed the relationship between the low standards of music in the schools and in the population at large, an argument that was resonant of Sir Thomas Wyse's almost one century previously:

> The real cause of failure to appreciate good music in Dublin is that the people have never been taught to do so: that is the reason for their apathy and their impoverished taste. Our system of musical education is not merely wrong, it is fundamentally unsound. . . . The position allotted to music in most of our secondary schools is, with a few honourable exceptions, lamentable. Music is usually pushed into the darkest corner of the curriculum. As a rule the children are lucky if the time given to it is not filched from their recreation; their musical talent is stultified, and, in the case of boys, successfully crushed.[26]

While Larchet and other critics blamed the educational system for the poor state of musical life,[27] some connected it to conditions outside the schools. In 1926, Cork school teacher (and later music inspector with the Department of Education) Donnchadh Ó Braoin addressed 'the national indifference to and contempt for music', and argued that the state of music in education was a reflection of its state in national life, each institution being 'a little microcosm of the people with all their faults and virtues displayed'.[28] What was needed, in Ó Braoin's opinion, was a comprehensive national policy for music in order to defeat 'the universal indifference' towards music so obvious in Irish life and resulting from historical circumstances.[29]

TOWARDS A NATIONAL MUSIC POLICY

Since music was regarded as an important expression of national identity and a strong ancestral trait, in the early years of independence the role of traditional music was central to discussions of Irish cultural development. Successive governments of the new state, while recognising the value of music education in the context of strengthening national identity, ignored their responsibility for formulating policy regarding the development of the arts and arts education in Ireland. The second Dáil did in fact have a Ministry for Fine Arts directed by George N. (Count) Plunkett which lasted nineteen weeks, from 26 August 1921 to 9 January 1922. However, after the Treaty the ministry was merged with the Department of Education and did not gain an independent ministry until 1982 when the office of Minister of State for Arts and Culture was created. Joseph Ryan commented on the lack of continuity between the agenda of cultural nationalists and arts policy in the new state: 'It is ironic that a state that had so strongly founded its claim to political autonomy on its distinctive cultural heritage should prove so reticent in fostering the arts when it came within its power to do so.'[30]

The low level of support for the arts may have resulted from a number of sources: the arts were associated by nationalists with colonial culture, they were regarded as a luxury of the sociocultural élite,[31] their role in culture was not understood by the majority of government officials, and the economy was not sufficiently stable to support the development of the arts in governmental agendas. In addition, music as a constituent of culture seems to have been viewed apart from the other arts. An Advisory Committee for Cultural Relations, appointed in 1949 by the Minister for External Affairs to promote the development of cultural relations with other countries, did not include a musician on its sixteen-member committee.

Whatever combination of factors prevailed against the development of a comprehensive national policy for the arts, there is abundant evidence that some musical leaders were acutely aware of this situation and provided ongoing commentary on the underdeveloped state of musical culture in Ireland. In their plan for music in national life, it functioned not merely to promote language or religious tenets. It was seen rather as a pervasive, enriching element in the life of the nation. There was a deep concern to improve Ireland's musical image and to pave the way for a school of native composers and audiences to receive and appreciate their compositions.

University music professors John Larchet (1884–1967)[32] and Aloys Fleischmann (1910–92)[33] maintained strong leadership profiles during the early decades of independence in advancing an agenda for improving Irish musical culture. Fleischmann was aware of the standards of musical culture in renowned musical nations and was conscious of the cultural lag in Ireland. In his opinion, not only did the country lack a proper system of music education and normal standards of music appreciation, but 'in attempting to bring in a new set of standards and values there is no established tradition to which we might reach back, such as existed for a recent generation of English composers'. Fleischmann's interest in developing art music was rooted in his own academic, classical background. He was aware that many advocates for a music revival were 'mainly concerned with the welfare of folk-music'.[34] Different agendas existed with a similar goal of developing musical culture in Ireland.

No forum or organisation existed to further their ideas and recommendations until the late 1940s. At that time the state of the arts became a national concern. A report on the arts was commissioned by the government in 1949 and published in 1951 as the Bodkin report. One of the primary criticisms was aimed at ministers of education since 1922:

'We have not merely failed to go forward in policies concerning the Arts, we have, in fact, regressed to arrive, many years ago, at a condition of apathy about them in which it has become justifiable to say in Ireland that no other country of Western Europe cared less, or gave less, for the cultivation of the Arts.'[35]

In submitting the Arts Bill to the Dáil in April 1951, Taoiseach John A. Costello said that since the establishment of the state, successive governments had been so fully preoccupied with other matters that they had little opportunity of adopting any kind of policy in regard to the arts.[36]

The 1950s witnessed increased official attention to the arts in Irish culture. The year 1951 stands as a landmark in the recent history of music education in Ireland with a number of significant institutions founded in that year: the Arts Council, Comhaltas Ceoltóirí Éireann (a movement to promote Irish traditional music, song, dance, and language), and Ceol Chumann na nÓg.[37] The subsequent expansion of these foundations influenced the musical education of Irish youth. Ceol Chumann na nÓg, founded in Dublin by Lady Mayer, had an immediate impact on school music education since it organised regular orchestral concerts in Dublin courtesy of the Radio Éireann orchestras and with financial assistance from the Arts Council.

Another national organisation which was active in the development of music in the 1950s was Foras Éireann. Its objective was to assist and promote the general development of rural Ireland 'in accordance with our Christian and National ways of life'.[38] The organisation's commitment to music was evident when it commissioned Professor Joseph Groocock in 1957 to survey music in the Republic of Ireland. A basic assumption of the survey was that any attempt to assess the state of music in the country or to suggest plans for its development needed to begin with the examination of the part that it played in the lives of children.[39]

Musical culture in Ireland underwent many contextual changes between 1922 and 1960, due in large part to the achievement of the new nation state. Daunting challenges faced policy-makers, scholars, and practitioners who attempted to reconcile the musical heritage of a traditional and colonial society with the musical needs of a modern Irish nation state. Supporting the challenges of building a national identity was an ever-expanding network of mass media which on the one hand helped to institute and diffuse the cultural canon of nationalism and on the other served to disseminate new ideas and expand cultural horizons.

MUSIC IN THE CULTURE OF FORMAL EDUCATION

National schools

The infusion of nationalist ideals was more remarkable in national schools than in secondary schools, in keeping with the history of both these educational sectors in colonial Ireland. National schools, Brown argues, seemed 'a representative Irish institution in the new state, a peculiarly resonant symbol of a society where authoritarian control enforced ideals of nationalism, religion and language'.[40] Now, in the aftermath of political independence, nationalists were free to transmit the ideals of Irishness to the next generation through the education system. In 1922 Pádraig Ó Brolcháin, chief executive officer of National Education, declared: 'It is the intention of the new Government to work with all its might for the strengthening of the national fibre, by giving the language, history, music and tradition of Ireland their natural place in the life of Irish schools.'[41] In practice, it was the Irish language that dominated the agenda of national schools,[42] and music, considered by many as 'a great educational instrument too long neglected',[43] became a servant to the teaching of the language.

MUSIC AND THE IRISH LANGUAGE MOVEMENT

Irish language songs dominated the curriculum of the new state, with official policy requiring that singing be taught through the medium of Irish, and that all songs be in the Irish language.[44] The official emphasis on language continued with the change of government in 1932. The new minister for education, Thomas Derrig, confirmed that:

> 'the Heart and Core of all our work in the creation of a Nation State must be the revival of the national language as the spoken language of the people, for in the Irish language lies enshrined for us the genius of our race. If we lose our language, we lose our national heritage. In its songs, its prayers and its proverbs are expressed the Gaelic soul of our people.'[45]

A *Revised Programme for National Schools* was issued under Derrig's ministry and, contrary to changing attitudes on the role of the Irish language in the shaping of national and cultural identity in the 1940s, its status was maintained in the schools. The emphasis on

Irish language songs was still in place during the 1950s,[46] although the 1956 *Programme of Primary Instruction* broadened the repertoire recommended for primary-school music.[47] The situation changed only marginally before the introduction of the new curriculum, in 1971.

The policy of reviving the language through song was successful in national schools from an official standpoint, in that the programme was implemented by the teachers. Its success from an educational standpoint is questionable, based on the number of problems encountered by teachers and students. Many educators claimed that Irish language songs were not psychologically suited to children and should not be taught even in senior classes.[48] Children (and frequently teachers also) encountered great difficulty in learning the words of the songs. With little emphasis on the song's meaning, children had no background from which to relate to its content and function; instead, mere mastery of the words was sufficient.[49] Due to the powerful demands of the Irish language movement, other areas of the music curriculum were neglected.[50] For example, an inspector reporting from the Midlands-North region for the 1929–30 school year, was critical of the fact that many children he met in schools had never heard any of Moore's melodies,[51] a situation that revealed the narrowness of music instruction.

Teaching Irish traditional singing was not a primary goal of official programmes in this period but teachers, particularly those in schools where such singing still survived in the neighbourhood, were encouraged to teach it and to notate and teach any unpublished tunes still alive in their locality.[52] Teachers were cautioned 'to tread very warily' in imparting the tradition to their pupils. In addition to technical proficiency, a teacher needed the traditional method, 'the distinctive attitude or outlook which is part of the mental make-up of the true traditional singer', which could only be acquired by personal contact with someone who had grown up in the tradition.[53] Even with optimum conditions, was traditional singing, a solo art form, compatible with collective classroom instruction? Given the developmental state of music pedagogy at the time and the status of folk music in education, it was unlikely that transmission of this music would be successful in national schools. Other more accessible aspects of Irish music were introduced into the curriculum.

From the early years of independence, many educational spokespersons advocated a much broader vision for music in education than merely serving the Irish language through song. It seems reasonable to assume that a Department of Education with a commitment to implementing a comprehensive Gaelic revival plan would strive to integrate all aspects of indigenous musical traditions into educational practice. With a variety of Irish music at hand – Irish and Anglo-Irish songs and ballads, instrumental music, dance music and dances – a narrow selection was made from some of the richest sources of folk music in Europe. However, instrumental music education was not sufficiently developed in colonial Ireland for such a project to succeed in the Irish Free State. Economic factors may also have impeded such a development, and the individualised method of traditional music pedagogy was not suitable for class instruction. Another area that was neglected was Irish dance. The Annual Report of the Irish Dancing Commission for 1934 expressed regret that 'the Department of Education cannot see its way to making special provision for the teaching of dancing'.[54] Instruction in Irish dancing was not neglected in the culture at large, but it operated only in private or community contexts.

Two forms of Irish music that gradually did gain popularity in schools were national songs in English, and to a lesser degree instrumental music such as tin whistle and percussion bands. Pádraig Ó Dálaigh's *A Ballad History for Schools*, published in the late 1920s, drew on the work of Thomas Davis in the 1840s as a reference point.[55] Unlike Davis' ballads of the 1840s, which seldom if ever reached the classrooms of national schools in the mid nineteenth century, there were no such obstacles to the use of Ó Dálaigh's collection. Due to pressure on teachers to teach Irish language songs, it seems that the teaching of ballads was not widespread until the 1930s, or beyond. Liam Redmond warned teachers in 1940 that in the heat of the language revival they must not forget that it was 'these old ballads, written in English, kept the national spirit intact through dark and hopeless years'.[56] About the same time, music inspector Seán Ó Casaide also addressed the need to teach national songs in English, simply because the people liked to hear them, and also 'to bring home to the generations growing up then the sacrifices that past generations had made in the name of nationality'.[57] This reasoning was in keeping with the movement away from an essentialist approach to nation-building in the 1940s, to embrace a more realistic view of contemporary life and the needs and values of the people.

Instrumental music that promoted 'Gaelic tunes' was also introduced into the schools in the late 1930s. Given the low cost of a tin whistle, it is not surprising to find that tin whistle bands become popular. Composer, arranger and collector of folk-music, Carl Hardebeck, arranged Irish tunes for tin whistle, and they were published in 1937 as *Ceol na nGaedheal*. 'The formation of whistle bands in our schools', he wrote, 'would aid considerably in raising the standard of musical appreciation throughout the country, and would constitute a tremendous force in the revival of our national tunes.'[58] Hardebeck seems to have been the first to address formally instrumental music in national schools using Irish repertoire and an instrument associated with Irish traditional music.

Tin whistle bands did become a feature of primary schools after this proposal was made by Hardebeck, and gained in popularity in the 1940s. One example of a successful band comes from Garryhill National School in Co. Carlow. A band was organised in 1943 and with much local support for the project, it thrived and on many occasions was invited to broadcast performances on national radio. When the band performed at local community events, the members were described as stepping out 'in green cap and blazer, cream skirt or trousers, carrying a green and gold banner embroidered "Foireann Cheoil Garrdhachoille"'.[59] This example from rural Ireland of the 1940s illustrates how music assisted children in identifying with aspects of Irish culture such as the language, the Irish tricolor, and Irish national radio.

MUSIC EDUCATION AND CATHOLICISM

Catholicism, a second marker of Irish identity in the emergent nation state, continued to affect the direction of music in national schools. One striking example was the plain chant movement. In 1926 Fr John Burke set up a summer school in plain chant for teachers.[60] This school, and others with a similar goal that operated from the 1920s through the 1940s, served to prepare teachers to teach chant, and thus to improve the quality of church music nationally. Part of the motivation for teachers to attend such courses was to help them prepare students to participate in the liturgical festivals which were a regular and popular event in many provincial towns such as Limerick and Kilkenny.

Based on the close alliance between the Catholic Church and national education, it is not surprising to find that a main feature of plain chant festivals was 'the massed singing of the Ordinary of the Mass by thousands of children'.[61] For example at the 31st International Eucharistic Congress held in Dublin in June, 1932 a children's High Mass choir consisted of 2,700 boys and girls who sang not only the mass, *Ecce Sacerdos*,[62] but also hymns in Irish. Where Irish versions were not available, translations were made especially for the occasion.[63] Liturgical festivals were media events and in that context they celebrated the triumphs of Catholic culture. As participants in these events, children were further inducted into the practices of Catholicism, while simultaneously fostering Catholic Church music through their performance.

One interesting feature of many of the festivals was the examination of choirs that took place after the mass.[64] This tradition, rooted in the festivals of St Cecilia held in Dublin in the 1890s, was a curious juxtaposition of sacred music in worship and in the arena of competition. Liturgical festivals provided motivation for teaching plain chant, a forum for performing it, and a medium for evaluating performance. In turn, the choirs' performances contributed in large measure to the success of the festivals held throughout the country.[65]

From the early years of the state, the Catholic Church expressed interest in school music and its efforts were supported by the Department of Education, although it seems that no official statement of educational policy regarding the role of Catholic musical traditions emerged until the 1950s. The INTO report of 1947, *A Plan for Education*, described the role of religion in national schools: 'We begin with the axiom that religion should permeate the whole schooling of the child, that it should be regarded as the first aim of education and its co-ordinating factor.'[66] The *Report of the Council of Education* published in 1954 confirmed this axiom:

> 'The claims of religious music (plain chant, hymns, etc.) to a place in the regular curriculum cannot be disregarded and wherever circumstances permit such music should find a place in the Music class. The influence of church music on musical standards has always been considerable and its importance in religious worship demands that it should be taught in the schools.'[67]

In practice, the ethos of national schools was permeated by the ideals of Catholicism. Music served as a religious socialiser in the context of nationalist ideology, serving locally to create a Catholic ethos in schools and to improve singing in churches, and serving nationally to reinforce Catholicism as a marker of Irish identity.

SCHOOL MUSIC AND CULTURAL DEVELOPMENT

The spread of nationalist ideals was facilitated by the growing network of mass media that was a feature of Irish life in the middle decades of the century. The goal of developing musical appreciation reached its zenith in the 1930s and early '40s with intense educational activities organised by Radio Éireann, the Army Band, and a limited number of other musical ensembles. Increasing access to gramophones and recordings popularised the idea of music listening and music appreciation in education.[68] In 1930 John D. Sheridan claimed that as a result of broadcasting and the gramophone public taste for music was improving; he advocated a system of musical training to develop critical listening skills.[69] The use of a gramophone in the classroom was also advocated to improve the standard of singing.[70]

The first efforts to use recordings and broadcasting for the purpose of teaching music in primary schools consisted of a series of broadcasts organised by 2RN in consultation with the Department of Education and the Department of Defence which controlled the No. 1 Army Band.[71] Beginning on 12 March 1936, a series of music programmes was broadcast every week.[72] It consisted of concerts played by the Army Band with commentary describing the instruments, composers' lives and the music played.[73] A more varied and elaborate series of music programmes was broadcast beginning on 11 January 1937. One striking feature of the series was its comprehensive treatment of Irish music. The programmes included not only Irish language songs with Pilib Ó Laoghaire but also a variety of other musical traditions: the Dublin Metro Garda Céilí Band performed and explained its musical selections, Irish history was illustrated through ballads, children's percussion bands were demonstrated, Fr Burke provided lessons on plain chant, and instruction was given on playing tin whistle, mouth organ, and bamboo pipe. Each programme ended with the national anthem.[74] Similar series were broadcast until 1941 when conditions arising out of World War II reduced the number of participating schools and caused the series to terminate.

As an experiment in educational broadcasting, these series were highly successful in promoting a variety of Irish musical traditions, and in serving to mediate between official nationalist policy and the musical education of the nation's youth. The newly established national ensembles such as the No. 1 Army Band and the Garda

Band became familiar to school children who listened to the series. In effect, the programmes were a direct manifesto of Irish identity, emphasis being placed on Irish music and musicians and the musical traditions of the Catholic Church.

The impact of these programmes was limited to those schools in a position to secure radio sets. Although the Department of Education supported the production of the broadcasts, it did not provide radio sets for schools, most likely due to economic factors. A small proportion of schools availed of the programmes – in 1937, approximately 400,[75] by 1939 the number had risen to 750,[76] but by 1941 only 76 schools were participating and the series ended. Enthusiasm for use of the radio in education waned and, following 'an exhaustive survey' by minister for education General Mulcahy in 1948, he came to the conclusion that 'educational benefits that might accrue from radio programmes for schools would not be commensurate with the cost involved'.[77]

In his appraisal of Irish broadcasting, Maurice Gorham concludes that Radio Éireann did important work for music in Ireland with its regular broadcasts to schools.[78] It is unfortunate that economic circumstances did not support the widespread participation of schools, especially in rural areas deprived of musical opportunities available to town and city children. Although the music education broadcasting series ended in 1941, Radio Éireann continued to include children's performances as a regular feature of its programming from the 1930s forward, from feis winners to céilí bands, tin whistle players to concerts of youth music.

Live musical performances for children represented yet another way to develop musical culture and educate the young generation. Starting in the winter of 1932–3, a series of band concerts for Dublin primary schools was initiated by Colonel Fritz Brase, director of the Army School of Music,[79] and supported by the ministers for defence and education. The aim of the project was to introduce and create in children a taste for good music and to advance the development of musical culture in national schools.[80] At the same time, the concerts were aimed at advancing 'more serious educational school work'.[81] For example, students wrote essays about the music they heard at concerts and on the lives of composers. The scheme was taken up in other cities. Cork Orchestral Society organised concerts and accommodated three thousand children every season. Classwork was integrated into the event by having essay competitions connected with each concert.[82] In the 1930s Waterford Orchestral Society organised a series of school concerts with the cooperation of the Department of Education.[83] By 1948 the Radio Éireann orchestra, founded in 1926, had grown to a sixty-two-member ensemble and Waterford hosted the first schools' concert given by this orchestra in January 1950.[84] Beginning in 1952, similar concerts were organised by Ceol Chumann na nÓg in Dublin.[85] These concerts became a popular annual attraction for schools.

Music concerts which involved child performers continued to be a feature of primary-school culture in independent Ireland. As early as 1925 the Cork School Music Committee, chaired by Donnchadh Ó Braoin, organised a school choir concert in Cork city. In addition to a massed schools' choir from city schools, a variety of other choral, instrumental and dance performances were included. This model was 'probably the first attempt of its kind in Ireland', with implications 'whose limits are not easily defined', according to a writer in the *Irish School Weekly*.[86] A significant feature was the commitment to develop community spirit and local music talent, and to extend Irish music repertoire. For example, prizes were awarded for compositions written for school choruses with Irish words, scholarships to the Cork Municipal School of Music were granted 'to the most promising pupils of National Schools',[87] and at the conclusion of concerts, one of the city's anthems, 'Sweet Cork by the Lee', was sung. Cork's school concert model was suggested for use in rural communities.[88] However, its adoption tended to occur in urban rather than in rural areas. The original Ceol Chumann na nÓg was formed in Dublin in 1937,[89] and its first concert was held at the Mansion House in July, 1937. Similar to Cork, the organisation was affiliated to a Municipal School of Music, a massed school choir was a feature of the concert, Donnchadh Ó Braoin directed the choir, and the funds accruing from performances provided scholarships for pupils to attend the School of Music.[90]

Educational broadcasting and public concerts represented two different avenues to the development of national identity through music in national schools. The national agenda was also a feature of other cultural institutions and movements that operated outside the schools: the feiseanna and féilte that were established in a number of towns between the late 1920s and the '40s, the activities of Coimisiúin na Rinnce, or the Claisceadal and other movements supported by Conradh na Gaeilge. In particular, feiseanna and féilte played a central role in developing national-school music; they motivated teachers to prepare students to perform in these celebrations of Gaelic culture. In addition to the feiseanna already established before 1921, others were founded in the post-independent years – Feis Maitiú, Cork (1927); Feis Shligigh, Sligo (1930); Feis Cheoil an Iarthair, Galway (1937); Feis na Bóinne, Drogheda (1941); Féile Luimní, Limerick (1944); Féile Chluain Meala, Clonmel (1945), and Cor Fhéile na Scol, Cork (1948).[91] In describing her schooldays in the 1940s at Limerick's model school, Angela Deasy wrote: 'There were certain annual events which influenced our school life greatly. These were: Féile Drámaíochta na Scol, Cor Fhéile na Scol, Féile Luimní, the Plain Chant Festival, Feiseanna around the countryside'.[92]

At these musical festivals, children performed on a variety of instruments. From the late 1930s forward, tin whistle and later percussion bands became a feature of junior classes.[93] In senior classes tin whistles and accordions, instruments associated with Irish traditional music, were the most popular instruments used in group performance. Instrumental music in primary schools between 1922 and 1960 was influenced by the ideology of cultural nationalism where 'pride of place is given to the cultivation of native music'.[94] Feiseanna and féilte became part of the calendar of school music and connected Irish children to a wide range of music and dance from native traditions that were closely associated with the agenda of political nationalism.

UNEQUAL PROVISION FOR MUSIC IN NATIONAL SCHOOLS

Although a considerable number of the nation's children was participating in musical performance, concerns were expressed in the 1940s and '50s about the standard of music education for national-school pupils. One concern originated in the lack of educational opportunity in rural schools and the other in the impact of radio on musical taste. Official reports indicated that music in rural schools was in a sad state and that children were deprived of opportunities to grow musically. Problems peculiar to teaching music in one- or two-teacher schools – such as the lack of available teachers – were frequently acknowledged.[95] The phenomenon of the 'non-singer' was associated largely with rural schools.[96] In many districts, the primary teacher was the 'sole source of local musical inspiration'.[97] In that capacity he was operating with many impediments. The dynamic traditional culture that was typical of rural communities in former years was diminished by at least two socioeconomic factors.

First, in the period between 1922 and 1960 there was a mass exodus of population from rural areas. Second, with a developing inferiority about things indigenous, there was an ambivalent attitude towards traditional music and motivation to pass it on was somewhat weakened. In 1926, Ó Braoin summarised the rural scene when he observed the universal silence of the countryside, 'broken only by the quavering ineffectual sound of a shattered, forgotten, and self-doubting tradition'.[98]

To fill this 'universal silence' many believed that the rural school ought to act as the nucleus for creating a musical atmosphere in the community and thereby developing a loyalty to the community and a love of the countryside. School music had a vital role to play in making life 'brighter and better' in rural communities, in slowing down the rate of emigration,[99] and in raising the self-esteem of communities by nurturing the development or ensuring the maintenance of local musical traditions.[100] No practical steps were taken to develop musical life in rural schools, nor was the recently developed British model of the rural music school adopted.[101] Except for a few efforts in certain counties, no professional support system existed in the form of a music advisor or agency to organise and coordinate music instruction in rural national schools. It is ironic that cultural nationalists found the ideals of Irish-Ireland in the values and life-style of rural communities; yet, those same leaders and their disciples failed to nurture cultural life in the very communities they idealised.

A second concern of educational leaders centred around the narrowness of the music curriculum and its failure to reach all children and counteract the 'mass-indoctrination by radio'.[102] The INTO report of 1947, *A Plan for Education*, criticised the department's vague policy with regard to the cultivation of musical taste and appreciation, warning that 'both our own treasury of native music and the masterpieces of Europe have all but been suffocated by the all-pervading jazz. And yet we stand by, impotent and unseeing, our only antidote being a meagre stock of school-songs – and a tin whistle!!'[103] A similar criticism was voiced in the 1954 *Report of the Council of Education*. While recognising the value of public performance, the report stated that the training of bands and choirs was secondary to the training which should be given to *all* pupils. In addition to practical instruction, the national school needed to provide the 'elements of cultural and aesthetic education'. Music was seen to have several functions in the education of the child – as a mode of self-expression, as an instrument of refinement, and as a source of pleasure to the child and to others.[104] The role and value of music in education was broadened with a shift away from the preoccupation with nationalist ideology which dictated the role of music in national schools in the early decades of independence.

MUSIC IN SECONDARY SCHOOLING

Continuity and change in the new era

The models used to design and implement the music curriculum in intermediate education between 1878 and 1921 continued to play a significant role in secondary-school music in the Irish Free State. Continuity was evident in the syllabus, the modes of evaluation, the Victorian attitude towards music education, and the payment of bonuses to schools based upon the results of choral and orchestral examinations. New trends also emerged in this period: the formation of an Irish examining body for practical music within the system, the gradual introduction of Irish compositions into the lists of set choral and orchestral works, the development and organisation of a professional body of music teachers, and the use of broadcasting in music appreciation classes.

Already in 1922, the Music committee of the Dáil Commission on Secondary Education, under the aegis of the Association of Secondary Teachers of Ireland, recognised the unsatisfactory position of music in the curriculum. The committee's recommendations reflected a strong desire to place music at the core of secondary education, available to all students. In the committee's opinion, the system in vogue was educationally unsound, owing to the limited number of songs prescribed, the difficulty of the tests in sight reading, and the utter neglect of national music. Recommendations advocated that music be taught in all schools, that there be a competent music teacher attached to every secondary school, and a permanent choral class and orchestra be drawn from all classes in the school.[105]

The strong commitment to music coming from the teaching profession was not reflected in the Department of Education's policy and music curriculum. In the early decades of independence, music was not considered as part of the general education of all secondary-school students. Under the new Intermediate Education

Act (Amendment) of June 1924, it became an optional subject for the Intermediate Certificate in a group with science, domestic science, and drawing.[106] The *Rules and Programme for 1924–25* contained the first official curriculum statement on music in secondary education.

> The course followed in Music should provide for ear-training, cultivation of taste, study of Musical History, development of technique, exercise in creative work, and training in the principles of composition. Provision should also be made for bringing the pupils into contact with the works of the great composers. It is essential that throughout the course the foreground should be occupied by the music itself and not by the system of names and symbols by which it is represented.[107]

In the official rhetoric, there seemed to be a movement away from an exclusive emphasis on music theory, and a more comprehensive curriculum was recommended. Music appreciation in particular was identified as basic and separate from technical skill development.[108] This statement remained the same until the *Rules and Regulations* of 1943–44 when music became more clearly defined.[109]

In practice, the music curriculum remained basically the same in structure and pedagogical orientation in independent Ireland. Music as an academic subject for certificate examinations continued to be a minority subject whose primary aim was to prepare students for entry into university music degree programmes.[110]

Enthusiasts for the advancement of national music and a national school of composition looked to the secondary school as one important nursery for young musicians. They were critical of secondary music education practices. Aloys Fleischmann considered it little more than 'a system of education by examination – surely the most negative of all methods'.[111] Emily Hughes focused on the confounding effects of music pedagogy on the creative potential of students, with music literacy continuing to dominate, and technical accuracy equated with musical excellence.[112] In many ways the Department of Education carried on the traditions bequeathed to it by the British system. Music continued to be an exclusive school subject; it was closed to the majority of students; it was conservative in structure and adhered strictly to the traditional model; it discriminated against boys' participation, and it was locked into the conservatory type of music education that stressed theoretical knowledge and evaluation by examination.

It was not until the late 1940s that the use and value of music in secondary education were officially endorsed. In 1948 the first music inspector for secondary schools was appointed, representing the official recognition of music in the secondary-school curriculum and its clarification as an academic discipline worthy of national supervision.[113] The early 1950s witnessed official encouragement for schools everywhere to make provision for the teaching of singing. This paralleled an increased interest in music in secondary education with greater numbers taking the subject for examination.[114]

A second boost for music in secondary education was the growth of the music profession. The year 1948 marked the foundation of the Music Association of Ireland (MAI) which took up issues of teacher education, something that had been discussed since the early years of the Irish Free State.[115] Although the registration of music teachers continued to present a problem, since the majority did not possess a university degree in music,[116] the MAI did initiate dialogue addressing this important area of secondary music education.

Secondary-school music and the nationalist agenda

Compared to music education in the primary sector, the influence of the language revival movement was less visible in secondary schools. Irish music was gradually included in the curriculum, defined by the standards of 'high', classical culture already in place. Beginning in 1924, the works of Irish composers – Delany, Esposito, Field, Harty, Ó Braoin, Larchet, Hughes, Ó Gallchobhair, and Stanford – were included in the syllabus of set pieces for certificate examinations.[117] In addition, each candidate was required to submit the names of twelve Irish melodies on which he would be examined.[118] The inclusion of Irish composers in the history component of the Intermediate Certificate programme was negligible. It was not until 1934–5 that composer John Field was introduced, the only Irish composer deemed worthy of historical study during the entire period between 1935 and 1960. Considering the rich musical heritage of Ireland and the range of contemporary composers, this was a narrow choice.

The choice of musical instruments recommended for practical examinations was also narrow with no reference to instruments associated with Irish traditional music. In general, Irish musical traditions were either excluded or were adapted to concur with the values and practices of the classical tradition. The function of music education as an agent for promoting classical culture continued to be a dominant value in secondary schools. While the music curriculum in other sectors of education, primary and vocational, was responsive to change in the national culture, the development of music in secondary schools did not reflect such change in its curriculum content. It was not until the 1950s, when the status of Irish folk music was elevated and its social acceptance became widespread, that more serious attention was paid to native Irish music.[119]

In the second principal area of music activity – practical music – the situation seemed somewhat more egalitarian and democratic in those schools where ensembles were organised and trained. The *Programme and Regulations for 1925–6* recommended that suitable provision be made for singing in secondary schools. It would be erroneous, however, to assume that singing and music performance in general were widespread at a national level in the succeeding years. The percentage of schools that presented ensembles was small, with an average of 0.2 per cent of all schools for the years 1924–5 to 1930–1. Of those schools represented, 37 per cent were situated in Dublin. Cavan and Leitrim were not represented and there was a minimum representation from Clare, Donegal, Kerry, Kildare, Limerick, Longford, Meath, Offaly, and Roscommon.[120] Similar to national schools, inequality of educational opportunity in music was evident, with many schools in the provinces not providing for music in the curriculum.

The granting of bonuses to schools for choirs and orchestras was a legacy from the British system that was maintained in the Irish Free State.[121] The scheme continued to gain in strength and the total amount in bonuses granted to secondary schools increased from £1,000 in 1924–5 to £2,640 in 1959–60.[122] No doubt the bonuses earned by the presentation of musical groups provided a stimulus for participation. However, this had the effect of reinforcing traditions already in place rather than stimulating the growth of new music traditions in schools. The spread of choirs and orchestras to all geographical areas of the country and to all types of secondary schools did not occur during this period.

The repertoire used as set pieces for choir and orchestra examinations showed an increase in the number of Irish selections.[123] In comparison to national schools, minimal attention was paid to the Irish language movement in repertoire selection in secondary schools. There were at least three reasons for this. First, music was longer established and more widespread in national schools; second, the Irish language movement was more active there, with many national teachers strong advocates of language revival; and third, the ethos of national schools was more responsive to external cultural influences.

The manner in which music functioned in secondary school culture depended to a large degree on the religious denomination and musical traditions of the school. A past pupil of Alexandra College, a Dublin Protestant school, recalled the events of a student concert at the college in the mid-1930s. 'Some of us were surprised, fifteen years after independence, to find the proceedings ending with "God Save the King". However, the following year this was remedied and we ended with "Auld Lang Syne".'[124] Anglicised traditions were slowly eroded and the canon of school music changed gradually. The classical education traditions on which many secondary schools were founded continued to dominate musical culture. Playwright Desmond Forristal, a pupil of Belvedere College, Dublin, in the 1940s, recalled the Gilbert and Sullivan operas which were a feature of the college calendar:

> 'There was drama, poetry, orchestral music, solo and choral singing, movement and dance, not to mention the arts of the scene designer and painter. As an introduction for youngsters to a cross-section of the arts, it could hardly have been bettered.'[125]

A number of factors acted as catalysts for change in the decade of the 1950s. Similar to national schools, the development of musical culture was increasingly highlighted, in large part the result of changing technology and the availability of music through mass media. Music appreciation courses were offered by the Department of Education as part of their summer programmes between the mid-1940s and the mid-'50s. In addition, Radio Éireann presented school concerts in various cities and towns, and this tradition was maintained throughout the 1950s.

Discussion about music in secondary schools occurred outside the system, focusing on the value of music education as an aesthetic subject that could refine musical sensibilities. This discussion was led by members of religious orders. Already in the 1940s, The Revd Maurice Weymes criticised the shallowness of the average response to music in Ireland.[126] He advocated the development of musical culture and appreciation based on 'reflective listening'[127] to good music. Br. Séamus V. O'Sullivan, professor of education at St Patrick's College, Maynooth, claimed that people had 'become drugged with material advance and remain insensate to the finer promptings from within'. Aesthetic education, in his opinion, would remedy this weakness and develop 'a truly Christian outlook and behaviour'.[128]

Given the religious composition of the population and the traditional role of the Catholic clergy in reinforcing national ideology and in shaping the Irish mentality, it was not surprising to find O'Sullivan equating the influence of aesthetic education with Christian values and lifestyle. Neither is it surprising to find Catholic clergy providing leadership with regard to music education. Aesthetic values, as advocated by the Church, were rooted in the traditions of Western classical music. Aesthetic values, as advocated by secular cultural nationalist movements such as the Gaelic League however, were rooted in the traditional musical heritage. One further example of these influences at work is found in vocational schools of this period. The technical sphere was generally thought to be socially inferior to the more academic institutions such as secondary schools[129] and this was reflected clearly in the type of music curriculum that was implemented in both school types.

MUSIC IN VOCATIONAL EDUCATION

Before 1930, vocational education in Ireland focused exclusively on developing technical skills and was designed for those pursuing occupations of a practical nature. The Vocational Education Act of 1930 expanded its role to provide continuing education for fourteen to sixteen year olds for whom secondary schooling was not available. The Act gave separate definitions of 'technical' and 'continuation' education and music was categorised under technical education with the exception of the county boroughs of Dublin and Cork where the municipal schools of music were affiliated to the Vocational Education Committee.[130]

Although music was not given a central role in the vocational curriculum in the 1930 Act, certain developments did take place. The rising interest in cultural subjects created an atmosphere that was receptive to music as a 'universal and most popular culture subject'.[131] The view of culture as belonging to all people and all people as being cultured, regardless of social class or ethnicity, was also becoming popular and underpinned the philosophy of music education in vocational education.[132] The school was seen as serving a predominantly rural, folk culture and, by inference, serving to transmit that culture.

Choral music was introduced into a certain number of schools in the 1930s. The Dublin Municipal School of Music held summer courses for teachers and considering that about seventy vocational schools were open by 1936 and that eighteen vocational school teachers attended the summer course that year, a reasonable amount of interest had been generated. In Dublin and Cork, Vocational Education Committees supported the municipal schools of music and they in turn served as agents for promoting music in schools in those borough areas.

Memorandum V. 40 issued by the Department of Education in 1942 changed the course of vocational education and added religious and cultural studies to the curriculum and made the vocational school a centre for fostering 'the Irish language and other distinctive features of the national life'.[133] Similar to national schools, music in vocational schools was viewed by the department as a cultural activity that could further the cause of the Irish language. Branches of Claisceadal, a movement to promote community choral singing in the Irish language, were founded in many vocational schools.[134] Schools inspectors encouraged the use of social activities i.e. choral singing and céilidhe dancing, in teaching the Irish language. The inclusion of cultural and religious studies in the curriculum heightened the school's function as a rural institution propagating Catholic, Irish values and ideals.

The 1940s witnessed an exodus of population from rural areas. The rural vocational school (which constituted the majority of schools) was seen as a centre for revitalising cultural life in rural communities and reducing the rate of emigration.

> The Rural Vocational School is the people's school, the folk school of Ireland of which we may be justly proud and the vocational teacher must be the leader in cultural pursuits and social activities – the philosopher, friend and guide to the whole parish.[135]

Besides preparing the student for a trade and for the workplace, she must also be prepared 'for the wise use of leisure time', so that she can enjoy and appreciate 'the higher things in life, such as religion, literature, music, art and courtesy, which are the constituents of culture'.[136] In the context of building musical culture, Fleischmann claimed that the most effective way of reaching the country as a whole was through the vocational schools.[137] This type of advocacy needed a lot of support at official and local levels in order to be implemented. In March, 1949, the minister of education extended the terms of the 1930 Act to include the formation and training of choirs and orchestras, theory, and music appreciation.[138]

The goal of integrating national ideals into the curriculum surfaced again in the 1950s. In a supplement to the *Vocational Education Bulletin*, 'An Saol Gaelach', the treatment of music was identical to that of primary-school journals. Irish language songs were presented accompanied by Tonic Sol-fa notation. The *Revised Memorandum V. 51* of 1955 provided a guide for teaching choral singing and it recommended the memorisation of 'as many songs as possible, particularly Irish songs'. In addition, emphasis was placed on the role of music in rural communities and in the general school culture, especially in providing 'the very desirable element of entertainment at school concerts, annual excursions and other gatherings'.[139]

Music in vocational schools served a number of functions – to teach the Irish language, to enrich community life in rural areas, and to develop a sense of place in young people and thus to arrest the flow of immigrants from the countryside. Given their affiliation with the schools of music, one might anticipate a conservatory-type music education similar to secondary schools. However, the function of vocational education in general, the cultural and musical background of the students and their vocational aspirations, ruled out this type of approach. The rural vocational school was 'the people's school, the folk school of Ireland'. Thus it was not surprising to find that Comhaltas Ceoltóirí Éireann, whose goal was to promote Irish traditional music, later held classes in vocational schools. The culture of these schools was formed around rural Irish life and folk and popular culture. When folk music was revitalised in the 1950s, this school culture was seen as open to the propagation of traditional music which, like vocational education, carried ambiguous and even negative cultural connotations.

CHANGING CONTEXTS FOR THE TRANSMISSION OF TRADITIONAL MUSIC

In parts of the country, traditional music continued to be passed on orally as an integral and natural part of growing up. Paddy Tunney recalled his grandfather singing to him as a child in his home

near the banks of Lower Lough Erne, Co. Fermanagh, in the
1920s: 'As he dandled me on his knee and repeated the verse I
found myself joining him in the song. I was a man of four sum-
mers then and very fond of my song-master.' His aunt Brigid
played the melodeon and he picked up many reels and set dances
from her. In contrast to national-school music education in the
Irish Free State at the time, where Irish songs dominated the music
curriculum, Tunney reported singing 'harmless inanities' in school,
songs that were culturally removed from the traditional singing he
learned at home.[140]

Although traditional music was legitimised in official policy and
education in the new state, social and economic factors acted
against its full integration and acceptance in Irish society. The fact
that its transmission had not been organised formally in schools and
institutions in colonial society (perhaps with the exception of the
pipers' clubs) meant that no infrastructure was in place to support
its transmission when socioeconomic and demographic conditions
changed in the middle decades of the century. Informal schools of
traditional music had been built locally around a skilled performer,
and these 'unassuming bardic parliament[s]' met regularly in various isolated areas throughout the country, but no effort was made
to connect the various communities of learners that gathered
around those master teacher-performers. Yet it was out of these
small, closely-knit musical communities that a national organisation for traditional music evolved.[141]

When emigration to towns and cities began in the 1920s, the
traditions of these schools were carried into the more populous centres[142] where pipers' clubs were already active. Within that network
of informal schools of traditional music and the already well-established feiseanna around the country, the foundations were laid for
Comhaltas Ceoltóirí Éireann (CCÉ) which was established in
1951. It was initiated when members of the Dublin Pipers' club
went to Mullingar to establish a branch of the club there. The project expanded into an organisation that would cater for all traditional instrumentalists across the country. CCÉ transformed the
way in which traditional music teaching was organised, and it created new opportunities for Irish youth to be immersed in the culture of the music. Just as its roots were in local communities of
music-makers so also was its philosophy based on a community
concept, with the local branch central to the welfare of the organisation. Its constitution reads:

The Branch is the fundamental and most important unit of the Comhaltas movement. It is the Branch which makes it possible for our native cultural characteristics to be propagated and strengthened in the community.[143]

From the beginning, education was central to the CCÉ mission to promote Irish traditional music. Four contextual features of the education process are noteworthy: being grounded in the concept of community music, intergenerational learning was common; learning the music was situated in the larger context of being immersed in traditional culture; the movement highlighted 'our common heritage rather than our differences'; and the competitive element, which can be traced back to the feis, was very strong in the organisation's pyramidal system of fleadh cheoil competitions.[144] This combination of factors determined the scope and impact of the organisation's educational efforts. In particular, the competitive element influenced how the music was passed on and in a sense directed the course of traditional music. Transmission at the local level was set in a national (and even international) context. Not unlike music in secondary education, standards and repertoire were set and judged by an official body of experts at a distance from the context of transmission. Traditional music learning assumed many of the pedagogical traits of classical music; where it was motivated by extrinsic rewards such as medals and cups, it was aimed at the perfect stage performance in a competitive arena, and it operated with a *caighdeán oifigiúil* (official standard) that determined content and criteria.[145]

ESTABLISHING NATIONAL MUSICAL CULTURE: CHALLENGES AND ACHIEVEMENTS

Music education and development in the period between 1922 and 1960 was an integral part of the highly complex and challenging process of constructing a new nation state. It functioned at one level to advance nationalist ideology and at another level to improve national cultural life. Within the nationalist agenda, the canon of Irish music and music in Irish culture were defined narrowly, with emphasis placed on reviving the language and promoting Catholic Church music. In formal education these influences were evident in the music curriculum. Primary and later vocational schools diffused the canon and reproduced the values of nationalist ideology in a more significant way than secondary schools whose foundations, student population, and social connotations dictated a slightly different function for music, one that was aimed at propagating the values of high culture.

The goal of building a national musical culture extended well beyond the narrow essentialist view of Irish identity. Musical leaders were aware of the low standards of music appreciation in Irish culture and education and advocated a much broader function for music in a modern nation state. Many sought to balance the role of tradition and the ideals of the past with a forward-looking agenda that focused on developing native composers, proficient performers, critical audiences, and a comprehensive system of music education. Government support for this musical and cultural agenda was not forthcoming until the late 1940s when deliberate attention began to be focused on the arts in Irish society.

The emergence of Ireland as a modern nation state coincided with the introduction and development of a broad spectrum of mass media. These media were broadcasting and recording, printing and publishing, live concerts and festivals, and organisations specific to music and music education. They functioned to control and develop musical culture and to link local, regional and national communities. Prior to this era, the transmission of classical music had been organised at the national level through centralised mechanisms such as examinations, national syllabi, or uniform performance standards. The transmission of traditional music did not have comparable mechanisms. As traditional music gained social status, popularity and academic respect and credibility in this era, we witness a movement towards an organisation of its practices and an assessment of its practitioners at the national level, culminating in Comhaltas Ceoltóirí Éireann. As it adapted to the values of Western education it instituted its own set of canons that in principle could be closely identified with the pedagogy of Western classical music – a competitive culture that encouraged standardisation, extrinsic rewards, and stage presentation.

Amidst all the daunting challenges of this era – economic, cultural, and political – considerable groundwork was laid towards building a dynamic musical culture. The primary challenge lay in uniting the essentialist and epochalist approaches in order to achieve a national consensus of the role of music in Irish culture. The scope of national organisations founded to promote music attested to the various strands of Irish musical heritage that were being redefined and made relevant to cultural and educational development. In essence, two levels of discourse and action existed, one centred in government and focused on the traditional, vernacular culture which was seen as essential to true Irish identity, the other coming from the musical leaders on the periphery who insisted that cultivated art music was the avenue towards a national music and an improved musical image abroad.

Political nationalists, in their eagerness to establish a national identity based on the essentials of Irishness, largely ignored the cultivation of art music and the criticisms of musical leaders, focusing instead on aspects of musical culture that advanced nationalist ideals. Given what we now know of policies in new nation states, this inward-looking, essentialist phase of cultural development was perhaps necessary to institute a canon of Irish culture and to build the nation state. In an era of highly prescribed cultural behaviour and values, the opportunity for innovation and the encouragement of cultural diversity were not concerns of those who directed the course of cultural and musical development. A modern nation state was yet to be realised in the post-1960 period, one that promoted an Irish identity based on diversity, and an educational system that provided a comprehensive music education for all young people, regardless of age, geographical location, gender, or socioeconomic class.

6

The Transmission of Music in Late Twentieth-Century Ireland

The emergence of Ireland as a modern industrial nation in the 1960s, followed by its entrance into the European Economic Community in 1973, were two dominant factors determining cultural and educational change in recent decades. In 1958 the government white paper, Economic Development, ushered in a new era in which public education began to be regarded as an agent for developing a skilled workforce. The next five years, according to Terence Brown, witnessed a new kind of Ireland coming to life.[1] Pluralism and heterogeneity began to take precedence over the narrow, essentialist view of Irishness as the basis for a cultural ideology. In the government white paper on the Irish language published in 1963,[2] the language was still to constitute a significant marker of Irish identity, but it was now to function in a plural, bilingual context which allowed it to play a more realistic role in Irish society. The general change in cultural policy, which allowed for new dimensions of Irishness to emerge, was welcomed by philosophers, statespersons and academics.[3]

Ireland's entrance into the European Economic Community (EEC, later EC, European Community, now EU, European Union) stimulated much debate concerning the cultural implications of this new bond. Discussions focused on issues of Irish identity, heritage, and developing a sense of place,[4] and they demonstrated a greater acknowledgment of the plurality of Ireland's cultures.

At the same time the arts began to receive increased attention in government publications. In 1980, a white paper on educational development issued by the Department of Education contained for the first time in any education white paper a separate chapter on the arts.[5] In 1982 the post of minister of state for culture and the arts was created and in 1987 the government issued *Access and Opportunity*, the first white paper on cultural policy in the history of the Irish state. The document stated that 'Irish culture is heterogenous, reflecting a complex and diverse social fabric'. A movement away from the concept of 'high culture' as a marginal element of Irish society to be appreciated by a select social group was evident throughout the paper. Instead, culture was seen as belonging to the mainstream of Irish life and accessible to all people.[6]

The definition of heritage also reflected shifting cultural values: in the paper, it was defined not as 'a static cultural element' but as 'a sifting process' that takes place in every generation, resulting in certain parts of the heritage being discarded and others being renewed and passed on. Each generation, the paper explained, makes a unique contribution to the heritage of the next generation.[7] In the context of Ireland of the 1980s, the challenge for the present generations included the recognition of common cultural values between the North of Ireland and the Republic of Ireland, and the formation of a European cultural identity.[8] Developing common cultural values was regarded by policy makers in the Republic as crucial to enriching Irish cultural identity, 'healing division, increasing mutual understanding and tolerance and promoting reconciliation'.[9] The promotion of the arts in general education was seen as central to achieving the goals of the white paper and to determining the future of artistic and cultural life in Ireland. Just as the outlook on the nature and role of culture in Irish life was changing, so also was music in Irish culture undergoing expansion and renewal.

A GOLDEN ERA FOR MUSIC IN IRELAND

A growing tolerance for pluralism in society in general was reflected in the emergence and broad acceptance of a variety of musical traditions, some of which had previously played a narrow role in Irish culture and education. Traditional music was one aspect of Irish musical heritage that was revitalised in this era. In light of the ambiguity and the social stigma that surrounded this music in the past, such a development was historically and culturally significant and, in John A. Murphy's opinion, 'the most enriching factor in Irish cultural identity' in the 1960s and early '70s. It created bridges between 'town and country, rich and poor, young and old and, to a certain extent, orange and green'.[10] The international revival of interest in folk music, exposure to this music in the media, the development of organisations such as Comhaltas Ceoltóirí Éireann, and the seminal work carried out by musicians such as Seán Ó Riada in creating new social contexts and performance practices for the music, all contributed to its rise in cultural status and power. Groups such as Ceoltóirí Cualann, the Chieftains, the Clancy Brothers and Tommy Makem, Planxty, the Furey Brothers, and Clannad contributed significantly to the revival, redefinition, and reform of traditional music and song. To assist with the work of scholars and musicians, radio and recordings, coupled with the introduction of television broadcasting in 1962, disseminated traditional music to a broad public.

Another stream of musical life that emerged in Ireland from the mid-century forward was that of popular music. In more recent years, it is unquestionable that Irish musicians such as Bob Geldof, Rory Gallagher, Van Morrison, U2, and the Cranberries have made major contributions to the world of rock music in an international context. Ireland's musical image abroad has been revitalised and boosted by both rock and traditional musicians. The development of classical music traditions was impeded by historical circumstances earlier in the century which were described by Ó Súilleabháin:

> Ever since the foundation of the Irish Free State, however, composers in Ireland have had to cope with the belief that European art-music produced in Ireland should either be based on Irish folk tunes or else should involve a setting of an Irish language text. Fruitless efforts were made to force a wedding between the Irish language and the European art-music tradition in the interest of 'de-anglicisation'.[11]

This situation has changed and now in the late 1990s there is abundant evidence that contemporary composers are no longer constrained by this post-independent mentality. In addition, the Contemporary Music Centre has made monumental strides in highlighting contemporary art music, in providing a support structure for composers, in encouraging and publicising the performance of works, and in educating and developing audiences.

The spectrum of music known as 'Irish' music expanded radically between 1961 and the late '90s. Formerly, it was regarded as synonymous with Irish folk or traditional music and the equation of the two, according to Ó Súilleabháin, had implied 'a tribal rather than a national definition of the term'. He argued for a definition that encompassed 'all creative music-making in Ireland'.[12] The last quarter-century was also a time of unprecedented developments in musical culture. Consider the wealth and diversity of contemporary classical music, the thriving practices of traditional music and dance, or the innovative developments in traditional and popular music, from Shaun Davy or Mícheál Ó Súilleabháin's merging of classical and traditional idioms to Enya's internationally popular compositions; from the reworking and renewal of ancient Irish spiritual themes in contemporary musical settings by Anúna, or Nóirín Ní Riain and the monks of Glenstal Abbey, to the Chieftains' collaborations with musicians from Galicia in northern Spain to Beijing in China, not to mention the global spectrum of music that is presented side by side with Irish music in *Riverdance – The Show*. In effect, it has been a time of musical interfacing of genres, of musicians, and the incorporation of new sounds into indigenous traditions, and of 'bringing it all back home'.[13] It has also been a time when musicians have drawn on the idioms of Ireland's rich musical heritage. The unprecedented activity in music was paralleled by prolific discussion and debate regarding the role of the arts in Irish education and national life.

THE ARTS AND EDUCATIONAL REFORM

The 1960s saw secondary education in particular heavily laden with utilitarian goals as a response to economic development. Consequently, educators became critical of the resulting curricular imbalance and called for reform. The 1962 Council of Education report on *The Curriculum of the Secondary School* addressed the minority position of music and the neglect of the arts in schools. It recommended a remodelling of the syllabus to accommodate the non-performing student, and an expansion of the repertoire.[14] In a similar vein, Br. Séamus Ó Súilleabháin criticised the lack of attention to emotional development in Irish education, and recommended that it be addressed through aesthetic education.[15] About the same time, the concept of cultural education was revitalised,[16] in which the school curriculum was viewed as being 'culturally determined and culturally determining'.[17] The notion of educating a 'cultured' person and transmitting a particular type of cultural experience was dispelled, at least theoretically. New awareness of the role of aesthetics and culture in education opened up discussion on the inclusion of the arts in general education from the late 1960s forward.

It was in such a climate that the Arts Council launched its campaign of advocacy for the arts in education, appointing a full-time education officer in 1979. The council's most active decade in education was between 1979 and 1989.[18] Discussions began formally with the Richards report of 1976 which contained a survey of the arts in education and identified weaknesses in the various sectors of the system.[19] This survey was a prelude to the Benson report of 1979, *The Place of the Arts in Irish Education*,[20] which examined the role of art in Irish society based on the perspectives outlined in UNESCO's 1977 report, *The Place and Function of Art in Contemporary Life*.[21] The Benson report pointed out that both functional and aesthetic uses of art had played a role in Irish society, 'but often in the service of two different traditions (frequently indifferent to each other), i.e., the native Irish and the Anglo-Irish traditions'.[22] In 1985, Ó Súilleabháin stated that if Irish music education could succeed in reconciling these 'opposing forces of our musical life, we will have hit upon a formula which may well prove to have an international significance'.[23] A year later, an American observing music education in Ireland, described the union of musical traditions in terms of a 'meeting of the waters' whose streams have come from very different sources and have always pursued widely different courses.[24] The challenge consisted of representing different musical traditions in the classroom, each legitimately a part of Irish heritage and cultural identity.

This theme of tolerance and cultural pluralism was popular in discussions of arts education not only in Ireland but in Europe in general. The 1981 Council of Europe document, *Music Education for All*, stated that

> Young people should be able, through confrontation with the music of their environment, to participate in the musical culture of our times. In our pluralistic society, music culture no longer offers a hierarchical scale of values. Music can be an enrichment and a source of pleasure on many intellectual levels and in the most varied ways.[25]

The philosophy of music education as a continuous part of general education for all students, basic to the council's statement, was also addressed by the Irish Arts Council during the 1980s. Already recommendations of the Benson report focused on issues of educational opportunity in the arts and in 1985, the Arts Council survey, *Deaf Ears?*,[26] criticised harshly the provision for music in Irish education, an issue discussed later in this chapter.

In addition to advocating and commenting on arts education through independent publications, arts education officers Ciarán Benson and Martin Drury served as arts consultants to the Curriculum and Examinations Board of the Department of Education, convened in January, 1984. In this forum their ideas were incorporated directly into the domain of public education. One of the broad goals of education identified by the board and elaborated in its 1985 discussion paper, *The Arts in Education*, was the transmission of the developing spiritual and cultural heritage. The neglect of this transmission in the Irish education system, according to the paper, was related to the low status of the arts in society at large, a point that had been made frequently since the foundation of the Irish state. Arts education was now seen as playing an important role in building national confidence and dignity, and in developing distinctive ways of knowing. The paper was highly critical of the imbalance created in schooling by the almost exclusive dependence on verbal and numerical symbol systems, to the neglect of the arts.[27]

If arts education was to improve the quality of cultural life in the nation, then change was needed in the curriculum. First, if contemporary culture was to be critically known and understood, then contemporary art forms needed to be presented and explored in education. On numerous occasions, the Arts Council was critical of the way arts education was constructed along the lines of history, heritage, and tradition, to the neglect of 'the ideas and practices of contemporary [Irish] culture'.[28] For example, neglect of twentieth-century music in the post-primary curriculum was addressed in the council's responses to both draft documents of the Curriculum and Examinations Board. If the music curriculum was to be culturally relevant to students' lives and reflect cultural heritage, it needed to include a variety of musical traditions – art, traditional, folk, and popular – past and present.

Second, the unique political situation in Ireland created cultural divisions between communities on the island. Public education was seen as a possible avenue for transcending cultural barriers, and the arts were regarded as particularly important for achieving this goal.[29] Besides functioning to create an empathy among various cultural groups within the island itself, arts education was seen as instrumental in developing European cultural identity and global awareness.

European Music Year was celebrated in 1985 and music was highlighted as part of a common European heritage.[30] For some music educators, the inclusion of European music in the curriculum was necessary but not sufficient. Mícheál Ó Súilleabháin advocated a tripartite British/European/global approach, claiming that musically, 'we must go further [than Europe] to embrace the globe if we are to spark the necessary fire of self-knowledge'. Only with the inclusion of such music as Javanese Gamelan and Gambian Kora, he argued, would Ireland find 'its place in a world musical cosmology'. Furthermore getting to know other traditional music would enable students to link their own experience with that of world cultures.[31] The same issue was addresssed in *The Arts in Education* when the report stated that the 'appreciation of *folk music* should also include the music of other nations including non-European music'.[32]

The climate of reform in arts education continued into the 1990s and it impacted a wider audience through the work of the Arts Council, the Department of Education, the Music Education National Debate, the PIANO Report, and Music Network, to name the major sources of action and influence. Throughout the 1980s the touchstone of Arts Council policy was the word 'access' – horizontal access in terms of geographical location and vertical access in terms of socioeconomic and educational circumstances.[33] This agenda had a ripple effect on many other efforts to improve the quality of music education in school and community settings.

The Music Education National Debate (MEND), although not limited to issues of access to music education, acted as a major catalyst for change in the way music functioned in education and in the culture at large. It was sponsored by the Dublin Institute of Technology and organised by its director of cultural affairs, Frank Heneghan. The debate focused on discussion of an eight-point agenda which included philosophy of music education, appraisal of the music education network in Ireland, the role of performance in education, the Leaving Certificate crisis in music education, music at third level and the training of professional musicians, the role of national culture in the music curriculum, and the establishment of a National Forum for Music Education. It took place in three phases during 1995 and 1996, beginning with a discussion of issues at the national level, and then opening the debate with input from the international music education community. The debate marked a significant milestone in the history of Irish music education in general, and in the development of music education as a discipline in this country in particular. It served as a forum for evaluating the strengths and weaknesses of contemporary music education and, in the context of arts education developments during the previous decade, it acted as a culminating dialogue on music education reform.

A second source of commentary on the state of music education was the PIANO report, produced by a review group set up by the minister for arts, culture and the gaeltacht in 1994 and chaired by John O'Conor. The group was briefed to report on the provision and institutional arrangements for orchestras and ensembles. In all, it received sixty-seven submissions representing a variety of interests. Many of the submissions called for a more developed and consistent approach to music education, as much to build audiences as to train performers. Among the recommendations that emerged were the provision of music specialists in primary schools, the development of two music syllabi for Leaving Certificate, one focusing on performance and composition, the other on music history and criticism, increased funding for music schools throughout the country, and the establishment of an Irish Academy for the Performing Arts.[34]

It is too early to assess the impact of the MEND and the PIANO reports but based on these and other efforts, it is clear that music education reform has been a central concern of both public and private institutions in the 1990s. This was also obvious in the deliberations of the Curriculum and Examinations Board of the Department of Education, the revised curriculum and syllabi for first- and second-level schools, and the 1995 government white paper on education which stated:

> The Government affirms the centrality of the arts within educational policy and provision, particularly during compulsory schooling. . . . The provision of arts education is an issue of social equality and there is an increasing recognition that cultural poverty is a significant part of disadvantage. The creative and performing arts have an important role as part of the whole school curriculum.[35]

Discussion on music education in the period between 1961 and 1998 was substantial, dealing with issues of access and opportunity, music as a cultural and cross-cultural attribute and music education leading to self-knowledge and the formation of a global musical identity.

MUSIC IN PRIMARY EDUCATION

The gradual shift away from a monocultural perspective of Irishness, combined with emerging international educational trends focused on child-centred education, brought challenges to the canon of repertoire which dominated the national-school music curriculum between 1922 and 1960. In Joseph Groocock's *A General Survey of Music in the Republic of Ireland,* published in 1961, he criticised the practices of school music. Instrumental music, he wrote, 'is often of the crudest kind: tin whistle bands, "flageolet" bands, harmonica bands'. He believed that students ought to be involved in 'more worthwhile musical channels' than popular and traditional music.[36]

The survey focused on school music festivals, the nucleus around which much school music had developed in the middle decades of this century. While Groocock had strong reservations about the quality of music performed at these non-competitive festivals, statements from the Department of Education emphasised their positive influence on school and community music education. Not only did festivals motivate and inspire teachers to form choirs and instrumental groups but they also impacted positively the children and their parents.[37] Between 1930 and 1960 school bands (tin whistle, harmonica, accordion, percussion) were a feature of many national schools and their strength in the 1960s attested to their success and relevance in school and community culture.

Contrary to Groocock's belief, the Department of Education's policy for music in primary education did not lack direction. Rather its direction evolved from a commitment to the social values of music and the power of music to bind school and parochial communities. Music festivals represented a strong social function of music education. A variety of musical genres were included, reflecting the democratic philosophy of the festival and the pluralistic social ethos which was emerging in the 1960s. School participation depended on a number of factors – the proximity of the event, the enthusiasm and talent of individual teachers, or the funds to buy instruments.[38]

The 1960s witnessed certain developments in vocal music education, in part the result of the new policy of bilingualism enshrined in the government white paper on the Irish language in 1963. The strong and militant all-Irish policy of former governments since 1922 had become ingrained in Irish primary education over four decades resulting in an educationally unsound emphasis on Irish language songs in the curriculum. Singing continued to dominate the curriculum, 'heavily weighted in songs of Gaelic and National origin', to the neglect of songs from other cultures, and without

sufficient attention to other aspects of music learning.[39] This repertorial canon was to change with expanding cultural consciousness
and a new curriculum in the early 1970s. As more attention was
paid to education within the context of the EEC, song collections
for schools seemed to expand to meet this change in orientation.
For example, in Mícheál Ó Ceallacháin's song collection, *Beidh
Ceol Againn,* published in 1969,[40] he presented international songs
with translations in Irish and English. It was an attempt to bridge
cultures through song, and in the context of early multicultural
music education in Ireland this was a laudable effort.

A new curriculum for primary-school music

As evidenced by cultural activities and language policy change in
the 1960s, the stage was set for curricular change. In contrast to the
1922 curricular manifesto, the cultural responsibility assigned to
primary education in the 1971, *An Curaclam Nua* new curriculum,
reflected a nation that had progressed from the insecurity of early
independence to a post-colonial confidence. 'A child born in this
country inherits certain privileges,' the document opened, 'Its civilisation, which is based on an ancient spiritual and cultural tradition, is part of his birthright'.[41] Now fifty years after the
achievement of political independence, knowledge about and
appreciation of Irish cultural traditions, past and present, were
accepted as basic to primary education rather than as functional to
establishing national identity.

In the new curriculum the role of music was expanded and the
curriculum revised. The monopoly of Irish language songs was subsumed under a more liberated view of music education, reflected in
the statement: 'Music should, therefore, be a pleasant and living
element of school life; it should be a vital means of self-expression,
a preparation for social life and a basis for future musical appreciation and creation.' The perceived poor musical skill of the Irish was
explained in terms of historical circumstances, and now it was time
to 'revive that tradition and keep it firmly and strongly alive'.[42] A
tolerance for the diverse traditions of music in Ireland was implied
and the determining factor in choosing repertoire was its potential
to instill 'good taste'.[43] In contrast to curricular policy in the post-
independent period, the new curriculum could be criticised for its
lack of a cultural thrust to reflect the unique Irish context.

The major components of the new music curriculum were singing, vocal technique, ear training, music and movement, notation, creative activity, and integration with other school subjects. Unlike previous eras when music teaching and learning functioned primarily in a rote system, here a definite stance was taken in relation to the role of music literacy in children's music education.[44] The curriculum was innovative in that respect, as it was in the area of musical creativity. An ambitious programme of music education was set out, one that needed to be supported by appropriate teaching materials and, more urgently, by a long-term plan for teacher in-service education.[45] Given the typical music education of primary teachers, both in their own schooling and in teacher training, intensive in-service workshops were needed to change the process of music education and to integrate the principles of the new curriculum into practice.[46] In addition, a comprehensive series of graded music textbooks and recordings was necessary for the curriculum to be implemented effectively.[47]

The impact of the music curriculum may be interpreted from the results of two surveys carried out in the mid-1970s. The INTO *Curriculum Questionnaire Analysis* revealed that while 79 per cent of respondents stated that they taught music, only 50 per cent felt that they were teaching it satisfactorily.[48] In a questionnaire issued by the Conference of Convent Primary Schools in Ireland, an overwhelming 86 per cent of teachers considered that pupils' musical appreciation had improved since the introduction of the curriculum.[49] This observation seems to have been related more to attitudinal change as a result of exposure to music than to cognitive and skill development resulting from music instruction. The section of the syllabus perceived by teachers as being the most difficult to implement was creative work, with singing perceived as being the easiest. The majority of teachers (76 per cent) agreed that implementing the music curriculum required teachers with special ability.[50]

Two surveys carried out in the 1980s also addressed the status of music education in the nation's primary schools and the implementation of the new curriculum. *Tuairisc ar Theagasc an Cheoil sna Bunscoileanna* (1983), conducted by the Department of Education, indicated satisfactory levels of achievement in song-singing, with very low levels of mastery in knowledge of intervals, musical literacy, and some aural skills.[51] The Arts Council marked European Music Year by commissioning Don Herron to survey and report on the provision for music education in Irish schools. The report *Deaf Ears?*

identified the weaknesses of music in primary (and secondary) education based on a comparison with music education in other European systems. The report concluded that the young Irish person was grieviously disadvantaged when compared with her European peers, and had 'the worse of all European "musical worlds" '.[52] According to the report, this resulted from the lack of a consistent support structure for classroom teachers teaching music, a clear rationale and policy for music education, the human and material resources necessary to inform and implement such a policy, and a formal scheme of instrumental music tuition in the schools.[53]

However dismal the results of these and earlier surveys may seem in relation to the implementation of the new curriculum in music, some positive developments did take place in primary-school music in the last three decades.

Positive developments in primary-school music education since the 1970s

Collections of Irish songs continued to be published, some reflecting the national bilingual policy and containing songs in both Irish and English. Three collections in the mid-1970s, *Éigse an Cheoil* (1975), *Cuisle an Cheoil* (1976), and *Cas Amhrán* (1975),[54] indicated a marked change in the presentation of Irish language songs for school use. Instead of Tonic Sol-fa, these songs were now accompanied by staff notation and chord indications. The primary challenge of presenting this music, as outlined in *Cuisle an Cheoil*, was to accommodate a solo, unaccompanied musical practice which functioned on the principle of variation within a group instructional setting. In addition, the rich variety of local dialects and performance styles made it necessary to choose one version of a song over another. Also challenging was the provision of song accompaniments to melodies which were traditionally sung unaccompanied.[55]

The radio educational series *Bímis ag Ceol*, broadcast between April and June of 1975, also promoted traditional music.[56] It was directed at Gaeltacht schools and presented thirteen Irish-language songs, in some instances using innovative ways to introduce them. The focus of this series was narrow in range, in broadcasting time-span, and in the school population for which it was designed. It did, however, add to the growing corpus of literature on native Irish music. The development of media for the teaching of Irish songs was paralleled by a similar development in the field of instrumental music.

Materials for class instruction in Irish song had been available since the early decades of the century, but tutors and repertoire collections suitable for teaching Irish traditional instrumental music in primary schools were not readily available. The orality of the tradition, its pedagogical orientation, and the social attitude towards it were significant factors holding back its widespread development in schools. As performance practices changed, social attitudes towards the music improved, and materials were made available, while schools became more receptive to its inclusion in the curriculum. Some of the first efforts to introduce Irish traditional instrumental music into primary education came from the North of Ireland.[57] Under the auspices of the Armagh Pipers' Club, Brian and Eithne Vallely published a series entitled *Sing a Song and Play It* in 1975, consisting of a complete three-year course of Irish music and song suitable for children.[58]

A second contribution from the North of Ireland was initiated in 1975 in the form of an educational project directed by Barry Burgess, 'The Primary School Irish Traditional Music Project'. Its aim was to meet the needs of primary teachers wishing to use traditional material in the classroom, and 'to give recognition to the fact that traditional music (both in performance and listening) cuts across all social, political, and religious divides and is, perhaps, the most single, unifying activity in Ireland today'.[59] The need to share the spiritual wealth of a common heritage was seen as transcending the border as a cultural barrier and traditional music was seen as a means to fulfill that need. Indeed the project was aimed at placing traditional music at the core of education. This project and its aims represented the first comprehensive statement on the role of Irish traditional music in education.[60]

Whatever the impact of this scheme, its overall significance lay in highlighting the value and use of Irish traditional music in education thus bringing it into the canon of Irish school music both as a musical practice with a rich repertoire and as a method of music teaching in the broadest sense. The project sought not only to reconstruct a rich element of Irish cultural heritage but also to develop understanding out of the diverse political and religious subcultures of the entire country. No doubt this aim was already basic to the activities of Comhaltas Ceoltóirí Éireann, but its implementation in primary education was only barely emerging.

The direct involvement of the Arts Council, especially through the Richards and Benson reports, provided a further impetus for the development of music in the primary curriculum. The recommendations of the Benson report in particular set a challenging agenda for establishing music at the core of the Irish educational system. The government *White Paper on Educational Development* (1980), similar to the Benson report, viewed arts education as aesthetic education, an approach that was popular internationally at the time. Given the increase in leisure time and the questionable value of the quality of music afforded by mass media in general, the paper argued that education should equip young people with aesthetic judgment and critical perspectives by enlarging their musical experience in every way possible, through song-singing, music-making and listening and moving to music.[61] The paper reflected a child-centered approach and this was particularly welcome in Ireland, in view of the often negative effects of cultural policy on the educational system in previous generations.[62] Although there was a clear absence of reference in this paper to the role of musical heritage in education, the *Programme for Action in Education, 1984–7* was based on the principle that 'the development of our linguistic and cultural heritage should be at the core of our education system'.[63] In the context of music education, this principle was evident during European Music Year in 1985.

One of the major musical events of this anniversary year was the founding of the National Children's Choir, brainchild of music inspector Seán Creamer. The idea of massed children's choirs was not unique to the 1980s. Donnchadh Ó Braoin operated on the same concept in Cork in the 1920s and in Dublin in the 1930s. The unique features of this project were its organisation at a national level and the group's participation in a grand European celebration. In addition to heightening awareness of music during that year, the project was intended to grant music a higher profile in primary education, to promote singing and expand the repertoire of songs currently taught in the schools, to highlight the importance of music in the social and intellectual development of children, and to give children an opportunity to perform to a high standard in venues otherwise unavailable to them.

In the first year, 4,500 children of fourth, fifth, and sixth class nationwide were taught the song repertoire which included J. S. Bach's *Peasant Cantata*, Benjamin Britten's *Friday Afternoons*, and Irish hunting songs.[64] Repertoire in subsequent concerts included

Irish language songs, folk music from around the world, and composed music.[65] The student preparation demanded for participation in such a performance and the enthusiastic response of schools throughout the country spoke of a deep commitment to choral music education. At no other time in the history of Irish primary music education were the national musical talents of classroom teachers tapped with such effectiveness as they have been in this creative project.

If the goal of primary music education was to have children perform a wide range of song repertoire, this project achieved the goal admirably. However, such achievement did not reflect the broad spectrum of music education goals outlined in *An Curaclam Nua* of 1971. A movement such as the National Children's Choir reinforced this reality since the children's limited ability to read music, the limited amount of class time for music, and the vast repertoire of songs to be learned could not allow for song material to be explored conceptually or to serve towards developing music literacy. In effect, the National Children's Choir and other music education projects such as Slógadh and Cor-Fhéilte, whose end was a stage performance, were responding to the idea of music education as cultural education. In those cases, the classroom was a training centre for the 'real' musical world, the stage and a live audience. The musical education of children, then, was aimed at group performance, uniformity, and cultural enrichment through music, song and dance. The long-term goal of cultivating musically educated children through conceptual, skill, and value development leading to music literacy and aesthetic perception was not possible given the lack of human and material resources granted to music in primary education.

The ideal curriculum would bind both music literacy and cultural goals in a sequential music curriculum that transmitted the unique Irish musical and cultural heritage. Also, it would develop in every child the understanding, skills, values, and aesthetic empathy necessary to recreate and reconstruct that heritage and to enrich it for future generations through creative endeavours. Arts Council Education Officer Martin Drury addressed the INTO in 1989 with a paper entitled 'Once More With Feeling' and advocated a new role for the arts in primary education. Viewed from the perspective of the two streams of primary music education identified in the 1970s and 1980s – the child-centered new curriculum and the social function of music education as evidenced by the response to organised stage performances and public competitions – Drury's paper synthesised both streams and provided a novel understanding of the value of music education as an arts subject.[66] Commitment to the child-centered approach was evident in his concern for developing the richness of 'the *interior landscape* of the child's own mind'.[67] This involved education of the child's artistic (i.e. the child as a maker of cultural images) and aesthetic (i.e. the child as a critical receiver of cultural images) intelligences.[68] The blending of the two, according to Drury, occurs when arts education facilitates

> the development of flexible creative intelligence which encompasses the interior and exterior worlds, the past and the present, the idea and the materials, reason and feeling, the individual act and the collective expression, the known and the unknown, the learned and the intuitive, the cerebral and the physical, – in equal measure.[69]

The seeds for change were sown in this valuable exposition on arts education. Philosophically, the ideas reconciled the former preoccupation with cultural and national transformation through primary music education and the emphasis on developing the individual's musical knowledge and skills.

Official documents made available in the 1990s indicate a considerable change in the direction of curriculum development in music. A report issued in 1994 from the arts education sub-committees of the National Council for Curriculum and Assessment stated that 'the ultimate aim of Music Education in the primary school is that children become literate'. Recommendations for a revised curriculum included more emphasis on the creative and appreciative aspects of music to balance performance, access for all children, and more opportunities for children to listen to a wide range of musical styles and traditions with particular emphasis on the national repertoire.[70]

INTRODUCTION OF INTERNATIONAL METHODS OF MUSIC EDUCATION

The Ward method of music teaching was introduced into Ireland in the 1960s. It was rooted in the musical traditions and culture of the Catholic Church, in particular Gregorian Chant.[71] Fr Seán Terry of St Colman's College, Fermoy, studied the method at the Cambridge Ward Method Centre in Cambridge, England, introduced it into St Colman's College in 1965, and subsequently advocated its use in Ireland. Between 1966 and 1972, the Department of Education and the Cork Vocational Education Committee (VEC) sanctioned teacher-training courses in the method. In 1973, Ward-Cheol, an independent Irish organisation, was established and teachers' courses continued until 1983. In the period from 1966 to 1983 over six hundred teachers participated in Ward method courses.[72] The adoption and official sanction of this method by the Department of Education is a further instance of the role of Catholicism in determining the nature of school music education in Ireland.

The introduction of the Ward method was only one instance of the influence of international trends in music education on developments in Ireland. Other methods found their way into Irish music education also. A Dublin teacher, Albert Bradshaw, studied the Kodály method at Kesckemet, Hungary, in 1974 and introduced it into Ireland on his return. In his doctoral dissertation he adapted the method to the Irish educational context. Subsequently, he provided teacher inservice training in the use of the method and published an extensive volume of Irish folk songs using the principles of the Kodály method.[73]

The 1980s witnessed an increased interest in this method. Numerous teachers attended courses at the Kodály Institute in Hungary, two seminars on the method were organised by Colm Ó Cléirigh in 1983 and 1985, and the Irish Kodály Society was founded by Ó Cléirigh in 1986.[74] The popularity of the method results in part from the well-established tradition of Tonic Sol-fa at primary school level, the clarity of the approach, and the strong focus on singing, all making it accessible to teachers. In addition, its emphasis on folk music was appealing to teachers who searched for a way to introduce traditional music into formal education.

The Carl Orff approach to music education has not yet been implemented to the same degree as the Kodály method.[75] Two aspects of the approach may well have limited its use in Irish schools – the cost of musical instruments and the emphasis on creative performance which would have required considerable teacher education for full implementation. In retrospect, the Orff approach could have provided a vital avenue for accessing and implementing the 1971 *Curaclam Nua*, a curriculum which sought to promote creativity and self-expression. Unlike the Kodály method, the principles and strategies of the Orff approach had few precursors in the history of Irish music education.

Of all the international music methods introduced into Ireland in the contemporary period, the Suzuki method has perhaps been implemented most extensively. The movement was initiated in Cork in the mid-1960s by two sisters, Renee Lane-McCarthy and Denise Lane. They were supported by the City of Cork VEC and the Cork Municipal School of Music. Buttevant was the first centre in Ireland to adopt the method in 1966 and in 1971 Charles Acton claimed that Cork was the only Suzuki centre in Europe. Whether this was the case or not, Cork was indeed significant as a European centre for the propagation of this method.[76] This example further illustrates Cork's historical role as a prominent innovative centre for music education in Ireland.

MUSIC IN POST-PRIMARY EDUCATION

A context for reform

Prior to the 1960s, secondary schools based on Catholic, classical ideals of education constituted the dominant type of post-primary school available to students. Groocock's survey of music in the late 1950s identified some weaknesses of secondary-school music: the limited scope and difficulty of the syllabus, the narrow range of musical experiences provided for students, and the lack of music education in boys' secondary schools.[77] Since the time of Groocock's survey, a climate of change, innovation, and expansion in post-primary education in general has influenced positively music curriculum development. Once an élitist subject aimed at propagating the values of one cultural group and transmitting one definition of 'good music', i.e. Western art music, the spectrum of post-primary music education has now broadened to include a diverse range of musical traditions and modes of expression. The increments of growth and change in this regard have been small, yet significant in light of the deep-rooted values in which post-primary music had been set for almost a century. Acknowledgement of the music and musical experiences that students engage in outside of school is but one indication that secondary-school music has become more inspired by and responsive to social and cultural changes than was true in previous eras.

The first report of the post-1960 period to survey music in post-primary education and to recommend curricular change was the Council of Education's report on the *Curriculum of the Secondary*

School in 1962. The difficulty of the music curriculum and the demands it made on the student's time were identified as the factors responsible for the minority position of music in the schools. The report recommended that the syllabus be remodelled with the non-performing student in mind, and that the prescribed repertoire be expanded to include 'some folk songs in Irish and in English, some good ballads, and some choral songs in unison or in harmony'.[78] A second report, *Investment in Education* (1966), also influenced the shape of music in post-primary education.[79] It identified the preparation of a skilled and technologically literate labour force as central to the mission of post-primary education.[80]

The year 1966 witnessed other developments that impacted music in post-primary education: a new type of post-primary school, the comprehensive school, was opened, a common Intermediate Certificate course was introduced for all post-primary schools, plans for 'free post-primary education' were announced, and a new multisyllabus for music in the Intermediate Certificate was introduced. In the opinion of one reviewer, the new syllabus released music 'from the shackles of the instrument, and automaton examinations', and removed that certain ' "Halo" of unreality' which characterised curricular music in the past.[81] Three courses – music, general musicianship, and general and practical musicianship – were now offered with an emphasis on critical listening to 'good music' and skill development for those with talent for instrumental performance.[82] However, similar to all other subjects, the syllabus lacked philosophical depth and a clearly expressed rationale with explicit aims.[83]

What impact did the introduction of this new syllabus (and subsequently a new syllabus for the Leaving Certificate in 1969) have on the development of music in post-primary education? Annual reports from the Department of Education indicate an increase in the percentage of students who sat for certificate examinations in music between 1966 and 1980,[84] although music continued to be chosen by a minority of students in their senior years. The new syllabi were not accompanied by a new form of assessment; thus the general student was assessed in a way similar to that of a student aiming to pursue a career in music. Only minimal change was evident in the department's scheme for choirs and orchestras. Its annual report for 1961–2 stated that every school was expected to provide for singing, and it encouraged group music activity based on its 'educational and cultural value'.[85] Reports indicate that while bonuses for choirs and orchestras increased approximately five and a half times between 1962 and 1983, those for science and equipment increased approximately fourteen times over the same period.[86] The allocation of public funds to educational schemes is determined partly by the current cultural value system so it can be concluded that although official rhetoric encouraged the expansion of music performance, it was not matched with appropriate funding for supporting such activity.[87]

Accommodation of diverse musical practices in the curriculum

In the new curriculum for certificate examinations, change was evident in the prescribed repertoire which included traditional Irish language songs, Irish ballads with English words, songs by modern Irish composers with Irish or English words, folk songs of other countries, and 'songs of the masters'.[88] This classification of song reflected the shifting cultural values so prevalent in the 1960s. For example, the inclusion of international folk songs indicated a need to expand students' cultural awareness beyond their own nation. The role of Irish music was extended. Set orchestral works did not reflect a similar inclusiveness, a fact that resulted in part from the poor perception generally held of Irish composers' works. A 'brief survey of Irish music' was introduced into the history component of the course.[89]

Since the content, pedagogical structures, and evaluation procedures of post-primary music education were rooted in Western art music from the beginning, the introduction of traditional music into the curriculum was a challenging one. Collections of songs did exist to promote such music, but no appropriate teaching materials were available. Gradually, music textbooks published in Ireland incorporated sections on Irish composers, collectors, and musicians, but as late as 1985 Mícheál Ó Súilleabháin criticised these publications, stating that the student

> opens his music-history book (often the Irish schoolbook industry's rehash of an outdated British colonial educational viewpoint) to be confronted with French, German, Italian, British and even Anglo-Irish names, but the great embarrassed silence is observed on the question of the musicality of the Gael.[90]

Meanwhile, conditions and contexts for the performance and analysis of Irish traditional music were expanding rapidly in Irish culture between the 1970s and the 1990s. In a study of attitudes to

Irish traditional music among secondary-school students in the late 1970s, Mary Devereux found that out of 127 urban and rural students surveyed, 62 per cent counted traditional music among their favourite types of music; 59 per cent stated that they would like to play a traditional instrument; of those who felt that Irish traditional music should be in the school curriculum, 80 per cent believed that it should be taught during normal school hours, and 87 per cent felt that emphasis should be on a practical rather than an academic curriculum and that teachers should be accomplished traditional musicians.[91] Other findings led the author to conclude that the average student's concept of traditional music had been formed by 'a series of disjoint and spurious experiences' shaped by the media who exploited 'the musical vacuum' which resulted from lack of official provision for music in the public education system.[92]

Since the early 1980s, efforts to disseminate Irish traditional music through post-primary education have been widespread. Rather than creating new curricular and pedagogical structures to accommodate this set of music practices, aspects were inserted into the current curriculum. For example, in the 1981–2 syllabus, the Irish harp was added to the prescribed instruments for practical examinations, with repertoire including the works of Carolan, Hempson, Cuthbert, and Larchet, and in 1984 a comprehensive practical music programme for traditional instruments was introduced thus placing these instruments on an equal academic standing with those of the classical tradition. Traditional music was also included as an option in the music history section of the certificate examinations, with emphasis on composers and collectors of the music, performance practices and styles, and instruments.[93]

In recent syllabi for certificate examinations, a more definite line of commitment to this genre has been adopted. Not only is traditional music endorsed strongly but syllabi provide a list of prescribed tunes and slow airs for performance, and they suggest the collection of a piece of traditional music as appropriate for a curriculum music project.[94] The most recent developments in post-primary school music in the late 1990s indicate a strong commitment to an authentic representation of traditional music in the curriculum, especially evident in syllabi, in teacher inservice education, and in the curriculum materials developed for teaching traditional music.[95]

The establishment or continued development of traditional music archives in a number of institutions was also significant in the development of educational resources for the transmission of traditional music. CCÉ maintains its own archives at Cultúrlann na hÉireann. A national Irish Traditional Music Archive (Taisce Cheol Dúchais Éireann) was founded in Dublin in 1987 and has grown 'from a concept without premises or holdings to the largest collection in existence of the materials of Irish traditional music'.[96] In addition, at University College, Cork, an innovative programme to prepare second-level music teachers was developed by Mícheál Ó Súilleabháin during the 1980s, where prospective teachers were trained in traditional as well as classical music.

In addition to traditional music, other genres of music beyond the canon of classical works were gradually included in the curriculum in the 1980s and '90s. Prior to that time, there was a general lack of attention to popular culture in secondary education. On the topic, Mulcahy wrote:

> Banished altogether from this domain [of cultural studies] is even the most modest attempt to devote attention to popular adolescent culture in the forms of popular music and dance. Furthermore, nowhere does one find an attempt to relate the aesthetic to the matter of everyday living. Art and culture are conceived in terms of the museum and the art gallery.[97]

In the larger cultural picture, from the 1960s forward, popular culture exercised a powerful influence over youth culture. Paul Hewson's (otherwise known as Bono) description of the musical influences that shaped U2's style attests to this omnipresence of popular culture through the media.[98] Although not included in his description of musical influences, members of the U2 group attended Mount Temple Comprehensive School in the mid-1970s, and participated in a music programme that catered for 'a wide range of tastes, from renaissance choral works to Spanish guitar'.[99] The ethos of this progressive, nondenominational school, coupled with an innovative music teacher, Albert Bradshaw, made this school the exception rather than the rule for the mid-1970s.

In the 1980s, efforts were made to link music in school culture with students' out-of-school experiences. *Musicscape*, a series of ten educational programmes broadcast during the 1980–1 school year, was designed to encourage an interest in music among first-year secondary pupils, especially those who had little or no formal musical background. To accomplish this, the series attempted to build on 'the musical experiences which young people might be expected to have assimilated from everyday life'. An attempt 'to broaden the musical tolerance of the listener' was evident in the first programme, 'That's Music', which presented music 'extending from Mozart to the Boomtown Rats to the music of the Far East'.[100] An isolated effort such as this may have inspired some teachers and students and its value cannot be underestimated, but no major impact could be anticipated in post-primary education as an outcome of this single series.[101]

As the 1980s progressed, other isolated efforts were made to integrate popular music into the music curriculum. Exposing students to a wide variety of music was basic to the revised Leaving Certificate syllabus in 1989, 'developing their judgment in forming an estimate of music of all kinds and of the quality of its performance'.[102] Yet no specific guidelines were provided to identify 'music of all kinds' which would be relevant to students. Again in the revised certificate syllabi of the 1990s there is clear commitment to including diverse musical traditions and in the process 'accommodating divergence in students' musical needs, interests, and ambitions'.[103]

School culture and the provision for music in the curriculum

Music education opportunities for post-primary school students have expanded and improved in quality during recent decades, especially at the junior-cycle level. In the proposed curricular framework of the Curriculum and Examinations Board in 1984, music, as part of the 'creative and aesthetic studies', was placed in the core curriculum which was defined as 'areas of experience which every pupil should have during the period of compulsory schooling'.[104] However, increases in the number of students taking music for certificate examinations have not been visible. Between 1990 and 1996 the numbers of students who sat for music at the junior-cycle level dropped from 17 to 13 per cent, and the senior-cycle level remained the same at 2 per cent of the total student population.[105]

The scope and nature of the music curriculum was largely determined by school type (secondary, vocational, or comprehensive and community), by gender, and by geographical location. Prior to the opening of comprehensive and community schools, music education assumed different roles in secondary and vocational schools, the latter perceived as venues for promoting the Irish language through *claisceadal* or community singing in Irish. Music in secondary schools, on the other hand, was linked inextricably to the propagation of classical music values. As late as the mid-1970s, one critic commented on secondary-school music as remaining 'little more than a social attribute on a level with a good dress sense or a refined palate for food'.[106] The value systems which stimulated the development of music education in both school types remained largely unchanged between the 1960s and the 1980s.

In 1966, measures were taken to unify the curricula of these schools through common subjects, common courses, and common examinations.[107] The introduction of the multisyllabus in music represented a step towards achieving this ideal. Due to the nature and structure of the Group Certificate, students in vocational day classes were not afforded the opportunity to elect music as a subject for examination. Their music education was also hampered by the weak provision made for music in these schools when compared to other post-primary schools.[108]

A different agenda underpinned music in vocational schools, one that was traditionally linked to cultural activities such as the promotion of the Irish language. Evidence of this was found in the government white paper on the Irish language of 1963. It recommended that each Vocational Education Committee employ a music supervisor to encourage and guide the development of choirs and community singing and to ensure that Irish songs were highlighted in the curriculum of their schools.[109] The fact that a large number of Comhaltas Ceoltóirí Éireann classes were held at these schools accentuated their role in promoting Irish traditional music. Describing the activities of the Vocational Education Committee in Co. Clare in the 1960s, Matt Power stated that

> Comhaltas Ceoltóirí Éireann co-operated with the VEC in organising Traditional Irish Dance and Music classes at many centres. These classes had a two-fold objective – the preservation of a very important aspect of our heritage and also the guarding of our youth against 'foreign influences'.[110]

Irish traditional music developed in both vocational and other second-level schools, its form influenced by the school ethos and local cultural values.

In addition to school type, another subcultural difference can be observed in relation to gender and the provision for music in schools, with a clear bias in favour of the subject in girls' schools and to a lesser degree in co-educational schools.[111] This bias is also evident in the gender distribution of those who sat for certificate examinations, even as recently as the 1990s.[112] A third major factor influencing the provision of music in second-level schools is geographical location. For example, the *Kerry Music Report* (1998) found that only ten of the thirty-two second-level schools in Kerry offered music at either junior- or senior-certificate levels in 1996. Gender imbalance was also a concern in this context, with far fewer boys taking music as an examination subject.[113]

While discourse on arts education was prolific during this period and advocated music as aesthetic and cultural education, the core structure of music in post-primary education did not change to accommodate this orientation until the decade of the 1990s. Criticism of the music curriculum was prolific throughout the period. It was perceived as being too academic, too élitist, socially irrelevant, and emanating from a philosophy which separated art from the fabric of everyday life. The erosion of this imperial, deep-seated structure of music instruction and evaluation has occurred in a very measured manner. Its most vulnerable point seems to have been in its response to the changing social meaning of Irish traditional music. Although this genre was accepted as worthy of study and practice, no new pedagogy accompanied its entry into the curriculum. If Comhaltas Ceoltóirí Éireann can be said to have approached this music from a social and cultural perspective, then the approach to the same genre in post-primary education may be regarded as an academic one on the lines of a classical education.

In general, the pace of social and educational change in Ireland since 1961 did stimulate new thinking and in some cases new practices in post-primary education. Consideration must be given to a number of factors determining the form of music in the curriculum – the strong utilitarian philosophy which undergirded post-primary education for much of this period and which prioritised areas for government financial support and encouragement; the emergence of new sociomusical values in Irish culture in conjunction with changing definitions of Irish music; the dearth of pedagogical materials and Irish textbooks treating Irish music, and the dilemma of accommodating a folk music based on communal social meaning within a curricular framework which evaluated solo performance, both at oral and written levels.

The years between 1961 and 1998 were transitional in the context of the role of music in post-primary education. The values of the old system were seen by many music educators to be socially obsolete; at the same time, the constant flux in Irish music subcultures was not conducive to establishing a clear philosophy upon which a new and socially relevant music curriculum might be founded.

NETWORKS FOR THE EXPANSION OF MUSIC EDUCATION

A striking feature of the contemporary era was the rich network of organisations and media that were founded or expanded to provide musical education for youth. Most notable was the unprecedented increase in the number of private and semi-private schools of music throughout the country, the role of Comhaltas Ceoltóirí Éireann in the transmission of traditional music and dance, and the development of partnerships between schools and a variety of organisations with an educational outreach programme. Smaller but no less significant developments were the organisation of Gael-Linn's Slógadh competition in 1969, the GAA's Scór competition in 1970, the Association for the Promotion of Music in Education (1970–6), the Music Awareness Agency in 1988, and the more recently established World Music for Youth Festival sponsored by the Royal Dublin Society.

Numerous factors contributed to the growth of institutions offering or stimulating music education outside the school classroom: demographic trends (by 1986, approximately 48 per cent of the population were under twenty-five years of age); the social attraction of music and music making; the propagation of a variety of music through the media, live concerts, recordings and videos; the resurgence of interest in traditional music and the popularity of Irish music on the world stage; the appeal of rock and other popular music to youth; the breakdown of barriers between musical genres and socioeconomic groups, and the greater official recognition of the role of music in Irish culture.

During the 1960s the role of the arts in national life and in education began to be discussed at a variety of levels. In 1969, a seminar on 'The Arts in Education' was held at University College, Dublin, and the Association for the Promotion of Music in Education (APME) was an outgrowth of this event. The primary aims of the association were to improve the status of music education in schools, to highlight its weaknesses, to provide support for teachers, and to promote an awareness among parents of the importance of music in their children's education.[114] In its short existence

(1970–6), APME provided a forum for expressing ideas, and its efforts highlighted music education as worthy of national attention; however, the association did not have the support or sponsorship of any influential body, thus limiting the advancement and impact of its agenda.[115]

MUSIC FOR YOUTH

A number of youth music ensembles at local and national levels were founded during this period. As early as 1958 the Cork Youth Orchestra was founded, an initial step towards establishing an Irish youth orchestra in 1967. National youth ensembles continued to grow in the 1970s and '80s with the founding of the Irish Youth Choir, Irish Youth Wind Ensemble, and the Irish Youth Jazz Ensemble. In addition, ensembles of the European Community (e.g. youth orchestra, jazz) are open to young Irish musicians.

Concerts for children continued to be organised by Ceol Chumann na nÓg, under the leadership of James Blanc. Whereas the Cumann's concerts were initially limited to Dublin, later they were extended to the National Symphony Orchestra's touring venues, with the children's programmes usually taking place on the morning following the public event. In more recent years, the orchestra's educational concerts (Music in the Classroom) have been supported by *The Irish Times*.[116]

The Music Association of Ireland (MAI) organised a Schools Recital Scheme in 1967 and a Music Workshop Scheme in 1986. The aim of the Recital Scheme was to bring live music regularly into schools in order to give young people the opportunity to listen to and enjoy music, and also to arouse their interest in music performance. Participation of provincial schools was considerable in this scheme.[117] In the Workshop Scheme, students explored the works of contemporary Irish composers and then participated in one-day workshops when the artist visited the schools and the work was performed. The active promotion of contemporary art music by MAI represents the association's commitment to this genre and its desire to involve students directly with the music and the composers. In MAI's statement on its role for the 1990s, it expressed grave concerns about music in schools and made several recommendations to improve the situation.[118]

Also involved in the promotion of contemporary art music was the Contemporary Music Centre (CMC), founded in Dublin in

1986 to improve access to the works of living composers, to promote Irish music, and to provide up-to-date information on contemporary art music in other countries. Besides being a storehouse for national and international contemporary music, CMC offers collaboration with schools in preparing events or exhibitions which encourage young audiences to explore 'the rich diversity of the music of our age'.[119] The centre provides a support system and a repertoire library for teachers. In the mid-1990s, CMC initiated a music series to publish simple instrumental music by composers experienced in writing for young students. The aim was

> to make Irish music of high quality readily available to teachers and their pupils from the very earliest stages of learning and in this way to make contemporary art music, and particularly music by home-grown composers, a normal part of their studies all the way from beginner to diploma level.[120]

The Ark, a cultural centre for children in Dublin, opened in 1995. Founded by Martin Drury, arts consultant and former education officer of the Arts Council, it is sponsored by the Arts Council, the Department of Education, FÁS, and Dublin Corporation, in addition to corporate sponsors and foundations. The Ark provides arts programmes for children aged between four and fourteen years, including those designed specifically for primary-school students, for individual children and family groups, and projects developed for children who are disadvantaged socially and economically.[121]

In 1997, The Royal Dublin Society (RDS) organised and sponsored a World Music for Youth Festival with workshops in gospel music, Ewe drumming, Javenese Gamelan, drum kit, electric guitar and world percussion. This model involved artists, clinicians and composers working in Dublin schools with students and bringing their performances to the RDS for a culminating concert that presented a variety of world music traditions.[122]

A number of agencies and organisations provided instruction for youth in traditional music, or supported it in formal education: Gael-Linn, Comhaltas Ceoltóirí Éireann (CCÉ), the Irish Folk Music Society, the Music Association of Ireland, and the Music Awareness Agency. Gael-Linn focused on music as a means of maintaining the Irish language as a socially relevant and living language among young people. In 1969, it launched an annual Slógadh competition which aimed at promoting the Irish language in youth culture through the arts.[123] A broad spectrum of music was reflected in the competition, ranging from sean-nós singing to punk-rock.[124] In effect, besides promoting the Irish language through the arts, the competition nurtured a variety of music relevant to youth culture and fostered a more tolerant attitude towards other forms of Irish music that were not neccesarily promoting the language. In the spirit of the bilingual policy of the 1960s, the Irish language in this festival was not linked exclusively with Irish traditional music; rather it functioned in the context of other musical genres such as art and popular music. The creative dimension of arts education was emphasised in Slógadh, and school groups were encouraged to regenerate, revitalise, and explore the possibilities of music in Ireland's multiple musical cultures. Social and academic barriers between music subcultures became blurred in the name of the Irish language, and the constant reworking of inherited traditions in the context of contemporary values and idioms has been a major thrust of this movement. In many primary schools, Slógadh became an annual event in the calendar.

Scór music competitions, organised by the Gaelic Athletic Association (GAA) in 1970, had a special section for youth performance, Scór na nÓg. The cultural agenda of this organisation is strong, with the promotion of traditional Irish dancing, music, song and other aspects of Irish culture in the forefront. A comparison of the aims of the GAA at the time of its foundation in 1884 and in the early 1970s provides insight into the radical change in cultural circumstances and also the changed role of traditional music as it is related to Irish identity. A century ago, education in Irish music was seen to ward against the daily importing of culture from England.[125] In the 1970s and thereafter the same threat to Irish identity was not present; what was present was the challenge of maintaining identity within the context of European unity.[126]

While Gael-Linn and the GAA promote the performance of traditional music by and for youth, the single most important agent and patron in the transmission of traditional music has been Comhaltas Ceoltóirí Éireann. Young performers are not only taught in regular classes but also exposed to the experience and expertise of the masters through sessions, workshops, concert tours, television programmes, and festivals. A rich learning context is provided, achieved primarily by the organisation being rooted in the community and working consistently at the local level: 'The importance of community based cultural activity is that it generates a pride in and a curiosity about local traditions – the keystone of our heritage'. The approximately 600 classes organised by CCÉ are but one step in the education process. Although no formal teaching takes place at sessions, young performers are exposed to the expertise of the generations of musicians who convene, and they are inspired 'to emulate their music elders'.[127] Ethnomusicologist Edward Henry observed sessions and noted that they provided 'a wholesome, family-like milieu for music-making that is a good environment for children'.[128] CCÉ also organised formal summer schools and workshops for learning traditional music – for example, Scoil Éigse founded in 1973 and Scoil Acla founded in 1985.[129]

As schools of traditional music became popular and a greater number of players were involved in teaching, the issue of certification for teachers of Irish traditional music arose. Teacher qualification was seen as an important safeguard for ensuring the authentic transmission of the music to the students and for establishing standards in the teaching of traditional music. In instituting a teacher's diploma, CCÉ collaborated with Mícheál Ó hEidhin, music inspector with the Department of Education, who designed and directed the project. In July 1980 the first course leading to a Diploma in Irish Traditional Music (Teastas i dTeagasc Ceolta Tíre, TTCT) was launched at the CCÉ headquarters, Cultúrlann na hÉireann.[130] From one perspective, traditional music was now legitimised in the music academy and took on some institutional traits such as a written examination as part of the assessment process. The informality and non-analytical approach to pedagogy, characteristic of traditional music prior to the 1960s, was no longer adequate. Now that the music had gained academic respectability, as it were, the need for an objective and scientific pedagogy and system of evaluating performance surfaced. Gemma Hussey's comment at the diploma ceremony in 1983 is significant in light of the history of traditional music in education. She urged that teachers must understand how 'to foster our own music without downgrading any other music'.[131] The wheel had come full circle: teachers who passed on traditional music, a music that for decades was itself downgraded by those who held control of cultural discourse, now needed to be careful not to downgrade other music and develop an ethnocentric attitude in students.

The Irish Folk Music Society, established in 1971, included the teaching of folk music as part of its agenda. Inspired by a conference of the International Council for Traditional Music at Bayonne in 1973, at which the topic of folk music in education was debated, the society addressed the same topic at its meeting in October 1974. A number of obstacles were identified in introducing folk music into education and recommendations were made to help overcome them. First, students without a background in traditional music found it difficult to identify with the music and appropriate attitudes needed to be formed in order for the music to become meaningful and relevant. Second, the tradition of harmonising airs was seen as inappropriate and 'could tend to dilute the true (monodic) tradition'.[132] Third, the suitability of the examination system in post-primary education for the assessment of folk music was questioned – for example, the standardisation of traditional tunes and playing styles was likely if the music was subjected to examination procedures. The question arose if the teaching of folk instruments ought to take place outside of school hours on an optional basis, or be granted full recognition and made part of the regular examination system in secondary education. Fourth, a methodology for teaching Irish folk music was needed and a specialist training for teachers and the provision of appropriate materials was necessary if this scheme were to be successful.[133]

Since the time of this debate, practical efforts have been made to improve the status and teaching of traditional music in Irish classrooms. In 1987, the Arts Council awarded a grant to the MAI to add a special Irish traditional music section within their existing 'music in education' schemes. The aim of the project was to 'spread the love of our Traditional Native Music and provide enjoyment for the students'.[134] Emphasis was placed on building positive attitudes towards participating in the music rather than in developing technical proficiency. A similar scheme was launched by the Music Awareness Agency, founded in 1988. Grant-aided by the Arts Council, the agency aimed to promote traditional music in primary schools by organising talks and concerts, by identifying resources which should be made available to teachers, and by assisting teachers in presenting this music with confidence.[135]

Until recently the inspiration and impetus to bring traditional music into formal education came primarily from cultural societies and institutions that operated outside the Department of Education. A striking feature of all the schemes has been the emphasis placed on exposure to the music and the development of positive attitudes towards it.[136]

COMMUNITY MUSIC

As cultural horizons broadened to embrace a more global view of and participation in music, so also did they refocus on cultural life in local communities. In Ireland, this movement had its origins in developing a sense of place and empowering local communities to develop a sense of self-confidence and self-discovery which, according to Kearney, is 'one of the best contributions we can make to the global community'.[137] In the 1990s in particular, local communities are increasingly active in preserving the identity of their towns and villages which now 'occupy a more powerful place in the national life and imagination'.[138] The empowerment of local communities was paralleled by a community arts movement beginning in the 1980s, coupled with an increased emphasis on developing musical life in provincial and rural communities, especially through the efforts of Music Network.

In 1983, Creative Activity For Everyone (CAFE) was established by the Arts Council to coordinate and strengthen the efforts of all groups and individuals interested in creative arts activity. An Arts Community Education Committee sought to foster the experience of the arts as part of everyday life 'at work, in school, or on the street'.[139] Working with a similar goal of cultural democracy in the arts, Music Network was established in 1986 to address the development of music in the regions of Ireland. It was sponsored by the Arts Council and viewed as a main channel for implementing its regional policy of universal access to the arts. In the initial years it was a small-scale regional touring agency; beginning in 1992 with the initiation of a music policy document, the Network entered what chief executive Niall Doyle described as 'a period of transformation' leading to a far more extensive, comprehensive and effective development of its brief. Concerns of access were fundamental to its goals: 'This access should be equal for all – independent of age, sex, financial circumstances or geographical location.'[140] Emphasis was placed on empowering local communities and giving them a sense of local ownership of initiatives. 'Access and education' was one of the six integrated programme areas outlined in the policy document. Education was viewed broadly as a process in all sections of the community and not simply equated with schools.

As part of a national effort to bring local music, education and community development organisations together county by county, the Kerry Music County 2000 project was launched in 1996 in cooperation with the Electricity Supply Board. The project committee consulted over 400 organisations, groups and individuals. The report, published in 1998, identified the need for unifying of disparate efforts and developing an integrated plan for music in the county. In addition to national projects and organisations, community music education is evident in developments such as Maoin Cheoil an Chláir, an independent music school in Ennis set up in 1993. In this context, we witness a democratic and comprehensive view of music education, reflected in the organisation of the school, the variety of musical traditions represented, and the celebration of the 'maoin cheoil' or musical wealth of the region. It is clear from the multiple developments in communities and private institutions that provision for music education outside the formal education system has increased in an unprecedented way in the last three decades.

TOWARDS DIVERSITY AND DEMOCRACY IN IRISH MUSIC EDUCATION

The predominance of monolithic structures in post-independent Ireland diminished as a pluralist vision for Irish society emerged in the 1960s. At the same time, an image of Ireland as a thriving industrial, technologically advanced nation within the European Union became dominant. Both of these developments expanded the concept of Irish cultural identity and impacted educational policy and practice. The changing cultural values were evident in the ongoing and extensive debate concerning the meaning of 'Irish music', and in increasing efforts to provide access to a variety of musical genres. An exceptionally rich, broad spectrum of local and national cultural and music organisations and activities emerged in conjunction with this debate, a trend that has become even more significant in the 1990s.

Due primarily to the efforts of the Arts Council from the mid-1970s forward, the importance of education in the arts gained unprecedented attention and came to be viewed as a government responsibility. The centrality of music education in cultural development was acknowledged officially, the canon of school music expanded to include a diverse range of musical traditions in the curriculum. The former essentialist agenda of nationalism that permeated primary-school music was less visible in this period. Now music education was linked in a variety of ways with cultural ideologies rooted in bilingual policy, the promotion of peace and tolerance among people in all parts of the island, the formation of an Irish musical identity within the consort of the EU, and the right of every young person to have access to Irish traditional music, a vital part of her heritage. The latter concern brought to the surface many challenges in reconciling an informal, orally transmitted, and unanalysed system of music education with an institutionalised, literacy-based formal education structure.

In no other period did mass media have as great an impact on the way music is known and transmitted. No longer is transmission limited to classrooms and informal instructional settings. Music is frequently learned through instructional materials such as recordings and videotapes; it can be composed using technological media that facilitate composition for students with limited formal music education; it can be produced using digital interface which enables a student to draw on a wide variety of sounds from diverse musical traditions worldwide. In effect, such media of communication have transformed the landscape of music learning. They facilitate the expansion of musical and cultural identity and make the process of music learning more accessible to the next generation.

The most striking feature of development in music education was increased access to music learning, especially in the context of cultural organisations, private music schools, and local community contexts. Some of these organisations functioned directly to improve the status of music education in schools, for example, the Arts Council, the Music Association of Ireland, and Music Network. The provision for music in schools improved significantly although it is clear that there is considerable scope for improvement so that every student who passes through the formal education system, regardless of age, geographical location, gender, or school ethos, has access to a high-quality education in music. In this period, issues of musical diversity and democracy dominated music education discussion and development, and it is in these areas that the greatest progress has been made towards developing the musical potential of school communities and meeting the musical needs of communities in general.

7
'The Given Note': Patterns of Music Transmission in Irish Culture

In his poem 'The Given Note',[1] Seamus Heaney captures the mystery, magic and myth that underlie the transmission of traditional music in Irish culture. The centrality of place in this process is highlighted as the musician is seen picking up an air 'on the most westerly Blasket . . . Out of wind off mid-Atlantic'. The image of music integrally related with place and inspired by and transmitted through the soundscape of the natural environment was also invoked by Donegal fiddler John Doherty when he said:

'The old musicians in them days would take music from anything. They would take music from the sound of the sea, or they would go alongside the river at the time of the flood and they would take music from that. They would take music from the chase of the hound and the hare'.[2]

Embedded in the myths about music in Ireland are beliefs in its magical source and its power to change behaviour. These perceptions of music assumed new meaning as colonial presence increased and 'the battle of two civilisations', as D. P. Moran put it,[3] embraced cultural as well as political domains. The transmission of music, as a subset of musical culture in general, came to be 'centrally involved in power relations and in the construction and reconstruction of identities of both colonised and coloniser'.[4] Colonists were suspicious and afraid of the effects that native Irish music might have on the cultural identity of their members: they outlawed native musicians and banned native instruments, which were viewed as symbols of native power and resistance. Thus music assumed a role as a marker of political identity, creating boundaries between self and other, constructing symbolic communities that provided meaning and identity for members of various subcultural groups.[5]

The manner in which music was practised and transmitted varied according to the subculture in question. At the beginning of the nineteenth century, music education within Anglo-Irish families, communities and institutions was typically aimed at reproducing the middle-class values of colonial culture. Emphasis was placed on teaching music that was appropriate for cultivating those values and the accompanying social skills, and for developing knowledge of the 'science of music'. This orientation to music learning was in many ways radically different to that of traditional communities where music served the social needs of lower-class communities and was 'eared down' to the young who experienced it as a natural part of the socialisation process. As the political status of traditional music began to change within the cultural nationalist movement, so also did the transmission of the music as it became institutionalised, formalised and in some respects aligned with the traditions of school music.

The site of music learning in all subcultural contexts was located at the intersection of local values and traditions and national political, religious, social, and economic realities. The breadth of instructional contexts in which music was transmitted, from the master-apprentice system of traditional rural communities to state-supported schools, was matched by the depth of political and cultural ideologies in which music learning was embedded.

The transmission of music functioned in at least two ways in Irish culture and education. In responding to various political movements of the time – colonialism, nationalism and post-nationalism – it contributed to the formation of cultural identity. It also created its own subculture as it developed in communal and school settings. David Elliott refers to the interdependence of both functions when he says that 'music education is not something that operates autonomously in a culture; it also functions powerfully as culture.'[6] Interaction between the two functions was frequently made explicit in written statements such as government documents and institutional philosophies, or was implicit in the repertoire chosen for transmission, the methods and media that facilitated transmission, and the manner in which music learning was evaluated and brought into the public domain.

Although the circumstances that guided the development of music education have changed over time, certain patterns can be gleaned from historical evidence that lend continuity to the narrative of music education in nineteenth- and twentieth-century Ireland. To access these patterns, I revisit the book's four points of departure introduced in chapter one, music as culture, as canon, as community, and as communication. These focal points provide insights into the influence of sociocultural, religious, political and economic developments, the overlapping bases of individual and communal identity, on the generational transmission of music. To disentangle these bases is all but impossible due to the 'complex web of interweaving narratives'[7] that underlie human motivation and behaviour. This analysis highlights the interactions between social and economic development and the growth of institutions and institutional influence in music education; the effects of political change on the canon of formal music education; the impact of shifting cultural and political values on the experience of music education as community; and the incorporation of new media and technology into the environment of music learning.

MUSIC AS CULTURE: FOUNDATIONS OF TRANSMISSION

At the beginning of the nineteenth century the most organised and institutionalised forms of music education were Dublin's two cathedrals schools, St. Patrick's Cathedral and Christ Church Cathedral, the University of Dublin, and private denominational schools throughout the country. In these contexts, musical values were aligned with middle-class social and ecclesiastical life. A worthy music education cultivated an appreciation of art music and was rooted in the values of Western aesthetics. Meanwhile, an informal system of music instruction existed throughout the country which ensured the generational transmission of traditional music. Due to the predominantly oral nature of music learning in this context, and the suppressed state of native culture in general, our knowledge of how traditional music was passed on is limited, and marked by an absence of reference to it in literature and government publications that described education.

The British government, through the establishment of the National School system in 1831, aimed at ameliorating the social and cultural life of the native Irish. The role of music in national education was to socialise and civilise the young, and to elevate their musical taste by exposing them to the pleasures of 'Victorian middle-class respectability'. Even Sir Thomas Wyse, who spoke on behalf of the native Irish, believed that young people needed an aesthetic education to help cultivate good musical taste and appropriate social sensibilities. Pedagogical emphasis was placed on formal knowledge and music literacy, diametrically opposed to the emphasis placed on social interaction and oral transmission in learning traditional music.

Community response to school music in the system depended on the location and type of school, and the social background of the students. In the context of model schools, it seems that parents viewed music as a valuable complement to the regular subjects taught and continuous with the middle-class values that underpinned such communities. Music performance served as an important public relations medium on examination days when parents and significant community members attended the proceedings. Lower-class parents, on the other hand, whose children attended ordinary national schools, typically regarded the purpose of education narrowly as a means to facilitate upward economic mobility and to prepare young people for emigration. To achieve those ends did not necessarily require learning the music of high culture. In many instances, children already belonged to close-knit musical communities, and besides, the songs taught in school and the Hullah method used to teach sight-singing were culturally discontinuous with parents' experience of music in their lives.

As the century progressed, Catholic teaching orders increased in number and influence, national schools became denominational, and the social values reproduced by school music developed to meet the cultural and musical needs of a rising middle-class Catholic population. Many religious men and women came from middle-class backgrounds; in some cases their orders originated in middle-class continental Europe and their educational philosophy was infused with the values of high culture. Sources indicate a strong social consciousness in nineteenth-century Catholic education, with consistent efforts to improve the social and spiritual life of the next generation of young Catholics. Such values were reflected in teaching art music, improving the quality of church music, preparing female students to fulfill the roles assigned to them in nineteenth-century middle-class society, and transforming the aesthetic dispositions of the young by developing the pupils' taste for 'good' music. It is reasonable to assume that parental support for music education in these schools was forthcoming. What is clear is that Catholic orders and Catholic clergy, in their teaching, school management and cultural leadership, provided patronage for music in education, strengthened the identity of middle-class Catholics with art music traditions, and bridged the worlds of lower- and middle-class musical values and practices. The value of music in the context of religious education is borne out by the fact that hundreds of harmoniums were purchased in the mid to late decades of the century to assist in the education of students and in the reform of church music. The work of the Cecilian Society as part of the greater effort abroad to reform church music from the 1870s onward, and the Catholic Church's encouragement of music competitions from the 1880s onward, brought together the worlds of the Catholic Irish and European art and ecclesiastical music. With the spread of the Gregorian chant movement in the late nineteenth century, and more especially after the papal legislation on sacred music in *Motu Proprio* in 1903, chant was introduced into parish communities throughout the country to enhance Catholic liturgy.

Sociomusical values were also transmitted through their endorsement in other institutions such as Intermediate schools, academies and colleges of music, and cultural institutions. When music was developed in the curriculum of Intermediate Education in the 1880s it was modelled directly after conservatory music education, in keeping with the middle-class values that dominated the schools of that system. The Academy of Music was founded in Dublin in 1848 to serve the children of middle-class parents and thus to propagate middle-class values. Originating in another subculture later in the century, the municipal schools of music in Cork and Dublin catered to children of all classes and, in a limited sense, broadened the musical values in the academy by introducing instruction in native music in the early twentieth century. In other institutions such as the Gaelic League and pipers' clubs, the sociomusical values of traditional rural communities became firmly established in the cultural spaces of colonial, urban music education. To learn traditional music in these new contexts implied learning the culture of a rising political Gaelic order.

In turn-of-the-century Ireland, music education flourished due to the liberating and empowering effects of cultural nationalism, the centralisation of musical culture in competitions and festivals, the founding of new institutions of music learning, and the changing climate of education, with emphasis on the developmental needs of the young. National teachers participated in in-service education; numerous collections of songs in the Irish language were published; music in rural communities such as those described in Foxford and Buttevant thrived; and local *feiseanna* began to be organised. In addition, numerous articles were published on music in Ireland and on the need for a national school of music and a comprehensive system of music education.

Positive musical developments in this period were short-lived. A climate of war in the early century, both at national and global levels, detracted attention from these positive cultural and educational forces, focusing instead on how music could serve in a time of political strife and tension. Efforts to broaden the definition of Irish music and to move away from the polarisation of native and colonial musical cultures[8] were marginalised as a narrow view of 'Irish' music was enshrined in the cultural policy of the new nation state. In addition, the challenges of political independence in terms of economic stability, and the economic depression of the 1930s, resulted in little official attention being paid to the development of musical culture. In some respects, this early post-independent period was also one of cultural depression, with little government support for or encouragement of music that did not directly contribute to the formation of Gaelic identity.

In incremental stages, especially after 1922, traditional music secured a social presence and respect beyond the parish communities of rural Ireland. Selected parts of the native repertoire, Irish language songs and other repertoire that served nationalist agendas were granted an honoured place in the school curriculums, especially in national, and later, vocational schools. Radio Éireann, in providing broad-ranging music programmes for schools and broadcasts of children's performances, counteracted the official neglect of music education in a small but significant way. The newly established national ensembles, through their participation in Radio Éireann broadcasts and the organisation of concerts for schoolchildren, also assisted in building concert audiences and a musically educated public, especially in urban areas. In general, music in national schools developed in response to the government's educational policy of building national identity. Music in second- and third-level institutions maintained the *status quo* of teaching art music and focusing on the education of professional musicians and music teachers.

Catholic teaching orders and the Catholic hierarchy also supported and encouraged art music in education in the Irish Free State, with a flourishing chant movement in the schools supported by summer schools in third-level institutions, and liturgical festivals in a number of provincial towns. By the 1960s when the monocultural view of Irish identity began to dissipate and Vatican Council II expanded the scope of church music to include vernacular music, the role of the Catholic Church as one of the primary patrons of art music in Irish culture diminished. One final effort to bring a Catholic influence to music in formal education was the introduction of the Ward method into Irish secondary schools in the late 1960s, inspired by the pedagogy and repertoire of the Benedictine monks of Solesmes. Over the decades, Catholic teaching orders played a major role in developing music education in schools and communities. They provided individual and group music instruction, prepared the young to participate in religious ceremonies, prepared students for examinations organised by royal and municipal colleges of music, and founded and maintained choral and instrumental ensembles in schools and communities that would otherwise be deprived of such musical culture.

Comhaltas Ceoltóirí Éireann, an important forum for the development of traditional music and dance in the 1950s and thereafter, highlighted the role of education in its efforts to disseminate these traditions. That institution's work, coupled with the growing international reputation of Irish traditional music (as well as folk music in general), broadened the social base of those choosing to learn traditional music and dance. This began a movement that not only allowed the music to develop in institutions that were rooted in middle-class sociomusical values, but gradually legitimised some aspects of traditional music instruction that in the past had been regarded as inappropriate for formal music education – for example, the methods of oral transmission and the instruments associated with the tradition. In the contemporary period, change in the school music curriculum was not limited to traditional music. It embraced a range of vernacular and popular music and, for the first time in the history of Irish music education, recognised the social and musical needs of young people.

Positive economic developments in the 1950s and '60s were also responsible for the change in attitude to the arts in education and in the culture at large. On the one hand, those school subjects that were viewed as crucial to economic growth were boosted while the poor status of artistic subjects such as music experienced no significant change; viewed from another perspective, there was a better economic environment for developing the arts. As the country became more affluent and Irish traditional music gained cultural status at home and abroad, the topic of music education came into the foreground in discussions of educational and cultural affairs. Beginning in the 1970s, this was evident in the attention and financial resources devoted to music education by the Arts Council. The momentum increased in the 1980s and reached a climax in the '90s with the state and semi-state sponsorship of projects and reports such as The Ark, MEND, the PIANO reports, and increased institutional commitment to broadening and improving music curriculums in schools and universities. Unlike former eras, music education is now being encouraged and supported by numerous private and public bodies such as arts councils, the Music Association of Ireland, Music Network, the Contemporary Music Centre, to name a few of the major sources of support. Increased government attention to arts education is also promising. An entreprenurial spirit is evident in the many schools of music that have been founded in provincial towns, serving populations that were traditionally deprived of formal music education due to geographical location, and social and economic circumstances. This spirit is also evident in the summer schools of traditional music and dance that have developed since the 1970s and now serve both native and foreign students – the Willie Clancy school, Scoil Éigse, Scoil Acla and Blas.

The social and political foundations for music transmission have shifted fundamentally since the beginning of the nineteenth century when access to particular forms of music instruction was determined primarily by ethnic group, socioeconomic class, and religious affiliation. In the late twentieth century, access to music education is determined less by these factors and more by traditions of music education in schools and communities, the presence of specialist music teachers in schools, and the availability of media and technology. What has remained constant is the biases in access created by geographical location and in some instances, gender. This seems to be changing with a new emphasis placed on access to music education for all populations, including disabled people, those who are economically deprived, living in geographically remote communities, or who for any reason might have been denied the opportunity of music instruction in the past.

As Irish musical culture thrives in this time of economic growth and stability, and Ireland's music and dance heritage is celebrated on stages from Chicago to Sydney, it is tempting to bask in the glory of musical heritage and its present high cultural profile. A deeper look at the status of music in the culture at large exposes the weak economic base that has been associated with musical development over the past two centuries. The educational juncture illustrates this reality clearly. Consider the legacy of music education – the absence of music specialists in primary and some secondary schools, the lack of instruments and instrumental music in primary schools,[9] the dearth of home-produced teaching materials and media, the amount of bonuses granted to secondary schools for establishing and maintaining ensembles, and the minimal government resources devoted to school music supervision and the professional development of music educators.

MUSIC AS CANON: TRADITIONS OF TRANSMISSION

The present history of music transmission in Ireland has provided striking evidence of the way in which canons and traditions of music education are instituted, diffused, and in turn can become deconstructed by counter-hegemonic movements. A school music canon represents a cluster of beliefs and values that organise instruction, determine the core repertoire of what is transmitted, and define what is excluded from a programme of instruction. A counter-hegemonic movement challenges that set of values by rejecting the repertoire, by refusing to have its members participate, and by gradually replacing the values of the dominant culture with its own set of values and musical traditions.

With the establishment of the National School system came the opportunity to institute a canon in public education, define a common curriculum for all young people, and diffuse a set of values that was resonant of middle-class colonial society. A school music canon was defined by the aesthetics, repertoire and methods of Western art music, and was framed within the context of British educational policy and the goal of multidenominational education. From the beginning, discussions of music in the system provided a forum for advancing a cultural counter-hegemony. The teaching of music was viewed by the various religious denominations with suspicion and a fear that proselytisation would occur through the teaching of hymns and other religious music. In addition, the system was criticised by Thomas Davis and others who were suspicious of its political intent and who advocated native Irish cultural content in the curriculum. Within the system, Sir Patrick Keenan, an advocate for teaching national culture, was also critical of the 'namby-pamby' music that he heard sung in schools, advocating instead the cultivation of Irish music, 'the class of music which the people could best understand and appreciate'.

This complicated set of political circumstances in mid nineteenth-century schooling inhibited the development of a dynamic school music culture in many of the system's schools. Diffusion of the official canon was met with a variety of responses – from successful implementation in model schools to indifference in many ordinary national schools, to resistance in cases where efforts were made to include songs perceived as religious music, to compromise in the case of Thomas Moore's *Irish Melodies* which mediated between the musical worlds of native Irish children and colonial society. Devoid of the emotional and political overtones of nationalist ballads, the melodies were thought to be acceptable to all subcultural groups.

As the nineteenth century progressed, the legitimacy and educational value of the school music canon were challenged on a number of fronts, and a counter-hegemonic culture grew in nationalist and Catholic institutions. The Catholic clergy, in the interest of developing sight-singing skills and ultimately improving the quality of Church music, regarded the Hullah method of sightreading as unsuitable for educating the schoolgoing population of Ireland at that time. In its place, the clergy promoted the Tonic Sol-fa method which had been used successfully in Britain to improve congregational singing. This effort represented the first phase of instituting a canon of school music based on the institutionalised values of the Catholic Church. The climate of competition from the 1890s forward provided a public forum in which the clergy could influence the direction and content of school music and validate the efforts of teachers and students to excel in the performance of sacred music.

The parish school increasingly became a musical nucleus in the community, with national teachers the pivotal figures in mediating between the ideals of nationalism and Catholicism and the dissemination of music traditions that furthered those ideals.[10] In this way, it bridged the political function of music in school, church and community, and helped transform the sociopolitical context of the school. A parallel movement of cultural nationalism, centred around the activities of the Gaelic League, began to institute Gaelic traditions in national schools, in festivals such as the Feis Ceoil and later local *feiseanna*, and in organisations such as the pipers' clubs in Cork, Dublin, and Limerick. The introduction of a bi-lingual programme in national schools in 1904 established Irish-language songs in the school music canon. In keeping with the dominance of text in Irish culture and the power of song to make a political ideology explicit, these songs in addition to Catholic hymns and plain chant, monopolised the curriculum in post-independent Ireland, creating a situation where music education served nationalist ends exclusively.

It was in response to the cultural nationalist movement that music in national and intermediate education became further differentiated, in terms of both purpose and content. Since the music traditions of high culture – literacy, art music, and formal musical knowledge – had not developed in the majority of national schools, there was little to deconstruct in terms of repertorial or pedagogical canons in these contexts. In addition, the close links between the institutions of education and religion at the parish level strengthened and facilitated the spread of Catholic and national ideals through music education. In contrast, Western art music repertoire and pedagogy did gain a foothold in Intermediate schools in the 1880s. Close association with music education in the Royal Irish Academy of Music and the Incorporated Society of Musicians led to the establishment of a conservatory music culture in which graded examinations in music theory and later performance were dominant.

As the twin powers of Catholicism and nationalism emerged triumphant in the 1920s, and a monolithic version of Irish national identity began to counteract the effects of centuries of colonial political and cultural domination, the school music canon changed accordingly. Selected images from Ireland's musical heritage – its Gaelic song traditions and medieval monastic song schools – were invoked to legitimise, support and define a new musical canon. The image of Ireland as the 'land of song' was narrowly interpreted through the singular promotion of Irish language songs in schools and communities. Intensive efforts were made to document and publish Irish song repertoire, typically accompanied by Tonic Sol-fa notation, thus enshrining the repertoire in 'a fixed, literate form'.[11] A standard version of songs was made available to schools, one that set up expectations and standards of performance for teachers and inspectors alike.

School music, at least in national and later vocational schools, advanced the canons of Gaelic culture through the transmission of Irish language songs, ballads, and, in some settings, the founding of tin whistle bands. Catholic Church music was also transmitted primarily in the preparation for church services and plain chant festivals. Thus, the musical traditions that were excluded from the official canon in the previous century found an honoured place in the schools of the young nation state. Public mass media such as Radio Éireann and national newspapers broadcast and reported on music and musical events that disseminated and affirmed the essentialist view of Irishness as Catholic, Irish speaking and nationalist.

At a distance from the core of the Gaelic canon were musical practices that functioned uneasily in the nation state. Without the unequivocal support granted to Irish language songs, instrumental traditional music, although clearly belonging to the dominant Gaelic culture, was nevertheless viewed with ambiguity in terms of its socioeconomic status and respectability as an art form. In another subcultural context, the role of traditional music in secondary schools was fraught with sociomusical conflicts. How could an orally transmitted music function in a literacy-based school culture and be appropriated to middle-class musical values? In the case of Catholic Church music in secondary schools, this issue did not arise since ecclesiastical and secular musical taste were rooted in the aesthetics of art music.

A further instance of ambiguity was in the government's attitude to and support of art music. This ambiguity seems to have been rooted in at least two sets of historical circumstances; first, art music was associated with colonial culture and marginalised in the Gaelic nation state; and second, those who came to power and instituted the cultural canon in the Irish Free State had limited formal music education and focused their energies on promoting the essentials of Irish identity which clearly did not include art music, jazz and other music perceived as 'un-national'. Instead the major patrons of education in art music were the Catholic Church, Radio Éireann, the developing national and regional orchestras, and those musical leaders such as Aloys Fleischmann and John Larchet who opposed the narrowness of the national vision for music education in Ireland. Opposition to the canon also came from the national teaching force and some school inspectors who were critical of the monopoly of Irish language songs in national schools, the lack of variety in song repertoire, and the neglect of other aspects of music instruction. Canons, although strict and rigid by their very nature and easy to institute in Church and state education settings due to uniform standards, values, and methods, seem to have had a troubled crusade in the democratic nation state as well as in the colonial context. As a cultural process, music is a dynamic force that thrives on variation and innovation as much as it does on maintaining tradition and displaying loyalty to heritage.

The 1960s witnessed the beginning of a period where the patronage of music education changed institutional hands, due to expanding cultural consciousness and changing economic conditions. Political and cultural ideologies which established the musical canon in the Irish Free State were gradually replaced by a broader philosophy of music's role in the education of youth, and a greater acknowledgement of children's developmental needs and their musical preferences. The broadening of the secondary-school music syllabus in 1966 and the introduction of a new primary-school curriculum in 1971 were symbolic of the shifting values of music education, not only in terms of how music ought to function in general education but also which music ought to be transmitted and to what ends. It was also during this period that the transmission of traditional music outside the formal education system began to incorporate some of the practices of school music. Simultaneously, in music curricula in formal education, there was a clear movement towards the inclusion of traditional music. As American educator Nancy Smith noted, 'a meeting of the waters' was taking place, the coming together of the formerly polarised worlds of school music and traditional music in educational settings.

And so began a period of transition in which established repertoire, methods, and syllabi changed incrementally to be more inclusive of Ireland's diverse musical traditions. In the absence of the driving forces of nationalism, linguistic ethnocentrism, and Catholicism as the *raison d'être* for music in education, other cultural forces began to influence school music. Ireland's membership of the EC brought about a new consciousness about Irish identity and the role of musical heritage and its transmission in forming that identity. From another perspective, a discussion on arts education led by the Arts Council focused on music's unique role in general education based on artistic and creative values, in contrast to former eras when its role as servant to various colonial and nationalist agendas was central to its mission in the schools.

In the new rationale, a comprehensive music education was seen as the right of every child. Subsequently, issues of access to, provision for, and quality of music education took precedence over the purpose and content of music teaching and learning. Government interest in and commitment to cultural development, evident in the institution of a ministerial post for culture and the arts in 1982, and in white papers on culture and education in the 1980s and '90s, also highlighted the importance of an arts education for all young people. Out of this unprecedented attention to arts education came a period of critical examination and debate on the status of music education in the nation. Calls to democratise and diversify the curriculum were consistent and compelling. In a sense, these calls served to question the current forms of music education and to improve the provision for and quality of music education.

Recent debate also questions the diversity of school music and particularly the role of art, ethnic and popular music in education. It also debates the relationship between performance, listening and appreciation, and creative activity in the musical education of the young, a more inclusive approach than the former emphasis on music performance and theory. It would be premature to predict the outcomes of this critical debate. It does seem that issues of universal access, musical diversity in the curriculum, performance opportunities for the amateur as well as the career-oriented music student, and a transformation of pedagogy using new music technologies will play a significant role in establishing an agenda for music education in the twenty-first century.

MUSIC AS COMMUNITY: CONTEXTS OF TRANSMISSION

The transmission of music occurs in the context of a community that provides meaning and identity for the music learner. Communities, as Anthony Cohen points out, are important repositories of symbols, the mental constructs that provide people with the means to make meaning and perceive the boundaries of a particular social group.[12] The generational transmission of music is a primary site for inducting the young into a group's musical practices and traditions, and through that process immersing them in communal values and passing on traditions that link the generations, symbolically and musically.

Observing developments in music transmission over the past two centuries in Ireland accentuates the changes that have taken place in the way music as a cultural phenomenon is related to community. It also highlights the variety of ways in which community can be experienced through music learning, from the master–apprentice system supported by a 'real', live community of significant adults, to a national system of music education whose meaning is created around standardisation and evaluation by examination and competition. These two contrasting examples of how music learners experience community were found in nineteenth-century Ireland in traditional and formal music learning contexts, respectively.

Music learning in traditional contexts was decentralised, an integral part of social development, and it connected the young generation to its cultural heritage through validating traditions and passing on a repertoire that could be shared in social settings. Community was experienced as immediate and intimate, 'real sharing by real people in real space'.[13] In contrast, institutionalised music learning in schools and academies functioned within a different set of aesthetic criteria. Here the cultural ideals and values underpinning Western art music were constantly in the forefront, thus linking the learner to the middle-class values and practices of all other learners with similar sociocultural aspirations. These ideals were crystallised in institutional philosophies of music education, in music syllabi, in graded examinations, and in the growing ritual involved in staged public performance.

As music learning became institutionalised, massed performing ensembles became popular, functioning to create communal identity through shared music experiences. In the context of feiseanna, the phenomenon of competition and public performance entered the world of traditional music learning, transforming the way learners experienced music as community and expanding the boundaries of music learning beyond the local and the personal.[14] At least two other developments contributed to this transformation. First, increased levels of literacy and general education among the native Irish coupled with widespread emigration shifted the mental boundaries beyond the immediacy of rural communities. Second, the rising movement of cultural nationalism depended for its dynamism on the re-creation of an imagined Gaelic community from the past. The creation of this 'imagined community' was facilitated by the growth of institutions that transmitted or sponsored 'national' music (national schools, institutions representing the Catholic Church, feiseanna), the popularity of public music performance in festivals and competitions, and the entrance of traditional music into the discourse and imagination of classically educated musicians, critics, and teachers.

As national consciousness grew and the nation state was established, the formation of Gaelic identity was at the forefront of official cultural agendas. All social and cultural institutions were encouraged to transmit the 'right' music, appropriate for developing the nationalist vision of a Gaelic Ireland. However, a political ideology alone cannot change the psychological boundaries of musical identity, as evident in the problems encountered in the long-term diffusion of the nationalist cultural canon. As long as musical traditions are maintained through transmission and education, reflecting the needs and motivation of particular communities, they continue to bestow meaning and form the musical identity of members of those communities. Although the transmission of art music was officially neglected in post-independent Ireland, the academies and schools of music continued their educational mission, regardless of the agenda of the nation state. Fragmented ideas of a musical education existed, some rooted in political ideology, others in sociocultural ideals, and still others in the social reality of growing up around active musical communities. For example, national and religious identity was developed through music in school and church, participation in organisations such as Conradh na Gaeilge and later Comhaltas Ceoltóirí Éireann. The ideals of high culture, as manifest in art music, continued to be transmitted in music schools, universities, and in many secondary schools, particularly in girls' schools. No effort was made to unite the aims and activities of these musical communities. Thus the fragmented view of Irish music was reproduced in the organisation and content of music education in schools and institutions of music learning.

At the same time, in the middle decades of the twentieth century, considerable attention was devoted to the national organisation of music and music education, evident in the founding of the Music Association of Ireland, music teachers' associations, a music inspectorate in secondary education, and the Arts Council. Consequently, the profession of music education began to form its own identity, bridging the worlds of general and specialised music education. As the profession grew from the 1950s forward, the process of music education began to be viewed as a separate, yet integral, part of musical culture. Even from the early years of independence, the poor state of musical culture was associated by musical leaders such as John Larchet with the poor state of music education in schools, yet it was not until the 1970s that the Arts Council undertook to examine the provision for and access to music education that any systematic inquiry was conducted.

With an ever-expanding cultural consciousness resulting from a new European identity in the contemporary era, and the omnipresence of global music made possible in large part by advanced technologies, music can now be transmitted in a way that encompasses a number of communities, from the real to the virtual, the immediate to the global, the individualised and private to the institutionalised and communal. The expanding sense of music as community has been paralleled by an equally powerful movement that refocuses music transmission in local communities.[15] This is evident, for example, in the number of local music schools that have been founded in the last decade and in the efforts of Music Network to promote and cultivate musical activity at the local level.

As young people learn to interact musically so also does that interaction frame their musical culture and constantly re-form their social, political, economic, or religious identity, depending on the context of transmission. In various historical eras, learning music was aimed at educating the young for membership in local, national, and more recently, in global communities. A unique and challenging feature of contemporary music education is accommodating the multiple communities that young people internalise as they are socialised. No longer can the physical confines of an island community or the cultural limitations of a colonial or a nationalist vision of community determine or guide the principles and processes of music education in Ireland. Philosopher Charles Taylor explains that people don't have simple identities any more where they relate primarily to a locality or nation, but rather complex identities where they relate to multiple communities.[16] In that context, music as community assumes new and expanded meaning that has repercussions for the scope and quality of music education afforded to young people in the next century.

MUSIC AS COMMUNICATION: MEANS OF TRANSMISSION

Media are an integral part of the communication of music in the learning process. They are instrumental in shaping the way music is received and perceived, the manner in which the learner identifies with a particular music, the contexts in which transmission is possible, and the efficiency with which a canon can be instituted and diffused. Multiple forms of media were used in the transmission of music in Ireland, from a variety of literacy-based media to mass media such as radio and television, to contemporary technologies that are transforming the landscape of music teaching and learning. The technology of music learning has changed radically over the last century, from a Curwen modulator of the 1890s that provided a visual to assist in learning scales and intervals, to interactive computer software of the 1990s that allows a student to hear and explore sounds in unprecedented ways.

Nineteenth-century schools and music academies functioned within a text-based, literate world. Music literacy (reading musical notation, and demonstrating formal musical knowledge) was central to the mission of music education in those contexts. As school music developed so also did instructional materials to support transmission. Prior to the 1870s and the introduction of the Tonic Sol-fa system, music textbooks were produced in Britain and imported into Ireland for use in schools. As the cultural nationalist movement and the Catholic Church gained power, indigenous music materials began to be published, such as Peter Goodman's *The Catholic Hymn-Book* and a prolific publication of native song collections in the early twentieth century. These collections were accompanied by Tonic Sol-fa notation which became the dominant method of sight-singing in general education.

Economic development and the process of modernisation also played a major role in how music was received and perceived in educational and cultural contexts. A striking example of how economic trends influenced directly the forms of school music can be found in the payment-by-results system in operation between 1872 and 1899. In this era of accountability, subjects and students were evaluated in terms of monetary rewards. As a result, the status and viability of music as a school subject suffered. Out of the same economic climate and period of 'mass-producing traditions'[17] emerged the capitalistic enterprise of competition, a medium that dominated music education for the next century. Music competitions and examinations penetrated not only the established music education systems in schools and academies but they also facilitated the organisation of traditional music and brought it into public spaces where performers could be judged and compared, and their performances reported in the media. The significance of competition in the development of Irish musical culture deserves to be treated in a separate study; suffice to say that it brought a degree of uniformity and standardisation to the transmission of music that left deep traces on the motivation to teach and learn music, and the way in which music performance was evaluated and rewarded.

The experience of massed group performance in festivals and competitions affected the way in which young people related to music and how they saw it mediate between their school life and other aspects of their life experience. So also did the spread of institutions of music education and the advent of mass media in independent Ireland. Learning traditional music occurred increasingly in institutional settings and, as Veblen points out, the institutions became part of the medium of learning, changing the way peopled learned music 'from casual and circumstantial contact to formalized instruction'.[18] With the introduction of mass media into music-learning contexts in the middle decades of this century, a common musical experience was possible through listening to radio broadcasts and recordings. No doubt the impact of these media was limited in the 1930s through the 1950s due to economic factors and the lack of attention to music in the formal education of the young generation. Yet students were increasingly to come into contact with music beyond their immediate experience as radios became a feature of every home. Sources from the 1940s and '50s indicated a serious concern about the kinds of music that young people were exposed to in the media, particularly jazz. Such music was not regarded as appropriate for use in schools. Thus a further rift was created between music as it was experienced in school and music as it was encountered in the everyday life of children and adolescents.

From the 1960s onward, mass media continued to provide a common musical experience for the schoolgoing population.[19] The music popularised by the media was an integral part of the youth culture that gained visibility and power in the late 1960s, a movement that was not unique to Ireland. It occurred at the international level and it can be argued that Irish music education in recent decades has become gradually aligned with international trends such as interfacing popular and school culture in the music classroom, acknowledging students' cultural diversity in the music curriculum, and developing a tolerance and appreciation of world music beyond the Western canon. Achieving some of these goals demands a heavy reliance on media in order to present music that is not immediately accessible to teachers and students.

In the 1990s, more music is learned though mass media and interaction with technological media than at any other time in the history of music education. The speed with which music is interconnected at the local, national and international levels increases steadily. Music literacy, in the narrow sense of reading standard notation (a skill that remains important), assumes new meaning for a generation that experiences music in a multisensory and multicultural context. The clearly defined worlds of literacy and orality in nineteenth- and early twentieth-century music instruction have become blurred as music literacy takes on new meaning in the electronic age of 'secondary orality', as Ong describes it. This change has impacted not only how music is received and perceived by students but also how the teacher functions in the transmission process. A century ago the teacher was typically the sole agent and authority in the process; now the teacher fulfills an extended role, not only as a musical model, but also as a provider, interpreter and monitor of media in the music classroom. The complexity of contemporary musical culture and the dominance of mediated music in the transmission of music are matched by the sophisticated media available to help teachers and students create meaning out of that complexity.

Music education in Ireland has not been served well by the media available in any given historical period, with the exception perhaps of the production of collections of Irish language songs in the early decades of this century to assist in the Irish language movement. Irish schools lack home-produced instructional music materials that present diverse Irish music traditions, both in historical and contemporary contexts.

LEARNING FROM THE PAST, LOOKING TO THE FUTURE

In the opening pages of this book I referred to the paradox that exists between the positive image that Irish music and musicians have earned abroad and the dominant perception at home that Ireland lacks a democratic and effective system of music education. Both views are easily accommodated when one considers the entire spectrum of music education in the country. The fine reputation abroad is based primarily on traditional, popular, and to a lesser degree, classical musicians, whose musical education occurred for the most part outside the formal education system.[20]

The strongest and most successful traditions of music education have developed outside the formal system in community settings, private and semi-private music schools, and in certain universities. However, it is also necessary to acknowledge the excellent music education practices that have developed in some primary and secondary schools. These practices, as Martin Drury observed in the context of contemporary music education, result from a system 'which allows for good practice to happen but which does not provide for it to happen'.[21]

The primary weaknesses of Irish music education are rooted in the cultural fragmentation caused by colonialism; lack of official support for the arts in independent Ireland; a weak economy that could not support the kinds of infrastructures necessary for the artistic development of a nation; an over-reliance on Ireland's past reputation as a musical nation as a means of musical development and cultural renewal; and the dominance of political ideologies as the *raison d'être* for music in education. In terms of infrastructures to support music education, no national school of music (or network of music institutions) has developed, although on many occasions such a proposal was made during the last century. This failure was symptomatic of the unstructured and circumstantial way in which music education occurred nationally. A young person's opportunity to receive an education in music was dependent on family environment, the presence of musically oriented teachers in primary school, the availability of a music curriculum in secondary school (which was frequently determined by the gender of the student population), the traditions of music performance in local churches and communities, as well as the region of the country in which the child was raised. Opportunities for rural children were inferior to those of town and city children and it would be erroneous to think that all rural children participated in vibrant traditional music communities. The transmission of traditional music was frequently limited to certain families and regions with strong traditions and minimal Anglo-Irish cultural influence.

Although music in education in Ireland occurred more as a result of local circumstances than national policy and support, some national structures did develop. For example, a national curriculum existed at the primary and secondary levels with national forms of assessment at the secondary level. The graded music examination system imported from Britain in the late nineteenth century impacted private instruction significantly as well as music education at the second and third levels. Perhaps the most powerful structure operating in the culture of music education was the competition, both as an event to evaluate music performance and as a total value system that motivated participation, shaped the way music was learned, set up hierarchies, rewarded a minority of performers, and caused divisiveness among students, teachers and institutions. In fact, it can be argued that the competitive climate exacerbated the already fragmented way in which music subcultures existed, and dashed any hopes of cooperation between the major institutions of music education.

The structures of competition and examination, underpinned by the aesthetic values of Victorian society, contributed to élitist, exclusive forms of music education. Exclusivity resulted also from the nationalist ideologies that dominated formal education, focusing music instruction on particular song repertoire, and imposing a parochialism on school music. Related to ideological dominance was a bias in favour of text-based music education, evident in the way music was rationalised and implemented in education.[22] Consequently, it could be argued that as a result of textual dominance and song a culture for choral music was nurtured successfully, even in those settings such as national schools and parish churches where music specialists or skilled musicians were not always available.

The discussion and debate of the last two decades on the status of music education was a necessary prerequisite to action for change. Armed with the self-knowledge gained in the process, it is timely to move forward with an agenda that is based on the principles of democracy, diversity and inclusiveness. Implementation of the agenda will require the participation of all institutions that influence, support or have a responsibility for transmitting music to the next generation – from government departments to semi-state bodies, cultural institutions to businesses, private music schools to community music groups, state schools to music industry and mass media, arts advocacy groups to institutions of higher education.

A democratic and dynamic system of music education in Ireland requires new standards of cooperation among these institutions and cultural forces; an infusion of creative thinking at administrative, organisational, curricular, and practical levels; an innovative and carefully planned approach to the creation and use of media and technology to communicate music to the young; and dedicated efforts to interface music in schools and communities. Most importantly, the needs, culture, voices and experiences of

children and adolescents need to take the limelight in all considerations and decisions. The task at hand is fundamentally a spiritual
one – connecting the generations through the at-once mystical and
tangible phenomenon of music.

The Given Note

On the most westerly Blasket
In a dry-stone hut
He got this air out of the night.

Strange noises were heard
By others who followed, bits of a tune
Coming in on loud weather

Though nothing like melody.
He blamed their fingers and ear
As unpractised, their fiddling easy

For he had gone alone into the island
And brought back the whole thing.
The house throbbed like his full violin.

So whether he calls it spirit music
Or not, I don't care. He took it
Out of wind off mid-Atlantic.

Still he maintains, from nowhere
It comes off the bow gravely,
Rephrases itself into the air.

                              Seamus Heaney

Notes and References

Notes to Introduction

1   Joseph C. Walker, *Historical Memoirs of the Bards* (Dublin: Luke White Publishing Co., 1786), p. 26.

2   Patrick W. Joyce, *Old Irish Folk Music and Songs* (Dublin: Hodges, Figgis, and Co., Ltd., 1909), p. 18, p. 38.

3   William B. Yeats, 'The Facts of Life', in *Autobiographies* (London: Macmillan and Co., Ltd., 1926), pp. 29–30.

4   Brian Boydell, in *Education and the Arts: A Research Report* (Dublin: Trinity College, University of Dublin, 1987), p. 210.

5   *Comhaltas Ceoltóirí Éireann: A Living Tradition*, 38th Annual Report (Dublin: Comhaltas Ceoltóirí Éireann, n. d.), p. 3, p. 5, p. 12.

6   'Bono: The White Nigger', interview with Paul Hewson, in *Across the Frontiers: Ireland in the 1990s*, ed. by Richard Kearney (Dublin: Wolfhound Press, 1988), p. 188.

7   Chris Curtin and Anthony Varley, 'Children and Childhood in Rural Ireland: A Consideration of the Ethnographic Literature', in *Culture and Ideology in Ireland*, ed. by Chris Curtin, Mary Kelly, and Liam O'Dowd (Galway: Officiana Typographica, Galway University Press, 1984), p. 30.

8   Donald Herron, *Deaf Ears? A Report on the Provision of Music Education in Irish Schools* (Dublin: The Arts Council, 1985), p. 41.

9   The entire island is considered in the pre-independent context; in post-independent Ireland, the scope is limited to the Irish Free State and later the Republic of Ireland.

10 J. H. Kwabena Nketia, 'Music Education in Africa and the West: We Can Learn from Each Other', *Music Educators Journal* 57 (November 1970), 48.

11 Barbara Reeder Lundquist, 'Transmission of Music Culture in Formal Educational Institutions', *The World of Music* 29 (1987), 73.

12 In his research on the use of terminologies associated with style in Irish traditional flute playing, Niall Keegan found that style exists 'within the context of various conceptual categories' that are held between musicians, that terminologies are 'purely descriptive in

nature and not operational as in Western classical music' (e.g. reference to the use of technique), and that speech about style 'places the performance both geographically and diachronically, in the context of a local social continuum in stark contrast with the reality of mass mediated music' which decontextualises and depersonalises performance. Verbal context then is vital to an understanding of performance style. 'The Verbal Context of Regional Style in Traditional Irish Music', in *Blas/The Local Accent in Traditional Irish Music*, ed. by Thérèse Smith and Mícheál Ó Súilleabháin (The Folk Music Society of Ireland and the Irish World Music Centre, University of Limerick, 1997), pp. 116–22.

13   F. S. L. Lyons, *The Burden of Our History*, The W. B. Rankin Memorial Lecture delivered 4 December 1978 (Belfast: Moyne, Boyd and Son, Ltd., 1979), p. 13.

14   Harry White, 'Musicology, Positivism and the Case for an Encyclopaedia in Ireland: Some Brief Considerations', in *Irish Musical Studies 1: Musicology in Ireland*, ed. by Gerard Gillen and Harry White (Dublin: Irish Academic Press, 1990), p. 296.

15   In the last two decades there has been a growing body of research on music education in Ireland especially in the form of theses and dissertations. The following studies represent a cross-section of this research. Martin E. Barrett, 'Continuity and Change in Music Education in Ireland, Northern Ireland, Wales, Scotland, and Britain, 1890–1992: Reflections', Ph. D. diss., University of Hull, 1994; Henry Carpendale, 'Music Education in the Primary School: A Comparative Study of Curricular Policy in the Republic of Ireland and Northern Ireland', M. Ed. thesis, University of Dublin, 1992; William Noel Kelly, 'Music in Irish Primary Education', MA thesis, University College, Cork, 1981; Marie F. McCarthy, 'Music Education and the Quest for Cultural Identity in Ireland, 1831–1989,' Ph. D. diss., The University of Michigan, 1990; Bríd Ní Shé, 'The Initial Education and Training of Music Teachers for Primary Schools in the Republic of Ireland, Northern Ireland, England and Wales', M. Ed. thesis, University of Dublin, 1994; Kari Veblen, 'Perceptions of Change and Stability in the Transmission of Irish Traditional Music: An Examination of the Music Teacher's Role', Ph. D. diss., University of Wisconsin, 1991.

16   Richard Kearney, *Postnationalist Ireland: Politics, Culture, Philosophy* (London and New York: Routledge, 1997), p. 189.

17   In her study of the teacher's role in the transmission of Irish

traditional music, Kari Veblen found that the actual processes of transmission which were employed were not documented closely, leading to a situation where contemporary musicians assume a continuity of tradition with the past which may or may not be justified. 'The Teacher's Role in Transmission of Irish Traditional Music', *International Journal of Music Education* 24 (1994), 24.

18 Kevin Whelan, 'The Region and the Intellectuals', in *On Intellectuals and Cultural Life in Ireland: International, Comparative and Historical Contexts*, ed. by Liam O'Dowd (Belfast: Institute of Irish Studies, 1996), pp. 121–3.

19 Cited in Kevin Whelan, 'The Bases of Regionalism', in *Culture in Ireland – Regions: Identity and Power*, ed. by Prionsias Ó Drisceoil (Belfast: The Queen's University of Belfast, 1993).

20 Richard Kearney, *Transitions: Narratives in Modern Irish Culture* (Manchester: Manchester University Press, 1988), p. 17.

21 Matthew Arnold, *Culture and Anarchy* (New York: The Macmillan Co., 1869, 1924). Arnold viewed culture as 'the best which has been thought and said in the world' p. viii.

22 'Polyhymnia: or, Singing for the Million', *Dublin University Magazine* 21 (January-June 1843), 17.

23 Patricia Shehan Campbell, *Lessons From the World: A Cross-Cultural Guide to Music Teaching and Learning* (New York: Schirmer Books, 1991).

24 This dictum was popularised by Marshall McLuhan and Quentin Fiore in their book *The Medium is the Message* (New York: Bantam Books, 1967).

Notes to Chapter 1

1 Musical 'knowledge' is used here as a multidimensional concept, drawing on David Elliott's categories of formal, informal, impressionistic, and supervisory knowledge. See *Music Matters: A New Philosophy of Music Education* (New York: Oxford University Press, 1995), pp. 53–68.

2 John Blacking, *How Musical is Man?* (Seattle, WA: University of Washington Press, 1973), p. 35.

3 Ibid., p. 43.

4 Brian Boydell, in *Education and the Arts: A Research Report*, p. 210. See also the quotation from Boydell in the 'Introduction' to this book, p. 2.

5   Patrick W. Joyce, *Old Irish Folk Music and Songs*, p. 3, p. 9, and p. 26.

6   Many issues of *Ceol* and *Treoir* also provide valuable biographical information on traditional musicians' early music education.

7   Yehudi A. Cohen, 'The Shaping of Men's Minds: Adaptations to Imperatives of Culture', in *Anthropological Perspectives on Education*, Ed. by Murray L. Wak, Stanley Diamond, Fred D. Gearing (New York and London: Basic Books, 1971). p. 22, p. 45.

8   Joann Keali'inohomoku, 'Culture Change: Functional and Dysfunctional Expressions of Dance, a Form of Affective Culture', in *The Performing Arts: Music and Dance*, ed. by John Blacking and Joann Keali'inohomoku (The Hague: Mouton, 1979), p. 47.

9   Ekkehard Jost, 'Musical Subcultures in Rural Communities of Hessen: Report on a Sociomusicological Research Project', in *Stock-Taking of Musical Life: Music Sociography and Its Relevance to Music Education*, ed. by Desmond Mark (Vienna: Dobinger, 1981), p. 66.

10   Catherine J. Ellis, 'Aboriginal Education through Music: Complexity within Simplicity', unpub. paper, The University of New England, New South Wales, Australia, *c.* 1987, p. 2.

11   Ibid., p. 4.

12   Cohen, 'The Shaping of Men's Minds', pp. 40–1.

13   David Cairns and Shaun Richards, *Writing Ireland: Colonialism, Nationalism and Culture* (Manchester: Manchester University Press, 1988), p. 15.

14   John Blacking wrote that if music can do anything to people, 'the best that it can do is to confirm situations that already exist'. *How Musical is Man?*, (Seattle, WA: University of Washington Press, 1973), p. 108.

15   *Ethnicity, Identity and Music: The Musical Construction of Place*, ed. by Martin Stokes (Oxford/Providence, RI: Berg Publishers, 1994), p. 7.

16   Paddy Tunney, *The Stone Fiddle* (Dublin: Gilbert Dalton, 1979), p. 52.

17   Luke Gibbons argues that from the onset of colonisation, 'culture in Ireland became ineluctably bound up with politics, a pattern that has persisted in many contentions and divergent forms down to the present day'. *Transformations in Irish Culture* (Cork: Cork University Press in association with Field Day, 1996), p. 8.

18   Christopher Small, *Music, Society, and Education*, rev. ed (London: John Calder, 1980), p. 80.

19   Alan P. Merriam, *The Anthropology of Music* (Chicago, IL: Northwestern Press, 1964), p. 225.

20 Rudolf E. Radocy and J. David Boyle, *The Psychological Foundations of Music Education* (Springfield. Ill.: Charles C. Thomas, 1979), p. 167.

21 Ricardo D. Trimillos, 'Itálau, Hochschule, Maystro, and Ryú: Cultural Approaches to Music Learning and Teaching,' *International Journal of Music Education* 14 (1989): 33.

22 This is illustrated by Raymond Williams in his insightful work, *Culture and Society, 1780–1950* (London: Chatto and Windus, 1958), vii. Williams identified five words which either came into common English use for the first time, or acquired new and important meaning in eighteenth- and early nineteenth-century Britain. These are industry, democracy, class, art, and culture. Of this group of terms, art and culture are the most pertinent in this context. Any discussion of art and culture in this politically, socially, and economically turbulent period will, of necessity, embrace the terms industry, democracy, and class as they impinge on the growth of those two terms.

23 Ibid., xvi.

24 Ibid., p. 63.

25 E. B. Tylor, *Primitive Culture*, 5th ed (London: S. Murray, 1929), p. 1.

26 Ibid.

27 See for example, Ernst Cassirer, *An Essay on Man* (New Haven and London: Yale University Press, 1944); Suzanne Langer, *Philosophy in a New Key*; Leslie White, *The Concept of Culture* (Minneapolis, Minnesota: Burgess Publishing Co., 1973), and Clifford Geertz, *The Interpretation of Cultures* (New York: Basic Books Inc. Pub., 1973).

28 Geertz, *The Interpretation of Cultures*, p. 5. His interpretation is based on Gilbert Ryle's notion of 'thick description', p. 6.

29 James Clifford, *The Predicament of Culture* (Cambridge, Mass., and London, England: Harvard University Press, 1988), p. 41, p. 46.

30 The distinction made between music in education, education in music, and music education, reflects changes in the relationship between music and education. Various components of culture were catalytic in this change. For an elaboration of this theme, see Peter Fletcher's introduction to *Education and Music* (Oxford and New York: Oxford University Press, 1987), xi–xii.

31 *The Canon in the Classroom: The Pedagogical Implications of Canon Revision in American Literature*, ed. by John Alberti (New York: Garland Pub., 1995), p. xi, p. xvii.

32   Nuala C. Johnson, 'Nation-building, Language and Education: The Geography of Teacher Recruitment in Ireland, 1925–55', *Political Geography* 11 (March 1992), 171; Maurice Goldring, *Pleasant the Scholar's Life: Irish Intellectuals and the Construction of the Nation State* (London: Serif, 1993), Introduction.

33   In her research on two song forms (the *rozgalica* and the *ganga*) of western rural Yugoslavia, Barbara Krader shows that 'each form creates a strong sense of identity in the group – for the singers and for their listeners, if the latter belong to the same culture'. Barbara Krader, 'Slavic Folk Music: Forms of Singing and Self-Identity', *Ethnomusicology* 31 (Winter 1987), 9.

34   Julia E. Bojus, 'Music Education in Poland', Ph. D. dissertation, The University of Miami, Florida, 1972, p. 58.

35   R. Seebauer, 'Erneuerungsversuche der Musikerziehung in der österreichischen Pflichtschule der 10–14 jahrigen (vom Reichsvolks-schulgesetz bis zur Gegenwart mit besonderer Berüchsichtigung Wiens)', (Attempts to revive musical education in Austrian secondary schools for children aged 10–14 (from the Reichsvolksschul Act to the present with special consideration of Vienna), D. Phil., The University of Vienna, 1978, 93–7.

36   Heitor Villa-Lobos, *Solfejos* (Rio de Janeiro: Cassa Arthur Napoleao, 1940), p. 4, quoted in Rex Eakins, 'Heitor Villa-Lobos: A Music Educator', *International Journal of Music Education* 10 (1987), 33.

37   Villa-Lobos, *A Música nacionalista no governo Getulio Vargas* (Rio de Janeiro, 1940), p. 10, quoted in David E. Vassberg, 'Villa-Lobos as Pedagogue: Music in the Service of the State', *Journal of Research in Music Education* 23 (Fall 1975), 166.

38   It is somewhat premature to predict the implications of this global approach to music repertoire in school music. Given the decreased attention to 'national' music, it seems that the role of school music in building national identity and patriotism is changing and, one could argue, diminished.

39   See *British Journal of Music Education* 10 (November 1993), Proceedings of the Music, Gender, and Education Conference, Bristol University, March 1993; Marcia Citron, *Gender and the Musical Canon* (Cambridge: Cambridge University Press, 1993); Susan McClary, *Feminine Endings: Music, Gender, and Sexuality* (Minnesota: Minnesota University Press, 1991); John Shepherd, *Music as Social Text* (Cambridge, UK: Polity Press, 1991).

40   Lucy Green, 'Gender, Musical Meaning and Education', *Philosophy*

of Music Education Review 2 (Fall 1994), 99–105. Elsewhere I argue that music in schools is a site for multiple levels of gendered discourse arising out of the institutional context, the discipline itself, and the interactive participants (teachers, students, and their related communties – peer, parental, cultural, and professional). Marie McCarthy, 'Gendered Discourse and the Construction of Identity: Toward a Liberated Pedagogy in Music Education', in 'Musings: Arts Education Essays in Honor of Bennett Reimer', *Journal of Aesthetic Education* (Fall 1999, in press).

41   B. Sugarman, 'Involvement in Youth Culture, Academic Achievement and Conformity in School', *British Journal of Sociology* 28 (1967), quoted in Frank Musgrove, 'Curriculum, Culture and Ideology', *Curriculum Studies* 10 (1978), 100.

42   Diamond, 'Epilogue', in *Anthropological Perspectives*, p. 305.

43   Mary Anne Raywid, 'Perspectives on the Struggle Against Indoctrination', *The Educational Forum* 48 (Winter 1984), 138.

44   Ibid., 141.

45   Musgrove, 'Curriculum, Culture and Ideology', 105.

46   Benedict Anderson, *Imagined Communities: Reflections on the Origin and Spread of Nationalism* (London: Verso Editions and NLB, 1983), p. 15.

47   Ernest Gellner, *Nationalism* (London: Weidenfeld and Nicholson, 1997), pp. 28–9.

48   For an exploration of traditional music, community, and place, see Mícheál Ó Súilleabháin, producer, *A River of Sound: The Changing Course of Irish Traditional Music* (Baile Átha Cliath: Radio Teilifís Éireann, 1995); also Marie McCarthy, 'Irish Music Education and Irish Identity: A Concept Revisited', *Oideas* 45 (Fómhar 1997), 5–22.

49   Allen Feldman and Eamon O'Doherty, *The Northern Fiddler: Music and Musicians of Donegal and Tyrone* (Belfast: Blackstaff Press, 1979), pp. 24–5.

50   For a discussion of the development of Irish rural life in this period, see Kevin Whelan, 'Towns and Villages', in *Atlas of the Irish Rural Landscape*, ed. by F. H. A. Aalen, Kevin Whelan, and Matthew Stout (Cork: Cork University Press, 1997), pp. 192–5.

51   *The Invention of Tradition*, ed. by Eric Hobsbawn and Terence Ranger (Cambridge: Cambridge University Press, 1983), pp. 1–7; Jeanne Sheehy, *The Rediscovery of Ireland's Past: The Celtic Revival 1830–1930* (London: Thames and Hudson Ltd., 1980), pp. 7–8.

52   Charles Taylor, in Richard Kearney, *Visions of Europe: Conversations on the Legacy and Future of Europe* (Dublin: Wolfhound Press, 1992), p. 55.

53   *Across the Frontiers – Ireland in the 1990s*, p. 187.

54   Kevin Whelan, 'Towns and Villages', p. 195; Hilary Tovey, Damian Hannan and Hal Abramson, *Why Irish? Language and Identity in Ireland Today* (Baile Átha Cliath: Bord na Gaeilge, 1989), p. 32.

55   James Clifford argues that twentieth-century identities no longer presuppose continuous cultures or traditions. He writes: 'Everywhere individuals and groups improvise local performances from (re)collected pasts, drawing on foreign media, symbols, and languages.' *The Predicament of Culture* (Cambridge, MA, and London, UK: Harvard University Press, 1988), p. 14.

56   David Hollinger, *Postethnic America: Beyond Multiculturalism* (New York: Basic Books, 1995), p. 105.

57   Ernest Gellner, *Nationalism* p. 96.

58   Walter Ong, *Orality and Literacy: The Technologizing of the Word*, reprin. ed. (London and New York: Routledge, 1988), p. 136.

59   Luke Gibbons, *Transformations in Irish Culture*, p. 3.

60   Ibid., p. 71.

Notes to Chapter 2

1   James Hardiman, *Irish Minstrelsy*, vol. 1 (London: Joseph Robins, 1831), p. iii.

2   Ann Buckley, ' "and his voice swelled like a terrible thunder storm . . ." Music as Symbolic Power in Medieval Irish Society', in *Irish Musical Studies: Music and Irish Cultural History*, ed. by Gerard Gillen and Harry White (Dublin: Irish Academic Press, 1995), p. 16.

3   Patrick Weston Joyce, *A Social History of Ancient Ireland*, vol. I, 2nd ed. (Dublin: M. H. Gill and Son Ltd., 1913), p. 572.

4   Book of Ballimote, cited in Hardiman, *Irish Minstrelsy*, vol. 1, v–vi. This manuscript contains miscellaneous tracts and poems of antiquity.

5   Ibid., cited in Hardiman, vi.

6   Hardiman, vii.

7   Dagda was considered to be the 'good god'.

8   Breandán Breathnach, *Folk Music and Dances of Ireland*, rev. ed. (Cork and Dublin: The Mercier Press, 1977), pp. 3–4. Breathnach

does not cite a particular source for this account but draws upon unnamed 'ancient legends', and 'references in the ancient literature'.

9   Ibid., p. 4. Breathnach cites another legend in which the three sons of Uaithne were named from the music played on the harp while Boand (the river Boyne, a goddess), their mother, was in labour. Elsewhere the three divisions are derived from the music played on a harp of three strings – iron, brass, and silver. The number three was of special significance both in Celtic mythology and Christian symbology. A further variant of this saga is provided in Jeffrey Gantz's selection of *Early Irish Myths and Sagas* (London, England: Penguin Books, 1981), pp. 117–18.

10 Ibid.

11 Ríonach Uí Ógáin, 'Traditional Music and Irish Cultural History', in *Irish Musical Studies: Music and Irish Cultural History*, ed. Gerard Gillen & Harvey White (Dublin: Irish Academic Press, 1995) p. 91.

12 In Alamnan's life of Columba, who died AD 596, one passage described Columba, his monks, and his poet Cronan in dialogue by the banks of the river Bos. When the poet retired, the monks expressed their regret that Columba had not asked him to sing some *Canticle* in *modulation,* according to the *Rules of His Art* . Reference to Alamnan's life of Columba is found in Hardiman's *Irish Minstrelsy,* vol. 1, xiii–xiv. This description confirms that a professional school of music existed in these monasteries.

13 Several sources mention a small eight-string harp used by clerics and carried around suspended from their girdles. *The New Grove Dictionary of Music and Musicians*, s. v. 'Music of the Celtic Rite'.

14 Joseph C. Walker, *Historical Memoirs of the Bards* (Dublin: Luke White Publishing Co., 1786), p. 26.

15 Uí Ógáin, p. 82.

16 Giraldus Cambrensis, *The History and Topography of Ireland*, trans. by John O'Meara (Portlaoise, Ireland: The Dolmen Press, 1982), pp. 102–3.

17 Breathnach, *Folk Music,* p. 7.

18 Buckley, 'and his voice', p. 24.

19 Mícheál Ó Súilleabháin, 'Irish Music Defined', *The Crane Bag* 5 (1981), 84.

20 The harp first appeared on coins about 1526 and was adapted as the national arms later in the century. Cited in Samuel Ferguson, 'Of the Antiquity of the Harp and Bagpipe in Ireland', in *The Ancient*

Music of Ireland, vol. 3, ed. by Edward Bunting (Dublin: Hodges and Smith, 1840), p. 45.

21 J. C. Beckett, *The Anglo-Irish Tradition* (Dublin: The Blackstaff Press, 1976). p. 23.

22 Ó Súilleabháin, 'Irish Music Defined', 84.

23 May McCann, 'Music and Politics in Ireland: The Specificity of the Folk Revival in Belfast', *British Journal of Ethnomusicology* 4 (1995), 52.

24 Seán O'Boyle, *The Irish Song Tradition* (Dublin: Gilbert Dalton, 1976), p. 10. Most escaped, it would seem, because by 1654, under the rule of Cromwell, all harpers, pipers, or wandering minstrels had to obtain letters from the magistrate of the district they came from before being allowed to travel through the country.

25 Ibid.

26 Gráinne Yeats, 'Irish Harp Music', in *Four Centuries of Music in Ireland*, ed. by Brian Boydell (London: British Broadcasting Corporation, 1979), p. 20.

27 The term 'Big House,' or its Irish equivalent, *Teach Mór*, have been used to describe the homes of the Gaelic chieftains and the newly arrived gentry from England and Scotland. See Daniel Corkery, *The Hidden Ireland* (Dublin: Gill and Macmillan, 1924), chap. 2.

28 Donal O'Sullivan, *Carolan: The Life, Times, and Music of an Irish Harper* (London: Routledge and Kegan Paul Ltd., 1958), p. 15.

29 *Songs of the Irish*, ed. by Donal O'Sullivan (Dublin: Browne and Nolan Ltd., 1960), p. 5.

30 Ascendancy refers to those who 'enjoyed access to political power in Ireland during the later seventeenth and eighteenth centuries'. It comprised of English families and a large number of descendants of colonists who had arrived in the seventeenth centuries. David Cairns and Shaun Richards, *Writing Ireland: Colonialism, Nationalism and Culture*, p. 167.

31 Arthur Young, who travelled in Ireland in the 1770s, described town life in Dublin as 'formed on the model of that of London'. Arthur Young, *A Tour in Ireland*, pt. 2 (London: Cadell and Dodsley Press, 1780), p. 75.

32 Boydell, 'Introduction', in *Four Centuries*, p. 11.

33 Boydell, 'Music in Eighteenth-Century Dublin', in *Four Centuries*, p. 28.

34 Dubourg, Geminiani, Arne, and Giordani made Ireland their home. Others like Handel and Corelli paid extended visits there. The

violinist Geminiani had an active teaching and performing career in Dublin between 1733 and 1740. One of his pupils, Dubourg, came to Dublin in 1724 and led the Viceroy's Band from 1728 to 1765. He maintained a school of violin playing in the city.

35 W. J. Starkie, 'The Royal Irish Academy of Music', in *Music in Ireland*, ed. by Aloys Fleischmann (Cork: Cork University Press, 1952), p. 104.

36 *Songs of the Irish*, Ed. Donal O'Sullivan (Dublin: Browne and Nolan 1960), p. 102.

37 Gerard Gillen, 'Church Music in Dublin, 1500–1900', in *Four Centuries*, p. 26.

38 Revd James Hall, *Tour Through Ireland*, 2 vols. (London: Wilson Printers, 1813), p. 74.

39 Ó Súilleabháin, 'Irish Music Defined', 84.

40 Breandán Ó Madagáin, 'Functions of Irish Song in the Nineteenth Century', *Béaloideas* 53 (1985), 131, 172.

41 Hardiman, *Irish Minstrelsy*, vol. 1, pp. 324–5.

42 In 1863 Kennedy referred to the dancing schools as 'rustic dance-academies', in 'Irish Dancing Fifty Years Ago', *Dublin University Magazine* 62 (October 1863), 438. See also 'The Dancing Academy', *Illustrated London News* 17 January 1852, 60.

43 Dancing was part of the military training of those who joined the French army, many of whom returned after the victory of Wellington at Waterloo. These musicians were a vital force in the music education of the Irish peasantry as well as the more affluent families in the eighteenth and nineteenth centuries. They introduced elements of French dance into an already vibrant and developing dance tradition in Ireland.

44 Young, *A Tour in Ireland*, vol. 2, p. 75.

45 Patrick Kennedy, *The Banks of the Boro: A Chronicle of County Wexford* (London: Simpkin, Marshall and Co., 1867), p. 135.

46 Trevor Fowler's painting of 'Children Dancing at Crossroads' provides an illustration of this phenomenon. In Barra Boydell, *Music and Paintings in the National Gallery of Ireland* (Dublin: The National Gallery of Ireland, 1985), p. 82.

47 William Carleton, *Tales and Stories of the Irish Peasantry* (Dublin: James Duffy Pub., 1845), p. 5.

48 T. Crofton Croker, *Researches in the South of Ireland* (London: John Murray, 1824), p. 117. This witness's description of the music being handed down with 'very little alteration' does not concur with what's

generally accepted about this genre. It is generally accepted that
variation, albeit in an incremental manner, occurred as an integral
part of the transmission of this music.

49   Hall, *Tour Through Ireland.* p. 37.

50   Liam de Paor, 'Ireland's Identities', *The Crane Bag* 3 (1978), 28.

51   Dublin, 'a kind of changing house' for these songs, 'reconciled them
      with native traditions, Gaelic and Old English, and sent forth new
      productions whose hybrid qualities are often apparent'. Hugh
      Shields, 'Ballads, Ballad Singing, and Ballad Selling', in *Popular
      Music in Eighteenth-Century Dublin* (Dublin: Folk Music Society of
      Ireland and Na Píobairí Uilleann, 1985), p. 31.

52   Ó Súilleabháin, 'Irish Music Defined', 87.

53   This aim was articulated explicitly in Bunting's collections of the
      ancient music of Ireland published in 1789, 1809, and 1840.
      Edward Bunting, *A General Collection of the Ancient Irish Music*
      (1796); *A General Collection of the Ancient Music of Ireland* (1809); *A
      Collection of the Ancient Music of Ireland* (1840).

54   Mary Trachsel, 'Oral and Literate Constructs of "Authentic" Irish
      Music', *Éire-Ireland* 23 (Fall 1995), 32.

55   Ibid., 37.

56   Edward Bunting, *A General Collection of the Ancient Irish Music*
      (1796), reprin. ed. (Dublin: Waltons, 1969), p. 8.

57   Thomas Moore, in *Irish Melodies with Miscellaneous Poems, with a
      Melologue upon National Music* (Dublin: John Cumming, 1833), pp.
      207–8. Seán O'Boyle summarised Moore's collection as 'nostalgic,
      pseudo-historical, whimsical, sentimental productions suited to the
      drawing rooms of the nineteenth century, and were in striking con-
      trast to the living Gaelic [songs] . . . of the Irish-speaking people'.
      O'Boyle, *The Irish Song Tradition*, pp. 13–14.

58   *Songs of the Irish*, p. 7.

59   John Coolahan stated that schooling was used 'as an agency of
      conquest with a view to spreading the use of the English language
      and the Protestant faith'. *Irish Education: Its History and Structure*
      (Dublin: Institute of Public Administration, 1981), p. 8.

60   This aim was restated in 1838 by the Select Committee on Foun-
      dation Schools and Education in Ireland. *Report from the Select Com-
      mittees on Foundation Schools and Education in Ireland* (1837), p. 6.

61   Quoted from 'Two Letters on the Subject of the Incorporated Soci-
      ety addressed to the Lord Lieutenant, the Archbishop of Cork by
      Two Catholic Citizens', 1809, in Joseph Robins, *The Lost Children:*

A Study of Charity Children in Ireland 1700–1900 (Dublin: Institute of Public Administration, 1980), p. 87.

62   The hedge schools of Co. Kerry seem to have been exceptional in their inclusion of dance in the range of subjects offered. Folkloric sources indicated that it was pointless trying to run a hedge school unless there was a dancing school in the vicinity. Frequently both schools shared the same premises, the schoolmaster at one end and the dancing-master at the other, both conducting their classes simultaneously. Department of Irish Folklore, MS. 27, p. 302, cited in Breandán Breathnach, 'The Pipers of Kerry', *Éigse Cheol Tíre* 4 (1982–85), 5.

63   Mary Carbery, *The Farm by Lough Gur* (London: Longmans, Green, and Co., 1937), p. 9.

64   Coolahan, *Irish Education*, p. 9.

65   Ibid.

66   Carbery, in describing her mother's boarding school education in the early nineteenth century, said that among the things she had learned to appreciate was 'good music'. *The Farm by Lough Gur*, p. 11.

67   William Shaw Mason, *A Statistical Account or Parochial Survey of Ireland* (Dublin: Graisbury and Campbell, 1814), p. 81.

68   James Glassford, *Notes on Three Tours in Ireland, in 1824 and 1826* (Bristol: W. Strong and J. Chilcott, 1832), pp. 43–4.

69   Mason, *A Statistical Account*, p. 158. Mason mentioned the use of Isaac Watts' hymns in a Protestant charity school in Drogheda. Ibid., p. 4. Isaac Watts' hymns and his *Divine and Moral Songs for Children* were popular in England at that time.

70   Hall, *Tour Through Ireland*, p. 140.

71   Graham Balfour, *The Educational Systems of Great Britain and Ireland* (Oxford: The Clarendon Press, 1898), xviii.

72   Henry Kingsbury, *Music, Talent, and Performance: A Conservatory Cultural System* (Philadelphia: Temple University Press, 1988), p. 76.

73   Ibid., pp. 77–9.

Notes to Chapter 3

1   Joseph Lee argues that the process of modernisation began to impact Ireland during the decade of the 1840s, *The Modernization of Irish Society, 1845–1918* (Dublin: Gill and Macmillan, Ltd., 1973).

2   The English language came to be viewed by the Irish-speaking population as vital to survival when they emigrated, and to improving

their social status. Use of the Irish language as the vernacular of the people declined so rapidly that by 1850 about half the population spoke English. Even to the Irish themselves, their language had become the mark of poverty, illiteracy, and social backwardness. F. S. L. Lyons, *Culture and Anarchy in Ireland, 1890–1939* (Oxford: Oxford University Press, 1979), pp. 8–9.

3   Donald H. Akenson, *Between Two Revolutions: Islandmagee, County Antrim, 1798–1920* (Don Mills, Ontario: T. H. Best Printing Co., Ltd., 1979), p. 126.

4   *Appendix to the Thirtieth Report of the Commissioners of National Education* (1863), p. 189. Hereafter all references to Annual Reports of the Commissioners of National Education are given in abbreviated form, e.g. *Appendix to Thirtieth Report* (1863).

5   Akenson illustrated this change in relation to the Islandmagee community. One example he cited described the change which occurred in musical values in the nineteenth century so that by 1906, when 'the music pupils of the brave Mrs Gibb gave a concert, it was not a concert of traditional music, but of a miniature symphony, and the instruments were not the traditional ones, but the piano, violin, and (yes) a solitary "cymbal" made from a teatray!!' Reported in *Larne Times and Weekly Telegraph*, 31 March 1906, quoted in Akenson, pp. 147–8.

6   English was adopted as part of a general political policy by leaders such as Thomas Davis and Daniel O'Connell.

7   *Dublin Musical Festival* (Dublin: Underwood Printers, 1831).

8   Joseph J. Ryan, 'Nationalism and Music in Ireland', Ph. D. thesis, University of Dublin, 1991, p. 197.

9   *The Royal Irish Academy of Music: Centenary Souvenir, 1856–1956* (Dublin: Corrigan and Wilson, Ltd, 1956), p. 6.

10   W. J. M. Starkie, 'The Royal Irish Academy', in *Music in Ireland*, p. 105.

11   Elizabeth Coulson left a sum of £13,000 to found an academy of music in Dublin where 'the children of respectable Irish parents' would receive instruction. In 1889 the academy was entrusted with the administration of the bequest. Ibid., p. 107.

12   Ibid., p. 106.

13   John Hutchinson, *The Dynamics of Cultural Nationalism* (London: Allen and Unwin, 1987), p. 79.

14   Quoted in John Stokes, *The Life of George Petrie* (London, 1868), p. 317.

15   Alf Mac Lochlainn, 'Gael and Peasant – A Case of Mistaken Identity', in *Views of the Irish Peasantry 1800–1916*, ed. by Daniel J. Casey and Robert E. Rhodes (Hamden, CT: Archon Books, 1977), p. 31.

16   The first Temperance society was founded in 1829 and by 1842 there were at least 300 bands in the country associated with the Temperance movement. Aiveen Kearney, 'Temperance Bands and Their Significance in Nineteenth-Century Ireland', M.A. thesis, University College, Cork, 1981.

17   'Music for the People', *The Dublin Journal (of Temperance, Science, and Literature)* 1 (July 2, 1842), 145–6.

18   Johann G. Kohl, *Riesen in Ireland* (London: Chapman and Hall, 1843), pp. 57–9.

19   James Johnson, *A Tour in Ireland with Meditations and Reflections* (London: S. Highley, 1844), p. 68.

20   Kearney, 'Temperance Bands', pp. 54–5.

21   In the *Dublin Magazine* (continued as *The Dublin Journal*) a section was devoted to 'The Native Music of Ireland.' Included were both Irish airs and Temperance band music. *Dublin Magazine* (January 1843). In 1843 'The Companion to the Native Music of Ireland' was issued, being intended for 'the gentlemen of the Temperance Bands – bands of brass and of wood – on which the ladies *reserve* their right of playing and do not practice'. Ibid., 1.

22   'Revival of the Irish Language: Mechanics Institutes – Temperance Societies', *The Dublin Journal* 1 (July 2, 1842), 178.

23   The Young Ireland Movement was a group of Catholic and Protestant modernist intellectuals that emerged in the 1840s. Their main objective was 'the reconciliation of the Protestant minority with the native majority on the basis of a common allegiance to Ireland as a unique historic civilization, and they advocated a moral regeneration of Irish life by a return to its traditional language, literature, music and arts.' Hutchinson, *The Dynamics of Cultural Nationalism*, pp. 95–6.

24   'T.', 'On the Cultivation of Music in Ireland', *Carlow College Magazine* 1 (March 1870), 627.

25   Amhlaoibh Ó Súilleabháin, *The Diary of Humphrey O'Sullivan*, trans. by Tomás de Bhaldraithe (Dublin and Cork: The Mercier Press, 1979), pp. 95–6.

26   Blind village piper, Rory Oge of Kincora, Co. Clare, complained bitterly to Mr and Mrs Hall about the Temperance Bands' lack of commitment to national music, having heard them play 'God Save the

Queen'. Mr and Mrs S. C. Hall, *Ireland: Its Scenery and Character* (London: Hall, Virtue, and Co., n. d., [tours were made subsequent to 1825]), p. 427.

27 Joseph Ryan, 'Nationalism and Music in Ireland', p. 197.

28 *Report from the Select Commmittees (of the House of Commons) on Foundation Schools and Education in Ireland*, pt. 1, Minutes of Evidence taken before the Committee, 1835. Nine out of the twenty-one witnesses examined before the House of Commons by the Select Committee gave evidence about or commented on music in education. Due to the fact that the majority of those who gave witness were British or Scottish, their ideas could not reflect the heterogeneity of Irish culture nor could they assess the musical state of contemporary Ireland.

29 Thomas Wyse, *Education Reform*, vol. 1 (London: Longman et al., 1836).

30 Knight, professor of natural philosophy at the University of Aberdeen, responded positively to the introduction of music into public education believing that it would provide a worthwhile pastime for the Irish classes 'who spend a great part of their days in the alehouses'. *Report from the Select Committees*, pt. 1, Ibid., p. 345.

31 One witness, The Very Revd Dean Mc Namara of Bruff, Co. Limerick, isolated music as being 'extremely useful' in its application to religious purposes. Ibid., p. 377. The Revd Charles Mayo, pioneer of Pestalozzian methods and educational reformer in England, also regarded music as making 'a valuable adjunct to devotional exercises.' Ibid., p. 507.

32 Prior to the establishment of the National School system, the primary aim of education agencies operative in Ireland under British authority was religious proselytisation. The explicit intent of the Board of National Education was, conversely, to maintain an educational system which accommodated mixed denominational groups without interfering with the religious beliefs of any pupils. However, the repeated efforts to proselytise in the past cast shadows of suspicion over the new system. Denominational reactions to it were negative and this applied not only to the Catholic Church but also to the Church of Ireland (Established Church) and the Presbyterian Church.

33 The use of the book of *Sacred Poetry* serves to illustrate this point. (*Sacred Poetry adapted to the understanding of children and youth for the use in schools* (Dublin, 1845)). The book was compiled, published,

and sanctioned by the Board of National Education. It consisted of 'a collection of religious verse and hymns selected from Isaac Watts, Jane and Emly Taylor and other sources'. *An Analysis of School Books* (Dublin: Authority of the Commissioners of National Education in Ireland, 1853), p. 12. Use of this collection in many of the national schools would be viewed with skepticism and animosity since the content was rooted in Protestant doctrine.

34 John Coolahan, *Irish Education*, 1981, p. 58; James Auchmuty, *Sir Thomas Wyse, 1791–1862* (London: P. S. King and Son Ltd., 1939), p. 303.

35 This was recognised by Joeph Mainzer in his *Music and Education* as early as 1848. Mainzer, a German teacher and musician, was himself an important figure in British and Scottish music education in the 1840s. He was familiar with Wyse's educational ideas and identified him as 'almost the first who brought the question of music, in its connection with a national system of education, before the British public and the British Parliament'. Joseph Mainzer, Appendix to *Music and Education* (1848) Intro. by Bernarr Rainbow (Kilkenny: Boethius Press, 1985), p. 106.

36 Thomas Wyse, *Speech of Thomas Wyse, Esq., M.P., in the House of Commons on Tuesday, May 19, 1835* (London: Ridgway and Son, 1835), p. 8. Rainbow stated that Wyse's proposal was greeted with a shout of laughter by the members of the House of Commons. Bernarr Rainbow, *The Land Without Music* (London: Novello and Co., Ltd., 1967), p. 41.

37 Wyse's education abroad, his obvious breadth of reading on educational matters, his travel, and the social milieu in which he functioned, all influenced his definition of music as a national attribute and as an educational component. His bias in favour of classical music was evident in his writings on 'Music' and 'Aesthetics' in *Education Reform*.

38 Wyse, *Education Reform*, p. 187. Wyse offered three reasons for this situation: 1. The jobbing system of our professors and publishers. 2. The deficiency of academies and conservatories for the study of the higher branches. 3. The total neglect of musical education in our elementary schools. Ibid., p. 193.

39 Ibid., p. 187.

40 Ibid., pp. 186–7.

41 Ibid., p. 195, p. 197.

42 Ibid., pp. 197–8.

43 Wyse did suggest, however, the compilation of national airs as part of a teacher's music manual. Ibid., p. 194.

44 'An Apology for Harmony', *Dublin University Magazine* 17 (January–June 1841), 583.

45 'Prefatory Minute of the Committee of Council on Education', in John Hullah's *Wilhem's Method of Teaching Singing* (1842), intro. by Bernarr Rainbow (Kilkenny: Boethius Press, 1983), p. iv.

46 The development of pedagogical principles and tools to accommodate popular music education emanated from two continental movements in the early decades of the nineteenth century – the first was Johann Heinrich Pestalozzi and his disciples in Germany and Switzerland, the second the French school of music pedagogy led by Pierre Galin and later by J. L.B. Wilhem. Pestalozzi's philosophy of music education had a strong humanistic base, one which identified the potential of music to inculcate moral, religious, and social values in the young. Wilhem was employed by the French Society for Elementary Instruction in 1819 to develop a method of music teaching for French elementary schools. He designed a system for large groups and modelled instruction on how language was taught. He focused on a narrow, purportedly scientific, and analytical approach in which methodology took precedence over the humanistic values of music. See *Pestalozzi's Educational Writings,* ed. by J. A. Green (New York: Longmans, Green, and Co., 1916); *Source Readings in Music Education History,* ed. by Michael Mark (New York: Schirmer Books, 1982); Bernarr Rainbow, *The Land Without Music* (London: Novello and Co., Ltd., 1967).

47 John Hullah's, *Wilhem's Method of Teaching Singing* (1842), intro. Bernarr Rainbow (Kilkenny, Ireland: Boethius Press, 1983). A series of exercises based on various intervals followed by songs illustrated the particular interval being introduced e.g. 'First Song on the Interval of the Sixth', or 'The Violet', p. 57; 'Exercises for the Practice of 6/8 Time', or 'O Come Ye into the Summer Woods!!' pp. 162–3.

48 Budding native music methods did exist in Britain; yet the Committee of Council on Education rejected them. Bernarr Rainbow identified John Turner, William Hickson, and Sarah Glover as the native pioneers of music education in Britain. *The Land Without Music,* pp. 29–53. A forewarning as to the shortcomings of the Wilhem-Hullah method was given by Hickson after Hullah's *Manual* was published. He criticised it for being 'so overlaid with the technical pedantries of the science, so abounding in difficulties insuperable to children . . . The introduction

of this manual . . . will, we fear, lead to the impression that music is one of the most impracticable of the sciences'. William E. Hickson, 'Music, and the Committee of Council for Education', *Westminster Review* 37 (January-April 1842), 29, 41. Continental methods were perceived as being superior. The early nineteenth-century continental image of Britain as *Das Land ohne Musik* (the land without music) was partly responsible for this mentality.

49 *Seventh Report* (1840), p. 87.

50 *Appendix to Twenty-Second Report* (1855), p. 74. Examples from Hullah's manual to support Keenan's criticism might be: 'Evening', p. 46; 'The Flying Course', p. 156; 'The Labourer's Sleep', p. 176, and 'Leaving Port', pp. 178–9.

51 The number of schools associated with the Board of National Education rose from 1,978 in 1840 to 5,632 by 1860 with an increase in the number of pupils on the rolls from 232,560 in 1840 to 804,000 in 1860. *Annual Reports of the Commissioners of National Education*, cited in Coolahan, *Irish Education*, p. 19. By 1867, there were 6,520 schools registered by roll-number with the National Board. Ibid., p. 24. The steady increase in the school population may seem to contradict the general decrease in population due to famine and emigration. However, Ireland had a dense population of approximately eight million before the famine, a fact which in part explains the large school-going population.

52 Other educational agencies such as Mechanics Institutes and schools of the Poor Law Unions of Ireland were also affiliated to the Board of National Education. Due to denominational opposition to the National School system, many religious orders and churches maintained their own schools independent of the board. In 1871, there were 2,661 schools providing elementary education which were not associated with the National Board of Education. Coolahan, *Irish Education*, p. 20.

53 The influence of model schools was limited. They are included here because the manner in which music developed in these schools reveals the official goals for music education in the system; second, the first music teachers worked in model schools; and third, the Annual Reports of the Commissioners provide a detailed description of the growth of music education in these settings.

54 These schools were 'some of the earliest public schools fully financed by the state in any country . . . and were strictly conducted on the mixed denominational principle'. Ibid., p. 23.

55   *Sixteenth Report* (1849), pp. 282–3.

56   *Thirtieth Report* (1863), p. 36. In the inspectors' reports, a distinction was made between the *ordinary* branches, the 3Rs, and the *extra* branches, singing, drawing, navigation, and book-keeping, to mention but a few.

57   In Clonmel model schools in 1850, many of the boys were 'the children of respectable parents from the country, and from the neighbouring towns, who are sent to board and lodge in Clonmel, for the purpose of attending the Model School'. *Appendix to Seventeenth Report* (1850), p. 241.

58   The *Appendix to Nineteenth Report* (1852), described the status of music: 'This refining branch of education had been most acceptable to the pupils and their parents. At first, many of both did not understand why singing should be taught, and considered it a loss of time. The pupils, however, first began to like it, and next the parents. The former deriving pleasure and instruction from the music and poetry, and the latter finding their evening fire-side cheered by the voices of their children after the toils and labours of the day', p. 225.

59   Noel Kelly, 'Music in Irish Primary Education, 1831–1922', *Proceedings of the Educational Studies Association of Ireland* (Galway: Officiana Typographica, 1979), p. 49.

60   Other peripatetic music teachers were later employed by the Board: Mr George Washington in Belfast, Mr Quin in Galway, Mr Goodwin in Dublin and Trim, Mr Shiel in Bailieborough, and Mr Wotzel in Limerick.

61   Evidence as to the status and development of music in model schools is found in the Annual Reports of the National Commissioners. These documents consist primarily of reports submitted by district and head inspectors to the Board of National Commissioners on the countrywide state of education. They are valuable in supplying information on who taught music, the method and repertoire used, the effect music education had on the pupils, and how this effect was brought to the notice of parents and community. In the reports, reference was frequently made to the appropriateness of songs sung on such occasions, 'care being taken that nothing of an objectionable nature is introduced'. *Twenty-First Report* (1854), p. 102. The performance of 'several appropriate airs' was often the language used by inspectors to express their satisfaction with music in the schools.

62   For example, songs performed on examination days between the late 1840s and early 1860s included: 'The Canadian Boat Song', 'The

Last Rose of Summer', 'The Meeting of the Waters', (Moore), 'The Irish Emigrant's Farewell', 'The Four-leaved Shamrock', 'The Vesper Hymn', 'The Hardy Norseman', 'The Shamrock', 'Dulce Domum', 'Druids' Chorus' from *Norma*, Scotch Air, 'March of the Cameron Men', 'Hurrah for Education' (a Christmas Carol), 'Rule Britannia', 'Farewell to Old Tennessee', 'Dear Harp of My Country', 'God moves in a Mysterious Way', and selections from composers such as Bellini and Donizetti. These songs are taken from the Programmes of Clonmel Model Schools, 1849, Trim, 1852, and Ballymena, 1861. *Appendix to Sixteenth Report* (1849), p. 268; *Appendix to Nineteenth Report* (1852), pp. 222–3; *Appendix to Twenty-Eighth Report* (1861), p. 127.

63   A description provided by Sir Francis Head of his visit to Marlborough Street Model Schools, Dublin, in 1852, captured the spirit surrounding the performance of this song: 'The whole of the three hundred girls rose, and, as with one voice, commenced with great taste and melody to sing together 'God Save the Queen!!' . . . Their performance was not only admirable, but deeply affecting.' Sir Francis B. Head, *A Fortnight in Ireland* (London: John Murray, 1852), p. 33.

64   *Appendix to Twenty-Seventh Report* (1860), p. 93.

65   *Appendix to Sixteenth Report* (1849), p. 273.

66   Since Catholic parents were suspicious of religious indoctrination in schools, political strategies were used to alleviate this suspicion. In Clonmel, it was reported: 'Advantage has also been taken of the singing in order to give effect to the devotional exercises of the Roman Catholic pupils at the hour of religious instruction, and they are now able to sing and chant creditably the hymns and litanies of their Church.' *Appendix to Sixteenth Report* (1849), p. 269.

67   *Twenty-Ninth Report* (1862), p. 72.

68   'Her Majesty's Visit to the Female Infant School of the National Board of Education, in Marlborough-Street, Dublin', in *Illustrated London News* (11 August 1849), 87.

69   In cases such as Dunmanway and Newry where a decline in music teaching was noted, the inspectors urged the board to send a teacher to improve the situation. Other centres built a strong tradition of music education due to the musical talent and enthusiasm of individual teachers. Music flourished in the Belfast model schools due to George Washington's instruction. In 1865 he stated: 'The pupils evince considerable aptitude in the study of vocal

music, a circumstance which enables me to produce a superior class of music at the annual public examinations. For instance, the following have been performed: – 'Glory to God', and 'Hallelujah', from the 'Messiah'; the Gloria ('How Glorious is Thy Name!!') from *Mozart's No. 12*; Locke's music to 'Macbeth'; the glees 'Here in Cool Grot', from 'Oberon in Fairy Land'; 'Awake Aeolian Lyre'; and many part songs of high character.' *Appendix to Thirty-Second Report* (1865), p. 87.

70   *Appendix to Twentieth Report* (1853), p. 117.

71   Akenson, *Between Two Revolutions*, p. 174.

72   For example, describing schools in Londonderry, Inspector Macaulay stated: 'Very little musical taste appears to exist amongst the poorer classes of this district.' *Thirty-Third Report* (1866), p. 225.

73   *Twenty-Seventh Report* (1860), p. 133.

74   'T.', 'On the Cultivation of Music in Ireland', 627.

75   The Orange Order was founded amid religion-tinted agrarian troubles in 1795 in Co. Armagh for Protestant self-defence. It functions to this day and makes use of music in the expression of its political and religious beliefs. The fife-and-drum ensembles are most typical of the tradition and seem to have evolved from the British military fife and drum corps of the eighteenth century. Gary Hastings, 'The Orange Musical Tradition', *Ceol Tire* 30 (January 1987), 2.

76   In July 1862, for example, a fife-and-drum band was organised in the Coleraine Model Schools, the first of its kind in Ireland, according to head inspector Fleming. This group performed Irish, English, and Scottish airs at the 1863 Public Examinations. The idea of establishing a fife-and-drum band in this instance originated with the district inspector, Mr M'Ilroy. *Appendix to Thirtieth Report* (1863), p. 56. The experiment influenced other educational institutions, among them the Workhouse School of the Poor Law Union of Ireland at Larne who organised the Larne Workhouse Boys' Band. A report of 1866 stated: 'The band became a regular feature of civic and ceremonial occasions, and although from the perspective of our own times it may seem a bit patronising to have the pauper children drilled as civic minstrels, for them the business must have been a great deal more interesting than sitting in the workhouse being conventionally and tediously industrious.' *Northern Counties Advertiser*, 3 March 1866, in *Between Two Revolutions*, p. 111.

77   Songs performed at the Public Examinations held at Coleraine in 1852 attest to this wide-ranging repertoire – music of classical

composers (Mozart, Morley), glees, Irish melodies by Moore, German anthem, Scottish melodies, and national songs. *Appendix to Nineteenth Report* (1852), p. 164.

78   The 1849 report of the infant school stated that the pupils started each day with a hymn and that much of their time was devoted to 'the repetition in song of their little hymns and rhymes'. *Sixteenth Report* (1849), p. 229. A list of hymns was given in the 1853 report: 'The Hosanna'; 'Lord dismiss us'; 'Infants' Alleluia'; 'The Morning Hymn'; 'The Evening Hymn'; 'Hark!!' 'The Evening Hymn' is stealing; A Hebrew Melody; Great God, and wilt Thou Condescend'. *Twentieth Report* (1853), p. 132.

79   For a description of musical traditions in the Big Houses, see chapter 2.

80   *Twentieth Report* (1853), p. 113.

81   Newell's reference to 'political excitement' and ballad singers reflected the role designated to music in the Young Ireland movement of the 1840s. Song lyrics were perceived as powerful in the educational process and, in that context, the effect of the melody was secondary to the indoctrinatory potential of lyrics. In relation to Trim Model School, Inspector Lavender remarked: 'While the airs are pretty, cheerful, and well selected, the words carry with them information either upon the ordinary trades and manufactures, or awaken the feelings of benevolence and devotion'. *Appendix to Nineteenth Report* (1852), p. 236. A similar remark was made by Newell in 1858 as he described his efforts to supply song materials to schools, in which the songs 'are chosen as much for moral sentiments they contain, as for the melody of the music'. *Twenty-Fifth Report* (1858), p. 23.

82   *Twenty-Second Report* (1855), p. 267, p. 157, p. 51, p. 100.

83   Ibid., p. 132.

84   Referring to a teachers' efforts in Cove, Co. Cork, in 1855, Newell stated that he had introduced 'drawing and music, with great success, even against the prejudices of the parents'. *Twenty-Second Report* (1855), p. 45.

85   *Twenty-Third Report* (1856), p. 51.

86   Patrick Weston Joyce, *English as We Speak it in Ireland*, 2d ed. (Trowbridge and Esher: Redwood Burn Ltd., 1979), pp. 158–9.

87   McHale wrote: 'To introduce these Melodies to my humbler countrymen, robed in a manner worthy of their high origin, has been my object in the following translation.' *A Selection of Moore's*

Melodies, trans. by Revd John McHale (Dublin: James Duffy, *c.* 1842, 1871), x.

88 *Appendix to Twenty-Second Report* (1855), p. 73.

89 Ibid.

90 Ibid., p. 74.

91 Kelly, 'Music in Irish Primary Education', p. 50.

92 *Royal Commission of Inquiry, Primary Education, Ireland,* vol. III (1870), p. 88, (hereafter the *Powis Commission*).

93 *Thomas Davis: The Thinker and Teacher,* ed. by Arthur Griffith (Dublin: M. H. Gill and Son Ltd., 1914), p. 35.

94 Ibid., pp. 52–3.

95 Thomas Davis, 'Schools and Study', in *Essays and Poems with a Centenary Memoir 1845–1945* (Dublin: M.H. Gill and Son, Ltd., 1945), p. 80.

96 By 1848, British music pedagogue Mainzer identified the monopolising effect of this method in Great Britain. He said: 'All other methods or systems of teaching, are under the ban of the Board of Education: . . . If you really wish that music should lay hold of the young population, and permeate into the very heart of the British islands, throw widely open the gates of instruction; surround yourself with a whole army of different teachers and different systems!!' Mainzer, *Music and Education,* pp. 94–5.

97 In 1859, in an effort to encourage teachers to teach music, the board offered an annual gratuity to those holding a Certificate of Competency in music teaching. In its first year of operation, only 31 out of 5,496 ordinary National Schools received gratuities for teachers of vocal music. The gratuity for music was £2–£5, for drawing was £3–£10, for navigation £5–£10. In 1869, Inspector Eardley criticised the inequality among the gratuities paid for various subjects. He stated: 'Singing is surely of more value as an educational instrument, particularly among a musical people as the Irish are admitted to be, than drawing; yet the gratuity attainable for the latter subject is double that for the former'. *Appendix to Thirty-Sixth Report* (1869), p. 260.

98 T. H. M. C., 'Musical Reform', *The Irish Magazine and National Teachers Gazette* 1 (1 July 1860), 47.

99 *Appendix to Twenty-Fourth Report* (1857), p. 7; *Thirty-Sixth Report* (1869), p. 346.

100 Correspondence to the Editor, 'Vocal Music', *Irish Teachers Journal* 2 (1 May 1869), 112. It is worthy of note that in March, 1868,

Keenan reported that within the previous seven or eight years, 433 harmoniums had been sold for use in national schools at a reduced rate. This seems to indicate that music in these schools was related to church services. *Powis Commission Report,* vol. III, p. 88.

101   *Irish Teachers Journal* 1 (February 1, 1868).

102   Ibid., 5 (1 September 1872), 444.

103   Ibid., 5 (15 September 1872), 466.

104   Ibid., 5 (1 October 1872), 478.

105   Ibid., 5 (15 November 1872), 518.

106   These orders included the Presentation Sisters (1782), The Irish Sisters of Charity (1813), the Loreto Sisters, (1822), the Mercy Sisters (1831), and the Holy Faith Sisters (1860).

107   Cumin stated that 'the only good specimens of music and sewing were found in convent schools'. *Powis Commission Report,* vol. III, p. 284. Earlier reports of music in convent schools were also very favourable: Keenan found singing 'very good' and part singing 'very pleasing' in the Presentation Convent, Mullingar, where 'the object aimed at is to educate the heart as well as the intellect'. *Twenty-Third Report* (1856), p. 184. He also praised the singing of the pupils at St Columb's Sisters of Mercy in Derry, stating that it was as good as that of the Model Schools. *Twenty-Second Report* (1855), p. 120. In Patterson's report on the Convent of Mercy in Gort, Co. Galway, he stated that the school excelled in musical instruction. Cited in Sr. Mary de Lourdes Fahy, *Education in the Diocese of Kilmacduagh in the Nineteenth Century* (Gort, Co. Galway: Convent of Mercy, 1972), p. 95.

108   *Powis Commission Report,* vol. III, p. 211; Ibid., vol. II, p. 139. At Kenmare, the elder girls and monitoresses formed 'the choir of the church to which the convent is attached, and in other towns where the Mass is chorally celebrated, the vocal portion of the music is contributed in part by convent pupils'. Ibid., p. 467.

109   In his study of elementary education in Co. Kerry, Joseph Carroll found evidence in the domestic annals of the Presentation Convent in Killarney of the presence of trained musicians and singers in the community from 1865 onwards. Joseph Carroll, 'A History of Elementary Education in Kerry, 1700–1870', M. Ed. thesis, University College, Cork, 1984.

110   Anne V. O'Connor, 'The Revolution in Girls' Secondary Education in Ireland 1860–1910', in *Girls Don't Do Honours: Irish Women in Education in the 19th and 20th Centuries,* ed. by Mary Cullen (Dublin: Women's Education Bureau, 1987), p. 40. This observation is conso-

nant with the conclusions drawn in two studies of education in the nineteenth century. Carroll, 'A History of Elementary Education'; Jane McCarthy, 'The Contribution of the Sisters of Mercy to West Cork Schooling, 1844–1922, in the Context of Irish Elementary Educational Development', M. Ed. thesis, University College, Cork, 1979.

111   McCarthy, 'The Contribution of the Sisters of Mercy', pp. 237–8.

112   Keenan reports this of both convent and model schools. McCarthy, p. 55; Richmond's report on Belfast convent schools stated: 'The monitoresses especially receive [music] lessons with a view to qualifying themselves as teachers in afterlife. . . . A good many girls at these schools learn to play the piano; . . . and they pay 10s a quarter for it'. *Powis Commission Report*, vol. III, p. 211.

113   In issues of the *Irish Teachers Journal* of 1868, governesses seeking employment in the homes of the wealthy offered tuition in piano, French, music, drawing, and English.

114   McCarthy, 'The Contribution of the Sisters of Mercy', p. 302.

115   Evidence was gathered from the Powis Commission report and sources written from within the Christian Brothers community. In the Christian Brothers' *A Manual of School Government*, published in 1845, a typical horarium included singing as part of the school day. 'Singing at seats' for two periods in the day was recommended for a junior classroom. Joseph Hearne and Bernard Duggan, *A Manual of School Government: being a complete analysis of the system of education pursued in the Christian Schools* (Dublin: The Christian Brothers, 1845), pp. 33–4. From the specimen timetable included in the Christian Brothers' returns to the Powis Commission of 1868–70, music was reported as being taught in the 'First or Junior School', but less time was given to it in the 'Second School', and there was no mention of it in the 'Third' and 'Fourth' schools. *Powis Commission Report*, vol. VIII, p. 93. It would seem, then, that music instruction was provided only in the lower grades. However, this distinction was not observed by individuals who visited the schools and who reported to the Powis Commission. Vocal music was taught in all the Christian Brothers' schools which King visited in the Dublin district. Ibid., vol. II, p. 7. Balmer found music taught regularly in their schools in the Killarney district. Ibid., p. 467. Sources written from within the community such as *A Manual of School Government, The History of the Institute,* or more general works such as Hennessy's *A Century of Catholic Education*, provided further evidence of the role and scope of music education in the Christian Brothers' schools.

116   'The Christian Schools', *The Standard*, 9 June 1928, 12.

117   Donal Blake, 'The Christian Brothers and Education in Nineteenth-Century Ireland', M. Ed. thesis, University College, Cork, 1977, p. 178.

118   Ibid., p. 179.

119   This was Br. Duggan's response when asked by members of the Royal Commission on Education in Endowed Schools in Ireland about the effect of music education on pupils. Cited in *History of the Institute*, vol. II (Dublin: Bray Printing Co., 1958–61), p. 248.

120   Ibid., p. 258.

121   P. J. Hennessy, *A Century of Catholic Education* (Dublin: Browne and Nolan, 1916), p. 126.

122   Blake, 'The Christian Brothers and Education', p. 179. The Christian Brothers published their own set of textbooks to reflect their educational and national philosophy. In the list of publications submitted by the Christian Brothers to the Powis Commission (1868–70), no music book was included. *Powis Commission*, vol. VIII, p. 94. However, one cannot conclude from such evidence that music was neglected in the schools. The foregoing example of the printing of music books in Cork confirms its role in the Christian Brothers' curriculum. The Cork Christian Brothers' schools, in Blake's opinion, were among the first in Ireland to adopt the Tonic Sol-fa method of music teaching.

123   Hennessy, *A Century of Catholic Education*, p. 139.

124   *History of the Institute*, vol. II, p. 279. This event invites a fruitful comparison with that of the lord lieutenant's visit to Belfast model schools in 1862.

125   An official report of 1854 showed that the Church Education Society used Watts' *Divine Songs*. These hymns originated in a Protestant context and functioned to confirm Protestant beliefs.

126   Baptist W. Noel, *Notes of a Short Tour through the Midland Counties of Ireland, in the Summer of 1836* (London: James Nisbet and Co., 1837).

127   Ibid., p. 202.

128   Thackeray, *The Irish Sketch-Book,* pp. 190–3.

129   Kohl, *Riesen in Ireland*, pp. 123–4.

130   'T.', 'On the Cultivation of Music in Ireland', 627.

131   *Report of Her Majesty's Commissioners on Endowed Schools, Ireland* (1857–58), p. 216.

132   For example, Horncastle's *Music of Ireland* (1844); Conran's *National Music of Ireland* (1850); the founding of the Society for the

Preservation and Publication of Irish Melodies in 1851, and Petrie's *Ancient Music of Ireland* (1855).

Notes to Chapter 4

1   Benedict Anderson, *Imagined Communities*.
2   Clifford Geertz, *The Interpretation of Cultures*, p. 239; John Hutchinson, *The Dynamics of Cultural Nationalism*, pp. 2–4. Maurice Goldring states that 'the golden age of nationalism in Ireland was also that of the modernisation of the state and of the education system'. *Pleasant the Scholar's Life: Irish Intellectuals and the Construction of the Nation State* (London: Serif, 1993), p. 172.
3   *Report of the Gaelic League for the year ended 30.9.1894* (Dublin: Dollard Printinghouse, 1895), p. 9.
4   Mary Daly pointed out that this attempt to encapsulate true Irish identity led to enthusiasts 'flocking to the western seaboard in search of native Irish speakers and the remnants of their indigenous culture'. In the process, the peasant life-style and values were idealised and elevated in an exaggerated manner. 'An Alien Institution? Attitudes Towards the City in Nineteenth and Twentieth Century Irish Society', *Études Irlandaises* 10 (December 1985), 181.
5   Maurice Goldring, *Pleasant the Scholar's Life*, p. 128.
6   George Moonan, *The Spirit of the Gaelic League*, Gaelic League Pamphlets No. 33 (Dublin: The Gaelic League, n. d.), p. 7.
7   Douglas Hyde, 'The Necessity for De-Anglicising Ireland', in *Language, Lore, and Lyrics,* ed. by Breandán Ó Conaire (Dublin: Irish Academic Press, 1986), p. 167.
8   Grace O'Brien, 'The National Element in Irish Music', *The Irish Monthly* 43 (November 1915), 710.
9   Annie Patterson, 'The Interpretation of Irish Music', *Journal of the Ivernian Society* 2 (September 1909), 32. Annie Patterson (1868–1934), Irish folksong collector, organist, composer and writer on music and music education, exerted considerable influence on the development of music in Ireland from 1895, when she organised the *Feis Ceoil*, to her death in 1934. *The New Grove Dictionary of Music and Musicians*, s. v. 'Annie Patterson.'
10   *Report of the Gaelic League for the two years ended 30.9.1896* (Dublin: Doyle Publishers, 1896), p. 6.
11   In George O'Neill's description of the aims of the Feis Ceoil, he stated that in this context, 'the word Irish is used in a strict but not narrow

sense. It describes all music which is charcteristically Irish, whether of the remotest antiquity or of to-day, whether the simplest tune or the elaborate work of the artist, whether Irish from intrinsic pecularities or from the instrument on which it is meant to be played'. 'The Work of the Feis Ceoil Association: A History and An Appeal', *Irish Ecclesiastical Record*, 4th series 8 (June–December 1900), 347.

12 R. I. Best, 'The Feis Ceoil', *Leabhar na hÉireann: The Irish Yearbook* (1908), p. 154.

13 *Feis Charman* (1902), Sligo *Feis Ceoil* (1903), *Feis Átha Cliath* (1904), *Feis Láir na hÉireann*, Muileann Cearr (1904), *Feis an Athar Maitiú*, Baile Atha Cliath (1908), in Ó Gallchobhair, 'The Cultural Value of Festival and Feis', in *Music in Ireland*, pp. 215–16.

14 *Feis Ceoil, Irish Musical Festival, Dublin May 18th, 19th, 20th, and 21st, 1897* (Dublin: Dollard Press, n. d.), pp. 10–11.

15 *Seventy-Third Repo*rt (1906–7), p. 165. For many Gaelic League advocates, the development of fluency in the Irish language was the primary function of these music competitions. This is an important distinction, since the promotion of the Irish language through song became a *tour de force* in Irish national schools in post-independent Ireland.

16 A further example of the development of cultural institutions with a competitive base was the *Oireachtas* (assembly or convocation), an annual festival founded by the Gaelic League in 1897 to encourage and create high standards in language, literature, music, art, and other aspects of native cultural traditions. *Oireachtas* competitions for young people never flourished in the same way as *feiseanna* did. Éamonn Ó Gallchobhair, 'The Cultural Value of Festival and Feis', in *Music in Ireland*, p. 215.

17 Best, 'The Feis Ceoil', 154–5. 'Singing in the Irish language was also provided for, and prizes given for unpublished Irish airs, and for performances on the Irish pipes, etc.'

18 Harry Bradshaw, *Michael Coleman 1895–1914* (Dublin: Viva Voce, 1991), pp. 36–7.

19 Pádraig Pearse, 'Traditionalism', in *An Claidheamh Soluis* (June 1906), cited in Donncha Ó Súilleabháin, *Scéal an Oireachtais, 1897–1924* (Baile Átha Cliath: An Clóchomhar, Tta., 1984), p. 109.

20 Carl Hardebeck, 'Traditional Singing: Its Value and Meaning', *Journal of the Ivernian Society* 3 (January–March 1911), 93.

21 Breandán Breathnach, reported in Hugh Shields, 'Recent Meetings: The Feis Ceoil and Irish Music', *Ceol Tíre* 22 (October 1982), 4.

22   'Niamh', 'Music Notes', *Journal of the Ivernian Society* 7 (October-
      December 1914), 44.

23   Annie Patterson, 'The Interpretation of Irish Music', 33.

24   Richard Henebry, 'Irish Music', *The Irish Year Book* (1908), p. 238.

25   Ibid., p. 233.

26   Competitions such as the Feis Ceoil highlighted the need for
      improving the standard of music in Ireland and expanding the way
      in which music was transmitted to Irish youth. In addition, as Irish
      traditional music entered the market place and the world of profes-
      sionalism, the need for providing formal training for traditional
      musicians emerged. Annie Patterson saw the need for 'training
      schools preparatory to competition and public performances'.
      'Notes on Music, Art, Etc.', *Journal of the Ivernian Society* 1 (March
      1909), 201.

27   Hyde, 'The Necessity for De-Anglicising Ireland', pp. 167–8.

28   *The Irish Song Book,* ed. by A. P. Graves (London: T. Fisher Unwin,
      1894), xvii.

29   Brendan Rogers, 'An Irish School of Music', *The New Ireland Review*
      13 (March-August 1900), 149.

30   For historical background on these institutions, see Bernard Curtis,
      Centenary of the Cork School of Music: Progress of the School 1878–1978
      (Cork: Cork School of Music, 1978), and Jim Cooke, *Coláiste an
      Cheoil, College of Music: A Musical Journey 1890–1993* (Dublin,
      1994).

31   He complaining bitterly that at a concert given by the Dublin
      Municipal School of Music, 'out of twenty-two items not one was
      Irish'. 'Lectures by Mr W. H. Grattan Flood', *Irish Musical Monthly*
      1 (April 1902), 24.

32   Curtis, *Centenary of the Cork School of Music;* Cooke, *Coláiste an
      Cheoil.*

33   Revd H. Bewerunge, cited in 'Lecture on Irish Music', *Irish Musical
      Monthly* 1 (January 1903), 116.

34   Patterson, 'The Interpretation of Irish Music', 41.

35   'Notes on Art, Archeology, and Music', *Journal of the Ivernian Soci-
      ety* 1 (June 1909), 262. It is thought that this article was written by
      'Niamh' who was author of this section of the journal in later years.

36   Joep Leerssen, *Remembrance and Imagination: Patterns in the Historical
      and Literary Representation of Ireland in the Nineteenth Century* (Cork:
      Cork University Press in association with Field Day, 1996), p. 151.

37   Ordinary subjects referred to the basics, subjects which were taught

in every national school i.e. reading, spelling, arithmetic. Extra subjects were not compulsory and their presence in the school curriculum was haphazard. Inspector Connellan considered this change of status for music in the curriculum as 'the first recognition of what all educationalists and all men of reflection regard as one of the most potent and subtle elements of culture'. *Appendix to Fiftieth Report* (1883), p. 211.

38 Singing exercises, reading, transposition, six approved songs for second and third classes, and harmonised songs for upper classes. *Appendix to Fortieth Report* (1873), p. 88.

39 Although the fee paid for vocal music was equal to that paid for arithmetic, it was available only to those pupils who passed the 'basic' subjects, i.e., reading, spelling, writing, and arithmetic. For vocal music, one and sixpence for each pass in second class, and fees equal to arithmetic in higher classes; no fee for a child who was not a member of a regularly constituted class for instruction in the theory and practice of vocal music, or of a regularly constituted class in operation in the school; no fee for a child who did not pass in reading and at least two other subjects of instruction; no fee for children in second and third classes unless the children in the higher classes showed a satisfactory proficiency.

40 Teachers in ordinary national schools who chose to teach music within school hours received no gratuity. Rather the examination results' fees accruing from their pupils went into a common fund divisible among all the teachers in that school. *Thirty-Ninth Report* (1872), p. 25.

41 *Sixtieth Report* (1893), p. 234.

42 In 1884 Tonic Sol-fa was granted official recognition and a programme was designed for teachers using this method. *Appendix to Fifty-First Report* (1884), pp. 82–3.

43 *Appendix to Fifty-Fifth Report* (1888), p. 139.

44 Edmund M. Sneyd-Kynnersley, *H. M. I.: Some Passages in the Life of One of H. M. Inspectors of Schools* (London: Macmillan and Co., Ltd., 1908), p. 287.

45 Head Inspector Fitzgerald believed that since 'Irish children have quick ears . . . singing by ear could be cultivated with advantage, as it is in most infant schools'. *Appendix to Fiftieth Report* (1883), p. 144. His observation may be interpreted in the context of Irish children growing up around music making, and learning music in an aural, oral context, thus responding well to 'singing by ear'.

Inspector Connellan made a similar observation: 'I believe Irish children are at least as well adapted as those of other nations for this culture. And yet, go where I will through the country, I can find no trace of this traditional native taste. Can it be that it is disappearing because of the feeble efforts made in our schools to teach the dull theory of music to a lively and sentimental race?' *Appendix to Fiftieth Report* (1883), p. 211.

46   Inspector Molloy warned teachers not to allow 'the extra branches to interfere with the attention due to the essential subjects of the school course'. *Appendix to Forty-Fourth Report* (1877), p. 145. For Inspector Roantree, 'public time that could ill be spared from pressing and important duties had to be frittered away in barren examinations on extra subjects'. *Appendix to Forty-Third Report* (1876), p. 72. Inspector Meeke considered music inspection as 'adding materially to the already excessive duties of the Inspectors, for in no subject are more care and time required to determine each individual's merit than in music'. He suggested that the fees to be paid for singing should be determined by the proficiency of the class on the whole, except in the upper classes. *Appendix to Forty-Eighth Report* (1881), p. 48.

47   Joseph Sleith, 'Music in the Schools – What is was, What it is, and What it Ought to be', *Irish School Weekly* 67 (6 March 1915), 1345–6.

48   The Tonic Sol-fa method was propagated by Curwen's own publications – *The New Standard Course, The Staff Notation, The Blackbird, Modern Part Songs.*

49   Advertisement in the *Irish Teachers Journal,* 9 (15 April 1876), 221. A second publication by Glover, *Singing Hand Books,* contained a selection of Irish melodies and was placed on the prescribed book list of the National Commissioners.

50   In 1873, a memorial of the managers and teachers of Irish National Schools was submitted to the Commissioners of National Education, requesting them to reconsider the status of music in the new results' system. 'Drawing and Singing of National Schools', *Irish Teachers Journal* 6 (12 April 1873), 101. *Appendix to the Thirty-Ninth Report* (1872), p. 295.

51   1871, £61.0.0; 1872, £51.3.2; 1873, £31.8.6; 1874, £33.0.0. *Annual Reports of the National Commissioners* (1871–1874).

52   1876–77, 76.7 per cent; 1884, 78.9 per cent, 1892, 82 per cent, and 1899, 89.0 per cent. *Annual Reports of the National Commissioners.*

53   *Report of Royal Commission on Manual and Practical Instruction in Primary Schools* (1898), p. 54.

54   Leerssen, *Remembrance and Imagination,* p. 221.

55   *Appendix to Fifty-Eighth Report* (1891), p. 191.

56   The location for the event, as described in the *Cork Examiner,* was the Cork School of Art. See 'School Singing Competition in Ireland', in *The School Music Review* 1 (1 November 1892), 95. However, the *Fifty-Ninth Report* (1892), p. 36, states that it was held in the Cork School of Music. See also *Fifty-Ninth Report* (1892), p. 36. There is no evidence to show that competitions were held in this format after 1894.

57   Quoted in Kieran A. Daly, *Catholic Church Music in Ireland, 1878–1903: The Cecilian Reform Movement* (Dublin: Four Courts Press, 1995), p. 142. Daly points out that from the inception of *Lyra Ecclesiastica,* it had raised the question of singing in schools and 'regularly called for countrywide school choirs, particularly those of primary school pupils'. Ibid., p. 141.

58   In his report of 1893, Goodman provided evidence of Keenan's role in the formation of the competitions: 'Early in October 1892, the Right Hon. Sir Patrick Keenan gave me to understand that he wished a Public School Competition in Singing should be held in Dublin. And in order that primary schools of all denominations might take part in it, he proposed that it should be conducted under the auspices of the RIAM [Royal Irish Academy of Music], of which he is a Vice-President'. *Appendix to Sixtieth Report* (1893), p. 331. No evidence was found to show that the Cork singing competition of 1892 influenced Keenan's thinking or that it provided the model for the Dublin competitions.

59   Ibid., p. 332. Goodman, aware that 'just about this time the Annual Singing Competitions of the London Board Schools was announced to take place', he went over to see how they were organised. On his return, schools were chosen by him to enter for the Dublin contest based on their examination record in music.

60   The sight-reading test was designed by John Curwen himself while Mrs Spencer Curwen was one of the judges. Members of choirs who read by the Tonic Sol-fa method were provided with individual copies for the sight-reading test while the 'Hullahists' had to read the piece from a blackboard, 'which many of them could see but indifferently'. Ibid., p. 333.

61   In an address delivered by the Archbishop of Dublin at the St Cecilian Festival in November 1893 where choir competition winners

sang, he praised the pupils and those 'enlightened teachers' who 'instinctively saw the advance that could not fail to be made if they introduced into their schools that one truly scientific system of musical instruction. . . . I mean of course that which is known as the Tonic Solfa system'. *Appendix to the Sixtieth Report* (1893), p. 335.

62 *Sixtieth Report* (1893), p. 334.

63 *Seventy-Second Report* (1905), p. 195. The nature of the event changed in 1897 when it became a public examination. One writer in *The Irish Musical Monthly* noted that, after that transition, participants from large schools (and especially convents) decreased and more small schools came forward. 'Vocal Music in the Dublin Schools', *The Irish Musical Monthly* 1 (August 1902), 61. *The Irish Musical Monthly* was issued between March 1902 and February 1903. Edited by Revd H. Bewerunge, it was 'A Journal devoted to the Interests of Music in Church and School', 1 (March 1902). It had similar objectives to that of the nineteenth-century journal, *Lyra Ecclesiastica*.

64 For example, the three winning choirs of the 1893 Dublin Singing Competition were chosen to perform the 'Mass of the Vatican Council' for the festival in Francis Xavier Church in November of that year.

65 *Sixty-Second Report* (1895), p. 312.

66 *Fifty-Fourth Report* (1887), p. 242.

67 Peter Goodman, *The Catholic Hymn-Book* (Dublin: J. Duffy and Sons, n. d. [*c.* 1886]). Goodman's promotion of Catholic hymns in the National School system was carried out in conjunction with his promotion of the Tonic Sol-fa system. In Sleith's appraisal of Goodman in 1915, he stated: 'The personality and popularity of the late Mr P. Goodman, one of its [Tonic Sol-fa's] chief exponents, helped very much to develop the system through the country'. 'Music in the Schools', 1346. Goodman's publication was described by the author of 'New Music', in *Lyra Ecclesiastica* 7 (1 June 1886), 66. For further description of Goodman's work in church and school music education, see Kieran A. Daly, *Catholic Church Music in Ireland, 1878–1903*.

68 Numerous references to the excellence of music instruction in convent schools were made by board inspectors. The 'School Examiners' Reports' in the *Christian Brothers Educational Record* of the 1890s show that the Brothers' philosophy for music education remained the same with emphasis placed on 'conveying sound moral, and

religious instruction'. J. F. R., 'Schools Examiners' Reports', *Christian Brothers Educational Record* 2 (1892–94), 336.

69 In reference to Dublin children, Newell observed: 'The children in this district, especially in the city, are extremely musical. Singing is taught in a large number of schools and generally with success'. *Forty-Seventh Report* (1880), pp. 83–4. This observation was reinforced in 1883 when he stated: '*Singing* is almost entirely confined to the city and suburban schools. The Dublin children have excellent ears'. *Fiftieth Report* (1883), p. 220. The pupils of Cork city were also assessed favourably as 'quite as good as the Dublin children'. *Fifty-Sixth Report* (1889), p. 70.

70 *Appendix to Sixtieth Report* (1893), p. 334.

71 *Appendix to Sixty-First Report* (1894), p. 210.

72 *Fifty-Sixth Report* (1889), p. 137.

73 Commenting on Downpatrick schools, Inspector Roantree stated that, with the exception of one or two schools, 'singing is as harsh and rude as can well be imagined; and the attempts that have been made at singing in parts have in most instances proved failures'. *Appendix to Forty-Third Report* (1876), p. 72. Inspector Kelly was more conservative in his evaluation of the perceived nonmusical nature of Down people when he stated that 'the predominance of the drum in Ulster may account to some extent for the lack of musical culture'. *Sixth-Fifth Report* (1898), p. 146. Identification of the Ulster drum with the politics of the Orange tradition and with religion brought music education into these domains also.

74 *Sixty-Sixth Report* (1899), p. 193.

75 Educational movements in Europe and America influenced reform in Irish education at the turn of the century – the Practical Educationists, the Social Reformers, the Naturalists, the Herbartians, the Scientific Educationists, and the Moral Educationists. R. J. W. Selleck, *The New Education 1870–1914* (London and Melbourne: Pitman and Sons Ltd., 1968), pp. 102–238.

76 Ibid., xviii.

77 One of the primary catalysts for change was the *Final Report of the Commission on Manual and Practical Instruction* in 1899. The report highlighted the weaknesses of music in national education. Another stimulus for change came from a survey of music in foreign educational systems. Goodman reported: 'In requiring that Vocal Music shall form a subject of instruction in all their schools, the Commissioners only repeat what is prescribed in the programmes of

elementary schools throughout the whole civilised world.' *Sixty-Eighth Report* (1901), p. 147.

78   *Reports of the Commissioners of National Education.*

79   Between 1900 and 1904, 168 teachers' classes were held, attended by about 6,400 teachers, nearly equally distributed over all parts of Ireland.

80   Peter Goodman stated: 'It is in such schools – small schools with one teacher only, in out-of-the-way places – that the brightening, gladdening influence of music is most needed. And as such schools form the majority of the Schools of Ireland, I felt that we could not give them too much attention'. *Seventy-First Report* (1904), p. 4. Ibid., p. 129.

81   *Appendix to Sixty-Seventh Report* (1900), pp. 90–1.

82   Joseph Sleith asked: 'Is music a *real* thing? Is it a personal possession – a feeling of our own which we can use at will to cheer or sadden ourselves and our friends as we desire? Is it a national asset infecting a nation, moving us to great things and mighty efforts, as all good music should do if we properly felt it?' 'Music in the Schools', 1346. Inspector Hollins criticised the music teaching he saw in Limerick schools around 1910 as 'lifeless and inefficient. The same modulator exercises are repeated day after day *ad nauseum*, the songs are sung in an uninterested, lifeless manner, without due attention to time'. *Seventy-Seventh Report* (1910–11), p. 101.

83   In Limerick schools, for example, Inspector Hollins reported that a number of students in most schools 'are spoken of as non-singers, and apparently content to be so regarded, sit for the half-hour period, disregarded by the teacher, and without an effort to improve themselves'. Ibid. A similar evaluation was made in the following year in the Omagh district, where the greater proportion of pupils in country schools, especially boys, 'can't sing'. Ibid., p. 173. In the following year, Inspector Gorman found many 'non-singers' in rural districts while music education in towns and cities was reported as satisfactory. *Seventy-Eighth Report* (1911–12), p. 42.

84   Ibid., p. 86.

85   *Fifty-Fourth Report* (1887), p. 69.

86   *Fifty-Eighth Report* (1891), p. 322.

87   *Annual Reports of the National Commissioners.*

88   Eibhlín Ní Niocaill identified the role of education in preserving nationality – 'the permanent identity of a people, what constitutes the past, the present, and the future generations into a historical

unity'. 'Nationality in Irish Education', *Irisleabhar na Gaedhilge* 19 (19 Meitheamh 1909), 258.

89   Ibid., 260.

90   'Notes', *Journal of the Ivernian Society* 2 (October 1909), 124. Authors for the *Journal of the Ivernian Society* (1908 to 1915 in particular) maintained a lively discourse on the progress of Irish music and the role of music in the primary and secondary education systems.

91   *Appendix to Sixty-Seventh Report* (1900), p. 76.

92   'Circular to Training Colleges – Music', *Irish School Weekly* 36 (6 December 1902), 10.

93   Evidence suggests that British hegemony in Irish culture was on the decline. The return visit of Queen Victoria in April, 1900, provided insight into schools' loyalty to the crown. During her 1849 visit fifty years previously, her contact with children was limited to the metropolitan centres of Dublin and Cork. In 1900, however, a nationwide scheme was organised by the Commissioners of National Education to bring children to the Phoenix Park, Dublin, to greet the queen and to sing 'God Save the Queen'. In return, they would receive a breakfast. This scheme was met with little positive response. Michael Mc Carthy, *Five Years in Ireland* (Dublin: Hodges; London: Simpkin, 1902), p. 494.

94   Goodman selected and arranged thirty songs. His publication was sanctioned by the Commissioners of National Education. A native Irish stamp was evident from the first song 'Go Raibh Éire Ceolmhar Arís' (may Ireland be musical again). He did not include Anglo-Irish political ballads but some of Moore's *Irish Melodies* and six songs in the Irish language. Also included were airs from the Petrie, Joyce, and Horncastle collections.

95   Fr Patrick Walsh [An tAthair Pádraig Breathnach], comp., *Fuinn na Smól* (Dublin: Brown and Nolan, 1913); *Songs of the Gael* (Dublin: Browne and Nolan, 1915).

96   Other articles in the *School Music Review* dealing with the topic of folk-song in education included, 'The Choice of Songs for Schools', 11 (1 February 1903), 162; 'The School Music Situation: Mr A. L. Cowley', 12 (1 November 1903), 148–150, 160; 'Folksongitis', 12 (1 November 1903), 105; 'Folk Songs for Schools', 12 (1 March 1904), 185–6; 'When is a Folk-Song not a Folk-Song?' 15 (1 June 1906), 1; 'Mr Cecil Sharp on "Folk-Songs for Schools"', 15 (1 June 1906), 3–5.

97   Séamus Ó Casaide, 'Father Walsh's Irish Song Books', *The Irish Book Lover* 7 (September 1915), 33.

98   Following is a list of collections and the year they were advertised. *An Ceoltóir* (1903), *The Educational Songster* (1912), *Song and Play for Infants* (1914), *The Harmony Songster* (1914), *Patriotic School Songs* (1914), *Songs of Our Land* (1915), *Songs of Our Home and Country* (1914), *Dia Linn Lá 'Gus Oidhche* (1917), *Raint Amhrán* (1917), *An Craoibhín Ceoil* (1920).

99   *Dia Linn Lá 'Gus Oidhche 's Pádraig Aspal Éireann* (Baile Átha Cliath: Brún agus Ó Nualláin Teor., 1917). Issued by the Columbian League, it was a collection of eight hymns in the Irish language.

100   Patrick Shea, 'Sounds of Thunder', from *Voices and the Sound of Drums*, in *An Irish Childhood*, ed. by A. Norman Jeffares and Antony Kamm (London: Collins Sons and Co. Ltd., 1987), p. 24.

101   Paddy Crosbie, *Your Dinner's Poured Out* (Dublin: The O'Brien Press, 1981), p. 31.

102   Music instruction included choral singing in Irish and English for all pupils and optional instrumental music (harp, violin, piano or pipes) and a special course in solo singing. By 1909, a piper was employed at the school. Irish dances or *Céilí* took place regularly. An operetta composed by Pearse, *Mac-Ghníomhartha Chúchulainn*, had its thematic roots in Irish heroic tales and used Irish language choral pieces with original Irish airs. *An Macaomh: St Enda's School Journal* II (May 1913).

103   The school's annals of 1910 reported that the pupils 'marched, eighty-five strong, in the Language Procession behind our piper and banner'. Ibid., 75.

104   'Irish National Teachers Organisation Congress: An Influential Gathering', *Irish School Weekly* 61 (6 and 13 May 1916), 453.

105   'Memorandum on Suggested Changes in Present School Programmes', *Irish School Weekly* 63 (3 March 1917), 122.

106   'A New Song', *Irish School Weekly* (3 October 1914), 714.

107   *Seventy-Third Report* (1906–07), p. 165. Advertisements in the *Irish School Weekly* attested to the demand for materials appropriate for concerts.

108   For a detailed description of the Maidstone Movement in Britain and its introduction into American education, see Robin K. Deverich, 'The Maidstone Movement – Influential British Precursor of American Public School Instrumental Classes', *Journal of Research in Music Education* 35 (Spring 1987), 39–55.

109 Headmaster of a London School, 'Organising and Maintaining a "Maidstone" Violin Class', *Irish School Weekly* 14 (11 July 1908), 687–88. In the *Irish School Weekly* of July and October, 1908, this method was promoted. A London headmaster described in detail the organisation and maintenance of a 'Maidstone' violin class. See also *Irish School Weekly* 14 (3 October 1908), 225; ibid., (31 October 1908), 348.

110 'Foireann Cheoil: Scoil na mBan Riaghalta, Béal Eas, Co. Mhuigh Eo', *Irisleabhar na Gaedhilge* 13 (July 1903), 345.

111 Sr. Elizabeth, Sisters of Charity, Foxford, Co. Mayo, to writer, August 30, 1988. See also Revd T. A. Finlay, *Foxford and the Providence Woollen Mills* (Dublin: Alex Thom and Co. Ltd., n. d.), p. 26.

112 'The Buttevant School Band', *Irish School Weekly* 57 (11 July 1914), 430.

113 Sr. M. Oliver, Convent of Mercy, Buttevant, to writer, 13 January, 1990.

114 Coolahan, *Irish Education*, p. 52. Diocescan schools such as St Patrick's College, Carlow, St Kieran's College, Kilkenny, and Thurles College, acted as seminaries for the training of Catholic clergy. Other colleges – Clongowes Wood (1814) and Tullabeg (1816) – were founded by the Jesuits. Catholic religious sisters provided for the education of girls while the Church of Ireland provided for its members. Any efforts to develop secondary education on the mixed-denominational principle met with opposition by the various churches.

115 Ibid., p. 53. At St Kieran's College, Kilkenny, 'in addition to the core curriculum of classical, English, scientific and mercentile education, religious practice, music, singing, dancing, drill and fencing were part of the general activity of the school'. Dr Peter Birch, *St Kieran's College, Kilkenny* (Dublin: Gill, 1951), p. 155. Maurice Hime, Headmaster of Foyle College, Londonderry, believed that 'Classics, . . . with or without music and drawing, are quite as much as any schoolboy, unless gifted with a peculiarly strong mind and a peculiarly strong body, ought to be asked to learn'. *A Schoolmaster's Retrospect of Eighteen and a Half Years in an Irish School* (London: Simpkin, Marshall, and Co., 1885), p. 21.

116 Cited in T. J. Mc Elligott, *Secondary Education in Ireland, 1870–1921* (Dublin: Irish Academic Press, 1981), p. 8.

117 'College Academies', *Carlow College Magazine* 1 (1869–70), 406–8.

118 T., 'On the Cultivation of Music in Ireland', 624.

119 For example, Alexandra College, Dublin, 'a most highly thought of seminary for the daughters of the gentry and superior tradesmen of Dublin', developed a music curriculum that was modelled on the contemporary English high school and reproduced the musical values of 'high culture'. Anne O'Connor and Susan Parkes, *Gladly Learn and Gladly Teach: Alexandra College and School, 1866–1966* (Dublin: Blackwater Press, 1983), p. 25.

120 Intermediate Education Board (Ireland), *Rules and Programme of Examinations for the year 1880*, p. 3 (hereafter cited as *Rules and Programme for [year]*).

121 At the meeting of 7 December, 1878, the following scale of marks was sanctioned: Greek, Latin, English – 1,000 marks; French – 700 marks; Music and Drawing – 500 marks; Italian and German – 500 marks; Celtic – 600 marks. None of the science subjects reached 500 marks. In monetary terms, music was worth half the price of English and equal to the price paid for Italian or drawing. Intermediate Education (Ireland), *Minutes of the Proceedings of the Commissioners Meetings,* vol. 1 (1878–1886), pp. 6–7 (hereafter cited as *Minutes of the Proceedings for [year]*).

122 When the Intermediate Board of Education was established, the Board of the RIAM submitted a memorandum to the government on the place of music in education and they offered their cooperation in directing music within the system. Their offer was accepted. W. J. M. Starkie, 'The Royal Irish Academy of Music', in *Music in Ireland*, p. 107. Links between the Commissioners of National Education and the RIAM were already in place since Sir Patrick Keenan, resident Commissioner of National Education, was on the Board of the Academy.

123 *Rules and Programme for 1880*, p. 18, p. 25, p. 32.

124 *Rules and Regulations for 1882*, p. 13, p. 18, p. 22.

125 The attitude to music instruction in the RIAM captured the thinking of the day. 'A class for ladies in violin playing was started in 1878, with Herr Lauer as the professor, since the Council believed the violin to be admirably adapted for female performance'. Starkie, 'The Royal Irish Academy', p. 107. A similar but more democratic agenda was evident in the founding of the Dublin Municipal School of Music which was to serve 'the sons and daughters of respectable Irish parents, possessing natural talent, who may be taught and instructed in instrumental music, and particularly on the piano'. J. Cooke, Coláiste an Cheoil, p. 2.

126   The report on music in 1882 stated that 'the answering, on the whole, was fairly satisfactory in the case of girls; the examiners complain that the boys were badly prepared'. *Report of the Intermediate Board* (1882), vii.

127   *Minutes of the Proceedings*, vol. II (1886–1893), p. 153.

128   'Some Remarks on the "Theory of Music" Papers Set at the Intermediate Education Examination, 1902', *Irish Musical Monthly* 1 (1 August 1902), 65.

129   T. O. Russell, 'Our Irish Music: What is to be Its Future?' *Evening Telegraph* 8 September 1894, 8.

130   *Final Report of the Commissioners on Intermediate Education, 1899*, p. 22.

131   *Minutes of the Proceedings* (1901–02), p. 136, p. 190. See also *The Irish Musical Monthly* 1 (May 1902), 34–5; and the *Journal of the Incorporated Society of Musicians* (1 April 1902), pp. 82–3. Already in the report of the Palles Commission in 1899, the Leinster Branch of the Incorporated Society of Musicians had commented on the fact that: 'There is no provision whatsoever for practical examinations in Vocal or Instrumental Music. In our opinion this constitutes the most serious defect in the system.' *Final Report of the Commissioners on Intermediate Education* (1899), p. 190.

132   H. C. Colles, *The Royal College of Music, 1883–1933* (London: Macmillan and Co. Ltd., 1933), p. 21. The formation of the Associated Board of the Royal Academy of Music and the Royal College of Music in London in 1889 focused music instruction on graded examinations.

133   Ibid. The RIAM was not the only examining body interested in setting up an alliance with the Intermediate Education Board. A competing body of examiners, the Leinster Branch of the Incorporated Society of Musicians, were also in correspondence with the board. *Minutes of the Proceedings* (1903), p. 385.

134   This society, at first called the Society of Professional Musicians, was founded in Britain in 1882. Centres were established in Dublin, Belfast, and Cork, which became known as the Leinster, Ulster, and Munster branches, respectively. Fleischmann, 'The Organisation of the Profession', in *Music in Ireland*, pp. 77–8. It is noteworthy that the secretary of the Leinster branch of the Society, T. R. Jozé, had been examiner in music theory with the Intermediate Board in former years.

135   Fr Finlay, a member of the Board's Music Committee, suggested designing honours and pass courses with the honours course catering

for those intending to pursue music professionally, and a pass course having a minimum theory component and a strong practical orientation. In 1919 this recommendation was implemented.

136   One observer described them as 'the greatest absurdity' in a programme that is rife with 'confusion and incongruities'. In his opinion, those who constructed the tests seemed to have one desire only, namely, to puzzle and discourage the children. Theo Gmur, 'The Choral Singing in Our Schools: The Intermediate System', *Journal of the Ivernian Society* 5 (October-December 1912), 35.

137   *Minutes of the Proceedings* (1912), p. 1435.

138   *Minutes of the Proceedings* (1916–1918), p. 7.

139   In 1888 The Revd Heinrich Bewerunge became professor of sacred music at St Patrick's College, Maynooth, and remained in that position until 1923. A lectureship in music was created at University College, Cork, in 1906 and it was converted into a professorship in 1908. Frederick St John Lacy held the position between 1906 and 1934. At University College, Dublin, a part-time chair of music was created in 1913 and held by The Revd Heinrich Bewerunge (1914–16), Charles Kitson (1916–20), followed by John Larchet; in addition a Dublin Corporation part-time professorship of Irish music was created in 1913 and first held by Robert O'Dwyer (1914–1939). *Music in Ireland*, pp. 23–9.

140   Gmur, 'The Choral Singing', 37.

141   'Intermediate Education', *The Irish Year Book* (1908), p. 214.

142   The following is a selection from this list: 'Echoes', by A. S. Sullivan; 'A Message from the Sea', by W. Griffiths; 'Now the Golden Morn', by Sir J. Stainer; 'A Canadian Boat Song', by T. Moore, and 'Glorious Apollo', by S. Webbe. *Minutes of the Proceedings* (1907–1909), p. 1040.

143   *Minutes of the Proceedings* (1916–1919).

144   *Rules and Programme for 1904*, p. 7.

145   *Annual Reports*, 1905–1916. In 1905, five girls' choirs and three orchestras, no boys groups; in 1907, ten girls' choirs and seven orchestras, two boys' choirs and one orchestra; in 1912, three girls' choirs and no orchestra, five boys' choirs and one orchestra; by 1916, two girls' choirs and no orchestra, three boys' choirs and one orchestra.

146   Brendan Rogers, 'Music in Our Intermediate Schools and Its Effects on Public and Ecclesiastical Taste', *Lyra Ecclesiastica* 2–3 (1880–81), 6–8; 66–8; 84–6.

147 Robert Lynd, *Home Life in Ireland* (London: Mills and Boon, Ltd., 1909), p. 102.

148 Reported in the *London Times* (April 1887), cited in Carroll, 'A History of Elementary Education in Kerry, 1700–1870', p. 167.

149 The argument that music was an élitist subject in intermediate education is based on the small, select group of student participants at music examinations, the perception of musical ability as synonymous with theoretical proficiency, and the narrow repertoire used in the music curriculum.

150 Richard Henebry, *A Handbook of Irish Music* (Cork: Cork University Press, 1928), p. 57.

151 Hardebeck, 'Traditional Singing', 93.

152 Bewerunge, 'The Special Charm of Irish Melodies Sung "Traditionally"', a paper delivered before St Mary's Literary Society, Maynooth College, *Irish Ecclesiastical Record*, 4th series 8 (July–December 1900), 140, 152–3.

153 Ibid., 140.

154 Breandán Breathnach, 'The Use of Notation in the Transmission of Irish Folk Music', Ó Riada Memorial Lecture I (University College, Cork: Irish Traditional Music Society, 1986), p. 4.

155 Ibid., p. 3.

156 O'Keeffe, a native of Sliabh Luachra in Co. Kerry, is regarded as one of the great fiddle masters. He trained as a national school teacher in Dublin and read both Tonic Sol-fa and staff notations. After a short teaching career in national schools, he concentrated on teaching and playing the fiddle. One of his pupils, Julia Clifford, described his routine in the 1920s. She reported that besides teaching some pupils at his own house on Sundays, he used 'to walk the roads and tracks of the area, perhaps travelling 20 or 30 miles a day, calling at the farms and houses where he gave lessons on the fiddle'. Since O'Keeffe taught so many pupils and their lessons may have been irregularly scheduled, he was forced to devise an easy code to help them recall the tunes he taught them. Clifford stated that O'Keeffe 'was always in a hurry. He used to just write the tune for me in his own code and I'd learn it'. His code was a system of tablature on the staff which illustrated graphically how a tune was to be played on the fiddle. Alan Ward, 'Music from Sliabh Luachra', *Traditional Music* 5 (1976), 11.

157 A second example of an indigenous system of notation was devised by Bartly McMagh, a fiddler from Newtownsaville, Co. Tyrone, to teach his own children. Only three lines were used to represent the

D, A, and E strings. This was sufficient as the tunes being taught did not extend to the G string. The music was divided into bars with little indication of duration of notes other than a tie to represent the first two notes of the triplets of quavers in jig time. Breathnach, 'The Use of Notation', p. 7.

158   Ward, 'Music from Sliabh Luachra', 8.

159   D. L., 'The Music of the Home in Kickham's Country', *The Irish Monthly* 59 (November 1931), 723.

160   Breathnach, 'The Use of Notation', 7.

161   D. L., 'The Music of the Home', 723.

162   Cited in Ward, 'Music from Sliabh Luachra', 7.

163   Ibid., 9.

164   John O' Donoghue, *In a Quiet Land* (London: B. T. Batsford Ltd., 1957), pp. 197–8.

165   Ibid., p. 199.

166   Robert O'Dwyer, 'The Modern Aspect of Irish Music', *The Irish Year Book* (1908), 252.

167   Seán Donnelly, Dublin, to author, November 13, 1997.

168   'Best performance on the Union Pipes by a Learner. Prize, a Gold Medal; presented by the Pipers' Conference. Open to all learners of the Union Pipes.' Donnchadh Ó Súilleabháin, 'Cumann na bPíobairí', *Treoir* 13 (1981), 35.

169   In a letter to the Gaelic League's journal *An Claidheamh Soluis* in 1904, Kent pointed out that due to the club's educational scheme, for the first time Dublin residents had the opportunity of acquiring the genuine style of traditional singing. Cited in Ó Súilleabháin, 35.

170   Jacques Attali, *Noise: The Political Economy of Music,* trans. by Brian Massumi (Minneapolis: University of Minnesota Press, 1985), p. 19.

Notes to Chapter 5

1   Francis Stewart, quoted in 'Eighty years with the storm troops of life', *The Sunday Press*, 18 April 1982, 23.

2   The religious composition of the Irish Free State changed drastically, reducing the size of the Protestant minority from approximately 25 to 6 per cent. This minority population was replaced by 'an increasingly self-confident and somewhat triumphalist Catholic culture'. Garrett Fitzgerald, 'Ireland's Identity Problems', *Études Irlandaises* 1 (December 1976), 138. In addition, 61 per cent of the

population lived outside towns and villages. Terence Brown, *Ireland: A Social and Cultural History,* p. 18.

3   Ernest Gellner, *Nationalism,* p. 45, p. 68.

4   Margaret O'Callaghan, 'Language, Nationality and Cultural Identity in the Irish Free State, 1922–7', *Irish Historical Studies* 24 (November 1984), 244.

5   Clifford Geertz, *The Interpretation of Cultures,* pp. 240–1.

6   Two articles written by Fr Corcoran a decade apart, 1923 and 1933, indicated his consistent philosophy for the union of music, language, and religion in education. T. Corcoran, 'Music and Language in Irish Schools', *The Irish Monthly* 51 (July 1923), 338–40; 'National Literature Through National Music', *The Irish Monthly* 61 (July 1933), 410–12. A similar link between language and Irish song was made by Elizabeth O'Boyle who looked to the Jesuit school of the Renaissance and adopted its model of language contests as an examplar for song contests to improve the Irish language and to propagate Irish song. Having described the 'noble singers' of the past and the rich heritage of Irish song, she stated that the answer to the contemporary musical 'silence' of the country was with 'the schools of Ireland, manned to-day and piloted by those who in religious and racial tradition descend directly from the masters of the great ancient schools'. In 'Irish Song Schools: A Memory and a Hope', *The Irish Monthly* 59 (April 1931), 225.

7   Brown, *Ireland: A Social and Cultural History,* p. 146.

8   Fr Corcoran quoted from a speech given by Sir Richard Terry in the late 1920s, stating that in Ireland, the plain chant movement to restore 'that *musica perenni'* had achieved results not equalled, not even approached, in any other European country. T. Corcoran, 'An Issue Concerning Music', *The Irish Monthly* 61 (June 1933), 338. See also Hubert Rooney, 'The Plainchant Movement', in *Music in Ireland,* pp. 219–21.

9   At Templenoe, four miles from Kenmare, a choir started in 1939 consisted of boys (aged eight to fourteen) from the parish school and men from the community. 'The true liturgical spirit was there, and the known wishes of the Holy Father as regards the formation of a Plain Chant Choir were kept steadily in mind.' J. P. Boland, 'Plain Chant in a Kerry Country Church', *The Irish Monthly* 79 (October 1951), 446.

10   Fintan O'Toole, *The Ex-Isle of Erin: Images of a Global Ireland* (Dublin: New Island Books, 1996), p. 99. *The Capuchin Annual* (1930–77) featured the arts, and heightened awareness and knowledge of Irish art

forms including music. Brian P. Kennedy, *Dreams and Responsibilities: The State and the Arts in Independent Ireland* (Dublin: The Arts Council, 1990), p. 35.

11 McKim Marriott explored cultural policy in new states and observed that whoever commands mass communications 'cannot avoid taking decisions and choosing among alternatives that shape cultural development'. 'Cultural Policy in the New States' in *Old Societies and New States*, ed. Clifford Geertz (New York: The Free Press, 1963), p. 29.

12 Luke Gibbons, *Transformations in Irish Culture* (Cork: Cork University Press in association with Field Day, 1996), p. 75.

13 Pádraig Ó Fearaíl, *The Story of Conradh na Gaeilge* (Baile Átha Cliath: Clódhanna Teo., 1975), p. 47.

14 Gibbons, *Transformations in Irish Culture*, p. 75.

15 Other organisations included the Dublin Musical Association of Ireland (1939), The Musicians' Guild of the Writers, Actors, Artists, and Musicians Association (1941), and The Irish Federation of Musicians (1944).

16 *The Music Association of Ireland*, ed. by Edgar Deale (Dublin: The Irish and Overseas Publishing Co., Ltd., 1957), pp. 3–4.

17 'Atavism', the renewed manifestation of heredity after remaining latent during one or more generations. Fleischmann used the term in the sense of 'ancestor-worship' in 'Composition and the Folk Idiom', *Ireland Today* (November 1936), 38.

18 Aloys Fleischmann, 'Ars Nova: Irish Music in the Shaping', *Ireland Today* 1 (July 1936), 45.

19 Seán Neeson, 'When Gaelic Tunes are Whistled in the Streets', *The Irish Press* (12 April 1935), 8.

20 Cited in Brown, *Ireland: A Social and Cultural History*, p. 147.

21 John F. Larchet, 'A Plea for Music', in *the Voice of Ireland*, ed. by William G. Fitzgerald (Dublin, Manchester, London, and Blackburn: John Heywood Ltd., 1924 [?]), p. 511.

22 Frederick May, 'Music and the Nation', *Dublin Magazine* 6 (July-September 1936), 53–5.

23 For example, in John O'Conor's contribution to The Thomas Davis Lecture Series in 1998, he presented a case for the establishment of an Irish Academy for the Performing Arts. 'Towards a New Academy', in *Music in Ireland 1848–1998*, ed. by Richard Pine (Cork and Dublin: Mercier Press, 1998), pp. 140–48.

24 Eamonn O Gallchobhair, 'Music: Academies and Professors', *Ireland Today* 2 (March 3, 1937), 63–5.

25 Robert O'Dwyer continued as Dublin Corporation professor of Irish folk music at University College, Dublin, until 1926 when the Dublin Corporation grant was discontinued. O'Dwyer continued in a college professorship of Irish Music from 1928 to 1939 when a lecturership position in Irish music was filled by Colm Ó Lochlainn. A Department of Irish Folk Music was founded in 1951 and directed by Donal O'Sullivan. At University College, Cork, a professorship of Irish music was established in 1922 by Cork Corporation and filled by Carl Hardebeck; this position was changed to a lectureship in 1923 and taken over by Annie Patterson, followed by Seán Neeson in 1933.

26 Larchet, 'A Plea for Music', p. 509.

27 As this period progressed, the monopoly of the Irish language movement over music in education, and the use of the Tonic Sol-fa system were cited as reasons for the low standard of music in schools and subsequently in the culture at large. At the opening of a teachers' summer music course at University College, Cork, in 1939, Fleischmann was reported as stating that the contemporary system of teaching Tonic Sol-fa in the schools was to a large extent to blame for the depressed condition of music in the country. At the same meeting, Larchet 'thought it possible that the British had imposed the Tonic Sol-fa system on this country as part of a well-designed plan to prevent our children from being educated in Music'. 'Organisation Jottings', *Irish School Weekly* 41 (22 July 1939), 695. In 1958 Landers observed that 'the chances of school-work in music having any long-term effect in making the country musical are diminished by a number of impediments. The principal one is the adherence to the tonic sol-fa notation'. T. A. Landers, 'Music for the Juniors', *An Múinteoir Náisiúnta* 3 (1958), 23.

28 Denis Breen, 'School-Music: Its Place in the National Life', *The Irish School Weekly* 77 (1 May 1926), 558.

29 Ibid., (15 May 1926), 620.

30 Joseph Ryan, 'Nationalism and Music in Ireland', p. 460.

31 Brian P. Kennedy, *Dreams and Responsibilities*, p. 30.

32 A leading figure in Irish music in independent Ireland, John Larchet deserves special consideration. He was a composer, professor, and scholar, and he advanced national music education in a variety of ways. In December, 1923, the Department of Education invited him

to be director of examinations in music and he continued to fill that post until 1948. As professor of music at University College, Dublin, he established his subject as a university discipline in the newly founded Irish state. He was also professor of composition at the RIAM and an inspirational figure in the foundation and advancement of an Irish school of composition. The *New Grove Dictionary of Music and Musicians*, s. v. 'John Larchet'.

33 Aloys Fleischmann studied music abroad and returned to his native Cork in 1934. He was professor of music at University College, Cork, from 1934 to 1980. As composer, educator, conductor, and music scholar, he has made a significant contribution to music in Ireland. *The New Grove Dictionary of Music and Musicians*, s. v. 'Aloys Fleischmann'.

34 Aloys Fleischmann, 'The Outlook of Music in Ireland', *Studies* 24 (March 1935), 122, 123.

35 Thomas Bodkin, *Report on the Arts in Ireland* (Dublin: The Stationery Office, 1949).

36 Cited in Bruce Arnold, 'Politics and the Arts in Ireland – the Dáil Debates', in *Unequal Achievement: The Irish Experience 1957–1982*, ed. by Frank Litton (Dublin: Institute of Public Administration, 1982), p. 285.

37 A fifth, although less significant, event in 1951 was the publication of *Music World*, claimed to be the first Irish magazine devoted exclusively to music. Its first issue of May–June 1951 stated that the lack of such a publication 'has impeded the development of the art of music, the proper appreciation of music by the public and the propagation of a wider general interest in the subject, so important to the development of the cultural life of a nation', p. 1.

38 Dinah Molloy, *Find Your Music*, 2d ed. (Dublin: The Arts Council, 1979), p. 162.

39 Joseph Groocock, *A General Survey of Music in the Republic of Ireland* (Dublin: Foras Éireann, 1961), p. 9. This survey was begun in 1957 and published in 1961. In the introduction to the published report, the Chairman of Foras Éireann stated that it was 'the first step in a campaign to revitalise music in Ireland'. p. 1.

40 Brown, *Ireland: A Social and Cultural History*, p. 249.

41 *Minutes of the Proceedings of the Commissioners of National Education at their Special Meeting on Tuesday, the 31st January, 1922*, pp. 2–3.

42 A Divisional Inspector in the mid-1920s argued that the teaching of Irish did not provide fully 'for all national desiderata in education'.

He asked for 'some more direct call to awaken the feelings of our people to a sense and appreciation of their national heritage'. An Roinn Oideachais, *Report of the Department of Education for the School Years 1925–26–27 and the Financial and Administrative Year, 1926–27*, p. 26.

43 Michael Tierney, *Education in a Free Ireland* (Dublin: Martin Lester Ltd., 1919), p. 46.

44 National Programme Conference, *National Programme of Primary Instruction* (1922), p. 14. In a second report issued in 1926, it was again recommended that 'as a general rule, all the songs taught through the course should be in Irish, especially in the lower standards'. *Report and Programme of Second National Conference* (1926), p. 42. The progress of the Irish language in schools seemed to be a preoccupation of the 1920s, evident in a caption in *The Teacher's Work* in 1927, 'To Our Language through Our Music'. *The Teacher's Work* 18 (November 1927), 119.

45 'Report on Annual Congress', *Irish School Weekly* 34 (April 2, 1932), 368.

46 A variety of sources provided evidence. For example, 'A New Song for Schools', advertised in *The Irish School Weekly* in 1950, brought the cause of the language to the heart of the music lesson. Its title was, 'O Labhraimís Gaeilge', (O, let us speak Irish). It was set to the tune of 'Bonnie Dundee', revealing that the use of an Irish melody was not vital to the cause of the language revival. 'A New Song for Schools', *The Irish School Weekly* 52 (28 October and 4 November 1950), 470. An example of a teachers' summer course further illustrated the intensity with which all curriculum subjects were made subservient to the Irish language. One of the courses advertised for teachers in 1951 was titled 'The teaching of Irish through music, art, and other activities'. *The Irish School Weekly* 53 (26 May and 2 June 1951), 259.

47 The programme recommended that 'in Junior Standards as a rule only Irish songs should be taught', while in senior classes, part songs and good arrangements of Irish tunes should be introduced. An Roinn Oideachais, *Programme of Primary Instruction* (1956), p. 16.

48 Denis Breen [Donnchadh Ó Braoin], 'School-Music – Its Place in the National Life', *Irish School Weekly* 77 (15 May 1926), 622.

49 An Roinn Oideachais, *Report of 1929–30*, p. 38; *Report of 1930–31*, p. 22; *Report of 1932–33*, p. 26. When a New Music Programme was introduced in 1939, the Kerry Co. Committee of the INTO

condemned it as something far beyond the capabilities of pupils and teachers. The teaching of Irish language songs was not a musical process, they claimed, since the words presented such an obstacle that music learning was 'less a pleasure than a strain'. 'The New Music Programme', *Irish School Weekly* 41 (28 October 1939), 1014.

50   All official documents on music were conceived in terms of spreading the language. In 1933, for example, a fifteen-page booklet, *Téarmaí Ceoil* [musical terms], was issued by the Department of Education for teacher's use in teaching music through the Irish language.

51   An Roinn Oideachais, *Report of 1929–30*, p. 29.

52   *Report and Programme of Second National Programme Conference* (1926), p. 42; *Programme of Primary Instruction* (1956), p. 16.

53   An Roinn Oideachais, *Notes for Teachers: Music* (1959), p. 31.

54   'Irish Dancing Commission', *The Teacher's Work* 24 (June 1934), 343.

55   *A Ballad History of Ireland for Schools*, ed. and sel. by Pádraig Ó Dálaigh (Dublin and Cork: The Educational Company of Ireland, n. d.), preface. It is likely that this book was published in the late 1920s, since Ó Dálaigh makes reference to Davis's work in the 1840s as 'some eighty years ago'.

56   Liam Redmond, 'Our History in Story and Ballad', *Irish School Weekly* 42 (12 October 1940), 764.

57   'Roscommon Music Conference', *The Irish School Weekly* 42 (22 June 1940), 495.

58   *Ceol na nGaedheal*, ed. by Carl Hardebeck (Baile Átha Cliath: Brún agus Ó Nualláin, Teor., 1937), p. 6.

59   Anna Kelly, 'The Whistlers of Garryhill', *Irish Press*, 12 November 1949, 3.

60   Summer schools teaching plain chant continued into the 1940s, held at University College, Cork, in 1938; at Mount Anville Convent, Dublin, in 1940; and at the Royal Irish Academy of Music, Dublin, in 1941. The curriculum of the RIAM course covered 'the knowledge necessary for teaching the chant in schools, with particular reference to the Bishop's Programme'. Advertisement in the *Irish School Weekly* 43, 21 June 1941, 433.

61   Rooney, 'The Plainchant Movement', in *Music in Ireland*, p. 219. At the Limerick Liturgical Festival in June, 1942, for example, 2,000 children sang the Common of the Mass while a selected convent-school choir sang the Proper. '2,000 Children In Plain Chant Festival', *Irish Press*, 1 June 1942, 3.

62 *31st International Eucharistic Congress: Pictorial Record* (Dublin: Veritas Co. Ltd., 1933), p. 156.

63 *Eucharistic Congress Hymn Book* (Dublin: Juverna Press Ltd., 1931), p. 3.

64 Sixty choirs were examined as part of the Limerick festival in 1942. The *Irish Press* reported: 'There was no competitive element. The choirs were judged on their rendition of the music and credited on certificates of merit'. *Irish Press* (1 June 1942), 3. All media reports did not agree on the nature of these events. In the following year, the *Cork Examiner* boasted that eighty-four choirs competed at Limerick. 'Liturgical Festival: Eighty-four Choirs Compete at Limerick', *Cork Examiner*, 10 May 1943.

65 *Report of 1959–60*, p. 40.

66 Irish National Teachers Organisation, *A Plan for Education* (Dublin: INTO, 1947), p. 41.

67 An Roinn Oideachais, *Report of the Council of Education* (1954), p. 188.

68 The National Programme Conference of the INTO in 1926 recommended the gramophone 'for the purpose of developing the pupils' musical taste'. *Report and Programme of the Second National Programme Conference*, p. 42. The following year, Larchet advocated a cheap gramophone model for schools 'as an aid in the collective development of musical skill, taste, and culture'. 'Grampus', 'How the Gramophone Can Help Musical Education: Views of Dr Larchet', *The Irish Times*, 6 October 1927, 4.

69 John D. Sheridan, 'School Music – Today and To-morrow', *Irish School Weekly* 31 (6 December 1930), 1378.

70 *Report of 1928–29*, p. 66.

71 A circular was issued to all schools in January 1936 stating the department's consideration of 'the feasibility of periodic broadcasts of Music for the benefit of the pupils of the schools'. The Department of Education claimed that these broadcasts would 'help considerably towards the development of Musical culture in the schools and the creation of a taste for Music'. An Roinn Oideachais, 'Proposed Broadcasts of Music for the Benefit of Pupils of all Schools – Primary, Secondary and Vocational', An Roinn Oideachais, Circular 2, January 1936.

72 *Radio Éireann Annual Report for 1936*, 'School Broadcasts', p. 6. A contradictory date of February 20 (for the first broadcast) was given in the Department of Education circular to schools. Since the Radio Éireann report was written after the broadcast that date has been selected here as more likely to be correct.

73   *Radio Éireann Annual Report for 1936*, p. 6.

74   'Broadcasts to Schools', *Irish School Weekly* 38 (7 November 1936), 1084; 'Oide', 'Craolachán i gCóir Scoileanna', *Irish School Weekly* 39 (18 September 1937), 916.

75   *Radio Éireann Annual Report for 1936*, p. 8.

76   *Radio Éireann Annual Report for 1939*, p. 16.

77   'No Broadcasts in Schools', *Irish School Weekly* 52 (9 and 16 December 1950), 540.

78   Maurice Gorham, *Forty Years of Irish Broadcasting* (Dublin: The Talbot Press Ltd., 1967), p. 109.

79   James Doyle, 'Music in the Army', in *Music In Ireland*, pp. 65–73. On the request of the Irish Military School, Professor Grawert, director of the Royal School of Military Music in Berlin, recommended Fritz Brase for the position of music director. A distinguished graduate of the Leipzig Conservatory and Royal Academy of Music in Berlin, Brase accepted the post in February 1923. Also appointed to the Military School in 1923 was Sauerzweig who took up the position of instructional officer. Brase died in 1940 and was succeeded by Sauerzweig. The success of the concerts was evident in the fact that by the third school year, 1933–34, 20,000 children attended the concerts.

80   *Report of 1932–33*, p. 34.

81   'Army Band Concerts for Dublin Primary Schools', *Irish School Weekly* 36 (20 October 1934), 1008.

82   Aloys Fleischmann, 'Music in Cork', in *The Music Association of Ireland*, p. 15.

83   *Report of 1933–34*, p. 28.

84   'Over 3,000 Attend Concerts', *Waterford News*, 21 January 1950, 2.

85   The model used by this organisation was Sir Robert Mayer's Children's Concerts, the first of which took place in London on 29 March 1923. *The New Grove Dictionary of Music and Musicians*, s. v. 'Sir Robert Mayer'. After hearing a concert for children in New York, Sir Robert and Lady Mayer returned to Britain where Sir Robert organised children's concerts. 'After World War II he further extended his activities by founding Youth and Music after the example of the continental Jeunesses Musicales'. The Mayers, and the models they provided for organising children's concerts, are significant in the context of Irish music education from 1951 forward. Lady Mayer founded Ceol Chumann na nÓg and was present at its first concert on 5 February 1952. 'Orchestral Concerts for Schoolchildren', *Evening Mail* (5 February 1952), 5.

86 'Cuirm Ceoil: Successful Schools' Concert in Cork', *Irish School Weekly* 77 (11 July 1925), 852.

87 'Cork School Music Committee: A Most Successful Concert', *Irish School Weekly* 77 (6 February 1926), 176.

88 Ibid. This suggestion was also made by Breen in 1926, 'INTO Congress, 1926', *Irish School Weekly* 77 (17 April 1926), 492.

89 Its aim was 'to develop and exploit the large reserve of musical potentiality at present going to waste in our schools'. 'Ceol-Chumann na nÓg', *Irish School Weekly* 39 (25 November 1937), 1169.

90 By 1939 the choir's performance was broadcast and it is worthy of note that all songs performed during the broadcast were in the Irish language. 'Choir of 400 Children to Broadcast', *Irish Independent*, 17 March 1939, 9.

91 Eamonn O Gallchobhair, 'The Cultural Value of Festival and Feis', in *Music in Ireland*, p. 216.

92 Angela Deasy, 'Growing Up in the Model', *Modhscoil Luimnigh, 1855–1986*, ed. by Marcus Ó hEochaidh (Limerick: Mc Kerns Prin., Ltd., n. d.), p. 78. Féile Dramaíochta na Scol (schools' drama festival) was founded in 1934 and its primary aims were to promote drama and to make the learning of Irish language more interesting for pupils. Bríd Nic Gearailt, to writer, 24 January 1990. In its initial years, music was performed as entertainment between the various parts of the drama competition. In 1936 a competition for action songs was introduced and in 1953, operettas in Irish formed a new competition. Donnchadh Ó Súilleabháin, *An Cumann Scoildramaíochta 1934–1984* (Baile Átha Cliath: An Clochomhar Tta., 1986).

93 A two-year series of articles on percussion instruction was published in *The Teacher's Work* between 1952 and 1954. This series was based on the method of Yvonne Adair and her arrangements were recommended. In addition, methods of accompanying Irish melodies with percussion were demonstrated.

94 *Report of 1959–60*, p. 40.

95 A special music curriculum was designed for such schools, but it was not supported by appropriate materials to assist in implementing it. In the 1928–29 school-year report, a divisional inspector advised the Department of Education on appropriate assistance for rural schools, recommending a gramophone with records of the songs to be taught. *Report of 1928–29*, p. 66.

96 When Ó Braoin became music inspector of schools in 1932, he observed that 'it was quite common to find in most of the schools in country districts from 20 per cent up to 90 per cent of the children classed as "non-singers"'. Donnchadh Ua Braoin, 'Music in the Primary Schools', in *Music in Ireland*, p. 37.

97 A. E. Mac Artuir, 'Staff Notation in the Schools', *The Teacher's Work* 18 (October, 1927), 116.

98 Breen, 'School Music', *The Irish School Weekly* 77 (15 May 1926), 620.

99 Music inspector Sean Ó Casaide addressed this topic at a one-day conference held in Roscommon on 18 May 1940, saying that 'if the country-folk were able to sing pleasantly and to play even the simplest instrument, it would improve the quality of life for them'. 'Roscommon Music Conference', 495.

100 Describing life in Co. Kerry in the early 1930s, Jeremiah King advocated that since music and dancing were favourite pastimes in Kerry, 'the parish school should be used for promoting such culture, by training pipers and dancers; parish and county competitions should be held regularly to encourage local talent'. Jeremiah King, *County Kerry – Past and Present*, 2nd ed. (Cork and Dublin: Mercier Press, 1986), p. 254.

101 See Seán Crawford, 'Rural Music Schools', *Irish School Weekly* 48 (5 and 12 October, 1946), 449.

102 Landers, 'Music for the Juniors', 24.

103 INTO, *A Plan for Education*, p. 55.

104 *Report of the Council of Education*, p. 100, p. 188. Music was given a further boost in the Department of Education's *Notes for Teachers: Music*, in 1959. 'There is to-day no civilisation or system of education in which Music is not of prime importance. . . . It is at once a source and a product of civilisation, and the most democratic and elemental of the arts.' An Roinn Oideachais, *Notes for Teachers: Music* (1959), p. 3.

105 'Association of Secondary Teachers of Ireland: Commission on Secondary Education', *Irish School Weekly* 71 (January 1922), 80.

106 Coolahan, *Irish Education*, p. 76.

107 *Rules and Programme, 1924–25*, p. 56.

108 Ibid., pp. 56–7.

109 'The provision made for Singing and Physical Drill should be included in the school Time Table and if it be desired that the syllabus followed in either or both of these subjects be approved for the

purposes of this rule, such syllabi should be submitted to the Department'. *Rules and Regulations, 1943–44,* p. 8. A subtle alteration in this rule in the 1950–51 *Rules and Regulations* indicated the department's increased conviction about the role of singing in secondary education. 'The provision made for Singing and Physical Drill should be included in the school time-table and the syllabus followed should be submitted to the Department for approval.' *Rules and Regulations, 1950–51,* p. 8.

110 In 1925, 0.8 per cent and 0.1 per cent of the total student population took the Intermediate and Leaving Certificate examinations in music, respectively; by 1960, the figures showed 1.1 per cent and 1.1 per cent. *Rules and Regulations,* 1925–1960.

111 Aloys Fleischmann, 'The Outlook of Music in Ireland', 125.

112 Emily Hughes, 'Music in Ireland', *The Irish Monthly* 69 (October 1941), 468–9.

113 In previous years examiners were appointed by the Department of Education to design, implement, and evaluate examinations but these individuals were affiliated to other institutions. For example, Professor John Larchet directed the examinations between 1924 and 1948.

114 Also, it is worthy of note that the compulsory school-leaving age was extended to sixteen years in 1947; consequently the decade of the 1950s witnessed an expansion in the number of secondary schools and in the number of pupils in attendance. As secondary education became a more widespread phenomenon, so also did music within the system.

115 In 1923, a letter submitted from the Christian Brothers school at Our Lady's Mount, Cork, to the Assistant Commissioners queried the status of music teachers. The letter read: 'Kindly state if Teachers of Music, and especially of Choral Singing constantly employed in connection with choirs examined specially by the Board, are not fairly entitled to be regarded as "registered teachers".' *Minutes of the Proceedings* (1923), p. 12. In 1935 Fleischmann, aware of the lack of qualified music teachers in secondary schools, suggested the establishment of a Music Teachers' Registration Council. Aloys Fleischmann, 'The Outlook of Music in Ireland', 128.

116 When Fleischmann described the status of the music teaching profession in the early 1950s, he stated that 'only those music teachers on the staffs of secondary schools who possess a University Degree in Music and the Higher Diploma in Education are eligible for registration as secondary teachers, and only four music teachers in the entire

country at present fall into this category'. Aloys Fleischmann, 'The Growth of the Music Teaching Profession', in *Music in Ireland*, p. 82.

117   Music syllabi from the Department of Education's *Rules and Regulations*.

118   *Rules and Regulations, 1924–25*, p. 58.

119   One example was the inclusion of a course on Irish music as part of the music summer school held for teachers in Dublin from 1946 to 1956. In 1949, Fr S. C. Ó Floinn presented a course 'Ceol na hÉireann' and this was continued on an annual basis.

120   *Rules and Regulations*, 1924–32.

121   In their recommendations to the new Ministry of Education, Larchet and the Music Committee advocated that the system of bonuses be abolished. The recommendation was not adopted. *Minutes of the Proceedings* (1924–25), p. 207.

122   *Rules and Regulations*, 1925–1960. Larchet also provided evidence of the growth in this component of music education when he delivered a lecture on the music syllabus for secondary schools, broadcast from Radio Éireann and reported in the *Rules and Regulations for 1943–1944*. He said: 'In 1925, 73 choirs, 25 orchestras and 31 individual pupils were examined. The figures for 1944 were 167 choirs, 45 orchestras and 125 individual pupils.' p. 29.

123   'An Draighneán Donn' (Rooney), 'Fear a' Bhata' (Old Gaelic), 'Oft in the Stilly Night' (Moore), and 'The Minstrel Boy' (Moore) in 1923–24, and 'Ban-Chnuic Éireann Oighe', 'The Fairies' (Stanford), and 'Máire Bhéil Átha hAmhais' in 1924–5.

124   O'Connor and Parkes, *Gladly Learn, Gladly Teach*, p. 180.

125   In *Portraits: Belvedere College Dublin 1832–1982*, ed. by John Bowman and Ronan O'Donoghue (Dublin: Gill and Macmillan, 1982), p. 98.

126   For most Irish people, he wrote, 'listening to music is not an artistic pursuit at all. . . . Our countrymen are indeed musically timid, behave like poor swimmers, ever in dread of going beyond their depth; they voluntarily restrict their musical experience to what is obvious and safe.' Revd Maurice Weymes, 'General Musical Culture in Ireland', *Irish Ecclesiastical Record*, 5th series, 56 (November 1940), 440–41.

127   Revd Maurice Weymes, 'General Musical Education in Ireland', *The Irish Ecclesiastical Record*, 5th series, 60 (November 1942), 353. Weymes developed the same argument in his article, 'Question of Value in Music', *Irish Ecclesiastical Record*, 5th series, 59 (January–June 1942), 314–24.

128 Br. Séamus V. O'Sullivan, 'The Value of Aesthetic Subjects in the School Curriculum', *Christian Brothers Educational Record* 34 (1955), 137, 139, 148.

129 Brown, *Ireland: A Social and Cultural History*, p. 49.

130 Saorstát Eireann, *Statutes of the Oireachtas, No. 29 of 1930, Vocational Education Act, 1930*, p. 601.

131 'The Vocational School Curriculum: Vocal Music as a Nation-Wide Subject', *The Teacher's Work* 21 (November 1930), 113–14.

132 A writer in the *Vocational Education Bulletin* of July, 1938, stated: 'Primitive societies are . . . those in which the artist is not a special kind of man, but every man is a special kind of artist. . . . These societies are "naturally cultured".'

133 An Roinn Oideachais: An Brainse Ghairmoideachais, *Memorandum V. 40* (1942), introduction.

134 Pádraig Ó Conghaile, 'Cuirtear Craobh den Claisceadal ar bun in gach Ceard Scoil', *Vocational Education Bulletin* 28 (May 1943), 563.

135 'Twenty-Fourth Annual Congress of the V. E. O.: The Rural Education Problem', *Vocational Education Bulletin* 42 (November 1947), 891.

136 P. Burke, 'Education for Work and Leisure', *Vocational Education Bulletin* 41 (July 1947), 871.

137 Aloys Fleischmann, 'Music in Ireland', *The Bell* 13 (1947), 22.

138 Cited in Bernard Curtis, 'Music in the Vocational Schools', in *Music in Ireland*, pp. 46–7. Curtis was referring to Order S. I. No. 74 of 1949. The tradition of music in Cork vocational education was already established and it is not surprising to find that the Co. Cork Vocational Education Committee organised a summer course in 1949 for the training of junior choirs. Fifteen of the twenty-one students who attended the course returned to teach classes in seventeen centres in Co. Cork during the 1949–50 school year. This course served primary teachers, vocational teachers and choir members. Fleischmann, 'Music in Ireland', p. 22. Donnchadh Ó Braoin stated in 1952 that in fifteen of the twenty-six counties no music was taught in any vocational school. Ó Braoin, 'Music in the Primary Schools', in *Music in Ireland*, p. 43.

139 An Roinn Oideachais – An Brainse Ghairmoideachais, *Memorandum V. 51*, 'Choral Singing in Vocational Schools: Notes for Teachers', p. 1, p. 3. The Mary A. Hardiman Trust provided some funds for music in vocational schools from 1955 forward and they went to Cork City and County Vocational Education Committees. The funds were used

to develop teacher-training courses and to train musicians to give the courses. Strong traditions of music education in this region and the presence of significant music educators such as Aloys Fleischmann were highly influential in both initiating and organising projects, and in acquiring funds to support them.

140   Paddy Tunney, *The Stone Fiddle*, p. 1, p. 4, p. 16. He cited the songs 'Merry Little Gypsies Are We', 'O the Boat Lightly Floating Merrily Away', and 'Do You Ken John Peel'.

141   A striking example of this type of local school and its role in linking the local with the national was that developed by fiddle player Jack Mulkere in Galway and Clare. His teaching career began in the early 1920s and it spanned over fifty years, during which time he taught thousands of young traditional musicians and contributed to the national organisation of traditional music in the 1950s. See Gearóid Ó hAllmhuráin, 'Jack Mulkere: Teacher, Patriot and Gael', *Treoir* 14 (1982), 6–7.

142   Éamonn Ó Muireadhaigh, 'Traditional Music', *Clogher Record* 1 (1953), 29–30.

143   *Bunreacht Comhaltas Ceoltóirí Éireann*, reprin. ed. (Dublin: Comhaltas Ceoltóirí Éireann, 1996), p. iii.

144   *Comhaltas Ceoltóirí Éireann: A Living Tradition* (Dublin: Comhaltas Ceoltóirí Éireann, n. d.), pp. 3–4; Edward O. Henry, 'Institutions for the Promotion of Indigenous Music: The Case for Ireland's Comhaltas Ceoltóirí Éireann', *Ethnomusicology* 33 (Winter 1989), 67–73.

145   Kevin Whelan argues that 'traditional music's *caighdeán oifigiúil* had the same imperialist effect of blurring or erasing local traditions, as did the linguistic *caighdeán* on the vigour of Irish language dialects'. 'The Bases of Regionalism', in *Culture in Ireland. Regions: Identity and Power*.

Notes to Chapter 6

1   Terence Brown, *Ireland: A Social and Cultural History*, p. 241.

2   *Commission for the Restoration of the Irish Language: Summary of the Final Report* (Dublin: The Stationery Office, 1963).

3   The poet Eavan Boland wrote: 'Let us be rid at last of any longing for cultural unity, in a country whose most precious contribution may be precisely its insight into the anguish of disunity; let us be rid of any longing for imaginative collective dignity in a land whose final

and only dignity is individuality'. Eavan Boland, 'The Weasel's Tooth', *Irish Times*, 7 June 1974, 7, cited in Brown, *Ireland: A Social and Cultural History*, p. 322, p. 324; John A. Murphy, 'Identity Change in the Republic of Ireland', *Études Irlandaises* 1 (December 1976), 143.

4   In 1974, RTÉ broadcast a series of television lectures entitled 'A Question of Identity' which addressed itself to the historical strands comprising the Irish nation. Brown, *Ireland: A Social and Cultural History*, p. 293. From a similar perspective, a six-part television series, *The Heritage of Ireland*, broadcast in 1977, presented 'a vision of the country as a complicated mosaic of cultures and social forces'. Ibid. Even in the 1980s, the debate continued as evident in a series of lectures on the theme of a sense of place, sponsored by Radio Teilifís Éireann and delivered at University College, Cork, in January 1985. The lectures were subsequently published in *Ireland: Toward a Sense of Place*, ed. by Joseph Lee (Cork: Cork University Press, 1985).

5   Anne Kelly, *Cultural Policy in Ireland*, (UNESCO, 1989), p. 67.

6   *Access and Opportunity: A White Paper on Cultural Policy* (Dublin: Government Publications Office, 1987), p. 12, p. 13.

7   Ibid., p. 40.

8   Ibid., p. 73.

9   Ibid., p. 15. One response to this political aspiration was the first North-South schools concert series in 1995 sponsored by the Irish Peace Institute at the University of Limerick in cooperation with partner organisations. The purpose was to celebrate the fiftieth anniversary of the founding of the United Nations. Three-hundred and fifty students from four schools participated, and concerts took place in Limerick, Derry and Dublin. A long-term cultural project grew out of this series. Martin Barrett, artistic director, Irish Peace Institute, to writer, November 1997.

10   Murphy, 'Identity Change in the Republic of Ireland', 149.

11   Ó Súilleabháin, 'Irish Music Defined', 85.

12   Ibid., 85, 87; Charles Acton, *Irish Music and Musicians* (Dublin: Eason and Son Ltd., 1978), pp. 1–2.

13   Nuala O'Connor, *Bringing It All Back Home: The Influence of Irish Music* (London: BBC Books, 1991).

14   An Roinn Oideachais, *Council of Education Report: The Curriculum of the Secondary School* (Dublin, 1962).

15   Séamus V. Ó Súilleabháin, 'Young People at School', *Christus Rex* 12

(April 1968), 149–51. As early as 1955, this author discussed 'The Value of Aesthetic Subjects in the School Curriculum', in *Christian Brothers Educational Record* 34 (1955), 137–48.

16   This is reflected both in a conference on 'Cultural Studies in the School Curriculum' held at the New University of Ulster in 1975, and in an entire volume of the journal of the Irish Association for Curriculum Development being devoted to 'Culture, Society, and Education in Ireland'. *Compass* 5 (May 1976).

17   Malcolm Skilbeck, 'Education and Cultural Change', *Compass* 5 (May 1976), 13.

18   To celebrate its ten-year achievement, a special seminar and exhibition was organised in October, 1989. The Arts Council, *Art Matters* 10 (May 1989), 2. In addition to the seminar and exhibition, a publication was issued by the Arts Council to mark the decade. *The Arts Council and Education, 1979–1989* (Dublin: The Arts Council, 1989).

19   The Arts Council, *Provision for the Arts*, a report by J. M. Richards (Dublin: The Arts Council, 1976).

20   The Arts Council, *The Place of the Arts in Irish Education*, a report by Ciarán Benson (Dublin: The Arts Council, 1979). Considering that the Arts Council had no statutory role in formal education, this extensive report indicated a deep commitment to improving the status of the arts in Irish education. Internally, the function of the Arts Council had been broadened considerably by the Arts Amendment Act of 1973.

21   UNESCO, *The Place and Function of Art in Contemporary Life: Report of an International Symposium* (Paris, 1977), cited in the Benson Report, *The Place of the Arts in Irish Education*, p. 14. Two perspectives were presented, one viewing art as manifest in the day-to-day life of a society, the other as transcending day-to-day life.

22   Ibid., 26. Deep-rooted cultural and musico-aesthetic categories die hard. Even in 1977, Breathnach was critical of music institutes representative of the 'Anglo-Irish' tradition, claiming that they used tutors and texts 'which maintain a silent but effective boycott of the native music'. Breandán Breathnach, *Folk Music and Dances of Ireland*, p. 121.

23   Mícheál Ó Súilleabháin, 'Out of Tune with Reality: Music and the School in Ireland', *Irish Educational Studies* 5 (1985), 46.

24   Nancy Smith, 'Music Education in Ireland: The Meeting of the Waters', *Music Educators Journal* 73 (December 1987), 49.

25   Council of Europe, *Music Education for All*, prep. by J. Frommelt (Strasbourg: Council of Europe, 1981), p. 36.

26 Herron, *Deaf Ears?*

27 Curriculum and Examinations Board, *The Arts in Education: A Curriculum Examinations Board Discussion Paper* (Dublin: Curriculum and Examinations Board, 1985), pp. 5–6.

28 *The Arts and Education* (I), a submission to the Curriculum and Examinations Board (June 1984), p. 5. A similar response was submitted by the Arts Council regarding the draft document, 'Educational Development at Senior Cycle', in 1986. *The Arts and Education* (IV), a submission to the Curriculum and Examinations Board (September 1986).

29 *The Arts in Education* recommended that 'schools should be encouraged to organise a series of cross-border projects in the arts'. *The Arts in Education*, p. 22.

30 The idea for designating 1985 as European Music Year was born at a meeting of the European Parliament on 20 November, 1980. It was established initially to celebrate the tercentenary of the birth of J. S. Bach, G. Frideric Handel, and D. Scarlatti, 1685–1985. In all, twenty-three countries participated in a year-long celebration of all kinds of music.

31 Ó Súilleabháin, 'Out of Tune with Reality', 47, 55.

32 *The Arts in Education*, p. 15.

33 *Art and the Ordinary: The Report of the Arts Community Education Committee*, ed. by Ciarán Benson (Dublin, The Arts Council, 1989), p. 43.

34 *The P. I. A. N. O. Report: Report of the Review Group PIANO presented to the Minister for Arts, Culture and the Gaeltacht, Mr Michael D. Higgins, T. D., January 1996 on the Provision and Institutional Arrangements Now for Orchestras and Ensembles*, pp. 50–5.

35 An Roinn Oideachais, *Charting Our Education Future: White Paper on Education* (Dublin: The Stationery Office, 1995), p. 21, p. 48.

36 Joseph Groocock, *A General Survey of Music in the Republic of Ireland*, p. 14. Groocock discouraged these humble and dubiously worthy musical instruments due to their 'unfavourable tone quality, and the lack of artistic value in their repertoire'. In his opinion, these bands had been given as hearty a welcome as complete orchestras in popular school music festivals which encouraged 'every form of music making'. pp. 16–17, p. 34.

37 An Roinn Oideachais, *Report for 1961–62*, p. 51. The report also stated that 'small orchestras have been established, groups trained to play stringed instruments and bands instructed in the use of suitable

popular instruments'. From the reference made to the establishment of 'small orchestras' it cannot be inferred that this was a nationwide development. Some obvious reasons exist to disclaim any popularity of string orchestras in primary schools. First, there is an absence of reference to such a phenomenon in official reports and school-related literature of the period. Second, few primary-school teachers were qualified to provide class instruction in stringed instruments. Third, if orchestras had become a widespread phenomenon, traces of such a development would be evident in today's schools.

38   A survey of teaching aids in primary schools in the late 1960s addressed the general lack of musical instruments especially in rural schools. The survey was carried out in a randomly selected 102 Catholic primary schools. The authors concluded that 'well over half of Irish schools (sixty-five per cent) have no instruments at all. City schools fare considerably better than rural ones: seventy per cent of city schools, fifty-three per cent of town schools and nineteen per cent of rural schools possess some kind of musical instrument, the piano being the most common.' Thomas Kellaghan and Liam Gorman, 'A Survey of Teaching Aids in Irish Primary Schools', *The Irish Journal of Education* 2 (Spring 1968), 38.

39   Carmel Fahy, 'We are the Music Makers: a look at the position of music in our primary schools', *An Múinteoir Náisiúnta* 13 (1968), 17.

40   Mícheál Ó Ceallacháin, comp., *Beidh Ceol Againn*, Cuid I agus II (Dublin: Ó Fallúin, 1969). Translation into both Irish and English, moreover, reflected the bilingual policy of the day.

41   *An Curaclam Nua*, pt. 1, p. 12.

42   Ibid., pt. 2, p. 211. The entire music curriculum is found on pp. 209–86.

43   Good taste is 'built on experience and young people acquire standards and preferences according as new experiences come their way. All the music they hear, including 'pop' music, has something to contribute to their total experience, but it would be a pity if this total experience were limited to the type of music promoted by the entertainment industry. It is for our schools to play a positive role in supplying the balance and in setting the standard.' Ibid., p. 272.

44   Ibid., p. 214.

45   These very issues, among others, were identified by the Teacher's Study Group in 1969, in response to the department's draft curriculum for primary schools. The practical suggestions made by the

group were that (a) a certain number of talented student teachers be trained as specialists in school music; (b) the intraining courses mentioned in the draft should precede the introduction of the curriculum; (c) the teachers' handbook should include a comprehensive range of suitable songs (both words and music) for each standard; and (d) a radio programme similar to BBC's *Singing Together* should be produced on Radio Éireann. Teacher's Study Group, *Report on the Draft Curriculum for Primary Schools*, ed. by Kathleen Mc Donagh, March 1969, p. 39. In effect, the group's recommendations embodied a felt need for a support system for teaching music in primary schools in the form of professional music specialists, appropriate teaching materials, and home-produced music broadcasts.

46 A report by the Department of Education in the 1970s on 'Musical Education in Ireland' stated that comprehensive and intensive inservice courses on the teaching of various subjects including music were given every year. An Roinn Oideachais, 'Musical Education in Ireland', unpub. paper.

47 Publications such as Maureen Lally's *Listen, Sing and Play* (1975) provided some guidance to teachers for implementing the new curriculum. It was a comprehensive, detailed scheme of lessons on tape with accompanying notes for teachers. Materials assisted the teacher in approaching voice-training, ear-training, literacy, and rhythm.

48 *Primary School Curriculum: Curriculum Questionnaire Analysis* (Dublin: INTO, 1976), p. 17.

49 Ibid., p. 31.

50 *Evaluation of the New Curriculum for Primary Schools*, Conference of Convent Primary Schools in Ireland (Dublin: Ardiff Printers, Ltd., 1975), p. 31.

51 Cited in Herron, *Deaf Ears?*, p. 2; similar findings issued from Meany's research conducted in early 1985 in the Galway region. Mary Meany, 'Aspects of Music Education in the Primary School', *Irish Educational Studies* 6 (1986–1987), 172–9.

52 Herron, *Deaf Ears?*, pp. 40–1.

53 Ibid., pp. 1–8.

54 An Roinn Oideachais, *Éigse an Cheoil* (Baile Átha Cliath: Oifig an tSolatháir, 1975); An Roinn Oideachais, *Cuisle an Cheoil* (Baile Átha Cliath: Oifig an tSolatháir, 1976); *Cas Amhrán*, ed. by Mícheál Ó hEidhin (Indreabhan, Gallimh: Clódóirí Lurgan, 1975).

55 Selection and editorial decisions made by the Music Committee of the Department of Education with the assistance of Seán Óg Ó

Tuama were stated clearly in the foreword to *Cuisle an Cheoil*. First, the versions of the songs chosen were not to be viewed by teachers as the definitive ones. The object was not to standardise a song and banish the diversity of local settings but rather to present one version out of many. Standardisation, however, was applied to the spelling and grammar of the text. When it was felt that standardisation affected the meter or the style, the original text was maintained. Adherence to traditional style was also evident in the treatment of rhythm and in the suggestions for conducting the songs. Chord progressions were supplied for songs, a feature that reflected the stylistic developments which had taken place in Irish traditional music since the late 1950s. p. ix.

56   *Bímis ag Ceol*, in *Radio na Scoile* (Baile Átha Cliath: Radio Teilifís Éireann, 1975), pp. 27–39. Similar to Ó Ceallacháin's approach in *Beidh Ceol Againn*, two traditional folk songs were presented, one with original text and the other with lyrics written by Gabriel Rosenstock. The teacher's handbook offered background information to the songs and to the notated melodies and words.

57   Although this region lies outside the geographical scope of this study for the contemporary period, with respect to developments in traditional music materials for schools, the North of Ireland's contribution is significant and needs to be acknowledged.

58   Eithne and J. B. Vallely, *Sing a Song and Play It: A Book of Irish Music and Song for Children*, 3 vols. (Belfast: The Appletree Press, Ltd., 1975). The authors stated that the publication was a response to a demand from teachers for further teaching material, after the success of their *Learn to Play the Tin Whistle*. A fundamental principle of the series was that 'instrumental playing should be directly related to vocal music'. Besides embracing a broad spectrum of Irish songs (from lullabies and occupation songs to love songs and ballads) in the Irish and English languages, and providing settings for tin whistle and percussion accompaniments, a rich cultural context was created by the inclusion of illustrations, photographs, and biographical details of musicians, composers, and collectors of the music.

59   Barry Burgess, 'The Primary School Irish Traditional Music Project', *An Múinteoir Náisiúnta* 23 (October 1979), 27. Burgess was then head of the music department at the Dominican College, Portstewart, Co. Derry. The project was completed in collaboration with the Learning Resources Centre at Magee College, Derry.

60   Ibid. Aims of the project included: to stimulate an interest in and understanding of Irish traditional music in primary/first year secondary school children; to teach the fundamentals of the language of music through the Irish musical tradition; to teach performing skills on the whistle thus giving a pastime activity which could be carried into post-school life; to develop a trained, musical ear which is essential for all traditional musicians, and to give children an opportunity of making and listening to music together. Pilot scheme materials were designed to implement these aims and, in 1979, at the time of Burgess's description of the project, the pilot scheme had been carried out in several schools in Co. Derry. pp. 27–9.

61   An Roinn Oideachais, *White Paper on Educational Development* (Dublin: Government Publications Office, 1981), pp. 63–4.

62   Seán N. Farren, 'Culture and Curriculum or Dream and Realities', *An Múinteoir Náisiúnta* 26 (Spring 1982), 29.

63   An Roinn Oideachais, *Programme for Action in Education, 1984–87* (Dublin: The Stationery Office, 1984), p. 1.

64   The success and significance of the project was reflected in its repetition and expansion in 1987 and 1989. The number of counties represented rose from seven in 1985 to twenty-three in 1989; the number of children (approx.) involved rose from 4,500 in 1985 to 10,000 in 1989. By 1989, 143 schools participated. Programme Notes, 1985, 1987, 1989. Also, Seán Creamer, director of the choir, to writer, July 1989.

65   In 1987 the unifying theme was 'Draíocht na Mara' (The Magic of the Sea) with emphasis on folk song and dance from many lands and a review of songs by the 'Great Composers', from Bach to the Beatles. In the introduction to this section of the 1987 performance, it was stated that just as folk songs 'bring us into communion with other nations' the songs of great composers 'give us a fleeting glimpse into the minds of Great Men'. The association of folk music with 'peoples' souls' and composed music with 'the minds of Great Men' leads one to believe that attitudes to folk music were still bound by the values of 'high culture' and the equation of art music with greatness and artistic worth. Performance Programme, 20–21 June, 1987. Three categories of song identified by Creamer were integrated imaginatively into the 1989 concert: the theme of the cycle of life from cradle to grave, the genre of opera through the ages, and choruses from Mozart and Wagner to Gershwin and Lloyd Webber.

66   Martin Drury, 'Once More with Feeling: The Case for Arts-in-Education', paper delivered at the INTO Education Conference in Ennis, May 1989, p. 7.

67   Ibid., p. 13.

68   Ibid., p. 5.

69   Ibid., p. 11.

70   'Report of the Arts Education Joint-Level Sub-Committees (Primary) For Music and the Visual Arts to the National Council for Curriculum and Assessment', May 1994, pp. 6–7. In addition to increased attention at the official level, primary-school teachers with particular interest and expertise in music have initiated a forum called *Fuaim*, with the aim of improving the quality of music in primary schools.

71   Justine Ward (1879–1975), an American music educator, studied Gregorian Chant at Solesmes and developed music education materials for US Catholic schools. In her 1956 publication, *That All May Sing*, she stated: 'The object of this series of textbooks is to give a solid education in music to the children in the primary grades of our Catholic schools. This education covers, not only modern music but the liturgical melodies of the Church, in particular Gregorian Chant as has been urged so repeatedly by the Holy See.' Justine Ward, *That All May Sing* (Washington, DC: Catholic Education Press, 1956), p. 1.

72   Fr Seán Terry, to writer, February 1990.

73   Albert Bradshaw, 'An Experiment in Curriculum Development Based on an Adoption of the Kodály Concept of Music Education for Particular Use in Schools in the Republic of Ireland' (Ph. D. dissertation, The University of Dublin, 1981); Bradshaw, *Pentatonic Songs (Folksongs for Irish Wee Folk): Teacher's Manual; Pentatonic Folksongs and Reading Exercises*, vols. 1 and 11 (Dublin: Bradshaw Music Education/Dublin University Press, 1988); Albert Bradshaw, to writer, February 1990).

74   Colm Ó Cléirigh, to writer, February 1990.

75   A private institution named the Carl Orff School of Music, Dance, Speech, and Drama, was founded by Olive Mulcahy in Dublin in 1976 and it lasted until 1988. Olive Mulcahy, to writer, January 1990. The principal methods that were introduced into Ireland in the 1960s and '70s were those of Justine Ward, Zoltan Kodaly, Carl Orff and Shinichi Suzuki. The two methods that have exerted most inflence on Irish music education are the Kodaly method and the

Suzuki method. For a description of each of these methods, the following sources are recommended: Lois Choksy et al., Teaching Music in the Twentieth Century (Englewood Cliffs, NJ: Prentice Hall, 1996); Some Great Music Educators, Kenneth Simpson Ed. (Kent, UK: Novello, 1976); Shinichi Suzuki, Nurtured by Love: A New Approach to Education, Trans. By Waltrand Suzuki (NY: Exposition Press, 1969).

76 Charles Acton, 'Music Teaching: Economics and the Community', *Éire-Ireland* 6 (Winter 1971), 132. The Sixth Annual Workshop of the European Suzuki Association was held in Cork in April, 1985, with Suzuki himself directing it.

77 Groocock, *A Survey of Music*, p. 25, p. 27.

78 An Roinn Oideachais, *Council of Education Report: The Curriculum of the Secondary School* (1962), p. 200, p. 202. The report stressed that figures representing students who sat for certificate examinations did not reflect the 'honoured place' that music was granted in the curriculum of many secondary schools. It stated: 'While but a small percentage of pupils take music as an examination subject, nevertheless, music, both liturgical and secular, and musical appreciation find an honoured place in the curriculum of quite a large number of schools.' Ibid., p. 82. In his appraisal of the council's reports, Aloys Fleischmann contradicted the statement that 'the number of schools in which singing is not taught is negligible'. (Para. 338) Fleischmann continued: 'This statement is untrue, and the evidence which shows that it is untrue was available to the members of the Commission if they had troubled to glance at one of the tables appended to the Report itself', in 'Music Education in Ireland as Surveyed in the Reports of the Council of Education', unpub. MS, p. 7.

79 An Roinn Oideachais, *Investment in Education* (Dublin: Statistical Office, 1966).

80 D. G. Mulcahy, *Curriculum and Policy in Irish Post-Primary Education* (Dublin: Institute of Public Administration, 1981), p. 72.

81 Michael Murtagh, 'The Status of Music', *The Secondary Teacher* 5 (Winter 1975), 37–8.

82 An Roinn Oideachais, *Rules and Programme for 1966–67*, pp. 107–8.

83 Mulcahy, *Curriculum and Policy*, p. 56.

84 Those who sat for Intermediate Certificate music rose from 0.2 per cent of boys and 1.5 of girls in 1966, to 3.5 of boys and 17.5 of girls in 1974, to 6.1 of boys and 21.6 of girls in 1980. Leaving Certificate figures reflected a similar increase on a smaller scale: 0.2 per cent of

boys and 1.3 of girls in 1966, 0.8 of boys and 4.0 of girls in 1974, and 0.7 of boys and 3.5 of girls in 1980. *Annual Reports of the Department of Education.* A gender bias was evident throughout the period.

85 An Roinn Oideachais, *Rules and Programme for 1961–62*, p. 57.

86 *Annual Reports of the Department of Education*, 1962–63, 1982–83. In 1962 funding for music represented 2.7 per cent of the total granted to science and equipment, whereas in 1983 it represented only 1.1 per cent. In contrast to this comparative decrease, funding for the publication of Irish textbooks represented only 0.3 per cent of science and equipment funding in 1962 but increased to 3.1 per cent by 1983.

87 Besides the limited funding available, a rigid set of rules accompanied the foundation of ensembles, their presentation for the department's examinations, and the conditions under which bonuses were granted. The amount of the bonus granted was determined by the ensemble type (vocal or instrumental), the number of voice parts, the class level of the ensemble (junior, intermediate, or senior), and the result of the examination (first or second class). Bonuses ranged from £7 to £30 with a maximum bonus granted to a senior orchestra with first class results followed by a senior choir (three- or four-part) with a similar result. With effect from the school-year 1977–78, bonuses for instrumental ensembles were increased with the new range from £15 to £45 per ensemble. 'Bonus for Choirs and Orchestras', *The Secondary Teacher* 3 (Spring 1974), 30.

88 *Rules and Programme for 1966–67*, p. 108.

89 Ibid. Prior to this, there was no mention of Irish music in this section. The Leaving Certificate music-history syllabus suggested that 'the Higher course is contained in the *New Musical Companion*'. *Report for 1964–65*, p. 107.

90 Ó Súilleabháin, 'Out of Tune with Reality', 46.

91 Mary Devereux, 'The Perception, Knowledge, and Practice of Irish Traditional Music among Secondary School Students', B. Mus. thesis, University College, Cork, 1979, pp. 23–6, pp. 30–1, p. 43. Other findings included: 9 per cent of respondents played some traditional Irish instrument, but only 1 per cent was taking formal instrumental lessons; 20 per cent saw a direct link between traditional music and nationalist ideology; even though 50 per cent recorded a liking for the Irish language, only 13 per cent considered it necessary for a true appreciation of traditional music; a statistically significant relationship

was found between the students who linked the music with the nationalist cause on the one hand, and those who resented the international use of traditional music.

92   Ibid., pp. 42–3.

93   A musicological approach to this genre was evident from the kind of information requested in the examination questions. Such a narrow focus for a socially and culturally rich genre is understandable when viewed in the context of research and scholarship pertaining to this music. Harry White, writing in 1984, identified clearly the need for a sociology of Irish folk music. Unless such a study is undertaken, he claimed, 'a profoundly vital tradition of making music that has much to say about the Irish people will escape the attention it so richly deserves and so badly requires'. Harry White, 'The Need for a Sociology of Irish Folk Music', *International Review of the Aesthetics and Sociology of Music* 15 (June 1984), 13. The treatment of the history of Irish folk music in the post-primary music syllabus attested to the state of scholarship that White described.

94   The 1989 syllabus stated: 'Irish music should form an important part of each student's work.' An Roinn Oideachais, *Music: Leaving Certificate Syllabus*, rev., 1989, pp. 6–7, p. 9.

95   I refer in particular to the achievements of the Curriculum Support Team for music appointed by the Department of Education in 1996. The members of the team – Martin Barrett, Jean Downey, Kathryn Fitzgerald, and Christopher Kinder – cooperated with specialists in traditional music to develop curriculum materials and resources for use in second-level schools. This was but one of the numerous projects completed by the team in their effort to create a bridge between the official syllabus, the practising teacher, the student, and others who influence the nature and quality of second-level music education.

96   *Irish Traditional Music Archive: The First Ten Years* (Dublin: Irish Traditional Music Archive, 1997), n. p.

97   Mulcahy, *Curriculum and Policy*, pp. 124–5. In Mulcahy's opinion, post-primary education was not responding to 'the realities of the present day'. In the area of cultural studies, he claimed, 'one finds a preoccupation with traditional art forms'. p. 124.

98   See 'Introduction', p. 2. 'Bono: The White Nigger', interview with Paul Hewson, in *Across the Frontiers*, p. 188.

99   Eamon Dunphy, *Unforgettable Fire: The Story of U2* (New York: Viking Books, 1987), p. 83.

100   Radio Teilifís Éireann, Radio Scoile, 1980–81, *Musicscape* (Dublin: Radio Teilifís Éireann, 1980), p. 2.

101   In May 1981, Radio Teilifís Éireann formally announced the termination of the remaining skeleton service of educational broadcasting. Reacting to this situation in 1984, Coolahan concluded that 'unless there is a more enlightened policy forthcoming later times will view this neglect as a serious lapse by this generation. It will have failed the younger generation of Irish people by depriving them of a resource that would be intensely enriching for their development, their imaginations and their creativity.' John Coolahan, 'The Dilemma of Educational Broadcasting in Ireland', *The Crane Bag* 8 (1984), 160.

102   An Roinn Oideachais, *Music: Leaving Certificate Syllabus, 1989–90*, p. 1.

103   An Roinn Oideachais, *The Leaving Certificate: Music Syllabus* (Dublin: The Stationery Office, 1996), p. 1.

104   *Issues and Structures in Education*, pp. 16–17.

105   Department of Education, Second Level Public Examination Statistics, 1990–1996.

106   Frank Corcoran, 'Musings on Our Schools Music', *The Secondary Teacher* 6 (Winter 1976), 15.

107   Mulcahy, *Curriculum and Policy*, p. 34.

108   Statistics taken from the 1976–77 school year illustrated this discrimination. For example, 41 per cent of secondary schools, 5 per cent of vocational schools, 30 per cent of community schools and 36 per cent of comprehensive schools provided for music at the Intermediate Certificate level. The Arts Council, *The Place of the Arts in Irish Education*, pp. 149–53.

109   A subsection of the report was devoted to 'Saothrú an Cheoil Dúchais sna Gairmscoileanna', *Commission on the Restoration of the Irish Language: Final Report*, p. 296.

110   Matt Power, *Half a Century – Co. Clare V.E.C. 1930–80* (Ennis: Clare Printers Ltd., n. d.), p. 50. After a long campaign of encouraging support from public representatives and the Clare VEC, a request was presented to the Clare County Council to sanction traditional music classes. As a result, Clare became the first county in Ireland to organise official Comhaltas classes in the Winter of 1962, held at the Vocational School in Ennis under the supervision of Jack Mulkere. G. Ó hAllmhuráin, 'Jack Mulkere, Teacher, Patriot, and Gael', 7.

111 In an analysis of provision for music at the Intermediate and Leaving Certificate levels in post-primary schools in 1980, the following percentages were provided: 45 (Intermediate) and 5 (Leaving) per cent of boys' schools, 85 and 50 per cent of girls' schools, 69 and 29 per cent of co-educational schools, 12 and 0 per cent of vocational schools, and 75 and 20 per cent of community/comprehensive schools. The Economic and Social Research Institute, 'Schooling and Sex Roles: Sex Differences in Subject Provision and Student Choice in Irish Post-Primary Schools', Paper No. 113 (Dublin: Economic and Social Research Institute, May 1983), pp. 157–8. Strong music programmes existed in some boys' secondary schools but they were the exception rather than the rule. For example, in 1970 the Catholic hierarchy instituted a *Schola Cantorum* at St Finian's College, Mullingar. This college offers five-year scholarships to musically talented boys who participate in intensive music education programmes including organ performance, choral and instrumental performance and composition. Shane Brennan, director of Schola Cantorum, St Finian's College, Mullingar, to writer, 3 October 1989; 'Schola Cantorum', *Franciscan Magazine* (1985), 12–15.

112 In 1990, 8 per cent of boys and 25 per cent of girls took music at the junior-cycle level, gradually dropping to 6 per cent of boys and 20 per cent of girls in 1996; at the senior-cycle level, the distribution remained the same at 1 per cent of boys and 3 per cent of girls in 1990 and in 1996. Department of Education, Second Level Public Examination Statistics, 1990–1996.

113 *Kerry Music Report: An Overview of Classical, Jazz, and Traditional Music in Kerry,* A Report compiled by Kerry Music County 2000, ed. by Orla Moloney (Dublin: Music Network, 1998), p. 11.

114 Colin McKenzie, interview by writer, Dublin, 4 August 1988; *National Adult Education Survey: Interim Report* (Dublin: The Stationery Office, 1970), p. 70. Through its newsletter, the association informed members of items of interest in music and provided a review of new music publications. Besides its founding committee and members in the Dublin area, it had a sixty-member branch in Galway.

115 According to Charles Acton, who chaired the inaugural meeting of APME, invitations to participate were sent to various branches of the Department of Education, but they were not accepted or acknowledged.

116 A special 'Music in the Classroom' seminar was held in 1994, sponsored by RTÉ and *The Irish Times*. Pat O'Kelly, *The National*

Symphony of Ireland 1948–1998 (Dublin: Radio Teilifís Éireann, 1998), n. p.

117 Music Association of Ireland, *Schools Recital Scheme, 1989–1990*, information pamphlet. In 1987, 89 per cent of the 211 recitals took place in provincial centres outside Dublin.

118 Recommendations included: a basic music education should be part of every pupil's education up to Junior Certificate level; instrumental tuition should be available in schools for every pupil; the study of Irish music – both classical and traditional – should be a core part of the curriculum at all levels; the present certificate courses should be declared obsolete and a range of new courses designed to reflect the various music careers available to students; radio and television programs should be developed in conjunction with music teachers in the schools, and research is needed to document the state of music education. 'The Music Association of Ireland: A Role for the 1990s', unpub. paper.

119 The Contemporary Music Centre, information pamphlet.

120 *New Music News* (May 1996), 4.

121 Highlights of the Ark's programmes and projects are a 'Children Make Music' series which grew out of CMC's compositions-in-schools programme, *SoundWorks*, collaborations with Music Network and with the National Children's Choir, a series of 'Meet the Orchestra' concerts with students from the Royal Irish Academy of Music Intermediate Orchestra (ten–fourteen years), *Musicfest* – a three-week music festival for children, and professional inservice days for teachers. Breda O'Shea, Programme Staff (Music), The Ark, interview by author, 19 November 1997. Also Public Relations materials, 'Eight Things You Need to Know About the Ark'.

122 'RDS World Music for Youth Festival, 24th–30th November 1997', publicity materials. As part of the festival, a Gospel Music Singposium, led by US conductor, teacher and gospel music specialist Barbara Baker, provided an opportunity for teachers and choral directors to experience first-hand gospel music repertoire and its transmission to secondary-school students.

123 On visiting the Welsh Eisteddfodau, Brian Ó Baoill was impressed not only by the efficiency of the organisation but also 'by the happy acceptance of modern trends side by side with the proud cultivation of tradition and by the easy way in which the new and old blended to make a wonderful and varied programme'. Ó Baoill aimed at replicating the idea in Ireland. Michael Ward, Director of Slógadh,

interview by writer, Gael-Linn, Dublin, 18 August 1989. (The inspiration for the foundation of the Feis Ceoil in 1897 also came from the Welsh Eisteddfodau.)

124 Dónall Ó Ríogáin, in *The Universe*, cited in Gabriel Rosenstock, *Slógadh*, n. d.

125 'Archbishop Croke's letter to Micheal Cusack', *GAA Pamphlets*, quoted in Michael Mulcahy and Marie Fitzgibbon, *The Voice of the People* (Dublin: The O'Brien Press, 1982), p. 50.

126 At the Scór na nÓg finals of 1989, President of the GAA, Seán Ó Dubhlainn said that one of the best ways to face the challenges of cultural change and avail of opportunities will be 'to retain and strengthen our national culture and identity thereby contributing uniquely Irish threads to the fabric of European life'. *Scór na nÓg '89* (Baile Átha Cliath: Cumann Luthchleas Gael, 1989), p. 3.

127 'An 39ú Tuarascáil Bhliantúil', *Treoir* 21 (1989), 4–5.

128 Henry, 'Institutions for the Promotion of Indigenous Music', 71.

129 Scoil Éigse occurs in the week preceeding the all-Ireland Fleadh, in the same town. It offers an ideal opportunity for young performers to learn styles and techniques from the masters. Up to two hundred performers are accepted each year. *Comhaltas Ceoltóirí Éireann: A Living Tradition*, p. 5. Even though the Willie Clancy Summer School did originate in Comhaltas Ceoltóirí Éireann, it very soon became an event that operated independently of the organisation.

130 Comhaltas Ceoltóirí Éireann, Mícheál Ó hEidhin, *Teastas i dTeagasc Ceolta Tíre* (Baile Átha Cliath: Comhaltas Ceoltóirí Éireann, 1980). The instruments usually covered on the course are: fiddle, concert flute, tin whistle, two-row accordion, harp, banjo, uilleann pipes, and concertina. By the late 1990s, 350–400 traditional musicians had completed the Diploma Course, with 90 per cent success rate. S. Mac Mathúna, interview by author, 13 January 1998.

131 Anon., *Treoir* 15 (1983), 33.

132 Caitlín Uí Éigeartaigh, 'Report on Recent Meetings: Teaching Folk Music?', *Ceol Tíre* 5 (October 1975), 3. This point was also made in 1970 when Charles Acton spoke of those who were in despair because of the Department of Education's publications of school music by An Gúm. In his opinion, these publications of two- and three-part arrangements of Irish traditional airs 'are bound to inculcate into succeeding generations of Irish children the idea that Irish

traditional music could suitably be dressed up in Anglo-German 19th-century harmony, a notion which all lovers of the true tradition must oppose on all turns'. Charles Acton, 'The Schools and Music: Reflections on Promise', *Éire-Ireland* 5 (Spring 1970), 100.

133   Uí Éigeartaigh, 'Report on Recent Meetings: Teaching Folk Music?', 4–5.

134   Music Association of Ireland, 'Introduction to Traditional Irish Music in Schools: Bringing the Arts to Schools', circular to schools principals, 1987. A package of three workshops with demonstrations was made available for (a) uilleann pipes, flute, tin whistle, (b) fiddle, harp, and (c) concertina, melodeon, and accordion. Schools were encouraged to take all three components which together would provide a comprehensive and coherent introduction to traditional music.

135   Paul McGrattan, administrator of the Music Awareness Agency, to writer, 23 February 1988.

136   In line with this emphasis, the *Final Report of the National Youth Policy Committee* in 1984 stated that traditional Irish music was one of the aspects of culture 'to which our young people should be guaranteed access'. 'Cultural Education', in *Final Report of the National Youth Policy Committee*, September 1984, p. 246.

137   Richard Kearney, 'The Fifth Province: Between the Global and the Local', in *Migrations: The Irish at Home and Abroad*, ed. by Richard Kearney (Dublin: Wolfhound Press, 1990), p. 122.

138   Kevin Whelan, 'Towns and Villages', in *Atlas of the Irish Rural Landscape*, p. 195.

139   *Art and the Ordinary: The Report of The Arts Community Education Committee*, p. 22, p. 37.

140   *Music Policy Document* (Dublin: Music Network, 1994), p. 2, p. 4.

Notes to Chapter 7

1   Seamus Heaney, 'The Given Note,' in *Opened Ground: Selected Poems 1966-1996* (New York: Farrar, Straus and Giroux, 1998), p. 36.

2   In Feldman and O'Doherty, *The Northern Fiddler*, p. 50.

3   D. P. Moran, *The Philosophy of Irish Ireland* (Dublin, 1905).

4   May McCann, 'Music and Politics in Ireland,' 52.

5   Anthony P. Cohen, *The Symbolic Construction of Community* (Chichester, UK: Ellis Horwood Ltd., 1985), p. 9.

6   Elliott, *Music Matters,* p. 212.

7   Kearney, *Transitions,* p. 17.

8   Harry White concludes that one of the central themes and problems of music in the cultural history of Ireland has been the 'polarisation between ethnic and colonial ideologies of culture'. *The Keeper's Recital,* p. 151.

9   Unlike Britain and the United States, students in primary school are not afforded the opportunity to learn a musical instrument. No system of peripatetic instrumental teachers is in place for primary schools. Another example of lack of tradition in instrumental music is evident in the absence of the Orff approach in Irish school music teaching, an approach that relies considerably on playing instruments.

10 In a study of teacher recruitment in post-independent Ireland, Nuala Johnson described the role of the primary-school teacher as 'the mediating link between the state's conception of its identity and the population that composed it'. Teachers from Gaeltacht regions were recruited intensively in an effort to Gaelicise the teaching personnel. 'Nation-building, Language and Education: The Geography of Teacher Recruitment in Ireland, 1925-55.' *Political Geography* 11 (March 1992), 170-71.

11 Traschel, 'Oral and Literate Constructs of "Authentic" Irish Music', 37.

12 Cohen, *The Symbolic Construction of Community,* pp. 12-19.

13 Anthony Everitt, *Joining In: An Investigation into Participatory Music,* Gulbenkian Foundation Report (London: Calouste Gulbenkian Foundation, 1997), p. 31.

14 Anthony Cohen argues that 'members of different communities may use similar structures, yet think about them in quite different ways.' Ibid. The manner in which competition and centralisation of music performance impacted traditional music practices deserves to be considered in a separate study; so also does the institutionalisation of traditional music learning.

15 Everitt describes the Community Music movement as emerging from the ferment of the 1960s, being 'as much concerned with personal and social development among those disadvantaged by poverty, and with the failure of the educational system, as it is with music in itself.' *Joining In,* p. 15.

16 Charles Taylor, in *Visions of Europe: Conversations on the Legacy and Future of Europe,* ed. by Richard Kearney (Dublin: Wolfhound Press, 1992), p. 55.

17   *The Invention of Tradition*, ed. by Eric Hobsbawn and Terence Ranger
      (Cambridge: Cambridge University Press, 1983), pp. 263-307.

18   Veblen, 181. See Veblen's study for a survey of organisational spon-
      sorship and traditional music, the impact of organisations and mass
      media on the transmission of the music, and a description of orga-
      niation profiles. 'Perceptions of Change and Stability in the Trans-
      mission of Irish Traditional Music,' 35–38, 180–83, 274–96.

19   Krister Malm, 'Music on the Move: Traditions and Mass Media,'
      Ethnomusicology 37 (Fall 1993), 340.

20   In her recent book, *In Search of Music Education*, Estelle Jorgensen
      criticises the narrow and inadequate manner in which music educa-
      tion has come to be defined i.e. music instruction in school settings;
      she urges that we broaden our view 'to include a plethora of
      instances and approaches besides school music that may also count
      as music education.' Estelle R. Jorgensen, *In Search of Music Educa-
      tion* (Urbana and Chicago: University of Illinois Press, 1997), xi.
      From the outset I have attempted to identify other forms of music
      education beyond the school system. In fact, a narrative that was
      limited to formal education would provide a narrow historical per-
      spective of music education in Ireland.

21   Martin Drury, 'Tacit Approval,' in *The Boydell Papers: Essays on
      Music and Music Policy in Ireland* (Dublin: Music Network, 1997), p.
      16.

22   This emphasis on text-based music education is consonant with
      Harry White's argument that 'the relationship between music and
      text has always been dominant in the cultural history of modern Ire-
      alnd', music serving as 'an enabler of textual communication'.
      White, *The Keeper's Recital*, pp. 9, 151.

Bibliography

Official Publications and Documents

Access and Opportunity: A White Paper on Cultural Policy. (Dublin: Government Publications Office, 1987).

Annual Reports of the Commissioners of National Education, 1834–1921.

The Arts Council. *Art and the Ordinary: The Report of the Arts Community Education Committee.* Ciarán Benson, (ed.). (Dublin: The Arts Council, 1989).

———. *The Arts Council and Education, 1979–1989.* (Dublin: The Arts Council, 1989).

———. *The Arts and Education (I). A Submission to the Curriculum and Examinations Board,* June 1984.

———. *The Arts and Education (IV). A Submission to the Curriculum and Examinations Board,* September 1986.

———. *Deaf Ears?* A Report by Don Herron. (Dublin: The Arts Council, 1985).

———. *The Place of the Arts in Irish Education.* A Report by Ciarán Benson. (Dublin: The Arts Council, 1979).

———. *Provision for the Arts.* A Report by J. M. Richards. (Dublin: The Arts Council, 1976).

Bodkin, Thomas. *Report on the Arts in Ireland.* (Dublin: Stationery Office, 1949).

Commission for the Restoration of the Irish Language: Summary of the Final Report. (Dublin: Stationery Office, 1963).

Conference of Convent Primary Schools in Ireland. *Evaluation of the New Curriculum for Primary Schools.* (Dublin: Ardiff Printers Ltd., 1975).

Curriculum and Examinations Board. *The Arts in Education: A Curriculum Examinations Discussion Paper.* (Dublin, 1985).

———. *Issues and Structures in Education: A Consultative Document.* (Dublin, 1984).

Economic and Social Research Institute. 'Schooling and Sex Roles: Sex Differences in Subject Provision and Student Choice in Irish Post-Primary Schools.' Paper No. 113. (Dublin, 1983).

Final Report of the National Youth Policy Committee, September 1984.

Intermediate Education Board (Ireland). *Minutes of the Proceedings of the Commissioners of Intermediate Education Meetings, 1878–1921.*

———. *Annual Reports of the Intermediate Board, 1879–1920.*

———. *Rules and Programmes of Examination, 1878–1921.*

Irish National Teachers Organization. *A Plan for Education.* (Dublin: INTO, 1947).

———. *Primary School Curriculum: Curriculum Questionnaire Analysis.* (Dublin: INTO, 1976).

Kerry Music Report: An Overview of Classical, Jazz, and Traditional Music in Kerry. A Report complied by Kerry Music County 2000. Orla Moloney, (ed.). (Dublin: Music Network, 1998).

Minutes of the Proceedings of the Commissioners of National Education at their Special Meeting on Tuesday, the 31st January, 1922.

Music Policy Document. (Dublin: Music Network, 1994).

National Adult Education Survey: Interim Report. (Dublin: Stationery Office, 1970).

National Programme Conference. *National Programme of Primary Instruction.* (Dublin: Browne and Nolan, 1922).

———. *Report and Programme of the Second National Conference.* (Dublin: Stationery Office, 1926).

The New Primary School Curriculum: Its Implementation and Effects. Reported by Particia Fontes and Thomas Kellaghan. (Dublin: Educational Research Centre, 1977).

The PIANO Report: Report of the Review Group PIANO presented to the Minister for Arts, Culture and the Gaeltacht, Mr Michael D. Higgins, T. D., January 1996 on the Provision and Institutional Arrangements Now for Orchestras and Ensembles. (Dublin, 1996).

Programmes of Instruction for National Schools for the School Year 1919–1920. (Dublin: Office of National Education, 1919).

Radio Éireann. *Annual Reports for 1936 and 1939.* (Dublin: Radio Éireann).

Radio Telifís Éireann. *Radio na Scoile.* Baile Átha Cliath: RTÉ, 1975.

———. *Musicscape.* (Baile Átha Cliath: RTÉ, 1980).

Report from the Select Committees (of the House of Commons) on Foundation Schools and Education in Ireland, 1835–1837.

Report of Her Majesty's Commissioners Appointed to Inquire into the Endowment Funds and Actual Condition of all Schools Endowed for the Purposes of Education in Ireland, 1857–58.

Report of the Commissioners on Intermediate Education (Ireland) – Final Report, 1899.

An Roinn Oideachais. *Annual Reports of the Department of Education, 1924–1964.*

——. *Charting Our Education Future:White Paper on Education.* (Dublin: Stationery Office, 1995).

——. *Council of Education Report: The Curriculum of the Secondary School.* (Dublin, 1962).

——. *Cuisle an Cheoil.* (Baile Átha Cliath: Oifig an tSolatháir, 1976).

——. *An Curaclam Nua.* Teacher's Handbook, Parts I and II. (Dublin: Browne and Nolan, 1971).

——. *Educational Broadcasting Committee: Report and Recommendations.* (Dublin: Statistical Office, 1982).

——. *Éigse an Cheoil.* (Baile Átha Cliath: Oifig an tSolatháir, 1975).

——. *Investment in Education.* (Dublin: Stationery Office, 1986).

——. *Music: Leaving Certificate Syllabus, 1989–1990.*

——. 'Musical Education in Ireland.' Unpublished paper, n. d.

——. *Notes for Teachers: Music,.* (Dublin, 1959).

——. *Programme for Action in Education, 1984–87.* (Dublin: Stationery Office, 1984).

——. *Programme of Primary Instruction.* (Dublin, 1956).

——. 'Proposed Broadcasts of Music for the Benefit of Pupils of All Schools – Primary, Secondary and Vocational.' Circular 2, January 1936.

——. 'Report of the Arts Education Joint-Level Sub-Committees (Primary-) For Music and the Visual Arts to the National Council for Curriculum and Assessment.' May, 1994.

——. *Report of the Council of Education.* (Dublin: Stationery Office, 1954).

——. *Rules and Programme for Secondary Schools, 1924–1988.*

——. Second Level Public Examination Statistics, 1990–1996.

——. *Téarmaí Ceoil.* (Baile Átha Cliath: Oifig an tSolatháir, 1933).

——. *White Paper on Educational Development.* (Dublin: Stationery Office, 1981).

——. *Brainse an Ghairmoideachais. Memorandum V. 40,* 1942; *Memorandum V. 51.* Revised, 1955.

Royal Commission of Inquiry, Primary Education, Ireland (Powis Commission), 1870.

Royal Commission on Manual and Practical Instruction in Primary Schools under the Board of National Education in Ireland – Final Report, 1898.

Saorstát Éireann. *Statutes of the Oireachtas,* No. 29 of 1930,Vocational Education Act, 1930.

Teacher's Study Group. *Report on the Draft Curriculum for Primary Schools.* Kathleen MacDonagh, (ed.). March, 1969.

Books

Aalen, F. H. A., Kevin Whelan, and Matthew Stout, (eds.). *Atlas of the Irish Rural Landscape.* (Cork: Cork University Press, 1997).

Acton, Charles. *Irish Music and Musicians.* (Dublin: Eason and Son Ltd., 1978).

Akenson, Donald. H. *Between Two Revolutions: Islandmagee, County Antrim, 1798–1920.* (Don Mills, Ontario: T. H. Best Printing Co., Ltd., 1979).

———. *The Irish Education Experiment: The National System of Education in the Nineteenth Century.* (London: Routledge and Kegan Paul, 1970).

Alberti, John, (ed.). *The Canon in the Classroom: The Pedagogical Implications of Canon Revision in American Literature.* (New York: Garland Pub., 1995).

An Analysis of School Books. (Dublin: Authority of the Commissioners of National Education in Ireland, 1853).

Anderson, Benedict. *Imagined Communities: Reflections on the Origin and Spread of Nationalism.* (London: Verso Editions and NLB, 1983).

Anthropological Perspectives on Education. (New York and London: Basic Books, Inc., Pub., 1971).

Arnold, Matthew. *Culture and Anarchy.* (New York: The Macmillan Co., 1924, c1869).

Attali, Jacques. *Noise: The Political Economy of Music.* Brian Massumi, (trans.). (Minneapolis: University of Minnesota Press, 1985).

Auchmuty, James J. *Sir Thomas Wyse, 1791–1862.* (London: P. S. King and Son Ltd., 1939).

Balfour, Graham. *Educational Systems in Great Britain and Ireland.* (Oxford: The Clarendon Press, 1898).

Beckett, J. C. *The Anglo-Irish Tradition.* (Dublin: The Blackstaff Press, 1976).

Birch, Reverend Peter. *St Kieran's College, Kilkenny.* (Dublin: Gill, 1951).

Blacking, John. *How Musical is Man?* (Seattle, WA: University of Washington Press, 1973).

Blacking, John, and Joann Keali'inohomoku, (eds.). *The Performing Arts: Music and Dance.* (The Hague: Mouton, 1979).

Bowman, John, and Ronan O'Donoghue, (eds.). *Portraits: Belvedere College Dublin 1832–1982.* (Dublin: Gill and Macmillan, 1982).

Boydell, Barra. *Music and Paintings in the National Gallery of Ireland.* (Dublin: The National Gallery of Ireland, 1985).

Boydell, Brian, (ed.). *Four Centuries of Music in Ireland.* (London: British Broadcasting Corporation, 1979).

Bradshaw, Albert. *Pentatonic Folksongs for Irish Wee Folk: Teacher's Manual; Pentatonic Folksongs and Reading Exercises.* Vols. I and II. (Dublin: Bradshaw Music Education/Dublin University Press, 1988).

Bradshaw, Harry. *Michael Coleman 1895–1914.* (Dublin: Viva Voce, 1991).

Breathnach, Breandán. *Folk Music and Dances of Ireland.* Rev. ed. (Cork and Dublin: The Mercier Press, 1977).

Breathnach, An tAthair Pádraig, (comp.). *Fuinn na Smól.* (Dublin: Browne and Nolan, 1913).

——. *Songs of the Gael.* (Dublin: Browne and Nolan, 1915).

Brown, Terence. *Ireland: A Social and Cultural History, 1922–1985.* 3rd impression, with added postscript. (London: Fontana Paperbacks, 1985).

Bunting, Edward. *The Ancient Music of Ireland.* Vol. 3. (Dublin: Hodges and Smith, 1840).

——. *A General Collection of the Ancient Irish Music* (1796), Vol. I. Rep. ed. (Dublin: Waltons, 1969).

Cairns, David, and Shaun Richards. *Writing Ireland: Colonialism, Nationalism and Culture.* (Manchester, England: Manchester University Press, 1988).

Cambrensis, Giraldus. *The History and Topography of Ireland.* John O'Meara, (trans.). (Portlaoise, Ireland: The Dolmen Press, 1982).

Campbell, Particia Shehan. *Lessons From the World: A Cross–Cultural Guide to Music Teaching and Learning.* (New York: Schirmer Books, 1991).

Carbery, Mary. *The Farm by Lough Gur.* (London: Longmans, Green, and Co., 1937).

Carleton, William. *Tales and Stories of the Irish Peasantry.* (Dublin: James Duffy Pub., 1845).

Casey, Daniel J., and Robert E. Rhodes. *Views of the Irish Peasantry 1800–1916.* (Hamden, CT: Archon Books, 1977).

Cassirer. Ernst. *An Essay on Man.* (New Haven and London: Yale University Press, 1944).

Citron, Marcia. *Gender and the Musical Canon.* (Cambridge: Cambridge University Press, 1993).

Clifford, James. *The Predicament of Culture.* (Cambridge, MA, and London, UK: Harvard University Press, 1988).

Cohen, Anthony P. *The Symbolic Construction of Community.* (Chichester, UK: Ellis Horwood Ltd., 1985).

Colles, Henry C. *The Royal College of Music: A Jubilee Record, 1883–1933.* (London: Macmillan and Co. Ltd., 1933).

Comhaltas Ceoltóirí Éireann. *Teastas i dTeagasc Ceolta Tíre.* Prep. by Mícheál Ó hEidhin. (Baile Átha Cliath: CCÉ, 1980).

——. *Bunreacht Comhaltas Ceoltóirí Éireann.* Reprin. ed. (Dublin: Comhaltas Ceoltóirí Éireann, 1996).

——. *A Living Tradition. 38th Annual Report* (Dublin: Comhaltas Ceoltóirí Éireann, n. d).

The Contemporary Music Centre, Dublin. *The Contemporary Music Centre.* Information Pamphlet, 1989.

Cooke, Jim. *Coláiste an Cheoil, College of Music: A Musical Journey 1890–1993.* (Dublin: n. p., 1994).

Coolahan, John. *Irish Education: Its History and Structure.* (Dublin: Institute of Public Administration, 1981).

Corkery, Daniel. *The Hidden Ireland.* (Dublin: Gill and Macmillan, 1924).

Council of Europe. *Music Education for All.* Prep. by J. Frommelt. (Strasbourg: Council of Europe, 1981).

Crofton Croker, T. *Researches in the South of Ireland.* (London: John Murray, 1824).

Crosbie, Paddy. *Your Dinner's Poured Out.* Intro. by James Plunkett. (Dublin: O'Brien Press, 1981).

Cullen, Mary, (ed.). *Girls Don't Do Honours: Irish Women in Education in the 19th and 20th Centuries.* (Dublin: Women's Education Bureau, 1987).

Curtin, Chris, Mary Kelly, and Liam O'Dowd, (eds.). *Culture and Ideology in Ireland.* (Galway: Officiana Typographica, Galway University Press, 1984).

Curtis, Bernard. *Centenary of the Cork School of Music: Progress of the School 1878–1978.* (Cork: Cork School of Music, 1978).

Daly, Kieran A. *Catholic Church Music in Ireland, 1878–1903: The Cecilian Reform Movement.* (Dublin: Four Courts Press, 1995).

Deale, Edgar, (ed.). *The Music Association of Ireland.* (Dublin: The Irish and Overseas Publishing Co. Ltd., 1957).

Dia Linn Lá 'Gus Oidhche 's Pádraig Aspal Éireann. (Baile Átha Cliath: Brún agus Ó Núalláin, Teor., 1917).

Dublin Musical Festival. (Dublin: Underwood Printers, 1831).

Dunphy, Eamon. *Unforgettable Fire: The Story of U2.* (New York: Viking Books, 1987).

Education and the Arts: A Research Report. (Dublin: Trinity College, University of Dublin, 1987).

Elliott, David J. *Music Matters: A New Philosophy of Music Education.* (New York: Oxford University Press, 1995).

Essays and Poems with a Centenary Memoir 1845–1945. (Dublin: M. H. Gill and Son., Ltd., 1945).

Eucharistic Congress Song Book. (Dublin: Juverna Press Ltd., 1931).

European Music Year 1985: Yearbook for Ireland. (Dublin, 1985).

Everitt, Anthony. *Joining In: An Investigation into Participatory Music.* Gulbenkian Foundation Report. (London: Calouste Gulbenkian Foundation, 1997).

Fahy, Sr. Mary de Lourdes. *Education in the Diocese of Kilmacduagh in the Nineteenth Century.* (Gort, Co. Galway: Convent of Mercy, 1972).

Feis Ceoil, Irish Musical Festival, Dublin May 18th, 19th, 20th, and 21st, 1897. (Dublin: Dollard Press, n. d.).

Feldman, Allen, and Eamon O'Doherty. *The Northern Fiddler: Music and Musicians of Donegal and Tyrone.* (Belfast: Blackstaff Press, 1979).

Finlay, T. A. *Foxford and the Providence Woollen Mills.* (Dublin: Alex Thom and Co., Ltd., n. d.).

Finnegan, Ruth. *The Hidden Musicians: Music-making in an English Town.* (Cambridge, UK, and New York: Cambridge University Press, 1989).

Fitzgerald, William G., (ed.). *The Voice of Ireland.* (Dublin, Manchester, London, and Blackburn: John Heywood Ltd., 1924).

Fleischmann, Aloys, (ed.). *Music in Ireland.* (Cork: Cork University Press, 1952).

Fletcher, Peter. *Education and Music.* (Oxford and New York: Oxford University Press, 1987).

Gantz, Jeffrey. *Early Irish Myths and Sagas.* (London: Penguin Books, 1981).

Gaelic Athletic Association. *Scór na nÓg '89.* (Baile Átha Cliath: Cumann Lúthchleas Gael, 1989).

——. *Scór: Rialacha, Nótaí agus Eolas ar Scór 1990, 1991, 1992.* (Baile Átha Cliath: Cumann Lúthchleas Gael, 1989).

Geertz, Clifford. *The Interpretation of Cultures.* (New York: Basic Books, Inc. Pub., 1973).

——, (ed.). *Old Societies and New States.* (New York: The Free Press, 1963).

Gellner, Ernest. *Nationalism.* (London: Weidenfeld and Nicholson, 1997).

Gibbons, Luke. *Transformations in Irish Culture.* (Cork: Cork University Press, 1996).

Gillen, Gerard, and Harry White, (eds.) *Irish Musical Studies: Musicology in Ireland.* (Dublin: Irish Academic Press, 1990).

——. *Irish Musical Studies: Music and Irish Cultural History.* (Dublin: Irish Academic Press, 1995).

Glassford, James. *Notes on Three Tours in Ireland, in 1824 and 1826.* (Bristol: W. Strong and J. Chilcott, 1832).

Goldring, Maurice. *Pleasant the Scholar's Life: Irish Intellectuals and the Construction of the Nation State.* (London: Serif, 1993).

Goodman, Peter, (comp.). *The Catholic Hymn-Book.* (Dublin: J. Duffy and Sons, [*c.* 1886]).

Gorham, Maurice. *Forty Years of Irish Broadcasting.* (Dublin: The Talbot Press Ltd., 1967).

Griffith, Arthur, (ed.). *Thomas Davis: The Thinker and Teacher.* (Dublin: M. H. Gill and Son Ltd., 1914).

Groocock, Joseph. *A General Survey of Music in the Republic of Ireland.* (Dublin: Foras Éireann, 1961).

Hall, Mr and Mrs S. C. *Ireland: Its Scenery and Character.* (London: Hall, Virtue, and Co., n. d.).

Hall, Rev. James. *Tour Through Ireland.* 2. vols. (London: Wilson Printers, 1813).

Hardebeck, Carl, (ed.). *Ceol na nGaedheal.* (Baile Átha Cliath: Brún agus Ó Núalláin, Teor., 1937).

Hardiman, James. *Irish Minstrelsy.* (London: Joseph Robins, 1831).

Head, Sir Francis B. *A Fortnight in Ireland.* (London: John Murray, 1852).

Heaney, Seamus. *Opened Ground: Selected Poems 1966–1996.* (New York: Farrar, Straus and Giroux, 1998).

Hearne, Joseph, and Bernard Duggan. *A Manual of School Government: being a complete analysis of the system of education pursued in the Christian Schools.* (Dublin: The Christian Brothers, 1845).

Henebry, Richard. *A Handbook of Irish Music.* (Cork: Cork University Press, 1928).

Hennessy, P. J. *A Century of Catholic Education.* (Dublin: Browne and Nolan, 1916).

Henry, Nelson B., (ed.). *Basic Concepts in Music Education: The Fifty-seventh Yearbook of the National Society for the Study of Education.* (Chicago, IL.: The University of Chicago Press, 1958).

Hime, Maurice C. *A Schoolmaster's Retrospect of Eighteen and a Half Years in an Irish School.* (London: Simpkin, Marshall, and Co., 1885).

———. *History of the Institute.* 2 vols. (Dublin: Bray Printing Co., 1958–61).

Hobsbawn, Eric, and Terence Ranger, (eds.). *The Invention of Tradition.* (Cambridge: Cambridge University Press, 1983).

Hollinger, David. *Postethnic America: Beyond Multiculturalism.* (New York: Basic Books, 1995).

Hullah, John. *Wilhem's Method of Teaching Singing* (1842). Intro. by Bernarr Rainbow. (Kilkenny, Ireland: Boethius Press, 1983).

Hutchinson, John. *The Dynamics of Cultural Nationalism: the Gaelic Revival and the Creation of the Irish Nation State*. (London: Allen and Unwin, 1987).

——. *Irish Traditional Music Archive: The First Ten Years*. (Dublin: Irish Traditional Music Archive, 1997).

Jeffares, A. Norman, and Antony Kemm, (eds.). *An Irish Childhood*. (London: Collins Sons and Co. Ltd., 1987).

Johnson, James. *A Tour in Ireland with Meditations and Reflections*. (London: S. Highley, 1844).

Joyce, Patrick W. *A Social History of Ancient Ireland*. Vol. 1. 2nd ed. (Dublin: M. H. Gill and Son Ltd., 1913, c. 1904).

——. *Old Irish Folk Music and Songs*. (Dublin: Hodges, Figgis, and Co. Ltd., 1909).

——. *English as We Speak it in Ireland*. 2nd ed. (Trowbridge and Esher: Redwood Burn Ltd., 1979).

Kearney, Richard, (ed.). *Across the Frontiers: Ireland in the 1990s*. (Dublin: Wolfhound Press, 1988).

——. *Transitions: Narratives in Modern Irish Culture*. (Manchester: Manchester University Press, 1988).

——. (ed.). *Migrations: The Irish at Home and Abroad*. (Dublin: Wolfhound Press, 1990).

——. *Visions of Europe: Conversations on the Legacy and Future of Europe*. (Dublin: Wolfhound Press, 1992).

——. *Postnationalist Ireland: Politics, Culture, Philosophy*. (London and New York: Routledge, 1997).

Kelly, Anne. *Cultural Policy in Ireland*. (UNESCO, 1989).

Kennedy, Brian P. *Dreams and Responsibilities: The State and the Arts in Independent Ireland*. (Dublin: The Arts Council, 1990).

Kennedy, Patrick. *The Banks of the Boro: A Chronicle of County Wexford*. (London: Simpkin, Marshall and Co., 1867).

King, Jeremiah. *County Kerry – Past and Present*. 2nd ed. (Cork and Dublin: The Mercier Press, 1986).

Kingsbury, Henry. *Music, Talent, and Performance: A Conservatory Cultural System*. (Philadelphia: Temple University Press, 1988).

Kohl, Johann G. *Riesen in Ireland*. (London: Chapman and Hall, 1843).

Langer, Suzanne. *Feeling and Form*. (New York: Charles Scribner's Sons, 1953).

Lee, Joseph. *The Modernization of Irish Society, 1845–1918*. (Dublin: Gill and Macmillan, Ltd., 1973).

——. (ed.). *Ireland: Towards a Sense of Place*. (Cork: Cork University Press, 1985).

Leerssen, Joep. *Remembrance and Imagination: Patterns in the Historical and Literary Representation of Ireland in the Nineteenth Century.* (Cork: Cork University Press in association with Field Day, 1996).

Litton, Frank, (ed.). *Unequal Achievement: The Irish Experience 1957–1982.* (Dublin: Institute of Public Administration, 1982).

Lynd, Robert. *Home Life in Ireland.* (London: Mills and Boon, Ltd., 1909).

Lyons, F. S. L. *The Burden of Our History.* The W. B. Rankin Memorial Lecture delivered 4 December 1978. (Belfast: Moyne, Boyd and Son, Ltd., 1979).

——. *Culture and Anarchy in Ireland, 1890–1939.* (Oxford: Oxford University Press, 1979).

Mainzer, Joseph. *Music and Education* (1848). Intro. by Bernarr Rainbow. (Kilkenny: Boethius Press, 1985).

Mark, Desmond, (ed.). *Stock-Taking of Musical Life: Music Sociography and its Relevance to Music Education.* (Vienna: Dobinger, 1981).

Mark, Michael. *Source Readings in Music Education History.* (New York: Schirmer Books, 1982).

McCarthy, Michael J. F. *Five Years in Ireland.* (Dublin: Hodges; London: Simpkin, 1902).

McClary, Susan. *Feminine Endings: Music, Gender, and Sexuality.* (Minnesota: Minnesota University Press, 1991).

McElligott, T. J. *Secondary Education in Ireland, 1870–1921.* (Dublin: Irish Academic Press, 1981).

McHale, Rev. John, (trans.) *A Selection of Moore's Melodies.* (Dublin: James Duffy, *c.* 1842, 1871).

McLuhan, Marshall, and Quentin Fiore. *The Medium is the Message.* (New York: Bantum Books, 1967).

Merriam, Alan P. *The Anthropology of Music.* (Chicago, IL: Northwestern University Press, 1964).

Molloy, Dinah. *Find Your Music: A Guide to Music in Ireland.* 2nd ed. (Dublin: The Arts Council, 1979).

Moonan, George. *The Spirit of the Gaelic League.* Gaelic League Pamphlets, No. 33. (Dublin: The Gaelic League, n. d).

Moore, Thomas. *Irish Melodies with Miscellaneous Poems, with a Melologue upon National Music.* (Dublin: John Cumming, 1833).

Moran, D. P. *The Philosophy of Irish Ireland.* (Dublin: 1905).

Mulcahy, D. G. *Curriculum and Policy in Irish Post-Primary Education.* (Dublin: Institute of Public Administration, 1981).

Mulcahy, Michael, and Marie Fitzgibbon. *The Voice of the People.* (Dublin: O'Brien Press, 1982).

The Music Association of Ireland. 'Bringing the Arts to School: Music Workshops, 1989–90.' (Dublin: The Music Association of Ireland, 1989).

——. 'Bringing the Arts to School: Schools Recital Scheme, 1989–90.' (Dublin: The Music Association of Ireland, 1989).

Noel, Baptist Wriothesley. *Notes of a Short Tour through the Midland Counties of Ireland, in the Summer of 1836.* (London: James Nisbet and Co., 1837).

O'Boyle, Seán. *The Irish Song Tradition.* (Dublin: Gilbert Dalton, 1976).

Ó Buachalla, Séamus, (ed.). *A Significant Irish Educationalist: The Educational Writings of P. H. Pearse.* (Dublin and Cork: The Mercier Press, 1980).

Ó Ceallacháin, Mícheál, (comp.). *Beidh Ceol Againn.* Cuid I agus II.(Baile Átha Cliath: Ó Fallúin, 1969).

Ó Conaire, Breandán, (ed.). *Language, Lore, and Lyrics.* (Dublin: Irish Academic Press, 1986).

O'Connor, Anne V., and Susan M. Parkes. *Gladly Learn and Gladly Teach: Alexandra College and School, 1866–1966.* (Dublin: Blackwater Press, 1983).

O'Connor, Nuala. *Bringing It All Back Home: The Influence of Irish Music.* (London: BBC Books, 1991).

Ó Dálaigh, Pádraig. *A Ballad History of Ireland for Schools.* (Dublin and Cork: The Educational Company of Ireland, [ca. 1929]).

O'Donoghue, John. *In a Quiet Land.* Foreward by Seán Ó Faoláin. (London: B. T. Batsford Ltd., 1957).

O'Dowd, Liam, (ed.). *On Intellectuals and Cultural Life in Ireland: International, Comparative and Historical Contexts.* (Belfast: Institute of Irish Studies, 1996).

Ó Drisceoil, Prionsias, (ed.). Culture in Ireland – Regions: Identity and Power. (Belfast: The Queen's University of Belfast, 1993).

Ó hEidhin, Mícheál, (ed.). *Cas Amhrán.* (Indreabhán, Gallimh: Clódóirí Lurgan, 1975).

Ó hEochaidh, Marcus, (ed.) *Modhscoil Luimnigh, 1855–1986.* (Limerick: Mc Kerns Printers Ltd., n. d.).

Ó Fearaíl, Pádraig. *The Story of Conradh na Gaeilge.* (Baile Átha Cliath: Clódhanna Teo., 1975).

O'Kelly, Pat. *The National Symphony of Ireland 1948–1998.* (Dublin: Radio Teilifís Éireann, n. d.)

Ong, Walter. *Orality and Literacy: The Technologizing of the Word.* (London and New York: Routledge, 1988).

Ó Riada, Seán. *Our Musical Heritage*. (Portlaoise, Ireland: The Dolmen Press, 1982).

Ó Súilleabháin, Amhlaoibh. *The Diary of Humphrey O'Sullivan*. Trans. by Tomás de Bhaldraithe. (Dublin and Cork: The Mercier Press, 1979).

Ó Súilleabháin, Donncha. *An Cumann Scoildramaíochta 1934–1984*. (Baile Átha Cliath: An Clóchomhar Tta., 1986).

——. *Scéal an Oireachtais, 1897–1924*. (Baile Átha Cliath: An Clóchomhar Tta., 1984).

O'Sullivan, Donal. *Carolan: The Life, Times, and Music of an Irish Harper*. (London: Routledge and Kegan Paul Ltd., 1958).

——. (ed.). *Songs of the Irish*. (Dublin: Browne and Nolan, 1960).

O'Toole, Fintan. *The Ex-Isle of Erin: Images of a Global Ireland*. (Dublin: New Island Books, 1996).

Pine, Richard, (ed.). *Music in Ireland 1848–1998*. (Cork and Dublin: Mercier Press, 1998).

Power, Matt. *Half a Century – Co. Clare VEC 1930–80*. (Ennis, Co. Clare: Clare Printers Ltd., n. d.).

Radocy, Rudolf E., and J. David Boyle. *The Psychological Foundations of Music Education*. (Springfield, IL: Charles C. Thomas, 1979).

Rainbow, Bernarr. *The Land Without Music*. (London: Novello and Co. Ltd., 1967).

RDS World Music for Youth Festival, 24th–30th November 1997. Programme.

Report of the Gaelic League for the year ended 30.9.1894. (Dublin: Dollard Printinghouse, 1895).

Report of the Gaelic League for the two years ended 30.9.1896. (Dublin: Doyle Publishers, 1896).

Robins, Joseph. *The Lost Children: A Study of Charity Children in Ireland 1700–1900*. (Dublin: Institute of Public Administration, 1980).

Rosenstock, Gabriel. *Slógadh*. (Baile Átha Cliath: An Gúm, n. d.).

The Royal Irish Academy of Music: Centenary Souvenir, 1856–1956. (Dublin: Corrigan and Wilson, Ltd., 1956).

Sacred Poetry adapted to the understanding of children and youth for the use in schools. (Dublin, 1845).

Sadie, Stanley, (ed.). *The New Grove Dictionary of Music and Musicians*. (London: Macmillan, 1980).

Selleck, R. J. W. *The New Education, 1870–1914*. (London and Melbourne: Pitman and Sons Ltd., 1968).

Shaw Mason, William. *A Statistical Account or Parochial Survey of Ireland*. (Dublin: Graisbury and Campbell, 1814).

Sheehy, Jeanne. *The Rediscovery of Ireland's Past: The Celtic Revival 1830–1930.* (London: Thames and Hudson Ltd., 1980).

Shepherd, John. *Music as Social Text.* (Cambridge: Cambridge, UK: Polity Press, 1991).

Shields, Hugh. *Popular Music in Eighteenth-Century Dublin.* (Dublin: Folk Music Society of Ireland and Na Píobairí Uilleann, 1985).

Slobin, Mark. *Subcultural Sounds: Micromusics of the West.* (Hanover and London: University Press of New England, 1993).

Small, Christopher. *Music, Society, and Education.* 2nd rev. ed. (London: John Calder, 1980).

Smith, Thérèse, and Mícheál Ó Súilleabháin, (eds.). *Blas/The Local Accent in Traditional Irish Music.* (The Folk Music Society of Ireland and the Irish World Music Centre, University of Limerick, 1997).

Sneyd-Kynnersley, Edmund *M. H.M.I.: Some Passages in the Life of one of H.M. Inspectors of Schools.* (London: Macmillan and Co. Ltd., 1908).

Stokes, John. *The Life of George Petrie.* (London, 1868).

Stokes, Martin. *Ethnicity, Identity and Music: The Musical Construction of Place.* (Oxford/Providence, RI: Berg Publishers, 1994).

Thackeray, William M. *The Irish Sketch-Book.* 2 vols. (London: Chapman and Hall, 1843).

31st International Eucharistic Congress: Pictorial Record. (Dublin: Veritas Co. Ltd., 1933).

Tierney, Michael. *Education in a Free Ireland.* (Dublin: Martin Lester Ltd., 1919).

Tovey, Hilary, Damian Hamman and Hal Abramson. *Why Irish? Language and Identity in Ireland Today.* (Baile Átha Cliath: Bord na Gaeilge, 1989).

Tunney, Paddy. *The Stone Fiddle.* (Dublin: Gilbert Dalton, 1979).

Tylor, E. B. *Primitive Culture.* 5th ed. (London: S. Murray, 1929).

Vallely, Eithne, and J. B. Vallely. *Sing a Song and Play It: A Book of Irish Music and Song for Children.* 3 vols. (Belfast: The Appletree Press, 1975).

Walker, Joseph C. *Historical Memoirs of the Bards.* (Dublin: Luke White Publishing Co., 1786).

Ward, Justine. *That All May Sing.* (Washington, DC: Catholic Education Press, 1956).

White, Harry. *The Keeper's Recital: Music and Cultural History in Ireland, 1770–1970.* (Cork: Cork University Press in association with Field Day, 1998).

White, Leslie. *The Concept of Culture*. (Minneapolis, Minnesota: Burgess Publishing Co., 1973).

Williams, Raymond. *Culture and Society, 1780–1950*. (London: Chatto and Windus, 1958).

Wyse, Thomas. *Speech of Thomas Wyse, Esq., M. P., in the House of Commons on Tuesday, May 19, 1835*. (London: Ridgway and Son, 1835).

———. *Education Reform*. (London: Longman et al., 1836).

Yeats, William Butler. In *Autobiographies*. (London: Macmillan and Co. Ltd., 1926).

Young, Arthur. *A Tour in Ireland*. (London: Cadell and Dodsley Press, 1780).

Articles

Acton, Charles. 'The Schools and Music: Reflections on Promise.' *Éire-Ireland* 5:1 (Spring 1970), 98–110.

———. 'Music Teaching: Economics and the Community.' *Éire-Ireland* 6:4 (Winter 1971), 127–33.

'An Apology for Harmony.' *Dublin University Magazine* 17 (January-June 1841), 570–584.

'An 39ú Tuarascáil Bhliantúil.' 21 *Treoir* (1989).

'Army Band Concerts for Dublin Primary Schools.' *The Irish School Weekly* 36 (20 October 1934), 1008.

'Association of Secondary Teachers of Ireland: Commission on Secondary Education.' *The Irish School Weekly* 71 (January 1922), 80.

Best, R. I. 'The Feis Ceoil.' *Leabhar na hÉireann: The Irish Yearbook* (1908), 154–156.

Bewerunge, H. 'The Teaching of Music in Irish Schools.' *Irish Ecclesiastical Record*, 4th series, 2 (December 1897), 481–87.

———. 'The Special Charm of Irish Melodies Sung "Traditionally".' *Irish Ecclesiastical Record*, 4th series, 8 (July-December 1900), 140–54.

Boland, J. P. 'Plain Chant in a Kerry Country Church.' *The Irish Monthly* 79 (October 1951), 446–49.

'Bonus for Choirs and Orchestras.' *The Secondary Teacher* 3:3 (Spring 1974), 30.

Boydell, Brian. 'Music in Ireland.' *The Bell* 14:1 (April 1947), 16–24.

Breathnach, Breandán. 'The Pipers of Kerry.' *Éigse Cheol Tíre* 4 (1982–85), 5–29.

——. 'The Use of Notation in the Transmission of Irish Folk Music.' Ó Riada Memorial Lecture 1. University College Cork: Irish Traditional Music Society, 1986.

Breen, Denis. 'INTO Congress, 1926.' *The Irish School Weekly* 77 (17 April 1926), 490–92.

——. 'School-Music – Its Place in the National Life.' *The Irish School Weekly*, 77 (1 May 1926), 558–62; (8 May 1926), 590–92); (15 May 1926), 618–22.

British Journal of Music Education 10 (November 1993). Proceedings of the Music Gender, and Education Conference, Bristol Univeristy, March 1993.

'Broadcasts to Schools.' *The Irish School Weekly* 38 (7 November 1936), 1084.

Burgess, Barry. 'The Primary School Irish Traditional Music Project.' *An Múinteoir Náisiúnta* 23:3 (October 1979), 26–9.

Burke, P. 'Education for Work and Leisure.' 41 *Vocational Education Bulletin* (July 1947), 871–72.

'The Buttevant School Band.' *The Irish School Weekly* 57 (11 July 1914), 430.

Carolan, Nicholas. 'Report on Recent Meetings: Teaching Irish Music.' *Ceol Tíre* 12 (May 1978), 6–7.

'Ceol-Chumann na nÓg.' *The Irish School Weekly* 39 (25 November 1937), 1169.

'Ceol-Chumann na nÓg.' *The Irish School Weekly* 41 (29 April 1939), 421.

'Choir of 400 Children to Broadcast.' *Irish Independent*, 17 March 1939, 9.

'The Christian Schools.' *The Standard*, 9 June 1928, 12.

'Circular to Training Colleges – Music.' *The Irish School Weekly* 36 (6 December 1902), 10.

'College Academies.' *Carlow College Magazine* 1:1 (1869), 406–08.

Coolahan, John. 'The Dilemma of Educational Broadcasting in Ireland.' *The Crane Bag* 8:2 (1984), 157–60.

Corcoran, Frank. 'Musings on Our Schools Music.' *The Secondary Teacher* 6:2 (Winter 1976), 15.

Corcoran, T. 'Music and Language in Irish Schools.' *The Irish Monthly* 51 (July 1923), 338–40.

——. 'An Issue Concerning Music.' *The Irish Monthly* 61 (June 1933), 338–40.

——. 'National Literature Through National Music.' *The Irish Monthly* 61 (July 1933), 410–12.

'Cork School Music Committee: A Most Successful Concert.' *The Irish School Weekly* 77 (6 February 1926), 176.

Correspondence to the Editor. 'Vocal Music.' *The Irish Teachers Journal* 2 (1 May 1869), 112.

Crawford, Seán. 'Rural Music Schools.' *The Irish School Weekly* 48 (5 and 12 October 1946), 449.

'Cuirm Ceoil: Successful Schools' Concert in Cork.' *The Irish School Weekly* 77 (11 July 1925), 852.

Daly, Mary. 'An Alien Institution? Attitudes Towards the City in Nineteenth and Twentieth Century Irish Society.' *Études Irlandaises* 10 (December 1985), 181–94.

'The Dancing Academy.' *Illustrated London News*, 17 January 1852, 60.

De Paor, Liam. 'Ireland's Identities.' *The Crane Bag* 3:1 (1978), 22–9.

Dervan, Michael. 'A Long Road to Catch up with European Standards.' *The Irish Times*, 11 January 1990, 14.

Deverich, Robin K. 'The Maidstone Movement – Influential British Precursor of American Public School Instrumental Classes.' *Journal of Research in Music Education* 35 (Spring 1987), 39–55.

D. L. 'The Music of the Home in Kickham's Country.' *The Irish Monthly* 59 (November 1931), 723–26.

Donovan, T. 'New Programme of the Board of National Education – Singing.' *Irish Ecclesiastical Record*, 4th series, 9 (January-June 1901), 1–25.

'Drawing and Singing of National Schools.' *The Irish Teachers Journal* 6 (12 April 1873), 101.

Drury, Martin. 'Once More with Feeling: The Case for Arts-in-Education.' A Paper delivered at the INTO Education Conference in Ennis, May 1989.

Eakins, Rex. 'Heitor Villa-Lobos: A Music Educator.' *International Journal of Music Education* 10 (1987), 32–5.

'Eighty Years with the Storm Troops of Life.' *The Sunday Press,* 18 April 1982, 23.

Fahy, Carmel. 'We are the Music Makers: a look at the position of music in our primary schools,' *An Múinteoir Náisiúnta* 13:1 (1968), 17, 20.

Farren, Seán N. 'Culture and Curriculum or Dreams and Realities.' *An Múinteoir Náisiúnta* 26:1 (Spring 1982), 27–9.

Fitzgerald, Garrett. 'Ireland's Identity Problems.' *Études Irlandaises* 1 (December 1976), 135–158.

Fleischmann, Aloys. 'The Outlook of Music in Ireland.' *Studies* 24 (March 1935), 121–30.

——. 'Ars Nova: Irish Music in the Shaping.' *Ireland Today* 1:2 (July 1936), 41–8.

——. 'Composition and the Folk Idiom.' *Ireland Today* 1:6 (November 1936), 37–44.

——. 'Music in Ireland.' *The Bell* 13 (1947), 22.

'Foireann Cheoil: Scoil na mBan Riaghalta, Béal Eas, Co. Mhuigh Eó.' *Irisleabhar na Gaedhilge* 13 (July 1903), 345.

Gmur, Theo. 'The Choral Singing in Our Schools: The Intermediate System.' *Journal of the Ivernian Society* 5:17 (October–December 1912), 34–8.

Grampus. 'How the Gramophone Can Help Musical Education: Views of Dr Larchet.' *The Irish Times*, 6 October 1927, 4.

Green, Lucy. 'Gender, Musical Meaning and Education,' *Philosophy of Music Education Review* 2 (Fall 1994), 99–105.

Hardebeck, Carl. 'Traditional Singing: Its Value and Meaning.' *Journal of the Ivernian Society* 3:10 (January-March 1911), 89–95.

Headmaster of a London School. 'Organizing and Maintaining a "Maidstone" Violin Class.' *The Irish School Weekly* 14 (11 July 1908), 687–88.

Henebry, Richard. 'Irish Music.' *The Irish Year Book* (1908), 233–8.

Henry, Edward O. 'Institutions for the Promotion of Indigenous Music: The Case for Ireland's Comhaltas Ceoltóirí Éireann.' *Ethnomusicology* 33 (Winter 1989), 67–95.

'Her Majesty's Visit to the Female Infant School of the National Board of Education, in Marlborough-Street, Dublin.' *Illustrated London News*, 11 August 1849, 87.

Hickson, William E. 'Music, and the Committee of Council for Education.' *Westminster Review* 37:1 (January–April 1842), 1–43.

Hughes, Emily. 'Music in Ireland.' *The Irish Monthly* 69 (October 1941), 468–72.

'Intermediate Education.' *The Irish Year Book* (1908), 209–15.

'Irish Dancing Commission.' *The Teacher's Work* 24 (June 1934), 343.

'Irish National Teachers' Congress, 1926: Paper on Music in Schools.' *The Irish School Weekly* 56 (17 April 1926), 490–2.

'Irish National Teachers' Organization Congress: An Influential Gathering.' *The Irish School Weekly* 61 (6 and 13 May 1916), 451–67.

'Irish Traditional Music Teacher's Diploma.' *Treoir* 19:2 (1987), 12.

Johnson, Nuala C., 'Nation-building, Language and Education: The Geography of Teacher Recruitment in Ireland, 1925–55.' *Political Geography* 11 (March 1992), 170–89.

'J. F. R.' 'Schools Examiners' Reports – 1892–93.' *Christian Brothers Educational Record* 2 (1892–94), 325–37.

——. 'Songs and Hymns.' *Christian Brothers Educational Record* 3 (1894–96), 467–9.

Kellaghan, Thomas, and Liam Gorman. 'A Survey of Teaching Aids in Irish Primary Schools.' *The Irish Journal of Education* 2:1 (Spring 1968), 32–40.

Kelly, Anna. 'The Whistlers of Garryhill.' *The Irish Press*, 12 November 1949, 3.

Kelly, Noel. 'Music in Irish Primary Education, 1831–1922.' *Proceedings of the Educational Studies Association*. (Galway: Officiana Typographica, 1979).

Kennedy, Patrick. 'Irish Dancing Fifty Years Ago.' *Dublin University Magazine* 62 (October 1863), 429–39.

Krader, Barbara. 'Slavic Folk Music: Forms of Singing and Self-Identity.' *Ethnomusicology* 31:1 (Winter 1987), 9–17.

Landers, T. A. 'Music for the Juniors.' *An Múinteoir Náisiúnta* 3 (1958), 23–4.

'Lecture on Irish Music.' *Irish Musical Monthly* 1:11 (January 1903), 116–21.

'Lectures by Mr W. H. Grattan Flood.' *Irish Musical Monthly* 1:2 (April 1902), 24.

'Liturgical Festival: Eighty-four Choirs Compete at Limerick.' *Cork Examiner*, 10 May 1943.

Lundquist, Barbara Reeder. 'Transmission of Music Culture in Formal Educational Institutions,' *The World of Music* 29 (1987), 67–76.

Mac Artuir, A. E. 'Staff Notation in the Schools.' *The Teacher's Work*, 18:4 (October 1927), 116.

Martyn, Edward. 'Gregorian Chant at Loreto Abbey.' *The Irish Musical Monthly* 1:1 (1 March 1902), 8–9.

May, Frederick. 'Music and the Nation.' *Dublin Magazine* 6:3 (July–September 1936), 50–6.

McCann, May. 'Music and Politics in Ireland: The Specificity of the Folk Revival in Belfast.' *British Journal of Ethnomusicology* 4 (1995), 51–75.

McCarthy, Marie. 'Irish Music Education and Irish Identity: A Concept Revisited,' *Oideas* 45 (Fómhar 1997), 5–22.

——. 'Gendered Discourse and the Construction of Identity: Toward a Liberated Pedagogy in Music Education,' in Musings: Arts Education Essays in Honor of Bennett Reimer, *Journal of Aesthetic Education* (Fall 1999, in press).

Meany, Mary. 'Aspects of Music Education in the Primary School.' *Irish Educational Studies* 6:1 (1986–87), 172–9.

'Memorandum of Suggested Changes in Present School Programmes.' *The Irish School Weekly* 63 (3 March 1917), 122.

Murphy, John A. 'Identity Change in the Republic of Ireland.' *Études Irlandaises* 1 (December 1976), 143–58.

Murtagh, Michael. 'The Status of Music.' *The Secondary Teacher* 5:2 (Winter 1975), 37–9.

'Music for the People.' *The Dublin Journal (of Temperance, Science, and Literature)* 1:10 (2 July 1842), 145–6.

Musgrove, Frank. 'Curriculum, Culture and Ideology.' *Curriculum Studies* 10:2 (1978), 99–111.

Neeson, Seán. 'When Gaelic Tunes are Whistled in the Streets.' *The Irish Press*, 12 April 1935, 8.

'The New Music Programme.' *The Irish School Weekly* 41 (28 October 1939), 1014– 15.

'New Series of Broadcasts To Saorstat Schools.' *Irish Independent*, 13 January 1937, 12.

'A New Song.' *The Irish School Weekly* 57 (3 October 1914), 714.

'A New Song for Schools.' *The Irish School Weekly* 52 (26 October and 4 November 1950), 470.

'Niamh.' 'Music Notes.' *Journal of the Ivernian Society* 6:21 (October –December 1913), 55–7; 7:25 (October–December 1914), 40–5; 7:27 (April–June 1915), 178–80.

Ní Niocaill, Eibhlín. 'Nationality in Irish Education.' *Irisleabhar na Gaedhilge* 19 (19 Meitheamh 1909), 258–67.

Nketia, J. H. Kwabena. 'Music Education in Africa and the West: We Can Learn from Each Other.' *Music Educators Journal* 57 (November 1970), 48–55.

'No Broadcasts in Schools.' *The Irish School Weekly*, 52 (9 and 16 December 1950), 540.

'Notes.' *Journal of the Ivernian Society* 2:6 (October 1909), 124.

'Notes on Art, Archeology, and Music.' *Journal of the Ivernian Society* 1:4 (June 1909), 260–63.

Ó hAllmhuráin, Gearóid. 'Jack Mulkere: Teacher, Patriot and Gael.' *Treoir* 14 (1982), 6–7.

O'Boyle, Elizabeth M. 'Irish Song Schools: a Memory and a Hope.' *The Irish Monthly* 59 (April 1931), 215–25.

O'Brien, Grace. 'The National Element in Irish Music.' *The Irish Monthly* 43 (November 1915), 704–14.

O'Callaghan, Margaret. 'Language, nationality and cultural identity in the Irish Free State, 1922–7: the Irish Statesman and the Catholic Bulletin reappraised.' *Irish Historical Studies* 24 (November 1984), 226–45.

Ó Casaide, Séamus. 'Father Walsh's Irish Song Books.' *The Irish Book Lover* 7 (September 1915), 32–3.

Ó Conghaile, Pádraig. 'Cuirtear Craobh den Claisceadal ar bun in gach Céard Scoil.' *Vocational Education Bulletin* 28 (May 1943), 563.

O'Dwyer, Robert. 'The Modern Aspect of Irish Music.' *The Irish Year Book* (1908), 251–54.

O'Gallchobhair, Eamonn. 'Music: Academies and Professors.' *Ireland Today* 2:3 (March 1937), 63–5.

'Oide.' 'Craolachán i gCóir Scoileanna.' *The Irish School Weekly* 39 (18 September 1937), 916.

Ó Madagáin. Breandán. 'Functions of Irish Song in the Nineteenth Century.' *Béaloideas* 53 (1985), 130–216.

Ó Muireadhaigh, Éamonn. 'Traditional Music.' *Clogher Record* 1 (1953), 29–30.

Ó Murchada, Máire Caitlín. 'What!! Music? A Case for the Inclusion of Music in the General Education of Children.' *Irish Educational Studies* 6:1 (1986–87), 180–92.

O'Neill, George. 'The Work of the Feis Ceoil Association: A History and An Appeal.' *The Irish Ecclesiastical Record.* 4th series, 8 (June–December 1900), 347–57.

'Orchestral Concerts for Schoolchildren.' *Evening Mail,* 5 February 1952, 5.

'Organization Jottings.' *The Irish School Weekly* 41 (22 July 1939), 695.

Ó Súilleabháin, Donnchadh. 'Cumann na bPíobairí.' *Treoir* 13:3 (1981), 34–5.

Ó Súilleabháin, Mícheál. 'Irish Music Defined.' *The Crane Bag* 5:2 (1981), 83–87.

——. 'Out of Tune with Reality: Music and the School in Ireland.' *Irish Educational Studies* 5:1 (1985), 44–57.

O'Sullivan, Br. Séamus V. 'The Value of Aesthetic Subjects in the School Curriculum.' *Christian Brothers Educational Record* 34 (1955), 137–48.

——. 'Young People at School.' *Christus Rex* 12:2 (April 1968), 144–52.

'Over 3,000 Attend Concerts.' *Waterford News,* 21 January 1950, 2.

Patterson, Annie. 'Notes on Music, Art, Etc.' *Journal of the Ivernian Society* 1:3 (March 1909), 199–201.

——. 'The Interpretation of Irish Music.' *Journal of the Ivernian Society* 2:5 (September 1909), 31–42.

Pearse, Pádraig H. *An Macaomh: Saint Enda's School Journal, 1910–13.*

'Polyhymnia: or, Singing for the Million.' *Dublin University Magazine* 21 (January-June 1843), 16–28.

Programme Notes to National Children's Choir. Dublin, 1985, 1987, 1989.

Pseudonym used Rathcol. 'Music Teaching in the Schools.' *The Irish Musical Monthly* 1:9 (November 1902), 91–3.

Raywid, Mary Anne. 'Perspectives on the Struggle Against Indoctrination.' *The Educational Forum* 48:2 (Winter 1984), 137–54.

Redmond, Liam. 'Our History in Story and Ballad.' *The Irish School Weekly* 42 (12 October 1940), 764.

'Report on Annual Congress.' *The Irish School Weekly* 34 (2 April 1932), 367–68, 370, 372, 393.

'Revival of the Irish Language: Mechanics Institutes – Temperance Societies.' *The Dublin Journal* 1 (2 July 1843), 177–78.

Rogers, Brendan. 'Music in Our Intermediate Schools and Its Effects on Public and Ecclesiastical Taste.' *Lyra Ecclesiastica* 2–3 (1880–81), 6–8, 66–8, 84–6.

——. 'An Irish School of Music.' *The New Ireland Review* 13 (March-August 1900), 149–59.

'Roscommon Music Conference.' *The Irish School Weekly* 42 (22 June 1940), 495.

Russell, T. O. 'Our Irish Music: What is to be Its Future?' *Evening Telegraph*, 8 September 1894, 8.

'Schola Cantorum.' *Franciscan Magazine* (1985), 12–15.

'School Singing Competition in Ireland.' *The School Music Review* 1 (1 November 1892), 95.

Sheridan, J. D. 'School Music – Today and To-morrow.' *The Irish School Weekly* 31 (6 December 1930), 1378.

Shields, Hugh. 'Recent Meetings: The Feis Ceoil and Irish Music.' *Ceol Tíre* 22 (October 1982), 3–4.

'Situations Vacant.' *The Irish Teachers Journal* 1 (1 February 1868), iii; 5 (1 September 1872), 444; 5 (15 September 1872), 466; 5 (1 October 1872), 478; 5 (15 November 1872), 518.

Skilbeck, Malcolm. 'Education and Cultural Change.' *Compass* 5:2 (May 1976), 3–23.

Sleith, Joseph. 'Music in the Schools – What it was, What it is, and What it ought to be.' *Irish School Weekly* 67 (6 March 1915), 1345–46.

Smith, Nancy. 'Music Education in Ireland: The Meeting of the Waters.' *Music Educators Journal* 73 (December 1987), 48–51.

'Some Remarks on the "Theory of Music" Papers Set at the Intermediate Education Examination, 1902.' *Irish Musical Monthly* 1:6 (1 August 1902), 65–6.

Spelman, Brendan, and Maureen Killeany. 'Music Standards and Dispositions of Students Entering a College of Education.' *Irish Educational Studies* 7:1 (1988), 102–123.

'T.' 'On the Cultivation of Music in Ireland.' *Carlow College Magazine* 1 (March 1870), 620–27.

T.H.M'C. 'Musical Reform.' *The Irish Magazine and National Teachers Gazette* 1:3 (1 July 1860), 47–8.

'To Develop the School Music of a Whole Nation.' *The Irish Musical Monthly* 1 (May 1902), 25–7.

'To Our Language through Our Music.' *The Teacher's Work* 18:5 (November 1927), 119.

Traschel, Mary. 'Oral and Literate Constructs of "Authentic" Irish Music.' *Éire-Ireland* 23 (Fall 1995), 27–46.

Trimillos, Ricardo D. 'Hálau, Hochschule, Maystro, and Ryū: Cultural Approaches to Music Learning and Teaching.' *International Journal of Music Education* 14 (1989), 32–43.

'Twenty-Fourth Annual Congress of the V.E.O.: The Rural Education Problem.' *Vocational Education Bulletin* 42 (November 1947), 886–93.

'2,000 Children In Plain Chant Festival.' *The Irish Press*, 1 June 1942, 3.

Uí Éigeartaigh, Caitlín. 'Report on Recent Meetings: Teaching Folk Music?' *Ceol Tíre* 5 (October 1975), 3–5.

Vassberg, David E. 'Villa-Lobos as Pedagogue: Music in the Service of the State.' *Journal of Research in Music Education* 23:3 (Fall 1975), 163–70.

Veblen, Kari. 'The Teacher's Role in Transmission of Irish Traditional Music,' *International Journal of Music Education* 24 (1994), 21–30.

'Vocal Music in the Dublin Schools.' *The Irish Musical Monthly* 1:6 (August 1902), 61–4.

'The Vocational School Curriculum: Vocal Music as a Nation-Wide Subject.' *The Teacher's Work* 21:5 (November 1930), 113–14.

Ward, Alan. 'Music from Sliabh Luachra.' *Traditional Music* 5 (1976), 1–32.

Weymes, Rev. Maurice. 'General Musical Culture in Ireland.' *Irish Ecclesiastical Record*. 5th series, 56 (November 1940), 440–48.

——. 'Question of Value in Music.' *Irish Ecclesiastical Record*, 5th series, 59 (January-June 1942), 314–24.

——. 'General Musical Education in Ireland.' *Irish Ecclesiastical Record*, 5th series, 60 (November 1942), 348–55.

White, Harry. 'The Need for a Sociology of Irish Folk Music: A Review of Writings on "Traditional" Music in Ireland, with Some Responses and Proposals.' *International Review of the Aesthetics and Sociology of Music* 15:1 (June 1984), 3–13.

Unpublished Materials

Blake, Donal. 'The Christian Brothers and Education in Nineteenth-Century Ireland.' M. Ed. thesis, University College, Cork, 1977.

Bojus, Julia E. 'Music Education in Poland.' Ph. D. dissertation, The University of Miami, Florida, 1972.

Bradshaw, Albert. 'An Experiment in Curriculum Development Based on an Adaption of the Kodaly Concept of Music Education for Particular Use in Schools in the Republic of Ireland.' Ph. D. dissertation, Trinity College, the University of Dublin, 1981.

Carroll, Joseph. 'A History of Elementary Education in Kerry, 1700–1870.' M. Ed. thesis, University College, Cork, 1984.

Devereux, Mary. 'The Perception, Knowledge, and Practice of Irish Traditional Music among Secondary School Students.' B. Mus. thesis, University College, Cork, 1979.

Ellis, Catherine J. 'Aboriginal Education through Music: Complexity within Simplicity.' Unpublished paper, The University of New England, New South Wales, Australia, ca. 1987.

Fleischmann, Aloys. 'Music Education in Ireland as Surveyed in the Reports of the Council of Education.' Unpub. ms., ca. 1965.

Heneghan, Frank. 'M. E. N. D. A Survey of Music Education in Ireland sponsored by The Dublin Institute of Technology.' Interim Report, Phase I, September 1995.

Kearney, Aiveen. 'Temperance Bands and Their Significance in Nineteenth-Century Ireland.' M. A. thesis, University College, Cork, 1981.

Kelly, William Noel. 'Music in Irish Primary Education.' M. A. thesis, University College, Cork, 1978.

McCarthy, Jane. 'The Contribution of the Sisters of Mercy to West Cork Schooling, 1844–1922, in the Context of Irish Elementary Educational Development.' M. Ed. thesis, University College, Cork, 1979.

Music Association of Ireland. 'Introduction to Traditional Irish Music in Schools: Bringing the Arts to Schools.' Circular to school principals, 1987.

——. 'The Music Association of Ireland: A Role for the 1990s.' Unpublished paper, 1989.

Ryan, Joseph J. 'Nationalism and Music in Ireland.' Ph. D. thesis, University of Dublin, 1991.

Seebauer, R. 'Erneuerungsversuche der Musikerziehung in der österreichischen Pflichtschule der 10–14 jahrigen (vom Reichsvolksschulgesetz bis zur Gegenwart mit besonderer Berüchsichtigung Wiens)' Dr. Phil., The University of Vienna, 1978.

Veblen, Kari. 'Perceptions of Change and Stability in the Transmission of Irish Traditional Music: An Examination of the Music Teacher's Role.' Ph. D. thesis, University of Wisconsin, 1991.

Media

A River of Sound: The Changing Course of Irish Traditional Music. Produced by Mícheál Ó Súilleabháin. (Baile Átha Cliath: Radio Teilifís Éireann, 1995).

Index